PAMELA IN THE M

Samuel Richardson's *Pamela* (1740) is often regarded as the first true novel in English and a landmark in literary history. The bestselling novel of its time, it provoked a swarm of responses: panegyrics and critiques, parodies and burlesques, piracies and sequels, comedies and operas. The controversy it inspired has become a standard point of reference in studies of the rise of the novel, the history of the book and the emergence of consumer culture. In the first book-length study of the *Pamela* controversy since 1960, Thomas Keymer and Peter Sabor offer a fresh and definitive account of the novel's enormous cultural impact. Above all, they read the controversy as a market phenomenon, in which the writers and publishers involved were competing not only in struggles of interpretation and meaning but also in the larger and more pressing enterprise of selling print.

THOMAS KEYMER is Professor of English and Leverhulme Major Research Fellow at the University of Exeter. His books include *Richardson's Clarissa and the Eighteenth-Century Reader* (Cambridge, 1992) and *Sterne, the Moderns, and the Novel* (2002). He is the editor of Fielding's *Joseph Andrews* and *Shamela* (1999) and Richardson's *Pamela* (2001) in the Oxford World's Classics series, and co-editor, with Jon Mee, of *The Cambridge Companion to English Literature from 1740 to 1830* (Cambridge, 2004).

PETER SABOR is Director of the Burney Centre, and Canada Research Chair in Eighteenth-Century Studies, at McGill University, Montreal. His books include *Horace Walpole: The Critical Heritage* (1987) and *Samuel Richardson: Tercentenary Essays*, co-edited with Margaret Anne Doody (Cambridge, 1989). He has edited several eighteenth-century novels, including Richardson's *Pamela* (1980) and Cleland's *Memoirs of a Woman of Pleasure* (1985), as well as the *Juvenilia* volume in the Cambridge Edition of the Works of Jane Austen.

THOMAS KEYMER and PETER SABOR are also General Editors of the Cambridge Edition of the Works and Correspondence of Samuel Richardson (in progress).

PAMELA IN THE MARKETPLACE

Literary Controversy and Print Culture in Eighteenth-Century Britain and Ireland

THOMAS KEYMER AND PETER SABOR

CAMBRIDGE
UNIVERSITY PRESS

CAMBRIDGE UNIVERSITY PRESS
Cambridge, New York, Melbourne, Madrid, Cape Town, Singapore, São Paulo, Delhi

Cambridge University Press
The Edinburgh Building, Cambridge CB2 8RU, UK

Published in the United States of America by Cambridge University Press, New York

www.cambridge.org
Information on this title: www.cambridge.org/9780521110181

First published 2005
Reprinted 2007
This digitally printed version 2009

A catalogue record for this publication is available from the British Library

ISBN 978-0-521-81337-2 hardback
ISBN 978-0-521-11018-1 paperback

For Prudence et pour Marie

Contents

Illustrations

Acknowledgments

We renew our thanks to colleagues previously acknowledged in our photo-facsimile edition of texts from the *Pamela* controversy (2001), and thank Pickering & Chatto for allowing us to draw on our editorial material. We are indebted to our exemplary editor at Cambridge University Press, Linda Bree, and to the anonymous readers of our proposal.

Several librarians and archivists have aided our research, including the late Hugh Amory (Houghton Library, Harvard), Gill Cannell (Parker Library, Corpus Christi College, Cambridge), Declan Kiely (Berg Collection, New York Public Library), John Mustain (Stanford University Library), Carl Spadoni and Adele Petroric (McMaster University Library), Liz Stacey (National Trust), Richard Virr and Lonnie Weatherby (McGill University Library), and Bruce Whiteman (Clark Library). Chapter 2 could not have been written without major archival work by William Keymer and Faith Keymer, and we have been fortunate in our research assistants: Kate Williams at the University of Oxford, and Gefen Bar-On and Elizabeth MacLean at McGill University.

We are also indebted in various ways to Adam Budd, Paul Burditt, Brian Corman, John Dussinger, Lindsay Holmgren, Heather Jackson, Nicole Joy, Maggie Kilgour, Shelley King, Laura Kopp, Devoney Looser, Jonathan Mallinson, William McCarthy, Keith Maslen, Claude Rawson, John Richetti, Valerie Rumbold, Emmi Sabor, Angela Smallwood, Patrick Spedding, Mark Spencer, Sophie Vasset, and our colleagues at Oxford and McGill.

Thomas Keymer gratefully acknowledges the generous funding of the Leverhulme Trust (Major Research Fellowship programme) and the warm hospitality of the Department of English, University of Toronto. Peter Sabor is grateful for support from McGill University, as well as from the Master and Fellows of Christ's College, Cambridge, the Social Sciences and Humanities Research Council of Canada, and the Canada Research Chairs programme.

Introduction

This is not a book about Richardson, nor even a book about Fielding. There could be no *Pamela* controversy without *Pamela* itself, of course, and like any other groundbreaking work Richardson's novel is valuably illuminated by the appropriations and transformations, the resistant readings and creative misreadings, that followed its publication. *Shamela* was the most brilliant and influential of these re-readings, and its parodic disruption of the original text, later amplified in *Joseph Andrews*, gave early shape to a struggle of interpretation that has been remembered ever since as a duel between two canonical titans. To *Pamela's* first audience, however, this duel must have looked more like a battle royal: a clash of multiple, mutually competitive adversaries, in which no sympathetic allegiance or satirical antagonism was ever complete or stable, and the many contestants in play not only defended Richardson or followed Fielding but also responded to, argued with, and stole from one another in an overlapping series of side-engagements. Something of the complex dynamism involved is caught by Solomon Lowe's wry comment to Richardson, a year after publication, that *Pamela* had been 'of so much Service to your very Brethren; witness the Labours of the press in Piracies, in Criticisms, in Cavils, in Panegyrics, in Supplements, in Imitations, in Transformations, in Translations, &c, beyond anything I know of'.[1] *Pamela* provoked and enabled a deluge of print, and in this context losses as well as gains have been entailed by a critical tradition in which 'Richardson and Fielding seem destined for eternal contrast' (as Allen Michie writes of this tradition)[2] while other participants in the controversy languish in eternal eclipse. As a cultural phenomenon, here was something bigger than even its foremost players, and of significance in its own right.

Within the last few years, republication of a much broader sample of *Pamela* writing has focused new attention on the controversy as a whole, both as an exemplary case of the disputatious, dialogic framework in which so much eighteenth-century literature was produced, and as a necessary context for understanding and interpreting individual contributions.[3] As the author of one such study concludes, 'any discussion of the political implications of *Pamela* and its many sequels and counter-fictions . . . is caught up in the multiple refractions of alternative readings and characterisations, made by Richardson himself and by his readers and rewriters'.[4] In light of these intricate entanglements, the purpose of the present study is to retrieve and analyse the output of *Pamela*'s quarrelsome progeny in all its plenitude and range. Rather than swell the existing body of criticism on *Pamela*, *Shamela* and *Joseph Andrews*, we undertake a compensatory project in which the presence of Richardson and Fielding, though always felt, is secondary to the recovery of their neglected allies and rivals: dramatists and novelists, journalists and artists, professionals and patricians, pirates and hacks.

The scale of the *Pamela* controversy is if anything more remarkable than Lowe alleges. By the date of his letter, the novel had appeared in six authorized editions (one of them in French), and Richardson had recently published his sequel. Piracies had come out in London and Dublin, an unauthorized newspaper serialization was in progress, and *Pamela* was shortly to become the first novel printed in America. Even more striking than the number of reprints, as Lowe's improvised taxonomy of reception indicates, was the related output of others. It is now clear that Richardson was underestimating his novel's impact when noting on this letter, late in life, that 'the History of Pamela gave Birth to no less than 16 Pieces under some of the above or the like Titles'; a similar late note, with the same conservative estimate, is scribbled elsewhere: 'no less than 16 Pieces, as Remarks, Imitations, Retailings of the Story, Pyracies, &c.'[5] *Pamela* inspired a swarm of uninvited appropriations, a Grubstreet grabfest in which a hungry succession of entrepreneurial opportunists and freeloading hacks – 'these Poachers in Literature', a book-trade colleague of Richardson called them[6] – moved in for a slice of the action. Items already published in whole or part as Lowe wrote include *Shamela*, *Anti-Pamela* and *The True Anti-Pamela*; *Pamela's Conduct in High Life*, *Pamela in High Life* and *The Life of Pamela*; *Pamela Censured* and *Pamela Versified*; and, most recently, *The Virgin in Eden* (proving 'Pamela's Letters . . . to be immodest Romances') and *Memoirs of the Life of Lady H------, The Celebrated Pamela*. London and Dublin had seen stagings of *Pamela. A Comedy*, and the text of this play had been published in competition with a rival comedy, *Pamela: or, Virtue Triumphant. Pamela* poems had appeared in the newspapers and magazines of London and Edinburgh, and even on an illustrated fan. Other engravings based on the novel were already in circulation, as published in *Pamela Versified*, *Pamela in High Life*, *The Life of Pamela*, and a London piracy of Richardson's text; an official illustrated edition was in preparation. *Joseph Andrews* was shortly to appear, and would be followed by 'Pamela the Second' in the *Universal Spectator*; *Pamela: or, Virtue Rewarded. An Opera*; *Pamela: or, The Fair Impostor. A Poem, in Five Cantos*; and a play recently discovered in a unique Dublin copy, *A Dramatic Burlesque of Two Acts, Call'd Mock-Pamela*. Another Irish play is recorded but lost.[7]

Further publications, without declaring the relationship in their titles, are little less closely connected with Richardson's novel, and less durable forms of cultural production and practice have assumed the dimensions of myth: the *Pamela* waxworks exhibited off Fleet Street for several months in 1745; the modish ephemera of London's pleasure gardens, one of which was decorated with *Pamela* canvases while at another 'it was usual for ladies to hold up the volumes of Pamela to one another, to shew they had got the book that every one was talking of'.[8] Other trends of this kind have been forgotten, including an equestrian *Pamela* vogue that is still faintly recoverable from records of the turf. The first racehorse to be named after Richardson's heroine ran at Reading in July 1741,[9] and by 1742 several Pamelas are regularly found in starting line-ups, alongside the usual displays of political allegiance ('Poor Robin', 'Bold Vernon') and crude innuendo ('Frisky Fanny', 'Bushy Molly', 'Stiff Dick'). Two Pamelas were entered for the same race at Epsom in May (both by baronets, one of them a Tory MP), but neither succeeded in beating 'Merry Pintle'; a third ran disastrously at Earlshilton in June ('*Foxhunter* run against a Post . . . upon which *Stradler* fell over or against him, and *Pamela* fell over *Stradler*'); a fourth was running in Ireland by July.[10] These horses had begun to age by mid-decade, when 'Mr. *Musters's* Ches[tnut] M[are] *Pamela*, six Years old' was the strongest survivor, but Richardson's novel retained sufficient currency for a new generation to take their place. The equestrian vogue was alive and well in 1748, when 'Capt. *Shafto's* Grey Filly, *Pamela*' was among the successes of the Yorkshire season, her virtues rewarded by the Mayday hundred guineas at Blackhambleton and several other prizes.[11]

More conventional indicators mark the *Pamela* controversy as a milestone in literary history, including a statistical spike in the production of new fiction that was unprecedented at the time and not reached again until the circulating-library boom of the 1770s. A key moment in the emergence of the novel as a generically self-conscious and culturally central form, the publication of *Pamela* not only established a compelling prototype for the domestic, epistolary and psychological fiction of the decades to come. By triggering the rival formulations of Fielding, drawing Eliza Haywood back to a mode of writing from which she had drifted, and stimulating a variety of fictional responses from the many other novelists, identifiable or anonymous, discussed in the chapters below, Richardson's novel also provoked enduring debate about the techniques and purposes of the genre, and elicited the much wider repertoire of fictional types that was to dominate production into the nineteenth century. This picture of the controversy as a watershed in generic development, familiar in outline since Ian Watt's *The Rise of the Novel* (1957), has been consolidated rather than overturned by the recent project of restoring to view the amatory novelists of earlier decades and reassessing their relationship to the established canon. Though Richardson no longer appears in his old (and always implausible) guise as an innovator *ex nihilo*, a new picture is emerging of a no less significant generic breakthrough, involving not insulation from earlier forms but instead a brilliant transposition and fulfilment of the potential latent in these forms. More work is needed on the connections between Richardson's novels and amatory fiction, especially in light of discoveries concerning his professional involvement with editions of Haywood and Aubin in the 1730s, but none of this will diminish the landmark significance of *Pamela* and the debates it engendered. Introducing a volume dedicated to the reassessment of Watt's thesis, David Blewett cites Janet Todd on the transformations of mode that make *Pamela* 'that secure contender for fictional originality', revisionist pressure on the canon notwithstanding.[12] 'In its density of social scene and sweep of historical reference radically absent in its amatory predecessors', as John Richetti puts it in reformulating the traditional view, '*Pamela* is a true original'; it is an original, moreover, that operates as antitype as well as model, generating in Fielding 'a style energized and to some extent organized by his rejection of the Richardsonian novel and its amatory predecessors'.[13] The formal consequences of this rejection continue to be illuminated in studies of representation and parody in Fielding,[14] and one purpose of the present book is to complement this work with corresponding attention to the cumulative role of other novelists in the process.

A second strain of scholarship moves on from questions of strictly generic history to stress the importance of the *Pamela* controversy as both an indicator of, and an agent in, the emergence of a thriving, dynamic, and fully commercialized marketplace for print in the *Dunciad* era. Figures for *Pamela*'s sale have not previously been known, but surviving evidence that a single edition (the third) sold 3,000 copies within two months lends statistical weight to the novel's reputation as, in Terry Eagleton's words, 'one of the century's best sellers'.[15] Even more arresting is the explosion of speculative print surrounding the work: bales of paper that seem to dramatize, or even decisively institute, the nightmare visions of *A Tale of a Tub*, in which books are like mackerel, fugitive commodities to be noisily hawked as their freshness ebbs. It is a nice paradox that Richardson courted the aging Scriblerians for endorsement of his novel, for in *Pamela* he unleashed the very phenomenon they most deplored, even as they drew on its energy: a market-led multiplication of lowbrow print, unregulated by traditional considerations of learning, decorum or taste. More recent perspectives emphasize this radical modernity. For Eagleton, *Pamela* is as brashly commercial as a Hollywood blockbuster, not so much a novel as 'a whole cultural event . . . the occasion or organizing principle of a multimedia affair, stretching all the way from domestic commodities to public spectacles, instantly recodable from one cultural mode to the next'. William Beatty Warner writes that 'the cultural location and meaning of novel reading took a decisive turn with the publication of *Pamela*', generating an unprecedented 'media event' in which the novel became 'an ambient, pervasive phenomenon' in the press and public sphere.[16] A defining moment in the history of print and consumer culture as well as that of a genre, the controversy gives special insight into the agility, responsiveness and entrepreneurial vigour of eighteenth-century Grubstreet, while also exhibiting the desperation that often drove its efforts. It is salutary to remember that the principal publisher of *Pamela's Conduct*, Richard Chandler, was shortly to kill himself under pressure of debt, and that *Shamela* was probably written in the bailiff's sponging-house where Fielding was confined in the month before publication:[17] the acquisition of money, in both these works, was no mere abstract theme.

To write about *Pamela* was not only to engage in commercial opportunism or a dispute about literary technique, however; it was also to take a position, whether consciously or not, on social and sexual politics. A third strain of criticism has stressed the ideological undercurrents of the controversy, finding in Richardson's euphoric tale of social mobility and transgressive marriage a set of provocative messages about gender and class, and interpreting the hostile interrogations of Pamela's character that proliferated after *Shamela* as evidence of a conservative backlash. By locating virtue in a voice from below, asserting the spiritual equality of servant and princess, and inserting this servant into the social elite as an agent of reformation, Richardson's novel disrupted many of the assumptions on which traditional hierarchy rested, and cried out for refutation. The text is laden 'with revolutionary moral and social implications . . . its impulses are insistently, even convulsively, antihierarchical', as Terry Castle writes, and in this context Fielding's parody is often read, for all its levity and exuberance, as a rearguard reassertion of patrician values.[18] At the most obvious level, debate turned on local ambiguities in Pamela's representation: the veracity of her narration, the sincerity of her motivation. Increasingly in play beneath the surface, however, were the larger uncertainties of an age in which social distinctions were coming to seem perilously fluid and their ideological foundations unstable – a trend crystallized for contemporaries by several high-profile breaches of endogamy in society to which the novel was publicly compared.

Critics have sometimes overstated Pamela's credentials as a working-class heroine, not only because of the anachronistic connotations of 'class' in a society still organized by traditional stratifications of rank, but also because Richardson was careful to modify her lowness with traces of ancestral respectability: as George Cheyne wrote, with only slight exaggeration, 'Your Heroine you have made a Gentlewoman originally and distinguished only [on her marriage] by some Ounces of shining Metal'.[19] Readings of *Shamela* as a reactionary critique of social levelling tend to rest, moreover, on a basic confusion between Fielding and the character of Parson Oliver (whose paranoid commentary, in neo-Scriblerian style, is part of the satire), while also neglecting the celebratory relish of Shamela's representation and the awkward fact that Fielding himself was later to marry a servant. Nonetheless, there can be no question that for other writers of the controversy *Pamela* did indeed present an affront (albeit sometimes a welcome affront) to hierarchical assumptions, and the novel remained an instinctive touchstone for decades when any question of marital misalliance came up. In Francis Coventry's *Pompey the Little* (1751), a girl with grand ambitions of social advancement locks herself up 'to read *Cowley*'s Poems, and the History of *Pamela Andrews*'; in Susan Smythies's *The Brothers* (1758), an eligible baronet is urged to 'have some regard to parity of birth . . . and remember every beautiful outside does not contain the soul of a *Pamela*'; in a satirical newspaper column of 1757, an earl's daughter elopes with her dancing-master, taking with her nothing but 'the second volume of Pamela, and the marriage service torn out of her Common-prayer book'.[20] These are only the jokier instances of a widespread unease, and make plain the extent to which Richardson's narrative of social disruption and moral disproportion had struck the rawest of collective nerves, in ways extending well beyond the positions of Richardson and Fielding themselves. The usefulness of this whole body of writing as an indicator of contemporary anxieties and tensions may be in inverse proportion, indeed, to the literary quality of the particular text involved. As Lady Mary Wortley Montagu observed when deploring a new 'Levelling Principle' at work in contemporary culture, it was in writers of the popular marketplace that the zeitgeist was most truly displayed: 'as they write merely to get money, they allwaies fall into the notions that are most acceptable to the present Taste'.[21]

Other issues at stake in the *Pamela* controversy, though more peripheral to modern critical preoccupations with gender and class, sparked no less fire among readers at the time. If Fielding's satire carried serious ideological freight, indeed, it lay more in religion and ethics than in questions of rank. By alleging the poverty of a notion of virtue that fails to go beyond chastity and justification by faith, *Shamela* implicates Richardson's narrative of virtue rewarded in larger theological controversies concerning the rival claims on the Christian soul of inward piety and outward action, and links the novel in particular with the self-regarding providentialism of George Whitefield. These objections were real and durable enough to resonate in Fielding's later works. In *Tom Jones*, the proposition 'that Virtue is the certain Road to Happiness' holds good for an inward-looking, stay-at-home prudence that unmistakably recalls his earliest responses to *Pamela*, but not for that more commendable benevolence 'which is always busying itself without Doors, and seems as much interested in pursuing the Good of others as its own'; a conspicuous instance of the former quality is the pious widow of a Turkey merchant, 'whose Virtue was rewarded by his dying, and leaving her very rich'.[22] Nor was Fielding the only writer to detect in *Pamela* a whiff of enthusiasm that alarmingly suggested – for all the confessional orthodoxy of its author – the dissenting radicalism of Defoe or the upswell of popular Methodism. Fifteen years later, when a survivor of the Lisbon earthquake described his deliverance with a mixture of providential rhetoric and circumstantial bathos that was now familiar ('I have been miraculously preserved . . . but I have no shoes to put on my feet'), there remained no more obvious or economical rebuke than to mock him as 'Master *Pamela*'.[23]

Even the proper pronunciation of Pamela's name became a matter of controversy, albeit one that was still inflected by the persistent issue of social hierarchy. 'Pamela' was originally the name of a romance princess (in Sidney's *Arcadia*), not an upstart servant, and had also featured in poems by Waller, Pope and others. For readers determined to prove the ignorance and vulgarity of the novel, Richardson's accenting, evident from the scansion of Pamela's verses on herself, was a solecism at odds with the etymologically correct accenting of the poets, and made offensively audible his perversion of established convention. Aaron Hill came ingeniously to Richardson's defence by concocting a new etymology for the name, involving a short Greek epsilon as opposed to a long eta, but a sense persisted that here was a symbolically important breach of propriety and tradition.[24] The dispute was heated enough to be recalled and satirized years later: 'all the pretty Gentlemen in the Kingdom were deciding the proper Pronunciation of the Name *Pamela*', remembers a character in Sarah Scott, and Sarah Fielding creates a pedant who, 'if the Question arose, whether the *e*, in *Pamela*, should be pronounced long or short . . . had immediate Recourse to the *Greek* Prosodia for a Determination'.[25] Mere vowels were now weapons of debate, and nowhere more so than in the devastating shift in orthography that became shorthand, in the work of Fielding's many imitators, for the subversive reinterpretation of Pamela's virtue. Fielding did not coin the term 'vartue' in response to Richardson, as is usually assumed (he uses it a decade earlier in his play *Rape upon Rape*, and may have borrowed it from a Vanbrugh comedy about moral and social affectation),[26] but the word sums up the fundamental question of identity on which everything in the controversy hinged.

This view of the radical divisiveness of Richardson's novel finds its classic statement in the unlikely shape of a plagiarized report, first published in English in 1750, but traceable to a Danish work of 1744:

There are Swarms of Moral Romances. One, of late Date, divided the World into such opposite Judgments, that some extolled it to the Stars, whilst others treated it with Contempt. Whence arose, particularly among the Ladies, two different Parties, *Pamelists* and *Antipamelists*. This Book describes a poor young Chambermaid, with whom a Gentleman of Fortune falls in Love, and endeavours, by Power and Subtilty, to corrupt; but her Virtue and Chastity prove so great, that she could not be prevailed upon to grant unwarrantable Favours. Hence, after some time, his impure Love turns to Esteem; insomuch, that, without regarding the Inequality of their Conditions, he marries her. Some look upon this young Virgin as an Example for Ladies to follow; nay, there have been those, who did not scruple to recommend this Romance from the Pulpit. Others, on the contrary, discover in it, the Behaviour of an hypocritical, crafty Girl, in her Courtship; who understands the Art of bringing a Man to her Lure. Both these Judgments, I think, are in the Extreme. For we cannot entirely rely upon the Conduct of such a Girl; because we frequently find, that Men are imposed upon by pretended Virtue: and yet every Instance of Virtue must not be deemed Hypocrisy. Women of real Religion may be found, who have no such sinister Views. I comply so far with the Ladies, whose Friendship I always cultivate, as to reckon *Pamela* of this last good Sort; especially as, in her Prosperity, her Conduct is similar to what it was before; so that she pleases every body by her Civility, Modesty, and obliging Behaviour. Her History, indeed, would have been more exemplary, and her Conduct less exceptionable, if this Heroine, after suffering so many Persecutions, had continued in her low Condition; for, thus she would have avoided the Censure now pass'd upon her. At least, she might have made her Admirer wait a few Years, before she concluded the Match. Nevertheless, I approve of this Romance, so far as it contains just Sentiments, and holds out an Example of Virtue and Honour. At the same time, I cannot allow it to be a Master-piece; and by no Means think it deserves to be recommended from the Pulpit. For tho' there are some instructive Parts in this Work; yet there are others too licentious. And certainly the Images it draws of a beautiful Woman, her Shape, Air, Neck, Breasts, &c. which are all fully display'd, cannot furnish a proper Text for a Sermon.[27]

The ostensible author of this discussion was Peter Shaw, a fashionable physician with prior business connections to the publishers of *Pamela's Conduct*, but Shaw's undeclared source was the introduction to Ludvig Holberg's *Moralske Tanker*. The key terms are Holberg's own ('tvende *Factioner* af *Pamelister* og *Antipamelister*'), and, having first gained currency as the eighteenth century progressed, they are frequently encountered as categories in modern criticism.[28] Like any other pair of binaries, they risk polarizing a body of writing that was rather more polymorphous and fluid than such language suggests, and Holberg's own evident ambivalence is a good reminder that Pamelist and Anti-pamelist currents could coexist and compete within a single writer or text.[29] With his talk of different factions or parties, however, Holberg nicely conveys the capacity of the *Pamela* controversy to outgrow its immediate source – as though resembling, or even eclipsing, the sensational politics of the day, when the long campaign against the great Whig kleptocracy of Sir Robert Walpole was in its climactic stages. There is a sense, indeed, in which the controversy provided an alternative channel or proxy arena in which these politics might be pursued, as happens not only in *Shamela*, which compares the heroine's dexterity in the art of thriving with that of '*his Honour* himself',[30] but also in the spurious continuation by John Kelly, whose zeal as an anti-ministerial satirist had previously landed him in prison, and whose political farce *The Levee* was banned in 1741.

Pamela became a site of contestation, in short, in which some of the most pressing anxieties, conflicts and stress-points of its culture can now be observed with unusual clarity. For all the capacity of reception studies to make visible the structures and fissures of mid eighteenth-century ideology, however, it may be that criticism has sometimes lost its sense of proportion on this issue, and that the larger dimensions of the controversy have been overplayed. Comparison with other print controversies is instructive here. At one level, a remarkable true-life analogue arises in the *cause célèbre* of Elizabeth Canning, a teenage scullery maid whose alleged abduction and imprisonment in 1753 by Mary Squires, a Jewkes-like gypsy, led to scandalous trials of both women and a pamphlet war in which Canning was accused, like her fictional precursor, of cynical falsification and hysterical religious enthusiasm. Writing of the furore, one author called Canning 'a realized Pamela', while another seemed to echo Shaw's version of Holberg: 'this intricate Affair had long engaged the Attention both of Town and Country, and divided all Ranks and Degrees of People into two Factions or Parties, the one distinguished by the Name of *Canningites*, and the other called *Egyptians*, each violently heated against the other's Favourite'.[31] There were also many differences, however, not least the fact that on this occasion Fielding was among the foremost champions of the calumnied victim as an exemplar, as he put it in his pamphlet on the occasion, of 'injured Innocence'.[32] The most significant difference lies in the sheer severity of the partisanship involved, which reached a pitch of violence when one leading anti-Canningite, the Lord Mayor Sir Crisp Gascoyne, was attacked by a mob in April 1754, the same month in which his attempt to enter Parliament as member for Southwark foundered disastrously on the issue.

Pamela broke no windows and threatened no lives, by contrast, and in this context a better analogy may lie in the much later dispute surrounding Henry James's *Daisy Miller* (1878). As with *Pamela*, James's exploration of changing gender roles and transgressive courtship in *Daisy Miller* became a kind of lightning conductor for debates about female identity and conduct. But this debate, though noisy and ubiquitous, was also shallow. 'The thing went so far that society almost divided itself in Daisy Millerites and anti-Daisy Millerites', as W. D. Howells writes in the aftermath of the affair, echoing Holberg's formulation about *Pamela* in a way that by now was doubtless coincidental. In this case the division was a matter of fashionable posture, however, and never more than superficial, as Howells adds: 'there has been a vast discussion of which nobody felt very deeply, and everybody talked very loudly'.[33] It is perhaps more apt to talk of this 'vast discussion' as a vogue rather than a controversy, a fashionable event whose character is best represented not by journalistic attacks but by the 'Daisy Miller hats' that become necessary accessories for a season; and so perhaps with *Pamela* too. In the most sober existing accounts of the novel's reception (such as the chapter on 'the *Pamela* Vogue' in the standard biography by Eaves and Kimpel), this is the preferred term, as though to register a resistance to cultural-historical flights of fancy in which the model of controversy is central. From this point of view, the true print controversies of the eighteenth century lie in directions rarely explored by literary scholars, most obviously in the virulent theological arguments that Swift satirizes in the ancient dispute between Big-Endians and Little-Endians in Lilliput, where 'many hundred large Volumes have been published upon this Controversy'.[34] The *Pamela*-related output of the 1740s is dwarfed in seriousness and scale, for example, by the 200 or more anti-deistical tracts published in response to Anthony Collins's *Discourse of the Grounds and Reasons of the Christian Religion* (1724), Thomas Woolston's *Discourse on the Miracles* (1727–9) and Matthew Tindal's *Christianity as Old as the Creation* (1730) – a body of writing on which Richardson drew when compiling his 'Cautions against Scepticism and Infidelity' in the closing section of *The Apprentice's Vade Mecum* (1734).[35] Although *Pamela* could become tangentially implicated in religious controversies of this kind, as it was, through Fielding's mischievous agency, in the war of sermons between Joseph Trapp and George Whitefield of 1739–41 that centred on the text 'Be not righteous over-much',[36] the stakes involved were not the same.

There remains an important contemporary sense, however, in which vogue and controversy were two sides of the same coin, and this sense is central to our analysis in the chapters that follow. The space between these two categories – one connoting modish posture, the other substantive argument – diminishes greatly if we think of controversy in a way that was second nature to many in the eighteenth-century book trade: not only, and perhaps even not primarily, as a forum of urgent debate, but as a mechanism for generating and selling print, in which contentiousness itself had commodity value. Even theological controversies were often viewed in this way, as disputes in which whatever doctrinal substance was originally at issue came to be overtaken, or at least accompanied, by the cynical multiplication of copy and pursuit of profit. The entire catalogue of the Bangorian controversy was dismissed as 'only mere battology' in an overview of 1718, and the same perception animates a farce of 1717 by J. Philips. Though acknowledging the rhetorical animosity between

Hoadly, Snape and their allies ('it is with Controvertists as with Cudgel-Players'), Philips also alleges a conspiratorial protraction of debate between these polemical divines: 'we have had Controversies that might have been decided in a Sheet of Paper, swell to Volumes, and last from Generation to Generation'.[37] In the 1730s, the *Grub-street Journal* is an ongoing repository of this idea, offering rules to hacks and their booksellers for the exploitation or perpetuation of controversies, and anatomizing the natural trajectory of these controversies from early directness, through declining vigour and desperate digression, to the graveyard of the waste-paper merchant. 'By the power of impudence,' as one number of this satirical journal puts it, 'the same stuff is vamp'd up in a thousand dresses; and arguments, which have been answered a thousand times over, set in battle array again and again, without the least notice taken that they have ever been answered at all'.[38] The most memorable source for this insight is the exuberant, unprincipled figure of Bookweight in Fielding's post-*Dunciad* comedy *The Author's Farce* (1730), for whom the contrivance of controversy is a lucrative professional technique. Rebuking a dilatory author for taking a fortnight to pen an anonymous attack on his own previous offering, Bookweight announces: 'I love to keep a Controversy up warm—I have had Authors who have writ a Pamphlet in the Morning, answered it in the Afternoon, and compromised the matter at Night.'[39]

Fielding is often thought to have had the notorious Edmund Curll in mind when creating the character of Bookweight, and Curll certainly had a keen sense of the commercial value of controversy. When Defoe launched a moralizing attack on *Onanism Display'd* and other pornographic works in Curll's list, Curll embraced the charge in a defiant pamphlet response, *Curlicism Display'd* (1718), thanking his antagonist for the free publicity; collusion between the two has been suggested.[40] Defoe himself was already a byword for the fabrication of bogus controversy, and his reputation for writing on both or all sides of any given issue is among the factors that continue to make his canon so intractable. As William Pittis alleged in 1714, Defoe could 'with a quiet Conscience publish a *Satyr* and a *Panegyrick* on the same Person, as very often he writes and answers himself', the only weakness in this Janus-faced professionalism being that, in adopting all positions, he was 'sometimes oblig'd to be honest by Necessity'. Defoe turned similar accusations freely on others, and in *The Secret History of the Secret History of the White Staff* (1715) – the labyrinthine title is entirely appropriate – he articulates a beautiful sense of the skill with which manufacturers of controversy could pull the strings of later participants, controlling the future course of any given debate by articulating its contrary extremes. The same people, he suggests, 'have been the Editors not only of the Books themselves, but also of several of the Answers to these Books, causeing the deceiv'd People to Dance in the Circles of their drawing, while these have enjoy'd the Sport of their own Witchcraft'.[41]

Authors, of course, were not always able to embrace attacks on their work with the freedom of a hard-nosed bookseller. Corneille was temporarily driven from the stage by the celebrated 'querelle du Cid' of the 1630s (a controversy that sprang immediately to the mind of one of Richardson's earliest French translators as he searched for a domestic analogue for *Pamela*'s English reception).[42] Samuel Johnson describes Alexander Pope's bravado in the face of pamphlet attacks as a tragic sham, reporting an anecdote in which Pope receives a lampoon by Colley Cibber with amused indifference, but then allows the mask to slip as he starts to read, 'his features writhen with anguish'.[43] Even so, pamphlets of this kind by Cibber, like 'the controversy betwixt the POPEANS and the THEOBALDIANS' a decade beforehand,[44] were grist to Pope's poetic mill, and many of the classic works of Scriblerian satire depended in direct and intimate ways on the texts they attacked and provoked. *Gulliver's Travels* quickly elicited a large body of writing, both sympathetic and hostile, on which Swift could play in the Dublin edition of 1735, and in later revisions to *A Tale of a Tub* he gleefully recycled into his apparatus several of the 'Pamphlets, and other Offensive Weapons' that had been launched against earlier editions.[45] Pope is the extreme case, his satire on proliferating print in the original *Dunciad* of 1728 provoking a cycle of further proliferations; when the Empire of Dulness struck back (as it did on a sufficient scale to fill four surviving albums in Pope's own collection), Pope wove these responses into the *Dunciad Variorum*, thereby eliciting further hostile material to plunder and mock.[46] This pattern of interdependency between creative text and controversial context persisted in later generations, and in Richardson's last years Sterne was unfailingly ebullient about the accumulation of attacks on *Tristram Shandy*. Sterne welcomed these attacks as promotional whatever their tone, and sometimes used them, as in his running mock-dialogue with the *Monthly Review*, as inspiration for further instalments. 'One half of the town abuse my book as bitterly, as the other half cry it up to the skies—the best is, they abuse it and buy it', as he wrote of *Tristram Shandy*'s second instalment.[47]

To place the *Pamela* controversy against this background is not to allege that Richardson deliberately contrived the entire dispute himself as a promotional gambit. There was no shortage of insinuations to this effect at the time, however, and their existence is a useful reminder that he was not only a victim but also a beneficiary of the controversy that raged around his novel. His multiple role as author, printer, and co-proprietor of *Pamela* (a role that gradually became public knowledge in spring and summer 1741) intensified suspicions that here was a peculiarly professional exercise in market manipulation. As author, Richardson had played all the catchpenny tricks of a Grubstreet hack or 'the Meanest of the Scribbling Tribe', alleged one antagonist; as proprietor he was accused of a wide range of worldly-wise manoeuvres, including sponsorship of a pamphlet denouncing *Pamela* as pornography in disguise.[48] There is an imaginative sense, moreover, in which Richardson did indeed engineer the controversy in its entirety, or make its participants dance in a circle of his drawing. Throughout the vast body of early writing about the novel, no allegation is made against *Pamela*'s character, conduct or narrative that is not unmistakably implied, and in most cases openly articulated, within the original text, in which Mr B., Lady Davers and others take turns to arraign the heroine as a mercenary adventuress, a devious hypocrite, a sanctimonious rhetorician, and more besides. In ways that look forward to *Clarissa*, the multiplicity of interpretations that competed around *Pamela* were all inherent in the conflicted character of the text itself. Nor did Richardson, in his many revisions to successive editions as the controversy wore on, do much to remove these ambiguities of representation, or to mute other controversial features of the work, including its erotic content. As Ian A. Bell describes this situation, 'the author fails to intervene decisively or to arbitrate between the contending positions, and readers are left to impose coherence on the text by selecting from it the particular emphasis that suits their reading appetite best'.[49] Richardson's persistence in this alleged failure makes it more accurate to talk, however, about a *refusal* to impose closure, the consequence of which was to replicate the controversial internal character of the text in larger public controversy. Individual contributions to this controversy frequently infuriated Richardson for both imaginative and commercial reasons, of course; but the phenomenon as a whole was always to his larger advantage.

In this sense, the *Pamela* controversy was the true product of the age inaugurated and satirized by *A Tale of a Tub*: 'so blessed an Age for the mutual Felicity of *Booksellers* and *Authors*' (p. 182). In this blessed age, to write about Richardson's novel was not only, and sometimes not even, to enter a high-minded debate about style and technique, gender and rank, or religion and ethics; it was also, or often simply instead, to enter a bustling forum that united all the 'Brethren' involved (to recall Lowe's guild-based term for Richardson's fellow book-trade professionals) as co-participants in the larger project of selling print. For some writers, *Pamela* was indeed a work that compelled attack or defence on moral or aesthetic grounds, or that inspired creative development irrespective of commercial motives. For many others, however, it was an opportunity to produce marketable books of their own, in which allegiance or outrage could be pragmatically faked as well as sincerely vented. While some of these books remain closely tied to Richardson's original in theme or approach, more-over, others use *Pamela* as a saleable pretext or available peg for purposes that sometimes leave the novel far behind. As books about *Pamela* multiplied, the controversy took on a self-sustaining dynamism in which new contributions could appropriate, recycle, or respond to other appropriations as much as to the original novel, in ways that kept the process alive and carried it forward well beyond the furore surrounding first publication. Nor does it diminish the significance of the *Pamela* controversy as either a historical phenomenon or a literary process to stress the pragmatism and opportunism of those involved. As Brean Hammond argues, this is a period in which 'writing for money provides the ongoing dynamic for literary production of all kinds, both at the "quality" and "popular" ends of the market'.[50] It is the age of Defoe and Johnson, when artistic creativity and financial motivation cannot be disentangled, and when to represent authoring as a trade, as Fielding wryly does in *Joseph Andrews* (p. 77), is by no means to denigrate its output. It may well be, indeed, that the minor novelist John Hill was right to claim a few years later that all recent fiction from *Tom Jones* downwards – he exempts only his own novel, *The Adventures of Mr Loveill* – had been 'written from the same source, the summons of the vacant pocket'.[51] Faced with this kind of choice between Parnassus and the marketplace, few would opt for Parnassus.

In this spirit, the following chapters, while situating and analysing individual contributions in various contexts of aesthetic, cultural and ideological debate, approach the controversy overall as a market phenomenon: as the product, agent, and uniquely visible trace of the new consumer culture that was taking hold, in which the novel genre was becoming an increasingly important commercial and literary mode and object of fashionable attention. In pursuing this interpretation, our aim is also to provide a definitive factual account, making good the omissions, errors and limitations of existing sources and incorporating the wealth of new information about *Pamela*'s presence in mid eighteenth-century culture made available by new research and modern reference tools. Despite the enduring and sustained upsurge of interest in the *Pamela* controversy in the past decades, there has been no book-length study of the phenomenon since Bernard Kreissman's critically obsolete, though still widely cited, *Pamela-Shamela*, and, before that, Robert P. Utter and Gwendolyn B. Needham's more ambitious but unfocused *Pamela's Daughters*.[52] For factual information, critics still rely on standard historical and bibliographical sources which, though formidable and groundbreaking works of scholarship in their time, now look increasingly inadequate. The biographical and bibliographical studies of Richardson published respectively by A. D. McKillop and W. M. Sale in 1936 miss important items and confuse others, especially in the areas of dramatic and verse adaptation, graphic illustration, authorship attribution and publishing mode.[53] Surprisingly little new information about the explosion of *Pamela*-related print in the early 1740s is added in the standard biography of Richardson by Eaves and Kimpel, who also perpetuate significant errors of description, attribution and chronology, and leave unexplored many of the controversy's most interesting aspects. These include the proliferation of engravings and illustrations long before the well-known 'earliest' illustrations commissioned by Richardson from Gravelot and Hayman; the scandalous rumours of Richardson's involvement in illegitimate promotional strategies, including his alleged sponsorship of *Pamela Censured*; the background of the single most influential participant in the controversy after Richardson and Fielding themselves, John Kelly, a former West Indian plantocrat and convicted seditious libeller. Our study lays emphasis on these and similar items of evidence (including several previously unrecognized contributions to the controversy in both manuscript and print) not simply to set the historical record straight, but because they challenge previously standard assumptions and pose productive new questions. To what extent was the authorized, high-end creativity surrounding *Pamela* indebted to, or dependent on, piratical, low-end appropriation; are we right to take at face value the moralizing rhetoric of many contributions, including Richardson's own; how far did personal background and political allegiance colour the stance of writers towards the novel's questions of power, rebellion and accommodation?

The publishing history of all relevant works is described in detail below, with special attention to questions of authorship and audience, to the stage history of dramatic adaptations and the circulation of visual representations, and above all to the promotional mechanisms and strategies that established the controversy as a major market phenomenon. Although the focus is on critical and historical interpretation, with all material subsumed into larger overall arguments about the economic dimensions, ideological configurations and aesthetic implications of the controversy, there is also a logic to the organization of chapters that is broadly chronological and generic. Here our intention is to bring out a previously unrecognized sense of *Pamela*'s controversial reception as unfolding in distinct, though overlapping, phases, in each of which a particular type of publication comes to predominate. Chapter 1 deals with publication and early promotion, and with a critical backlash following the publication of *Shamela* in April 1741, in which Richardson and Pamela are repeatedly conflated as writers seeking self-enrichment by means of bogus moral claims. Chapters 2 and 3 examine the spurious continuations, and thereafter the related narratives and counter-fictions that came to dominate the market after the opening volume of *Pamela's Conduct* in May and Haywood's *Anti-Pamela* in June. Chapter 4 traces a rash of stage adaptations in the winter theatrical season of 1741–2, the way led by Garrick's eighteen appearances in Henry Giffard's *Pamela. A Comedy* at Goodman's Fields. Chapter 5 approaches the celebrated illustrations of Hayman and Gravelot (1742) and Joseph Highmore (1744) by way of Richardson's abortive prior negotiations with Hogarth and a little-known cluster of visual representations in earlier piracies and appropriations. Chapter 6 registers the distinct geographical and cultural identity of *Pamela*'s Irish reception, but also pursues diachronic progression by documenting the particular longevity, as well as the characteristic satirical cast, of the controversy in Ireland, as manifested especially by *Pamela; or, The Fair Impostor*, a mock-Popean poem of 1743, and the previously unknown farce *Mock-Pamela* (1750), which conflates Fielding's *Shamela* with memory of much earlier Irish writing on the virtue-rewarded theme.

CHAPTER I

'The Selling Part': publication, promotion, profits

Visiting Richardson for the first time in 1743, Laetitia Pilkington was struck by the affluence on show: 'As I had never formed any great Idea of a Printer, by those I had seen in *Ireland*, I was . . . extremely surprized, when I was directed to a House of a very grand outward Appearance'.[1] The author of *Pamela* was a wealthy man, but Pilkington was right to associate this wealth primarily with his printing, not with his writing. Richardson had moved to the imposing house she saw, on the west side of Salisbury Court, in 1736, and in 1738 he also took on a spacious semi-rural retreat in the suburbs west of London. It was in these pre-*Pamela* years that he rapidly stepped up to a new plane of prosperity, and the key factor, alongside the expansion of other branches of his profession, was the lucrative contract he had secured a few years earlier as printer to the House of Commons.[2] His first novel, begun in November 1739 and published a year later, did not create his wealth as poetry had created Pope's, for he had already transformed his fortunes through strenuous application to what he liked to call, with ostentatious humility, 'a mechanic business'.[3] If anything, the link between Richardson's worldly success and his novel of virtue rewarded works the other way. In celebrating the upward mobility of its worthy protagonist, *Pamela* draws on energies that had already secured its author's rise, and teasingly reflects his own deserving path from obscurity to status and wealth.

If the commercial triumph of *Pamela* was merely a bonus for Richardson, however, this bonus was certainly substantial. Even in its own day, the novel was widely cited as a classic instance of the money to be made from print. In a satirical dialogue of 1748, a fictional bookseller urges an aspiring author to 'Invent, *Sir*, Invent; there's *Pamela (says he)* that was a rare thing, if you could do something like that, it would set all Things right.' Uninterested in aesthetic merit or moral tendency, this character thinks of *Pamela* above all as a lucrative market success: 'the Piece might be bad or good for any Thing I know, but this I am sure of, that it sold admirably'.[4] Two years later, these sentiments were sourly echoed by the author of *The Female Soldier: or, The Surprising Life and Adventures of Hannah Snell* (1750), who contrasts his real-life paragon of chastity and virtue with Richardson's fictional creation. Snell 'ought not to be entered on the same List with the late famous *Pamela*, who for some Time alarmed the Town with her extraordinary Virtues: Those, we are all sensible, were imaginary only, and the Result of an artful Bookseller, or Author's Brains, who entertained the Publick, to his no small Emolument, with a fabulous Story of a Lady of his own Creating' (pp. 166–7). Even two decades after *Pamela*'s publication, the protagonist of George Alexander Stevens's *The History of Tom Fool* (1760) could find no more natural way of arguing for the saleability of his own story than by declaring it 'as well worth Printing, as e're a *Pamela* of 'em all' (p. 135).

The exact scale of Richardson's 'emolument' is hard to quantify, but it was evidently a good deal more than he expected, and would have been larger but for an initial error of judgment. Rather than retain full copyright, he sold a two-thirds share to the booksellers Charles Rivington and John Osborn for twenty guineas. Richardson may have felt beholden to these men, who had approached him to compose the manual now usually known as *Familiar Letters* (1741) and were still awaiting delivery while he broke off, inspired by the task, to write *Pamela* instead. Even so, he was clearly underestimating the success in store. In 1763 a 1/18 share in *Pamela* changed hands for two guineas, implying a total valuation that had risen, long after the novel's vogue had abated, to thirty-six guineas; in 1776 a 1/16 share sold for as much as £18.[5] Another way of measuring Richardson's miscalculation is to compare the case, just a year after *Pamela*'s publication, of Fielding's *Joseph Andrews*. Desperately indebted, Fielding had been prepared to sell his manuscript for £25, but was instead offered almost eight times as much by the bookseller Andrew Millar.[6] In Samuel Johnson's eyes, Millar was the Maecenas of the modern marketplace for print, a commercial patron to be applauded by authors for having 'raised the price of literature'.[7] Millar was certainly quick to see what Richardson had failed to predict: that *Pamela* made nonsense of the old benchmarks, and had dramatically and permanently raised, in particular, the price of fiction. As a reviewer noted at the century's end, novels as consumer products took off in the 1720s, but Richardson's was the real breakthrough: 'two of the earliest fabricators of this species of goods, the modern novel, in our country, were Daniel Defoe, and Mrs. Haywood; the success of *Pamela* may be said to have brought it into fashion; and the progress has not been less rapid than the extension of the use of tea'.[8]

Few of Richardson's printing accounts survive, and none is relevant to *Pamela*. But the rapid succession of editions of the novel tells its own story. *Pamela* was first published on 6 November 1740, but in January Richardson was already announcing a second edition, and when this edition appeared on 14 February 1741 he could boast of 'a large Impression having been carried off in less than Three Months'.[9] Exactly how large is not known, but the fact that Richardson was forced to put out some of the work to another press yields tantalizing evidence. The claim to have occupied several printers at once was a standard ruse for talking up new books,[10] but Richardson's need was real. An entry in the ledgers of William Bowyer records that on 2 March 1741 Bowyer completed the printing of two sheets (the equivalent of forty-eight pages) in a run of 3,000 copies for an unspecified edition of *Pamela*.[11] There is little doubt that this was the third edition, published on 12 March; if so, the large print-run recorded here did not prevent the need for a fourth edition less than two months later, on 5 May. Only then was Richardson getting the measure of demand, and the fifth edition of 22 September 1741 did not have to be replaced by another in the same duodecimo format until 1746 – though in the interim he also oversaw the lavish octavo edition of 8 May 1742, an authorized French translation (printed by Bowyer in 1,500 copies, and published by Osborn on 23 October 1741),[12] and several editions of his two-volume continuation, first published on 7 December 1741. In view of Bowyer's figure, it is not unreasonable to estimate that 20,000 copies of authorized editions were produced and sold by the end of 1741, little more than a year after first publication, to which total must be added piracies of several kinds including abridgments, newspaper serializations and Dublin editions. The circulating-library system was still in its infancy, but informal practices of sharing copies and reading aloud in family or friendship groups mean that the number of readers involved was many times larger. Again, a useful point of comparison is provided by *Joseph Andrews*, easily the most successful of the early fictional responses to Richardson's novel: 1,500 copies were printed of the first edition (February 1742), 2,000 of the second (June 1742), and 3,000 of the third (March 1743), which was then sufficient to meet demand for a further five years.[13] By any standard, *Pamela* was selling at a prodigious rate.

What brought this spectacular success? Much of the explanation must lie, of course, in the compelling internal power of the text itself. Traditional identifications of *Pamela* as the first true novel, or again as the first commercial bestseller, have been tempered by the fuller picture we now have of existing trends in both the techniques of fiction and the commodification of literature in earlier decades. Yet both of these once-standard claims have much to say about the nature and breadth of the work's appeal. Structured as a series of letters from the heroine herself as the plot unfolds, its epistolary form seemed to offer intimate access to the ebb and flow of consciousness, unhindered by the distancing or flattening effects of retrospection. Richardson was later to name this technique 'writing, to the moment',[14] and the phrase catches to perfection its two associated qualities: not just its capacity to register the flux of consciousness over time, but more particularly its dramatic synchronizations of narration and crisis, with focus above all on the immediate psychological impact of 'moments' in the sense of turning-points or critical junctures. The potential effects of excitement and suspense, heightened by the interrupted nature of the epistolary form, could be fully exploited by a plot that turned on seduction, abandonment, and imprisonment; yet at the same time these more or less illicit pleasures could seem legitimated by the elaborate didactic claims and religious glosses that larded the text. Add to this the engagingly humble status of Richardson's heroine (not the aristocrat or princess of traditional romance, but a day-labourer's daughter in domestic service, describing the workaday world in demotic tones); add again the intoxicating fantasy of rags-to-riches advancement and providential reward that her story offered; and the capacity of *Pamela* to absorb – and, in terms of social spread, to maximize – its audience is plain enough.

Yet explanations must also look beyond this primary answer of literary genius. Or rather, they must accommodate a different but no less instrumental aspect of Richardson's genius, acquired during his long climb to the eminence he now occupied in his profession. As hard-nosed an entrepreneur as any subsequent player in the *Pamela* vogue (and materially more successful than them all), Richardson combined his growing parliamentary business with a keen eye for areas of growth in the commercial book-trade, and in the run-up to *Pamela* had devoted increasing attention to prose fiction – notably (see chapter 3 below) in his professional involvement with novels by Haywood and Aubin. The success of Haywood's *Love in Excess* (1719–20) had made amatory fiction a remunerative product in the 1720s, and it was not least as 'a Lover of Money' that Mary Davys contributed to the genre in *The Reform'd Coquet* (1724): as she announces of her amatory theme, 'would the Poets, Printers and Booksellers but speak the truth of it, they would own themselves more

obliged to that one Subject for their Bread, than all the rest put together'.[15] It is true that the fashion for amatory fiction waned as recyclings
of Haywood's formula grew increasingly stale (to be partly replaced in the
1730s by imports from France), but the potential for reanimating or
reinventing the mode remained. In this context, it is little exaggeration
to say that *Pamela*'s success lay as much in commercial strategy as in
literary achievement – or only in the second as a consequence of the first.
Through his shrewd identification of an emerging market to exploit, and
his ready skill in providing a product that was in growing demand but
limited, low-grade supply, Richardson could reach thousands of consumers for whom (as a reader of *Pamela* calling himself 'Eusebius' laconic-
ally put it) 'Things of that Sort in English but seldom appearing made me
a little curious to see it.'[16]

With the experience and resources of his publishers and co-proprietors
to back up his own, Richardson then did everything within his formidable
reach to boost the novel's sale, bringing to bear on *Pamela* an irresistible
range of promotional techniques, both traditional and innovative. Having
targeted his market, he manipulated it with a virtuoso publicity campaign
involving celebrity endorsements, newspaper leaders, a commendatory
sermon, and even, it was alleged, covert sponsorship of a pamphlet
denouncing the novel as pornography in disguise. One need not believe
this last allegation (which Richardson, unsurprisingly, denied) to recognize his genius for what 'Eusebius' pungently termed 'the Selling Part'.[17]
Though eventually the campaign took on a momentum of its own, with
Pamelists and Antipamelists alike carrying out Richardson's work for him
unbidden, his guiding hand is discernible in many of the first interventions, and the novel's early promotion took place amidst allegations of
greased palms and services rendered that may have had real foundation.
As time wore on, the campaign became not only a catalyst for *Pamela*'s
success but a focus of controversy in itself, and beneath many attacks
on the heroine's allegedly mercenary character lay analogies with its
thriving author, as though both were hypocritically engaged in converting
professions of piety, or fictions of virtue, into personal profit.

If *Shamela*'s Parson Oliver is right that *Pamela* had unleashed 'an
epidemical Phrenzy now raging in Town' (p. 312), the frenzy is clearly
traceable to the audacious promotional manoeuvres surrounding the text.
At first, moreover, this contagion was orally transmitted. In the immediate period of publication, Richardson used conventional advertisement no
more than was normal, and it was only the following summer, as he

attempted to fight off a spurious continuation, *Pamela's Conduct in High Life*, that the London newspapers came to be flooded with belligerent advertising. More deftly and effectively, the novel was launched with a gale of puffing behind it. 'The Pulpit, as well as the Coffee-house, hath resounded with its Praise', as *Shamela's* Tickletext puts it (p. 310), and his point is echoed by the author of *Pamela Censured*: 'both the *Pulpit* and the *Press* have . . . extoll'd it as the most perfect Piece of the Kind'.[18] Cried up and preached up, *Pamela* was promoted by word of mouth as much as in print, and in ways that skilfully exploited the key institutions and spaces of an emerging public sphere.

It is inevitable that only a trace of this spoken puffing survives, but reconstruction is possible. It is known from a letter from Aaron Hill to Richardson of 6 January 1741 that what amounted to a promotional sermon had been delivered by 'that hearty good Friend of yours, Doctr. Slocock, of St. Saviours':

So uncommon a Truth as he dared to recommend from his Pulpit did an Honour, not only to Pamela, but to the Speaker, and ye Place it was spoke from. I am charmed by ye brave Independence of Taste in the generous Doctor! Only *That* could impell him so nobly to avow his Approbation in the face of the World, without waiting ye Sanction of Time for safe-guarding his Sentiments.[19]

We cannot know exactly what was said by the preacher in question, Dr Benjamin Slocock (1691–1753), chaplain of St Saviour's, Southwark, but it seems likely that he had compared *Pamela* with *The Whole Duty of Man*, a standard devotional manual first published in 1658. That would explain, at least, why *Shamela* plays repeatedly on *The Whole Duty of Man* from its title page onwards, and why later in the year Charles Povey expressed outrage that 'they recommend it to Families equal to *The Whole Duty of Man*, to instill Religion into the Minds of both Sexes'.[20] A further clue is provided by the French poet Georges-Louis de Bar, who illustrates the extravagant praise showered on the novel by recalling '[le] bon Monsieur Slocock . . . qui en Chaire exhorta ses Auditeurs de mettre *Paméla* entre les mains de leurs enfans, comme un Ouvrage qu'on ne sauroit assez lire'. In a discussion echoing Holberg and anticipating Shaw, Bar contrasts this exhortation to place *Pamela* in the hands of children with the Antipamelist objection that it seduces youth, and wittily appeals to Horace to resolve the debate. The lines he quotes from the *Ars poetica* are telling, linking *Pamela's* dual appeal with that clever blend of instruction and pleasure that makes authors famous and the 'Sosii' – eminent booksellers – rich.[21]

Slocock's sermon won almost instant notoriety, as reflected not only in the framework of *Shamela*, where Tickletext's gushing enthusiasm for the novel is more sexual in origin than he knows, but also in the ironic dedication to Slocock of *Pamela Censured*, which rebukes him for lending an aura of sanctity to prose that was covertly pornographic. The same allegation – that *Pamela*'s spiritual pretensions merely legitimate an appeal that is carnal at root, and that Slocock's sermon both illustrates and advances this process – is more neatly made in the anonymous *A Voyage to Lethe*. In this blatant, though rather engaging, work of pornography, 'by Capt. Samuel Cock; Sometime Commander to the Good Ship the Charming Sally', a bogus subscription-list plays mercilessly on Slocock's name, which is listed alongside 'Alderman *Slycock*', 'Mr. *Nocock*', 'The Hon. Mrs. *Laycock*', and 'Madam *Handcock*'. Where these subscribers buy *A Voyage to Lethe* in tens and hundreds, no fewer than 3,000 copies are set aside for 'the Rev. Mr. *Slowcock*, for himself and Parishioners, to bind up with the Octavo Edition of *Pamela*'.[22] *A Voyage to Lethe* and *Pamela* were two of a kind, the implication is; there was nothing more dignified behind Slocock's recommendation of the novel, whether or not he knew it, than a relish for its erotic charge.

This was not the only interpretation of Slocock's sermon to have entered circulation, however. *The Life of Pamela* (1741) makes the damaging reflection that aspects of the heroine's conduct must 'destroy the Character that so much Pains have been taken with, even tho' a Parson should have ten Guineas to recommend it from the Pulpit' (p. 340 n.), and the casual tone of the allegation suggests that it had been voiced before. The rumour may even have been true. Richardson's biographers loyally discount it, but it is an arresting fact that years later Slocock, who by then was wealthy, pointedly bequeathed £10 to 'Mr Richardson author of Pamela'.[23] At a time when Richardson was now also the author of *Clarissa*, and prosperous enough for a gift of £10 to be otherwise an affront, this oddly worded and measured bequest has the ring of a private joke, and may have been a coded gesture of repayment on Slocock's part. Perhaps suspicions that Slocock had taken a bribe were already in the air when Aaron Hill wrote the letter quoted above. There must be some such reason, at any rate, for Hill's strangely emphatic remark that 'only *That*' (i.e. Slocock's 'brave Independence of Taste', as opposed to some material inducement) could have motivated the sermon.

Beyond the reach of any such bribery was the most eminent living poet of the day, Alexander Pope. But Pope too contributed invaluably to the *Pamela* campaign, and there is good reason to suppose that his famous commendation of the novel, spoken in Bath but rapidly circulating on the national grapevine, was just as actively solicited. When the physician George Cheyne told Richardson that Pope had charged him 'to tell you that he had read Pamela with great Approbation and Pleasure, and wanted a Night's Rest in finishing it, and says it will do more good than a great many of the new Sermons', we seem to be in the realm of private compliment.[24] A similar report by Richardson's business associate and brother-in-law James Leake, however, leaves a different impression. Leake was proprietor of an elegant bookshop and circulating library on Terrace Walk, which, with the famous Pump-Room, was one of the two main centres of society in Bath: 'one of the finest Bookseller's Shops in *Europe*', as Richardson called it, or in the words of another witness, 'the Asylum of all polite Literature'.[25] In a letter quoted by Anna Laetitia Barbauld, Leake reports Pope as saying that *Pamela* 'will do more good than many volumes of sermons' (this was clearly a standard routine); Leake adds that he had 'heard them both [i.e. Pope and his patron Ralph Allen] very high in its praises, and they will not bear any faults to be mentioned in the story'. This prompts Barbauld to comment that *Pamela* received 'spontaneous eulogiums from many of the first authors of the day',[26] but the spontaneity here looks rather doubtful. The later Pope was an accomplished performer of his own celebrity, his appearances choreographed, and his utterances calculated, for maximum public impression. He could silence a thronged auction-hall by walking in, and crowds would hang on his words: 'all was in an instant, from a scene of confusion and bustle, a dead calm', as was reported of a rare public appearance in 1742.[27] It is much more likely that Leake had persuaded Pope to speak his set-piece about *Pamela* publicly in the bookshop, and perhaps on an occasion as theatrical as the auction-hall appearance. Reports then travelled about town, and thereafter the country, with great effectiveness. In a culture of sociability and polite gossip, performances like these – a celebrity endorsement in a fashionable spa, a promotional sermon from a metropolitan pulpit – were worth whole bales of conventional newspaper advertisement.

Although the oral commendations that were so crucial to *Pamela*'s early impact are now only distant echoes, other influential puffs survive in printed form. In the first edition of November 1740, Richardson included two: one the work of a French translator then earning his living in London, Jean Baptiste de Freval (*fl.* 1737–51), the other unsigned but probably by William Webster (1689–1758), a 'friend and debtor' of Richardson (as Eaves and Kimpel economically put it) who had recently

become vicar of Thundridge and Ware, Hertfordshire.[28] Neither writer
had the distinction of Pope or even Slocock, and Webster is now remembered only for his walk-on part in the *Dunciad* (where his religious zeal
earns him a place, opposite the Methodist George Whitefield, in the
braying competition).[29] They were useful enough for Richardson's immediate purpose, however. Webster's commendation had already
appeared in advance of publication, having been used as a leader in the
Weekly Miscellany, the religious periodical he edited as a vehicle for his
high-church, pro-ministerial views, on 11 October 1740. In a preliminary
paragraph that Richardson did not retain in *Pamela*, Webster declares the
fictionality of the work ('He has written an *English Novel*, with a truly
English Spirit'), and adds that he has selected 'this publick Manner of
giving the Author my Sentiments upon it, in hopes by this Means to
quicken the Publication of it, and excite Peoples Attention to it when it
does come out'. Webster was to devote two further front pages to *Pamela*
following publication: the issue for 13 December reprints Richardson's
preface, and on 28 February 1741 Webster reprints part of the new
promotional matter of the second edition, acknowledging that he has
been 'censur'd . . . for taking too much notice' of the novel.

In praising *Pamela* so fulsomely, Webster must have had to overcome an
element of real antipathy. On doctrinal grounds, at any rate, it remains
hard to explain his promotion of the novel – a novel that reminded one
early reader of Defoe's providentialism and made others think Richardson
'too much of a Methodist' – in a journal that specialized in invectives
against Methodism and dissent.[30] Other factors must have been at work,
and Richardson's influence over the *Weekly Miscellany* was strong enough
for this prominent coverage to be attributed to him directly. He had
printed the journal for four years following its inception in 1732, and had
recently forgiven Webster a residual debt of £90; he may also have been one
of the creditors without whose help in 1732 Webster 'must have died', as he
later recalled, 'like a poisoned rat in a hole'.[31] Nor was this the first time that
Richardson had used the *Weekly Miscellany*, which aggressively promoted
The Apprentice's Vade Mecum in 1733–4, to such ends.[32] Similarly, the obscure Jean Baptiste de Freval was a Richardson client, and the same sense of
cravenly suspended allegiances is conveyed by the tactical Francophobia
of de Freval's text. Richardson had recently printed his English translation of the Abbé Pluche's *The History of the Heavens* (published March
1740) on favourable terms, and in closing his commendation de Freval was
rather obviously bidding for the commission to translate *Pamela* into
French: as the author of *Pamela Censured* drily puts it, he 'insinuates a

French Translation, and as I see one is since advertised to be published, it may not be amiss to congratulate the Gentleman, whoever he is, on his lucky Thought'.[33] Though no doubt sincere in aspects of their admiration, both de Freval and Webster were demonstrably in receipt or expectation of Richardson's patronage, which must have helped to lubricate their praise.

Preceding these commendations was Richardson's own brief preface, a genre in which he was already expert. Although he was often to solicit prefaces to his own work from others (confessing that 'of all the Species of Writing, I love not Preface-Writing'), he later revealed that before becoming a novelist he had built up a reputation among publishers for 'writing Indexes, Prefaces, & . . . *honest* Dedications'.[34] One such Richardson preface, to Penelope Aubin's posthumous *Collection of Entertaining Histories and Novels* (1739), has been convincingly identified by Wolfgang Zach.[35] This preface praises Aubin as achieving an exemplary purification of amatory fiction, and anticipates the thinking behind his brief *Pamela* preface. Where other women have brought 'a Disreputation' on the genre by seeming 'to make it their Study to corrupt the Minds of others' (Behn, Manley and Haywood are the unnamed targets), Aubin is a salutary alternative for youthful readers, working instead to 'instil into their Minds the Principles of Virtue and Honour, and that at a Time when they are most susceptible of such Impressions as may be attended with either happy or pernicious Effects'.[36] More clearly still, this argument looks forward to Richardson's private accounts of his own attempt to recuperate the risky immoralities of scandal fiction and seduction narrative. *Pamela* too, he told Cheyne, would 'catch young and airy Minds, and when Passions run high in them, to shew how they may be directed to laudable Meanings and Purposes, in order to decry such Novels and Romances, as have a Tendency to inflame and corrupt'.[37] The irony is that, in noisily repudiating amatory fiction, Richardson also reworks the distinctive language in which it was promoted, not least in a volume of Haywood's works, including *Love in Excess*, that he had printed in 1732. Here a commendatory poem by James Sterling hails Haywood for completing (after Behn and Manley) 'the fair Triumvirate of Wit', and celebrates her narratives for their exhaustive focus on, and final transcendence of, sexual distress. Readers of Haywood will glow with zeal and melt in desire, 'Till, pleas'd, rewarded Vertue we behold, | Shine from the Furnace pure as tortur'd Gold'.[38] In this context, for Richardson to speak of 'virtue rewarded' was to advertise sexual as well as pious content; in the very subtitle of his novel, he was craftily reminding readers of the illicit narrative pleasures he affected to eschew.

Shortly after publication of the first edition, magazine puffs began to appear from sources that look more objective, though even here Richardson's hand can plausibly be detected. Edward Cave's *Gentleman's Magazine* fed the *Pamela* frenzy by announcing in January 1741 that it was 'as great a Sign of Want of Curiosity not to have read *Pamela*, as not to have seen the *French* and *Italian* Dancers'.[39] But Cave and Richardson were on familiar terms (or so it would seem from a hudibrastic dinner invitation sent by Cave a few years beforehand, which offers the rotund Richardson 'two seats, whene'er you come, | This for your arms – and that your bum'),[40] and Cave may simply have been doing a favour to a friend. Less well known is the first formal review of the novel, which appeared in the December 1740 number of the *History of the Works of the Learned*, a monthly abstracting and reviewing periodical founded in 1737 by the bookseller Thomas Cooper, who was later joined by a co-proprietor, Jacob Robinson. Little evidence survives to connect Richardson with Robinson (who later published Henry Giffard's comedy *Pamela*), but he had dealt closely for years with Cooper. Keith Maslen lists Cooper among the booksellers and publishers for whom Richardson most frequently printed, and between 1732 and 1737 the two were jointly concerned in the *Daily Journal*. Cooper's pamphlet shop had served as the distributing agent for other Richardson-printed periodicals, and for separate works including Richardson's own *A Seasonable Examination of . . . Play-Houses* (1735). In 1739 Richardson had also been drumming up contributions for, and possibly printing without charge, another periodical published by Cooper, a short-lived weekly entitled *The Citizen*, and Cooper may well have been minded to perform a service in return.[41]

Literary reviewing was not firmly established in Britain until the launch of the *Monthly* and *Critical* reviews a few years later, and the *History of the Works of the Learned*, which folded in 1743, is something of an oddity. Conceived in an older, more highbrow tradition (Elizabeth Kraft identifies the magazine's prototype as a seventeenth-century French serial, the *Journal des Sçavans*),[42] it showed little interest in contemporary imaginative writing, and generally ignored fiction. Its stock in trade was the approving summary of new works by 'the most eminent Writers' of philosophy, divinity, history, and science, and in these conditions the mere existence of a *Pamela* review is remarkable. Even the magazine's indexer was taken aback, to judge from the uncertain wording of his entry in the 1740 index for 'Pamela, *an Account of a sort of Novel under that Title*'. More typical of the magazine's content was a lengthy review the previous May of *The Negotiations of Sir Thomas Roe*, which praises

Richardson handsomely enough (and with inside knowledge: 'The Printer of this Volume may, I think, be very justly stiled the Editor of it') to confirm that he and the magazine's management were on friendly terms.[43] Circumstantial factors apart, the *Pamela* review reads like an inside job. Long quotations from the prefatory matter are followed by a sympathetic synopsis, and only in the closing sentence is criticism ventured: 'The Language is not altogether unexceptionable, but in several Places sinks below the Idea we are constrained to form of the Heroine who is supposed to write it.'[44] The point is mildly put, but inaugurates a strain of objection (marking a deep-seated cultural resistance to Richardson's location of virtue in a 'low' voice) that would be a major theme of *Pamela*'s early reception. Though obviously inappropriate to a work attempting to simulate a servant's letters, criticisms like this followed inevitably from the standard assumption that good literature involved high style, and generated an equivocal reaction in Richardson himself. Though suspending this assumption as he wrote, he also craved approval from polite and learned readers who upheld it. The result was that later editions of *Pamela*, in progressive layers of defensive revision, would attenuate the stylistic daring of the original text.[45]

Buoyed by these friendly notices in the *History of the Works of the Learned* and the *Gentleman's Magazine*, Richardson chose in *Pamela*'s second edition (and in all subsequent duodecimo editions published in his lifetime) to retain his first-edition preface and the commendations of de Freval and Webster. He also added a more substantial introduction, which likewise survived in all lifetime duodecimo editions, though with removal or moderation of a few of the most extravagant passages from the fourth edition onwards.[46] The bulk of this introduction was drawn from letters sent to Richardson by his friend Aaron Hill, the poet, playwright, projector and critic, and it is here Richardson showed his true enthusiasm for (in a phrase later applied to Millar) 'the modern ART *and* MYSTERY *of* PUFFING'.[47] Hill is likely to appear somewhat absurd to modern eyes, but he was one of the most influential literary arbiters of his day, and his cultural importance has been recognized in a major biography by Christine Gerrard. Hill's involvement in the *Pamela* controversy gains added interest when we remember that he had previously been close to Eliza Haywood and friendly with both Henry Fielding and John Kelly, whose work he had also promoted.[48]

Hill's first letter, dated 17 December 1740, responds to Richardson's presentation of a copy of *Pamela* to his daughters, and was followed by at least five further letters in support of the novel, all of them couched in similarly flatulent style. From these sources (his critical faculties disabled by sheer pleasure), Richardson stitched together his lengthy introduction, rounding off the whole with a commendatory poem, also by Hill.[49] Almost immediately, Hill's effusions elicited much plainer language from a nauseated reader. In a letter to one of *Pamela*'s co-publishers, John Osborn, an anonymous clergyman declared that he and his 'Brethren of the Cloth' had been recommending the novel on pastoral visits, 'but you were bewitched to Print that bad stuff in the Introduction, for it has made enemies'. Though ready enough to follow Slocock, this cleric drew the line at Hill, and in mentioning the public enmity Hill was arousing – 'the Writer indeed calls us all Fools, and of coarse Discernment' – intriguingly suggests that the promotional matter, not *Pamela* itself, was the cause of the hostility to follow. Hill had been 'too full of himself, and too gross in his Praises of the Author'; Richardson, for his part, had 'done himself no good in accepting of such greasy Compliments. He wou'd do well to alter it, and make it shorter.'[50] Richardson began to do so in the fourth edition, but it is only in the immediately posthumous eighth edition that large-scale cuts are made.

Modern readers are unlikely to agree that Hill's commendations are 'some of the most beautiful Letters . . . in any Language' (*Pamela*, p. 509), and even Richardson had the wisdom to remove this claim from the fifth and later editions. Hill's letters have their moments – among them the tale of young Harry Campbell, whose tears of sympathy for Pamela 'form'd two sincere little Fountains' (p. 515)[51] – but the most interesting part of the introduction is the summary Richardson gives of a letter from another source, thereby working the emergent controversy among readers into the paratext of his novel. The passage is an enumerated series of objections to various aspects of *Pamela*, and derives from a letter sent anonymously to Osborn's co-publisher, Charles Rivington, a few days after the first edition appeared. The manuscript survives and, though sufficiently courteous and complimentary for Richardson to docket it as 'this good-natured letter', is rather more robustly expressed than in Richardson's published summary. The objection 'that if the sacred Name were seldomer repeated, it would be better' (p. 509), for example, is originally an objection 'that if [Pamela] repeated the Sacred Name much seldomer, it wou'd have so much less the Style of Robinson Crusoe'.[52] Richardson was sufficiently intrigued to append a note to several advertisements for the novel, appealing for further communication with the anonymous objector 'under what Restrictions he pleases'. But he was still fruitlessly publishing this appeal in mid-December, and there was to be no outcome here to compare with Richardson's long friendship with Lady Bradshaigh, which began in similar circumstances years later.[53] If any such possibility remained open in February, Hill's bludgeoning response to the objector would have closed it for good. As the clergyman who so disliked the new introduction added in the objector's defence, 'a Gentleman who seems to have intended well and honestly, is very ungratefully used, and it has given Offence'[54] – from which it seems possible that these two anonymous writers were one and the same.

The spoof preliminary matter of *Shamela* makes clear that it was the expanded paratext of Richardson's second and later editions, as much as the body of the novel itself, that provoked Fielding's parodic attack a few weeks later – thereby launching the controversy in earnest. Fielding's skit was published on 2 April 1741, three weeks after the third edition of *Pamela*,[55] and in the parodic framework that surrounds the burlesque, in which two clergymen debate the moral claims of the text, Parson Tickletext advises Parson Oliver and his neighbouring clergy to 'supply yourselves for the Pulpit from the Booksellers, as soon as the fourth Edition is published' (p. 311). *Shamela* thus responds to Richardson's promotional apparatus in its most bloated form, and in its own framing apparatus, from the preliminary letters headed 'The Editor to *Himself*' and 'John Puff, *Esq.*' (p. 309) to the enumerated closing objections of Parson Oliver (p. 343), it pays special satirical attention to Hill's letters.[56] Indeed, the second-edition introduction is kept in play even in the body of the work, as when Parson Williams's sermon on Ecclesiastes 7:16, '*Be not Righteous over-much*' (p. 324), picks up the objection, as summarized by Richardson and answered by Hill, 'That if the sacred Name were seldomer repeated, it would be better; for that the Wise Man's Advice is, *Be not righteous over-much*' (p. 509).[57] With these and other reworkings, *Shamela* must be seen as a parody not of *Pamela* in general but specifically of the expansions in later editions. A high proportion of its fire is turned on the new introduction, which Fielding deftly associates with other egregious acts of self-promotion from the same year, notably Conyers Middleton's oleaginous dedication to *The Life of Cicero*, and two self-serving autobiographies by favourite targets of Fielding's pen elsewhere, *An Apology for the Life of Colley Cibber* and *A Short Account of God's Dealings with the Reverend Mr. Whitefield*.[58] Fielding seems to have known the apparatus in its original form, and in his dedication 'To Miss *Fanny, &c.*' (p. 307) played obscenely on Richardson's incautious abbreviation of his title to 'PAMELA, *&c.*' above one of the first edition's commendatory

letters (at a time when 'etc.' had the same slang meaning – vagina – as
'fanny').[59] More of his energies are exercised, however, on the richer
source of comic innuendo that Richardson supplied even as he deleted
(too late) the '*&c.*' from the second edition: the letters by Hill, who is
conflated with Slocock into the ludicrous Tickletext. Where Hill writes of
'a poor Girl's little, innocent, Story' (p. 506), Tickletext allows his mind
to wander towards 'a poor Girl's little, *&c.*' (p. 311). Where Hill effuses
that '*Millions of* MINDS . . . are to owe new Formation to the future Effect
of [Richardson's] Influence!' (p. 508), Tickletext more strictly speaking
ejaculates that 'Millions . . . are to owe Formation to the future Effect of
his Influence. – I feel another Emotion' (p. 311).

Here and elsewhere, only a nudge is needed to tip Hill's commendations into open absurdity. The remarkable thing is that Hill had been
on friendly terms with Fielding in the 1730s, and had influentially promoted his *Pasquin* in a review that, 'though a little precious', as Battestin
tactfully puts it, comes closer 'than any other contemporary critic to distinguishing the qualities and intent of Fielding's experimental drama'.[60]
It remains possible that Fielding was unaware whose letters he was
mocking, but Hill's overwrought style has a signature all of its own,
and it may be that Fielding was knowingly picking a fight with his
former ally. Scholars have often assumed from *Shamela*'s elaborate play
on issues of authorship and anonymity that Fielding was unaware even
of Richardson's role, but he was hardly out of earshot of literary gossip,
and by the time of *Shamela*'s publication the identity of *Pamela*'s author
was an open secret played on in the public press.[61] Speculation had begun much earlier, and Fielding could have learned the truth through such
friends as the poet David Mallet, who had originally suspected Hill's own
hand in the body of the novel, perhaps because Richardson had inserted a
poem by Hill at one point (*Pamela*, pp. 288–9). As Hill bluntly replied
to Mallet in January, 'the sole, and absolute author is Mr. *Richardson
of Salisbury-Court*'.[62]

Fielding was not alone in attending as much to *Pamela*'s promotion as
to the text itself. Anonymously published on 25 April 1741, some three
weeks after *Shamela*, *Pamela Censured* shares with Fielding's satire a
hostile interest in the publicity campaign, and especially in the way in
which (as Tickletext writes) the clergy have combined 'not only to cry
[*Pamela*] up, but to preach it up likewise' (p. 310). Early advertisements
for *Pamela Censured* draw special attention to the fact that the pamphlet is
ironically '*Dedicated to the Rev. Dr.* SLOCOCK, *Chaplain of St. Saviour's,*

Southwark',[63] and this dedication works as a kind of replay of Oliver's rebuke to Tickletext in *Shamela*. No divine, the author insists, 'would recommend any Thing in his Sacred Function, but what might be repeated there, without Offence to Decency and Morality' (p. 3). Yet the burden of the pamphlet is that decency and morality are travestied throughout the novel, which has used pious preliminary matter to veil its true identity as a pornographic text. Where Fielding parodies the commendatory letters, *Pamela Censured* simply slates them. First Richardson's strategies of authorial disavowal and claims of factual authenticity are unpicked: *Pamela* is redefined as a mere novel in the tradition of Charles de Mouhy's *La Paysanne parvenue* (1735–7),[64] and Richardson is mocked as a vacillating 'HALF-EDITOR, HALF-AUTHOR' (p. 9). If *Pamela* is in truth an authored novel, moreover, no excuse can be made for the extravagant puffs preceding the work, in which Richardson comes to rival Cibber (again the cue is from *Shamela*) as 'sole Monarch of the Realms of *Effrontery* and *Vanity*' (p. 12). As a group, these fulsome commendations 'look like what the Booksellers are very often forced to say to make a bad Copy go off' (p. 10). Then comes the attack on the text itself, which is 'directly the Reverse of the Encomiums bestow'd in your Preface' (p. 19). Where Fielding had wittily hinted at *Pamela*'s potential as pornography in the masturbatory effusions of Tickletext, *Pamela Censured* catalogues the offending passages with dogged prurience. Drawing on a range of Antipamelist objection (which, according to the censurer, is now heard as widely as Pamelist praise), it makes shrewd and pithy allegations along the way: the charge, for example, that Pamela's '*Virtue* is only founded on *Shame*' (p. 33).

The overwhelming obsession, however, is with pornography. Breathily alert to every hint of the illicit, from Mr B.'s obscene punning on 'quick' in the sense of pregnant (p. 44) to the implied lesbianism of Mrs Jewkes ('There are at present, I am sorry to say it, too many . . . Women of Mrs. *Jewkes*'s Cast, I mean *Lovers of their own Sex*' (p. 50)), *Pamela Censured* not only warns against readerly arousal but vividly exemplifies the problem:

The Advances are regular, and the amorous Conflicts so agreeably and warmly depicted, that the young Gentleman Reader will at the best be tempted to rehearse some of the same Scenes with some *Pamela* or other in the Family, and the Modest Young Lady can never read the Description of Naked Breasts being run over with the Hand, and Kisses given with such Eagerness that they cling to the Lips; but her own soft Breasts must heave at the Idea and secretly sigh for the same Pressure; what then can she do when she comes to the closer Struggles of the Bed, where the tender Virgin lies panting and exposed . . . (p. 23).

These increasingly frenzied words are attributed in context not to the censurer himself but to another reader (whom the censurer characterizes, with wonderful implausibility, as 'a stay'd sober Gentleman'). But they only slightly exaggerate the tone of the whole.

The result is that *Pamela Censured* has traditionally been read, and laughed at, not only as a humourless exercise in scandalized paranoia, but also as the work of a writer rather too deeply absorbed in the lewdness he berates. Yet the pamphlet may be something more mischievous and sophisticated than simply the work of an excitable puritan who reads with one hand. Witnesses who understood the elaborate feints and charades of the book trade at the time suspected as much. John Kelly not only called this critic of *Pamela* a 'luscious Censurer' who 'charges his own luxurious Fancy on the Author';[65] he also took the effect to be very deliberate. Alluding to the most devious and scandalous bookseller of the day, Edmund Curll (whose latest ruse had been to publish a pornographic satire with false imprints implicating Richardson's brother-in-law),[66] Kelly calls *Pamela Censured* 'a Piece of *Curlism*; the greater Part a Transcript from *Pamela*'s Letters' (I, xiii). The implication is twofold: that the censurer is first a pirate, using his censorious pose as a pretext for reprinting the best-thumbed sections of Richardson's text, and second a pornographer, adding titillating commentaries to ensure that readers will 'imagine as lusciously as he does' (I, xv). In this light *Pamela Censured* changes completely: it becomes not moral denunciation but pornography disguised as denunciation – or, more dizzyingly, pornography disguised as the moralizing exposure of pornography in moral disguise.

It is hard not to feel here that Kelly (or, strictly speaking, his editorial persona 'B. W.') has a point. Though Charles Batten calls *Pamela Censured* 'a much more serious attack than *Shamela*', and Eaves and Kimpel concur in finding it 'earnest', 'a less frivolous attack' than Fielding's,[67] it looks more likely that the earnest surface was bogus. Or perhaps we should say that both these pamphlet attacks were driving in the same direction, satirically focusing as much on the extravagant absurdity of early responses (whether Pamelist or Antipamelist) as on the novel itself. It would not be impossible to read *Pamela Censured* as an ironic skit inspired by *Shamela*'s framework, written in the voice of a character in whom Parson Oliver's moral severity mingles disastrously with Tickletext's lust.

Contemporary reactions suggest one further possibility, even more intriguing. An unidentified friend of Aaron Hill (or perhaps simply, in the tactful phrasing of Hill's letter to Richardson, his own conjectures) went further than Kelly in refusing to take the pamphlet at face value. In his view, *Pamela Censured* was nothing less than 'a Bookseller's Contrivance, for recommending ye Purchase of *Pamela* to such Light and Loose Readers, as the names of Religion and Virtue might well have scar'd from any Purpose to look into it'.[68] Richardson and his co-proprietors, in other words, were behind the work themselves – an idea, however alien to our usual assumptions about Richardson, that should not be dismissed out of hand, coming from a source so close to him and his professional world. By implicating the owners of *Pamela* as clandestine sponsors of an attack on their own literary property, the allegation opens up a beautiful sense of how the dual appeal long noted by critics – the potential of Richardson's novel as both didacticism and erotica – might have worked as a marketing gambit. Overtly promoted by the moralizing puffs of the *Weekly Miscellany*, and covertly by the enticing denunciations of *Pamela Censured*, the novel is simultaneously recommended on divergent grounds to divergent tastes. Or rather, once three editions of *Pamela* have been exhausted in sales to the moral and pious, a new market of libertine readers is furtively tapped for the fourth, which followed *Pamela Censured* by ten days and was regularly advertised alongside it.[69] We might imagine *Pamela Censured* being offered as a risqué appendix to the novel, or as an index and finding aid – one of many suspect features being its studious provision of page-references for the passages it deplores, thus enabling interested readers to research the matter further. As another novelist was later to note, the insertion of bedroom scenes and 'a little of that same lascivious description, has been found an infallible receipt to promote the sale of works of this nature'; now the points of insertion were impossible to miss.[70]

Richardson denied the allegation of involvement, angrily protesting 'Quite mistaken!' in the margin of Hill's letter. But one sees how the rumour could have arisen. Whatever the case in London, the pamphlet was quickly enrolled as a promotional device in Amsterdam, where the publisher Dirk Swart brought out a volume juxtaposing an abridgment of *Pamela* with a full translation of *Pamela Censured*.[71] Nor does it strengthen Richardson's denial that *Pamela Censured* had been published by his close associate James Roberts, the publisher of his *Apprentice's Vade Mecum* in 1733, and a man for whom he printed more frequently than for any other after the Rivington and Osborn partnerships, Andrew Millar, and James Leake.[72] As James Grantham Turner notes, one of the lengthiest collaborations between Richardson and Roberts concerned the main repository of the earliest puffs for *Pamela* as a moral work, the *Weekly*

Miscellany.[73] More of a smoking gun is impossible to find, but a circumstantial case for Richardson's involvement is there to be made, and it was far from unknown for authors to encourage, or even compose, attacks on their own work as covert promotion. Roberts had published another such pamphlet at the start of his career, Pope's spoof re-reading of *The Rape of the Lock* as seditious allegory in *A Key to the Lock* (1715), which resembles *Pamela Censured* in claiming to lay bare the true subtext and motive – in 'proving, beyond all Contradiction', in Pope's subtitle, 'the dangerous Tendency of a late Poem, entituled, *The Rape of the Lock*, to Government and Religion'. Sterne gleefully welcomed attacks on *Tristram Shandy*, and may himself have had a hand in one of the first, entitled *The Clockmakers Outcry*, which like *Pamela Censured* focused on the indecency of the original. Sterne later projected a similar scheme with the French novelist Crébillon *fils*, in which each would denounce the other as a writer of bawdry: 'these are to be printed together—Crebillion against Sterne—Sterne against Crebillion—the copy to be sold, and the money equally divided'.[74]

We are left to choose between three alternative views of *Pamela Censured*: first, as a moralizing attack on *Pamela*'s eroticism, in which the writer denounces, while unconsciously demonstrating, the novel's corrupting power; second, as an opportunist work of pornography, which legitimates (and spices up) its compilation of *Pamela*'s erotic highlights beneath a façade of moral denunciation; third, as the most ingenious marketing ploy surrounding the novel, in which overt promotion of *Pamela*'s moral surface is stealthily followed by covert exhibition of its scandalous subtext. Modern readers have rarely looked beyond the first of these options, but the second – that *Pamela Censured* is 'a Piece of Curlism' – looks more persuasive, and the third – that it is a contrivance 'for recommending ye Purchase of *Pamela*' – should not be ruled out. Richardson was not only a religious didact but also a resourceful entrepreneur, and the didacticism, for all its centrality, was an approach to his own writing that he was capable of stepping outside. Whatever the truth, he evidently thought the aspect of the novel denounced in *Pamela Censured* important enough to protect in subsequent revisions. Though Batten suggests that it is under the censurer's influence that Richardson toned down his 'warm scenes' in later editions, he finds only one example. Where *Pamela Censured* protests at a description of Pamela 'extended on a Floor in a Posture that must naturally excite Passions of Desire' (p. 31), Richardson retains the description but specifies that she is face down, which creates as many problems as it solves.[75] Of nearly a thousand changes made to the text in the fifth edition, this amplification is the single adjustment that can be linked to *Pamela Censured*, and even so the connection is no more than a possibility.[76] *Pamela Censured* culminates by calling on Richardson to 'amend . . . or entirely strike . . . out' the many other inflaming passages it notes (p. 64), yet Richardson makes every one of these passages survive in its objectionable form in every subsequent lifetime edition. Only in the posthumous edition of 1801 do changes occur that coincide with the censurer's objections (the removal, for example, of the pun on 'quick'), and these bowdlerizations may well be the work of Richardson's daughters.[77]

Following the public mockery of his promotional apparatus in *Shamela* and elsewhere, Richardson prudently began to tone it down; in any case, it had done its job. He was to use verse eulogy again (notably in *Clarissa*'s third edition, which frames the text with poems by Thomas Edwards and John Duncombe), but in future novels there would be no extravaganza of prose puffing to compare with the *Pamela* introduction. Paratextual matter in the sequel is reticent and spare, and in the original novel, although the introduction survives in later lifetime editions (Richardson may have thought it too great a victory for his critics to remove it completely), some attempt is made, in various discreet adjustments to Hill's prose, to give fewer hostages to fortune. In the fifth edition, 'the wonderful AUTHOR of PAMELA' becomes simply 'the AUTHOR' (I, xvii); '20,000 inexpressible Delicacies' become 'a Variety of inexpressible Delicacies' (I, xxvii). The greatest concentration of changes falls on Hill's rough treatment of the anonymous objector, and from this point of view Richardson's revisions seem influenced more by the unidentified clergyman who protested to Osborn than by published attacks.

Even so, Richardson's ambitious marketing campaign had not quite run its course. Having sold *Pamela* once as piety, and arguably once again as pornography, he then gave a third identity to the novel by repackaging it as pedagogy. An early decision had been made to bring out a French translation under the imprint of Osborn alone (it was advertised in March as already in press), and on publication in October advertisements specified that it was intended '*For the Use of* SCHOOLS'.[78] Here was a masterstroke of market maximization, equipping *Pamela* with a new selling-point and thus enabling Richardson to sell the same product twice to the same consumers: young readers already have the novel by heart, the message is, so what better means of teaching them French? Similar gambits had been made before, as when a parallel-text edition of Guilleragues's *Lettres Portugaises* and L'Estrange's translation was advertised in 1702, 'the English being on the opposite page for the benefit of the ingenious of other languages'; Fénelon's *Telemachus* was published the same way in 1742 'as a sort of a Practical Grammar, shewing the idiom or genius of both languages at the same time'.[79] Richardson went a step further, however, by putting an English text into French for this purpose, rather than vice versa. No doubt the translation was also exported in volume to France (where the author of *Lettre sur Pamela* disparaged it as 'une assez mauvaise traduction d'un Original singulier'), but its primary purpose was always domestic. It even retained de Freval's prefatory denunciation of French taste: 'la legereté de cette inconstante Nation'.[80] The translator is nowhere identified, but as the author of *Pamela Censured* assumed, de Freval himself is the likeliest of several names to have been floated.[81]

In May 1742, Richardson was at last ready to publish his lavish sixth edition of the novel, presented in octavo format, illustrated with fashionable engravings, and 'beautifully printed on a Writing-Paper'[82] – a fourth identity for *Pamela*, then, as an ornament for a genteel library. Here he took the chance to drop Webster, de Freval and Hill (who survive, however, in later duodecimo editions), 'because the kind Reception which these Volumes have met with, renders the *Recommendatory Letters* unnecessary' (I, viii). Instead he supplied an 'Epitome of the Work' in thirty-six pages, following the method previously used in his immense table of contents to *The Negotiations of Sir Thomas Roe* (a table that the *History of the Works of the Learned* singled out as 'an excellent Pattern, which the Publishers of such Collections will always do well to imitate').[83] This synopsis heralds the controversial table of contents added in 1749 to the second and subsequent editions of *Clarissa*, though with little of the same interpretative tendentiousness. Perhaps because the controversial nature of *Pamela*'s reception had played such a central role in its commercial success, Richardson was not concerned at this stage to head off deviant readings; his priority, instead, was to provide the novel with an apparatus fitting the place to which he now aspired in a modern canon.[84]

A further item planned for inclusion in the octavo edition is the dedication to an unknown 'admirable Lady', now surviving in two separate manuscript drafts, that was 'once design'd, to be prefix'd to the Four Volumes of Pamela'.[85] It is not known whether Richardson thought better of the gesture, or whether the dedicatee declined to be identified as having 'sat in the Writer's Mind for the Graces both Personal and Intellectual' of his heroine. But in the event this edition came equipped with higher patronage still. Completing its handsome appearance was a

Royal Licence granted to Richardson and his co-proprietors on 13 January 1742, and like earlier components of *Pamela*'s paratext it combined claims to prestige with sound commercial motivation.[86] The document grants *Pamela*'s proprietors, for fourteen years, 'Our Licence for the sole Printing, Publishing, and Vending the said Work . . . strictly forbidding all Our Subjects within our Kingdoms and Dominions to reprint or abridge the same, either in the like, or in any other Volume or Volumes whatsoever, or to import, buy, vend, utter, or distribute any Copies thereof reprinted beyond the Seas'. Apart from the status it conferred, the Royal Licence (which was more often used in multi-volume reference works like the *Universal History* and *Biographia Britannica*, and would have been expensive to obtain)[87] thereby served a useful protective function. *Pamela* had already suffered kinds of piracy against which the Copyright Act of 1710 offered no defence. Jurisdiction did not extend to Ireland, where George Faulkner had undercut the price of Richardson's London editions, and it is even possible that Irish copies were returning to sell at a discount in the British market. The same went for America, where readers soon had imported copies (Eliza Pinkney had all four volumes by mid-1742, and thought Pamela's 'disgusting liberty of praising herself . . . a reflection upon the vanity of our sex'), but competition was to arise from the Philadelphia reprint by Benjamin Franklin, who sold his edition of 1742–4, the first and only novel printed unabridged in America until the eve of the Revolution, for less than half the price of the authorized imports.[88] Another loophole in the legislation, exploited on a heroic scale in magazines of the period, was that exercises in abridgment or summary remained exempt. Several farthing newspapers were already making a feature of serialized fiction, often in digest. Though fugitive half-sheets of this kind (which evaded stamp duty and relied on hawkers for distribution) rarely survive in extended runs, it has been established that *Robinson Crusoe's London Daily Evening Post* reprinted *Pamela* over eighteen months or more in 1741–2.[89] Other *Pamela* serializations may have existed, but it was probably *Robinson Crusoe's Post* that gave rise to the well-known tale, subsequently repeated in various versions, of the jubilant villagers who rang the church bells on hearing of Pamela's wedding. One version of the story locates it in Slough in Berkshire, but in Hester Thrale's account a wider provincial distribution is evidenced:

When [Richardson]'s Story of Pamela first came out some Extracts got into the public Papers, and used by that means to find their way down as far as Preston in Lancashire where my Aunt who told me the Story then resided: One Morning as She rose the Bells were set o' ringing & the Flag was observed to fly from the

Great Steeple; She rung her Bell & enquired the Reason of these Rejoycings when her Maid came in bursting with Joy, and said why Madam poor Pamela's married at last; the News came down to us in this Mornings Paper.[90]

This anecdote and others like it are usually cited with condescension, but one can see how the intimate reality effect of Richardson's fiction must have been enhanced by the rhythms of serialization. Just as Pamela writes to the moment, so the common readers of Preston and Slough would have read (or listened) to the moment, their access to her story and letters paced in something like isochronous relation to both.

Catering to a class of readers unable to afford a six-shilling novel, *Robinson Crusoe's Post* can have cost Richardson few direct sales, but usefully boosted the novel's profile. (The maid, with annual earnings of perhaps £3, would never have bought more than a chapbook; on the other hand, Thrale's aunt would never have touched a farthing paper, but may have been moved to buy the authorized text.) The episode demonstrates how, once initial interest had been aroused, newspapers and magazines then worked as conduits for ongoing promotion of Richardson's novel without further intervention of his own. Useful here is William Beatty Warner's idea of a self-sustaining 'media event', in which a profile is artificially contrived at first but then establishes a life of its own in the organs of print.[91] To Warner's point it should be added that the process rapidly took on an international momentum, unmistakably beyond the reach of personal influence. After the *History of the Works of the Learned* and the *Gentleman's Magazine*, indeed, the most significant attention in journals came in German and French. Systematic reviewing was further advanced on the continent, and in spring 1741 *Pamela* was reviewed in two of the most influential literary periodicals in Europe, the *Göttingische Zeitungen von Gelehrten Sachen* and the *Bibliothèque britannique*, well before the availability of French and German translations.[92]

Domestically, if *Pamela's* life in the periodicals began with reviews or puffs that were planted or actively solicited by Richardson himself, its most interesting continuation was as a stimulus to amateur creative writing. Journalists continued to exploit the commercial power of Richardson's title into the following year, as when the *Universal Spectator* attempted to restore its flagging fortunes by serializing 'Pamela the Second' across three numbers in April–May 1742 (see chapter 4 below). By this time it was clear, however, that response to *Pamela* was no longer the exclusive preserve of book-trade professionals in London, and that Richardson's novel was drawing into print a new class of writer, amateur and provincial, who only a generation earlier would have lacked any access to publication. That so many amateurs were moved to write about Richardson's novel not only demonstrates his success in rooting *Pamela* in the public consciousness, or even the public unconscious; in that much of the resulting writing then worked its way back into magazine columns, this trend also shows how *Pamela*'s promotion came to perpetuate itself automatically through the agency of enthusiastic readers – and indeed the agency of hostile readers, no publicity being bad. To the body of *Pamela*-inspired verse discovered by A. D. McKillop and other early scholars, several further poems may be added, which collectively conduct a vigorous debate on the moral implications of the original text, while also responding to some of the most prominent fictional rejoinders, notably *Shamela* and *Pamela's Conduct*.

Hill's disingenuously titled 'Verses, sent to the Bookseller, for the Unknown Author of . . . *Pamela*' was probably the first of the verse responses to be written, and certainly the first to be published. Its inclusion in *Pamela*'s second edition was followed by a speedy reprint in the *Weekly Miscellany* for 28 February 1741. Other poems remained in manuscript and now survive among Richardson's papers in the Forster Collection. Richardson's original index records, among others, the following unpublished poems: 'To the Author of Pamela a poetical Letter'; 'Mr. Ellis's Ode on the Virtue of Pamela'; 'Verses to the Author of Pamela'; 'To the Author of Pamela. By a Friend of Oxford'; 'Verses on Pamela by Philopaideias'; 'Philaretes to the Author of Pamela. Censure of Shamela, and Vindication of Pamela. With an Ode written by a Miss not 12 Years of Age'.[93] All are loyally 'Pamelist' in drift, some at a level of bland commendation, but others with interesting engagement in the controversy as it begins to unfold. For the Oxford poet, this controversy was in the first place an academic matter concerning Richardson's violation of neoclassical convention, but he also acknowledges, like 'Philaretes', Fielding's subversive re-reading of Pamela's motives:

> Let snarling Critics, and censorious Fools
> Who cramp the Genius with pedantic Rules,
> Thy well-formed Plan with Arrogance despise,
> Call Virtue Art, and Innocence but Lyes.[94]

No doubt these manuscript poems circulated privately among Richardson's friends. In the burgeoning print market of the 1740s, however, amateur poetry was no longer doomed to blush unseen. New outlets were developing in the periodical press, and in the 1730s the magazines, with their wide distribution and readership, offered a national platform to categories of writers whose voices had previously been unheard. The prototype and market leader among the new monthlies was the *Gentleman's Magazine*, founded in 1731 by Cave, who over the next few years pioneered poetry competitions as a way of boosting interest in his publication while also ensuring a plentiful regular supply of free copy. By the later 1730s the poetry section of the *Gentleman's Magazine* would regularly occupy eight double-column pages, with provincial clergymen, schoolteachers and women among the largest identifiable groups of contributors.[95]

It is even possible that some of the poems surviving in the Forster Collection were surplus submissions to the magazine, passed on by Cave. He certainly gave the impression of receiving more about *Pamela* than he could print. In his number for January 1741, apparently squeezed in as an afterthought before going to press at the end of the month, comes the full notice mentioned earlier in the present chapter:

Several Encomiums on a Series of *Familiar Letters*, publish'd but last Month, entitled *PAMELA* or *Virtue rewarded*, came too late for this Magazine, and we believe there will be little Occasion for inserting them in our next; because a Second Edition will then come out to supply the Demands in the Country, it being judged in Town as great a Sign of Want of Curiosity not to have read *Pamela*, as not to have seen the *French* and *Italian* Dancers.

The 'Encomiums' in question never appeared, and in the decade as a whole only two short poems on *Pamela* were ever carried by the magazine. Given Cave's unexacting standards ('It is never without great regret that we disappoint our Correspondents, by suppressing their Pieces', as he advertised the previous year),[96] the loss should not be lamented. We gain instead a vivid glimpse of the *Pamela* craze in its early flood, just as the metropolitan vogue is poised to ripple out, through the second edition, to readers nationwide. *Pamela*, the implication is, has become as necessary a cultural reference-point, and perhaps as lucrative an entertainment, as the show-stopping acrobatics that had packed the house at Drury Lane since late November. An earlier item from the same month's issue praises 'the celebrated Comic Dancers, Signior and Signiora *Fausan*, who were become the Topic of all polite Conversation from their Performances, which are as extraordinary as they are new'; it was later reported of the Drury Lane manager, Charles Fleetwood, that 'his Italian and French people last season' brought him over £70 per week, contributing 'more to the profits of a season than any actor whatsoever'.[97]

When the *Gentleman's Magazine* did include a poem on *Pamela*, in its April number, it was up to its old trick of reprinting verses from rival publications without crediting the source ('as stolen linen, handkerchiefs, &c. are rendered the fitter for sale', one victim of this practice complained, 'by taking out the mark of the owner's name').[98] 'Advice to Booksellers (After reading *Pamela*)' originally appeared in the *Daily Advertiser* for 7 April, just days after the *Pamela* vogue had been catapulted into a new phase by the publication of *Shamela*. Where *Shamela* targeted the disruption of social hierarchies entailed by Richardson's plot, however, this brief verse epigram plays instead on disruptions of professional function:

> Since printers with such pleasing nature write,
> And since so aukardly your scribes indite,
> Be wise in time, and take a friendly hint;
> Let printers write, and let your writers print.

This teasing play on the confusion of book-trade roles implied by Richardson's authorship shows not only that the poet knew who had written *Pamela*, but also that he expected his readers to know. Contrary to the common assumption that *Shamela*'s elaborate shadow-boxing around this issue results from ignorance on Fielding's part (as opposed to a satirical strategy of conflating Richardson with Cibber and others), the verse makes clear that the identity of *Pamela*'s author was already known.[99]

Shamela's appearance inspired a new spate of versification, published this time in the chief imitator and rival of the *Gentleman's Magazine*, the *London Magazine* (which, as its name suggests, targeted a more sophisticated metropolitan readership than the defiantly provincial *Gentleman's*). 'Remarks on *Pamela*. By a Prude', published in May, is a tongue-in-cheek interrogation of the heroine's motives, jauntily written in ballad metre. It also draws on *Shamela* for its view of Mr B. as an incompetent booby:

> The man, it seems, was frighted sore
>   At her pretended feint,
> So when he might have had a whore,
>   He took her for a saint.

The following month came a poem directly addressed 'To the Author of *Shamela*'. Here Fielding's burlesque is credited with overturning the public response to Richardson's heroine, though there is also a quiet nod to *Pamela Censured* in the wording of the poem's third line:

Admir'd *Pamela*, till *Shamela* shown,
Appear'd in ev'ry colour – but her own:
Uncensur'd she remain'd in borrow'd light,
No nun more chaste, few angels shone so bright.

Only in July did a third poet, 'R. D.', come anapaestically to Pamela's defence in the face of cynical readings that now seemed to have the upper hand:

If *Pamela* chance to be spoke of,
Or merit be suitably prais'd,
Why is virtue then made a mere joke of,
And laughter in libertines rais'd?[100]

North of the border, 'Remarks on *Pamela*. By a Prude' was reprinted in the July number of the Edinburgh-based *Scots Magazine*, and in October the *Scots* carried a long extract from *Pamela Versified*, a separately published poem that does not survive in its original form. This poem was launched as a serial in London in July, by which time *Pamela's Conduct* and other appropriations were already on the market, and it was perhaps because of this competition that the venture failed.[101] Something of its character can be reconstructed from two notices in the *Daily Advertiser*, and from the 110-line passage reprinted in the *Scots Magazine*. The first advertisement, on 24 July 1741, announces publication the same day of 'Number I. *of* PAMELA Versified: or, Virtue Rewarded. An Heroic Poem. Containing her Life, &c. Publish'd in order to cultivate the Principles of Virtue and Religion in the Minds of the Youth of both Sexes. Done from the Original. *By* GEORGE BENNET, *A. B. Late of St. John's College, Oxford*'. Then follows a quotation from Ovid (sufficiently mangled to suggest that the classical part of Bennet's Oxford curriculum was not his strong suit), the publisher's name ('A. Ilive, at the Queen's Head in the Old Baily'), and the following note: 'The whole will be compris'd in fifteen Numbers, and adorn'd with Copper-Plate Cuts.'

Nothing is known of the author, who is probably the 'George Bennet, A. M.' who later brought out *A New Translation of the Morals of Seneca* in 1745. *Alumni Oxonienses* gives no record of his matriculation, and in book-trade terms he was not keeping prestigious company. Abraham Ilive was an obscure printer and publisher of pamphlet material, whose repeated scrapes with the law include arrest on at least two occasions, the first in 1737 for illegally publishing the text of Walpole's unpopular Gin Act, and the second, during the Jacobite rebellion of 1745, on the more dangerous charge of publishing the Pretender's declaration.[102] Ilive's only other known publication of 1741, a low-grade Newgate biography entitled *Turpin the Second: or, Cooke Caught at Last*, probably typifies his stock in trade, and he seems also to have been the publisher of *All-Alive and Merry*, the illegal half-sheet that serialized Eliza Haywood's *Anti-Pamela* in 1741–2 (see chapter 3 below).

At twopence per instalment, *Pamela Versified* fits the downmarket profile of Ilive's establishment. Higher ambitions are suggested, however, by the copperplate cuts. The second advertisement (12 August, announcing publication of the second instalment on 18 August) describes part of the poem as printed on superfine Dutch demy paper, and the indications are that Ilive was over-reaching himself commercially. Though serial publication was an increasingly familiar and sometimes lucrative practice in the century's second quarter, it was also, in the absence of formal subscriptions from readers, precarious. The paper and engravings would have been expensive, and sales were clearly not brisk. Signs of anxiety show in the August advertisement, which assures readers that all numbers of the poem would be published with convenient speed, and promises a 'proper Introduction to the whole Tale'. No further advertisements have been discovered, and by October the *Scots Magazine*, though finding *Pamela Versified* 'the attempt of no mean genius', could also report that 'the work now seems dropt'.[103]

Without having seen the *Scots Magazine* extract, Sale suspects from the Ovidian tag in Ilive's advertisement a more dubious motive in *Pamela Versified* than is indicated by its retention of Richardson's 'Virtue and Religion' formula: 'Ovid is suggesting that a woman may be seduced without much difficulty.'[104] Perhaps the intention was to convey at once, in the English and Latin texts of the advertisement (and, presumably, the lost title page), different messages to different clienteles, rather as *Joseph Andrews* was later to promise 'the Classical Reader' levels of meaning unavailable to others (p. 4). The *Scots Magazine* extract, which seems to represent the poem's opening, is not explicitly subversive of Richardson's original, and continues to profess its purely didactic motive: 'Charms may decay, this column is design'd | To eternize the triumphs of the mind' (lines 15–16). But the poem also draws out the lubricious potential of its subject, returning Richardson's novel to the Haywoodian amatory mode from which, in important respects, it had emanated at first:

> When eager wishes sparkle from the eyes,
> And teach the tender virgin's breasts to rise,

Love in bewitching smiles assumes his throne,
Ruling with power despotic and alone;
Soft converse melts the yielding soul away,
And sighs and languid eyes the lovesick nymph betray.

(lines 25–30)

Pursuing such effects in iambic verse, Bennet often seems to look towards the teasing, ornate eroticism of *The Rape of the Lock*. Even the couplet on decaying charms quoted above carries a Popean echo ('frail Beauty must decay . . . | Charms strike the Sight, but Merit wins the Soul'), and the flirtatious action of Pope's poem is again in play when Pamela's 'wavy locks, in light brown ringlets flow, | And o'er the neck a golden shadow throw' (lines 93–4).[105] In this respect the surviving fragment of Bennet's poem, without quite crossing the line into mock heroic, looks forward to the more sophisticated conflation of *Pamela* and *The Rape of the Lock* later achieved by J---- W----, the Irish author of *Pamela: or, The Fair Impostor* (1743) (see chapter 6 below).

It is likely that other verse responses have not survived, or languish unidentified in rare existing runs of provincial journals. In the second volume of the spurious *Pamela's Conduct*, published in September 1741, Pamela writes from Bath that 'we have among us here some Satyrist who . . . has done me the Honour to mention me in his poems', and Kelly may well have had real examples of fugitive verse in mind. (Real or imagined, these poems are decidedly Antipamelist, and represent her as 'extremely vain, a false Devotee, mean-spirited, which is the Consequence of my former servile Condition'.)[106] Kelly may also have been aware of a poem attacking his own continuation, 'To the Unjust Author of *Pamela in High Life*' by Elizabeth Teft of Lincoln (b. 1723), first published in book form in 1747. Teft advertised her entire collection as 'Never before Published', but at least two poems had previously appeared in the *Gentleman's Magazine* under her pseudonym 'Orinthia',[107] and the occasional nature of the *Pamela* poem makes some such previous outing likely. For Teft, the continuation had soured the original happy ending by characterizing Mr B. as a domestic tyrant:

Please to inform me, Sir, in what Regard
The lovely *Pamela* meets her Reward.
I've read each Line, view-d her in ev'ry State,
Find her most Wretched when I see her Great.
Her Angel Form you gave to Mr. B—,
He fetters her with gilded Slavery.[108]

Here Teft seems to colour her response with memories of Pope's 'Epistle to Miss Blount, with the Works of Voiture' (1712), in which, rather presciently, Pope introduces a character named Pamela as an unhappy instance of social elevation through marriage. With her gilded slavery, Teft's heroine shares the paradoxical fate of Pope's Pamela in her 'gilt Coach', who 'glares in *Balls, Front-boxes*, and the *Ring*, | A vain, unquiet, glitt'ring, wretched Thing!'[109]

Another likely candidate for magazine publication is Josiah Relph's 'Wrote after Reading *Pamela*', a poem very much in the idiom of occasional magazine verse. Relph (1712–43) was a minor pioneer of dialect poetry who spent most of his short life in the Cumberland parish of Sebergham, where he became schoolmaster and curate. He left enough to fill *A Miscellany of Poems*, which was posthumously published in Glasgow in 1747.[110] As with Teft, other items in the volume (including a verse epistle to the printer of the *Kendal Courant* and another poem about the same journal) were evidently written for the poetry columns of periodicals, and it seems likely that the *Pamela* poem had found some such earlier billet in the regional press, probably at the height of the vogue. Loyally Pamelist in drift, and praising Richardson for his seeming artlessness in arousing sentiment and instilling virtue, Relph's poem also tacitly acknowledges the erotics of the text. Though sworn to virtue on reading the novel, he is also prepared by the text to admit a flesh-and-blood rival: 'Yet if a lovely Fair I spy, | Like her whose shade here charms my eye, | The hasty vow, I'll break in part; | For Pamela must share my heart.'[111]

Slightly less insipid is a later poem from the provinces, 'To the Author of *Pamela*', first published in the *Gentleman's Magazine* for February 1745 under the pseudonym 'Belinda'. Written on behalf of 'instructed country damsels' (and by one well enough instructed herself to throw in a tag from Virgil), it enthusiastically embraces the social politics of the novel, and praises Richardson for embodying in his heroine 'An honour far above the pride of courts'. It goes further than Richardson would have cared, indeed, in imagining the effect of the novel on maids 'Who, fir'd by thy *Pamela*'s merit, scorn | The servile deeds to which our rank is born'; but this alarming message is contained within conventions of form and diction that are reassuringly conformist.[112] Other than the somewhat Popean ring to her pseudonym, the most interesting thing about 'Belinda' is that she writes from Salisbury, then an important regional centre with its own poetry-bearing newspaper, and home to a flourishing literary circle centred on Fielding's friend James Harris and the talented Collier sisters, Jane and Margaret.[113] Margaret is thought to have entered Fielding's household as a governess at about this time, but Jane was still in Salisbury: best known as author of *An Essay on the Art of Ingeniously Tormenting* (1753), she became influential in Richardson's circle, and composed for the *Gentleman's Magazine* a defence of *Clarissa* which, having written a covering letter to Cave, she left unsent. 'Belinda' shows little sign of Jane Collier's flair, however. Perhaps this somewhat belated *Pamela* poem was written by one of the charges of Mrs Mary Rookes, to whose school in the cathedral close at Salisbury girls were sent (as Sarah Fielding had been in the 1720s) 'to be educated and . . . brought up as Gentlewomen'.[114] Alternatively, the author may have been one of Cave's established contributors: at least three other poems by, to or about 'Belinda' had recently been carried by the magazine,[115] and it is possible that the pseudonym, like 'Eliza' (Elizabeth Carter) or 'Melissa' (Jane Brereton), was reserved for a known individual.

Whether celebratory or critical in vein, the amateur verse of the vogue played a crucial role in maintaining *Pamela*'s currency in newspapers and magazines. Elicited at first by Richardson's promotional campaign and Fielding's mockery of it, and heavily influenced by this material in their discursive and interpretative choices, the poems came to work as voluntary auxiliaries in the campaign, shouldering much of its burden. In his classic study of modern public opinion, Jürgen Habermas identifies both *Pamela* and the magazines as early agents in the emergence of a critical public sphere, and in magazine poems about the novel we see these agents working in tandem, as private readers were stimulated to enter a national forum of debate.[116] As the period wore on, longer poems by established and/or professional writers show just how firmly *Pamela* had established itself as a touchstone in the culture of the day, a necessary point of reference in satirical writing on topics ranging from the rule of fashion and the role of women to social rank and corruption. In *Fashion: An Epistolary Satire* (1742), Joseph Warton's satirical persona is scandalized by a fop, 'this self-pleas'd King of Emptiness', whose trivial talk ignores a context of national crisis and international war: 'With him the Fair, enraptur'd with a Rattle, | Of *Vauxhall, Garrick*, or *Paméla* prattle'. For Fielding in his *Miscellanies* (1743), there was no better way of freshening up an early Juvenalian imitation than by citing *Pamela*, and he does so with a comically botched rhyme which (like Warton's accenting) calls satirical attention to the 'low' pronunciation of the name that Richardson had popularized: 'But say you, if each private Family | Doth not produce a perfect *Pamela*; | Must ev'ry Female bear the Blame | Of one low private

Strumpet's Shame?'[117] A year later, discussing the pains of social misalliance in his verse epistle *On Nobility* (1744), William Whitehead links
Pamela sympathetically with the romance figure of patient Griselda:
'Who does not, *Pamela*, thy Suff'rings feel? | Who has not wept at
beauteous *Grisel*'s Wheel?' The more hostile view returns in *Bribery: A
Satire* (1750) by César de Missy, a French protestant exile in London, in
which an ambitious maid 'dumbshews' with her master, 'smiles down-
ward at a Jest, | Lets loosely puff-and-blow her wanton Breast', and finally
imagines an even greater catch than Richardson's Mr B.: "'*I'd e'en to
Dukes ha'e been a* PAMELA!'"[118] *Pamela* was everywhere, and still selling.

CHAPTER 2

Literary property and the trade in continuations

The phenomenon of the sequel, and of seriality in general, is associated by Umberto Eco with a commercialized, post-Romantic aesthetics in which originality and innovation give way to repetition and variability as the exemplary mode of modern culture.[1] Yet comparable practices of extension and accretion were at work in ancient epic, and the attachment of continuations became routine in Renaissance romance.[2] Above all, the modern sequel is heralded in the eighteenth-century marketplace for print by the energies of the emergent novel. It is in this context that Richardson's *Pamela* continuation of December 1741 and the rival sequel that forced him to write it, *Pamela's Conduct in High Life* by John Kelly (*c.* 1684–1751), are best understood. In the public struggle for ownership of *Pamela's* future that surrounded these works, and in Kelly's prior career in the crucible of Grubstreet, we gain unusually intimate access to the commercial and creative forces that powered the controversy as a whole. Another continuation was published in the wake of Kelly's success, the anonymous *Pamela in High Life* (1741); further new episodes appeared in *The Life of Pamela* (1741), and it is on this proliferation of fictional extensions that Fielding plays in the celebrated walk-on part he contrives for Pamela at the climax of *Joseph Andrews*.

For here was a genre of writing in which, to adapt Henry James, relations really did stop nowhere. Defoe's *Robinson Crusoe* and Haywood's *Love in Excess*, two bestsellers published within months of one another in 1719, both generated pairs of sequels; behind them lay Behn's three-part *Love-Letters between a Nobleman and His Sister* (1684–7), in which reassuring continuity and pleasurable variation took precedence over the satisfactions of closure. As J. Paul Hunter has argued, this characteristic openness to continuation in early novels recognizes the arbitrary nature of fictional resolutions, and implies instead a life-like assumption 'that stories are interwoven, seamless, continuous, and relatively endless'.[3] The failure of Defoe's follow-up volumes to secure themselves lastingly to *Robinson Crusoe*, however, is also a reminder of the inevitable bathos of fictional revisits. As Terry Castle writes of *Pamela*, the paradoxical desire addressed in a continuation – 'that the sequel be different, but also *exactly the same*' – dooms to failure its attempt to reconstitute the full pleasures of its precursor.[4] Once achieved, the rags-to-riches thrill of the original text cannot be restaged afresh; the second part misses, by its very nature, the primary force of the first. Nor is this a new perception. In *Don Quixote*, Samson Carrasco's celebrated judgment 'that second parts are never good' is offered as an established truism,[5] and by *Pamela*'s time the number of tedious proofs of the point assumed daunting proportions. 'I dread any thing like the 4th. Vol. of Gil Blas, or y[e] Sequel to y[e] Beggar's Opera', as one anonymous reader told Richardson within days of *Pamela*'s publication.[6]

At first, Richardson was reluctant to add further volumes to his existing two, sensing that the tide of taste was turning against continuations, and showing here, as in so much else, the sure instincts of a seasoned book-trade professional. Concerned that 'Second Parts are generally received with Prejudice',[7] he resisted the encouragement of several advisers (including even the jaundiced reader of Le Sage and Gay) to cash in again on *Pamela*'s success, and resolved to quit while commercially and imaginatively ahead. In later years, he devised elaborate ways of parrying similar requests, and even appended to *Sir Charles Grandison* an ingenious rationale, based on the novel's time-scheme, for the impossibility of any sequel.[8] Only in private did he admit that bruises still remained from the experience of *Pamela*, when his hand had been forced by intrusive rivals. 'Perhaps some other officious Pen (as in Pamela in High Life, as it was called) will prosecute the Story', he wearily wrote of *Grandison*; 'But I hope it may be suffered to end where I have now concluded it.'[9]

Richardson was certainly referring here to *Pamela's Conduct in High Life*, though his wording also recalls a second and less prominent attempt, entitled simply *Pamela in High Life* and published in autumn 1741 by Mary Kingman, an obscure bookseller who had already produced a piracy of the original novel.[10] Perhaps by now there was no distinction to be drawn between these rival usurpations of his story, which together had taught him a lesson he should have foreseen: that he alone no longer controlled, and could not close down, the fictional world he had opened. The vicarious fulfilment that was central to *Pamela*'s appeal – the wishful identification of readers with Pamela's special providential status and upward social mobility – had created an obvious market for a second part, in which all her gains from the first might be savoured at length. Anyone could exploit this market, moreover, for though Richardson had all the protectionist instincts of a one-man Disney Corporation, he had none of the legal arsenal. Even after the legislation of 1710, the rudimentary nature of copyright law made it hard enough to protect an existing publication (as Kingman's piracy and Faulkner's Dublin reprints were already demonstrating), and prohibition of supplements by others was out of the question. Two decades later, after the first two volumes of *Tristram Shandy*, a spurious continuation forced Sterne to sign several thousand copies of his genuine further volumes, and the assumptions about copyright that would make it possible to assert intellectual property over a character or setting were still centuries away. Nor could Richardson turn for support, as Sterne was able to do in the next generation, to the powerful reviewing periodicals of the century's third quarter (which in 1760 were quick to label the upstart *Tristram* volume 'not genuine' and 'a spurious brat').[11] His predicament was closer to that of Cervantes when faced in 1614 by the *Quixote apócrifo* of the pseudonymous Alonso Fernández de Avellaneda – though Cervantes had seemed to solicit Avellaneda's invasion in the closing line of his original text,[12] and turned the problem to creative advantage in his authorized continuation, with its clever metafictional play on the existence of a spurious rival.

In the absence of institutional protection, Richardson's disinclination to declare his authorship of *Pamela*, and his pose of plain fidelity to real events, further limited his capacity for effective protest. If *Pamela* was merely a collection of found documents, there was little to stop others claiming equal sanction, or even greater authority, for their own alternative versions. Among the most shameless of the uninvited riders on Richardson's bandwagon was the anonymous author of *The Life of Pamela*, a third-person redaction of Richardson's original and Kelly's continuation, kicked off by a thirty-page 'prequel' of its own, who insouciantly claimed that 'whoever put together the other Account that has been published of *Pamela*, was entirely misinformed of the Cause of Mr *Andrews*'s Misfortunes'. (The true cause, we now learn, was the South Sea Bubble.) Having failed to declare himself the creator of Pamela's story, Richardson was now merely the compiler of a dubious 'other Account'. The present version, *The Life of Pamela* loftily adds, will rectify 'a thousand more Mistakes that have been made in that Work, as will plainly appear in the following Sheets, for which we have the best grounded Authority from the original Papers now in the Hands of the Reverend Mr. *Perkins* of *Shendisford Abbey*'.[13]

At the literal level, few readers can have fallen for this kind of gambit (though *Pamela*'s first audience did include a minority who, like the pious grandmother remembered decades later by Richard Griffin, 'believed every word of it, as she did her Bible').[14] Even when recognized as merely conventional, however, the claims to authenticity that multiplied and competed around *Pamela* subtly eroded Richardson's authority over his own imagined world. They violated the integrity of this world, destabilized its grounding assumptions, and rendered its distinctive features plural or blurred. The complex register of Pamela's voice is a case in point. Richardson had made her talk 'like a *Philosopher* in one Page and like a *Changling* the next', complained *The Life of Pamela*, promising to make her sound more consistent, and her husband 'more like a Gentleman'; her voice is different again in *Pamela's Conduct*, with occasional dramatic plunges in register, but for the most part conventionally polite; *Pamela in High Life* gives her amusing but probably accidental touches of faux-genteel over-correction, as when she considers the inheritance due to her son 'after the Decease of his Father and I'.[15] Even the basic time-scheme of the story, which Richardson indicates by implication in the original text and firmly locates 'between the Years *1717* and *1730*' in his continuation (III, iii–iv), became contested and increasingly confused. *Pamela's Conduct* has the heroine appear at court near the end of Queen Anne's reign (giving her date of birth as 1694), and was chided in *The Life of Pamela* for 'a great Anachronism here, for *Pamela* was not married 'till the year 1726'.[16] Still more wayward was *Pamela in High Life*, in which the heroine is presented to Charles II, some months after attending (in one of several giddying time-warps) a performance of *Love for Love*; her husband later becomes a key player in the Glorious Revolution, and is rewarded with various honours, including a dukedom. Finally, and as though to complete Richardson's dispossession, all three narratives sealed their appropriation of his story by killing its heroine off, so rendering the wedding bells of the original text a merely provisional closure, and staking claims to the higher definitiveness of obituary.

For all their irritating features, neither *The Life of Pamela* nor *Pamela in High Life* can have struck Richardson as more than a minor problem. Both were obviously pitched at a low target audience, and an audience, moreover, that proved slow to buy. Neither went into a second edition, and *The Life of Pamela* was still being advertised years later, optimistically priced at 4 shillings bound. Its level is suggested by one of these advertisements, in a cookery book of 1743, which bills its celebration of Pamela's 'Innocence and Chastity' alongside a scurrilous rogue novel, *The English*

Rogue; or, The Life of Jeremy Sharp, in which readers could enjoy 'the Exploits he performed in Bawdy-Houses; how he gets into a Boarding School in Woman's Apparel, as a Maid-Servant, and gets several of the young Ladies with Child'.[17] Hints of similar pleasures emerge when *The Life of Pamela* embellishes the plot of Kelly's sequel with an abduction attempt by a rakish baronet, but for the most part its flat retrospective account does little more than prove Richardson right about the advantages of first person and writing to the moment. Its main features of interest are paratextual: a series of illustrative plates, and a smattering of footnotes in which Richardson and Kelly are both accused of misrepresenting elite manners. As for *Pamela in High Life*, the serialization of which was pragmatically shortened after publication began, this work had even fewer pretensions. Much of the text is irrelevant padding, though the author shows glimmers of artistry when interpolating stories loosely connected to the 'virtue rewarded' theme: in one, a Turkey merchant buys but refrains from raping a beautiful slave, and is later showered with riches by her grateful father; in another, a street urchin grows up to marry a well-born girl whose life he has saved, and becomes through honest toil 'one of the greatest Builders in *London*'. In the main narrative, Pamela hosts lavish banquets for the local gentry and simpler entertainments for her tenants, the most eventful of which comes when 'Farmer *Roger* burst his Breeches a dancing; and . . . his unruly Member was discover'd'. Otherwise, the main appeal of *Pamela in High Life* is its salivating specification of Pamela's wealth, which she details with all the vigilance of Moll Flanders, though with a much more impressive bottom line: 'I have in Monies, Bank Notes, *East-India* Bonds, and other Securities 220,000 *l*.', she calculates in her will, leaving massive bequests to all her children except the eldest two, Thomas ('He is very rich') and Pamela ('Her Lord is very rich').[18]

Both these works build on aspects of *Pamela*'s appeal, in short, but neither could exploit it with sufficient skill to make much impact on the market. The real threat, and the work that compelled Richardson to reassert himself in an authorized sequel, was *Pamela's Conduct*. Commissioned from Kelly by an ambitious young bookseller named Richard Chandler (*c*. 1713–44), and published in two volumes of 28 May and 12 September 1741, it attracted immediate and widespread notice. Faulkner and Nelson brought out a Dublin reprint of volume 1 on 23 June, and when a second London edition of the opening volume followed on 3 October, *Pamela's Conduct* must have looked set for lasting success.[19] Chandler published the work with his usual partner Caesar Ward and three other booksellers, but he was always the driving force of the venture, as Richardson recognized when calling it simply 'the Chandlerian Continuation'.[20] Fresh from bringing out the first published account of Dick Turpin's trial, and a leading partner in Fielding's former vehicle the *Champion*, he evidently struck Richardson as a coming man in the trade, and one dangerously adroit in its tricks. Through clever production and marketing, Richardson feared, *Pamela's Conduct* would take on an air of definitiveness as the natural companion of his novel, and it is clear that Chandler had just this ambition. His brash title – stolen from Richardson's preface and conclusion, which celebrate Pamela's rise 'from low to high life' (pp. 3, 503) – was perfectly judged, and it was this title that lodged in the public mind, not the starchy second-best wording with which Richardson was left.[21] Even the format of publication was carefully planned. Chandler's earliest advertisements specify that *Pamela's Conduct* was 'Printed on the same Letter as *Pamela, or Virtue Rewarded*': a poor typeface, as George Cheyne had noted of Richardson's volumes, but exactly right for Chandler's purpose, which was to have readers bind *Pamela's Conduct* with the original novel, thereby materially uniting the two as a single cohesive set.[22]

Richardson's friends were quick to reassure him that Chandler's ploys would fail, if only because of his inferior product. 'The Public so distinguish between the original Pamela, and the attempted Imitation of in High Life, as may well give Vanity', wrote one anonymous reader in July; another added in August (on grounds of conservation of character) that 'Pamela in High Life as they call it . . . will bear no Comparison on any Account' with the original text.[23] A different tale is told, however, by sale catalogues of personal libraries over the following decades. Here *Pamela's Conduct* is regularly listed alongside *Pamela* itself, and sometimes alongside *Pamela* in only two volumes, as though the purchaser had contented himself with the spurious sequel, ignoring Richardson's continuation when it later appeared. In this respect *The Life of Pamela*, which notes a difference in style between *Pamela* and *Pamela's Conduct* but weaves their stories together as one, must have seemed a particularly ominous sign.

Our background knowledge of Chandler's initiative still relies on Richardson's letter of August 1741, which he later indexed under the heading 'History of the true and spurious Continuation of Pamela'.[24] Written to his brother-in-law James Leake, this account is worth quoting at length, above all for the light it sheds – in the dialogue between experts in the book trade and its ways, 'brethren' in the dual sense – on the disputed professional codes that came into play. Richardson later modified his intemperate wording, leading to the rather confusing editorial presentation of previous transcriptions.[25] The unrevised text is reproduced here, in all the heat of Richardson's anger, with squared brackets surrounding two small later additions retained to clarify the sense:

You desire to know when the 3$^{d.}$ Vol. of Pamela will come out; and you'll have seen several base Advertists. and Papers against me in the Champion, in Defence of the spurious High Life publish'd only to draw me into Controversy, to make that foolish Piece sell; and I will give you a Short Acc$^{t.}$ of the Affair.

Having heard that Chandler had employed one Kelly, a Bookseller's Hackney, who never wrote anything that was tolerably receiv'd, and had several of his Performances refused by the Stage [to continue my Pamela,] I remonstrated against it, to a Friend of Kelly's. This brought Chandler to me, who when he found I resented the Baseness of the Proceeding; told me that he understood I had said, I had neither Leisure nor Inclination to pursue the Story. I told him it was true I had said so to several of my Friends who had pressed me on the success to continue it; but that was upon a Supposition no one would offer to meddle with it in which case I had resolved to do it myself, rather than my Plan should be basely Ravished out of my hands, and, probably, my Characters depreciated and debased, by those who knew nothing of the Story, nor the Delicacy required in the Continuation of the Piece. I told him that still I would decline continuing it, if he and others did not force me to it in my own Defence; but if they proceeded I must & would; and Advertise against them, as soon as they Published. He had the Impudence to propose to me, to join my Materials to their Author's and so let it come out under my Name; A Proposal I rejected with the Contempt it deserved. Next he offered to cancel 4 Sheets he had printed (tho' it was no more than 4½ Sheets, as I found afterwards) and to lose 9 Guineas they had advanced to their Author, if I would continue it, for him and his Partners. I told him, that if, contrary to my Inclination, I was obliged to continue it, I would suffer no one to be concern'd in it; having a young Family of my own that was intitled to All I could do for them. And insisted that if their Piece was so well Written as he pretended (and much boasted to me, saying, they fell in nothing short of my two Volumes) he should have it publish'd under some other Title, and not infringe upon my Plan or Characters which I represented to him in the Light it wou'd appear in to every Body; and I urg'd the Insignificance of his Plea of what old Mr. Osborn had said, if he did say it, when he might have consulted me, and had my Answer from my own Mouth, and the Baseness as well as Hardship it was, that a Writer could not be permitted to end his own Work, when and how he pleased, without such scandalous Attempts of Ingrafting upon his Plan. He went from me, as I thought, convinced of this Baseness, wishing he had not ingaged in it, and saying he would consult his Partners, and give me an Answer. I never heard further from him only of his Boasts how well written their Piece was, and how determined they were to prosecute it, braving it out that if I did Advertise against them, they had Authors who c$^{d.}$ give me Advertisement for

Advertisement let me say what I wou'd, and that I was like the Dog in the Manger wou'd neither eat myself nor let them eat. Their Author sent me the 4 half Sheets by means of his Friend upon full Assurance I wou'd be pleased with his Performance; and by these I saw all my Characters were likely to be debased, & my whole Purpose inverted; for otherwise, I believe I shou'd not have prevailed upon myself to continue it; for Second Parts are generally received with Prejudice, and it was treating the Public too much like a Bookseller to pursue a Success till they tired out the buyers; and the Subject to be pursued as it *ought*, was more difficult and of Consequence, my Leisure, my Health and my Capacity to do it were all Objections to ye Attempt.

But, on the other Hand, when it was represented to me, that *all* Readers were not Judges, and that their Volume, and another Volume after it, which they design'd, and had intended to Publish with their 3^d. had not my Menaces to Advertise against them made them try the Success of one first; and still more and more intended possibly by them, so long as the Town would receive them would by the Bookseller's Interest and Arts, generally accompany ye Two [I had written] and moreover reflected upon the Baseness of their Proceedings; they likewise giving out; that I was not the Writer of the two (which, indeed, I wish, and did not intend should be known to more than 6 Friends and those in Confidence) but they were written by one of my Overseers, who was dead, and that I *could not* for that Reason continue them – I set about the Work, but began not till I found their Volume in great Forwardness, and they in Earnest to proceed, and that was in the middle of last April. By which you may judge that its Appearance cannot be very sudden.

Richardson then outlines the plan of his proposed continuation, an undertaking given renewed urgency by publication soon afterwards of Chandler's threatened second volume, and by the possible Shandean infinitude ('still more and more') of this rival project. When the opening volume of *Pamela's Conduct* compares its narrating heroine to 'certain Ministers about the Person of the *Chinese* Monarch, who minute down every Word and Action he says or does' (I, 123), the potential for future growth looks limitless. The second volume quickens the pace to the point of Pamela's death, but also tentatively floats a spin-off work: her literary correspondence with 'the honourable Mrs. S------', which 'we may hereafter publish . . . under the Title of *Select Letters*' (II, 314).

Most striking about Richardson's account of events, with its angrily disrupted prose, is his sheer outrage. There is a furious eloquence to his images of ravishment, debasement and engraftment, which swarm with lurid connotations: sexual despoliation; pecuniary corruption; monstrous, invasive propagation. As so often, one senses the novelist's deep inward identification with his embattled heroine, as the tale of virtue they share – and the material reward this tale should bring – is besieged and threatened from without. It is not clear, however, that Richardson's adversaries were quite the villains he describes, though they were certainly unprincipled (or differently principled) opportunists. Kelly's remarkable background is described below. Chandler, whose meteoric career vividly expresses the precarious nature of book-trade life in the period, comes across as oddly naive. Though Richardson represents his behaviour in their interview as cynical chutzpah, Chandler may genuinely have convinced himself (having apparently consulted Osborn, who owned as much copyright in *Pamela* as Richardson himself) that there was no moral objection to his plan. He seems genuinely surprised by Richardson's anger, as, too, was the feckless Kelly, whose ill-judged attempt to win Richardson round by showing him copy – four half-sheets would have corresponded to forty-eight pages – was a red rag to a bull. Other sources represent Chandler as essentially honest, though overstretched and increasingly desperate following his entry into partnership with Ward in 1734 and the pair's acquisition in 1738 (in addition to their shops in London, York and Scarborough) of a printing house in York. Chandler may be the shareholder whose rocky financial state Fielding tactlessly mentions in one of his last *Champion* papers, and in 1741–2 he overreached himself with another project that Richardson, as official parliamentary printer, may have interpreted as a trespass, the multi-volume *History and Proceedings of the House of Commons from the Restoration to the Present Time*.[26] By 1744, Chandler was irretrievably indebted, and a fellow bookseller reports that 'rather than become a despicable object to the world, or bear the miseries of a prison, he put a period to his life, by discharging a pistol to his head'.[27] Ward was declared bankrupt the following year, though he recovered to print, among other works, Sterne's *Political Romance* in 1759. The paradox is that all the 'High-Life Men' (as Richardson scathingly termed them) were struggling to stay afloat in a harsh commercial environment; it is hard not to feel sympathy for Chandler's Aesopian talk of dogs in the manger.

Whatever Chandler's original posture, the affair quickly became as acrimonious on his side as on Richardson's, and the advertising duel to which Richardson refers was soon a prominent feature of the daily press. Much has been written about 'the *Pamela* ad campaign' (in Warner's term),[28] as though the novel was launched in 1740 to saturation newspaper publicity. The less colourful truth is that it was only adequately advertised in print by the norms of the day: Richardson kept his big promotional budgets for expensive folios like *The Negotiations of Sir Thomas Roe* when involved on the publishing side, and early marketing took place by subtler means.[29] It is only with the appearance of *Pamela's Conduct* that large-scale newspaper advertising begins to happen. At that point, however, 'campaign' is exactly the word, though its characteristics on Richardson's part were not promotional but violently defensive – the work of a man daily studying every move of what his advertisements call an 'Invasion', and launching strategic counter-manoeuvres of his own. At the height of the war, columns of competing advertisements (see figure 2.1, from the *London Evening-Post* for 23–5 June 1741) were not unusual. The irony is that Richardson may eventually have done himself more harm than good: *Pamela's Conduct* did not deserve the publicity he was giving it, a correspondent reminded him, and if his own sequel could be 'finished up to Expectation, no premature Imitation will hurt y^c Profit of the Printer, nor the Credit of the Author'.[30]

Initially, Chandler favoured the opposition press as his vehicle, placing his first known advertisement for *Pamela's Conduct* in the *Champion* for 28 May, and advertising again in the *Craftsman* and *Common Sense* for 30 May. Richardson placed his most copious replies in the pro-ministerial *Daily Gazetteer*, which he was almost certainly printing at the time,[31] so that the earliest salvos between the two take on a proxy political colouring. Having heard in April (as he told Leake) that the volume planned by Chandler and his conger was 'in great Forwardness, and they in Earnest to proceed', Richardson fired his opening shot by appending the following note to his announcement of *Pamela's* fourth edition in the *Gazetteer* for 7 May:

Certain Booksellers having in the Press a spurious Continuation of these Two Volumes (in Letters from Pamela to Mrs. Jervis her *Housekeeper*) the Author thinks it necessary to declare, that the same is carrying on *against* his Consent, and without any other Knowledge of the Story than what they are able to collect from the Two Volumes already printed: And that he is actually continuing the Work himself, from Materials, that, perhaps, but for such a notorious Invasion of his Plan, he should not have published.

It is a measure of Richardson's anxiety that, having carefully adjusted the earliest newspaper puff for *Pamela* to avoid declaring the work a fiction (the *Weekly Miscellany* letter '*To my worthy Friend, the Author of* PAMELA' reappears in the novel with 'Editor' in place of 'Author'), he now felt forced to drop his pose. As 'Author' of the text, he now frankly claims a right of property in the matter of its projected extension; yet the

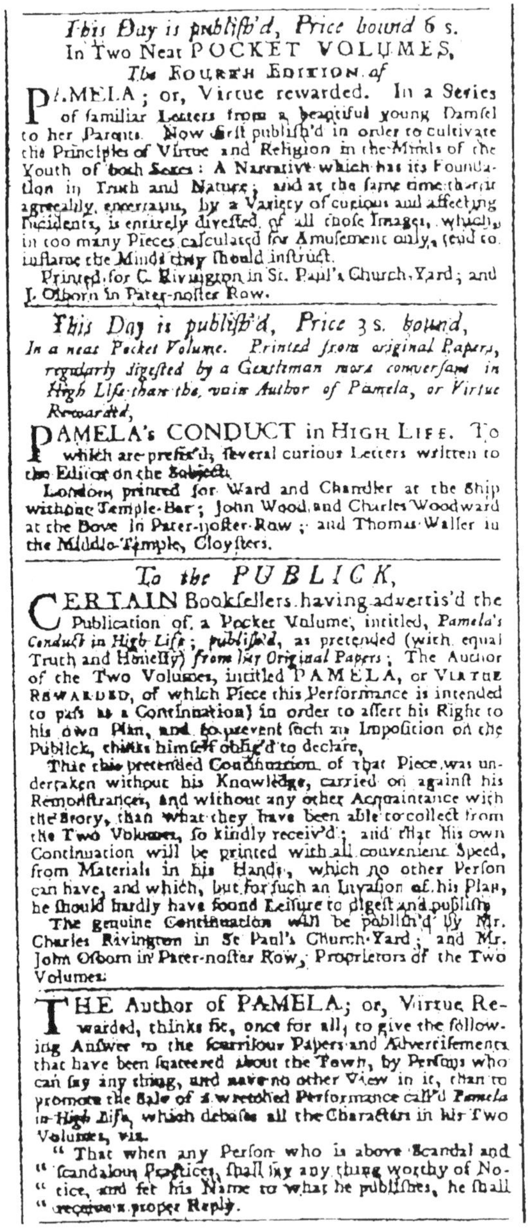

This Day is publish'd, Price bound 6 s.
In Two Neat POCKET VOLUMES,
The FOURTH EDITION of

PAMELA; or, Virtue rewarded. In a Series
of familiar Letters from a beautiful young Damsel
to her Parents. Now first publish'd in order to cultivate
the Principles of Virtue and Religion in the Minds of the
Youth of both Sexes: A Narrative which has its Foundation in Truth and Nature; and at the same time that it
agreeably entertains, by a Variety of curious and affecting
Incidents, is entirely divested of all those Images, which,
in too many Pieces calculated for Amusement only, tend to
inflame the Minds they should instruct.
Printed for C. Rivington in St. Paul's Church-Yard; and
J. Osborn in Pater-noster Row.

This Day is publish'd, Price 3 s. bound,
In a neat Pocket Volume. Printed from original Papers,
regularly digested by a Gentleman more conversant in
High Life than the vain Author of Pamela, or Virtue
Rewarded,

PAMELA's CONDUCT in HIGH LIFE. To
which are prefix'd, several curious Letters written to
the Editor on the Subject.
London, printed for Ward and Chandler at the Ship
without Temple-Bar; John Wood, and Charles Woodward
at the Bove in Pater-noster-Row; and Thomas Waller in
the Middle-Temple, Cloysters.

To the PUBLICK,

CERTAIN Booksellers having advertis'd the
Publication of a Pocket Volume, intitled, *Pamela's
Conduct in High Life*; publish'd, as pretended (with equal
Truth and Honesty) from her Original Papers; The Author
of the Two Volumes, intitled PAMELA, or VIRTUE
REWARDED, of which Piece this Performance is intended
to pass as a Continuation) in order to assert his Right to
his own Plan, and to prevent such an Imposition on the
Publick, thinks himself oblig'd to declare,
That this pretended Continuation of that Piece was un-
dertaken without his Knowledge, carried on against his
Remonstrances, and without any other Acquaintance with
the Story, than what they have been able to collect from
the Two Volumes, so kindly receiv'd; and that his own
Continuation will be printed with all convenient Speed,
from Materials in his Hands, which no other Person
can have, and which, but for such an Invasion of his Plan,
he should hardly have found Leisure to digest and publish.
The genuine Continuation will be publish'd by Mr.
Charles Rivington in St Paul's Church-Yard; and Mr.
John Osborn in Pater-noster Row; Proprietors of the Two
Volumes.

THE Author of PAMELA; or, Virtue Re-
warded, thinks fit, once for all, to give the following Answer to the scurrilous Papers and Advertisements
that have been scattered about the Town, by Persons who
can say any thing, and have no other View in it, than to
promote the Sale of a wretched Performance call'd *Pamela
in High Life*, which debases all the Characters in his Two
Volumes, viz.
"That when any Person who is above Scandal and
"scandalous Practices, shall say any thing worthy of No-
"tice, and set his Name to what he publishes, he shall
"receive a proper Reply.

Figure 2.1. The advertising war between Richardson and Chandler, *London Evening-Post*, 23–5 June 1741.

advertisement also keeps in play the alternative idea of a true underlying 'Story', and of necessary authentic 'Materials', to bolster his exclusive claim. Caught between these two uneasily compatible objections to Chandler's invasion (which subsequent advertisements never resolve), Richardson responded to the appearance of *Pamela's Conduct* three weeks later by intensifying his rhetoric further. The *Gazetteer* of 30 May marks his feelings in a riot of angry italics:

> *To the PUBLICK.*
>
> Certain Booksellers having advertis'd the Publication of a Pocket Volume, intituled, *Pamela's Conduct in High Life; Published*, as pretended (with equal Truth and Honesty) *from her Original Papers;* The Author of the Two Volumes, intituled, *PAMELA, or* VIRTUE REWARDED, (of which Piece this Performance is intended to pass as a *Continuation*) in order to assert his Right to his *own Plan*, and to prevent such an *Imposition* on the Publick, thinks himself obliged to declare,
>
> ☞ That this *pretended Continuation* of that Piece was undertaken *without* his *Knowledge*, carried on *against* his *Remonstrances*, and without any other *Acquaintance with the Story*, than what they have been able to collect from the Two Volumes, so kindly received: And that his OWN CONTINUATION will be printed with all convenient Speed, from Materials in his Hands, which *no other* Person *can* have. . .

Richardson then quotes from the *Champion* of 28 May (now lost, with other *Champion* numbers in which Chandler was advertising) the names of the publishers of this '*worthy Ingraftment*' and '*Honest Work*', reminding readers that 'the GENUINE CONTINUATION' will be published by Rivington and Osborn, 'Proprietors of the Two Volumes'.[32]

By now Richardson had forgotten his resolution not to be drawn into controversy and so promote what he wished to crush. Chandler's counter-advertisements were deftly provocative (*Pamela's Conduct*, he claimed in the *Daily Post* on 3 June, was done 'by a Gentleman more conversant in High Life than the vain Author of Pamela, or Virtue Rewarded'), and sucked Richardson, despite himself, into a slanging-match that continued to grow in volume. It reached its pitch on 4 June, when the *Gazetteer* led with an extract from *Pamela's Conduct*, tauntingly interspersed with Richardson's sarcastic notes. The chosen scene (pp. 125–7 of Kelly's opening volume, reprinted '*in order to convince the Publick how well the Volume call'd* Pamela in HIGH-LIFE, *deserves that Title*') shows Pamela bumpering wine from a pint glass while heavily pregnant. She hits the ground running the following day – on which 'nothing pass'd *worth*

sending you an Account, *except* my drinking a whole Bottle of Burgundy
at Dinner and two at Supper . . . without finding any Alteration'
(Richardson's italics) – and then muses in Socratic vein on the mysterious immunity to alcohol conferred by her condition: 'Well said the
Philosopher, *All that I know is, that I know nothing.*'

Richardson had certainly found an odd scene to reprint, and perhaps
this is simply the work of a clumsy hack. Perhaps, however, it is the work
of a writer losing patience with his source, and burlesquing either a
particular episode in the original (the wine-drinking scene, p. 352) or
the heroine's general characteristics: not only her moralizing reflections,
but also her low-life robustness, which Kelly indicates elsewhere in the
same passage by howling lapses of diction at moments of stress ('This
Answer set my Face in a Glow, for he had hit the Nail on the Head'). If a
satirical note was being attempted here, however (and we should not
forget Fielding's links with both Chandler and Kelly), Richardson chose
to ignore it. Taking the comedy as unintended, he uses heavy italics and
bracketed interjections to allege the absurdity of Kelly's style, and closes
by assuring the public 'that the *whole* Volume is written with *equal* Spirit
and Propriety; and if this succeeds, (as who can doubt it!) the honest
High-Life-Men in their Introduction give Hopes of another Volume'. His
main charge is ignorance of elite decorum (a weapon used by all sides in
this phase of the controversy), and his interjections mock the familiarity
of Kelly's Pamela with her upper servants. Where she addresses 'my dear
Jervis', Richardson reminds readers that this is '*the House-keeper, to whom
all her Letters are written, because she is now in* HIGH-LIFE *the Reader must
remember*'. Where she comments that 'the Knowledge of our own Ignorance is, in my own Opinion, knowing a great deal', he appends a sneering
footnote: '*What Pity the* HIGH-LIFE MEN *know not thus much!*'[33]

Pleased enough with this hatchet job to reinsert it in the *Daily Advertiser* two days later, Richardson repeatedly points back to it in later
notices, as in the *Gazetteer* of 12 June:

N. B. In the *Gazetteer* of Thursday June 4, and the *Advertiser* of Saturday June 6,
is a faithful SPECIMEN of this HIGH-LIFE *Performance:* And the Publick is
assur'd, that (*bad as it is*) 'tis one of the best-written Parts of their Volume.

☞ *The same Specimen may be had Gratis of Mr.* Rivington *and Mr.* Osborn,
abovementioned.

No copy of this separate flysheet is known to exist, and there were also
answers from the other side that have not survived. In the *Gazetteer* for 9
July, Richardson refers not only to a Chandler advertisement in a lost

number of his favourite vehicle, the *Champion*, but also to other flyers in circulation:

Fresh Irruptions of Scandal and Impertinence in the honest *High Life Men*, as advertis'd in the Champion of July 7, make it necessary to re-publish this Advertisement [first published in the *Gazetteer* of 12 June]:

THE Author *of* PAMELA; *or*, Virtue Rewarded, *thinks fit*, once for all, *to give the following Answer to the* scurrilous Papers *and* Advertisements *that have been scattered about the Town, by Persons who* can say any thing, *and have no other View in it, than to promote the Sale of a wretched Performance called* Pamela in High-Life, *which debases all the Characters in his Two Volumes*; viz.

"*That when any Person who is* above Scandal *and* scandalous Practices, *shall say any thing worthy of* Notice, *and set his* Name *to what he publishes, he shall receive a proper Reply*."

Presumably Chandler had now gone public with his allegation that *Pamela* was the work of a Richardson employee who had since died. A long advertisement in *Common Sense* (18 July and later numbers) develops this theme, holding Richardson mercilessly to the pose of authorial disavowal that he was now struggling to discard. *Pamela's Conduct* was 'published from original Papers, *without the Consent, or even Knowledge*, of the *pretended* Author of Pamela, or Virtue rewarded'. In a second volume now in press, they '*have been obliged to* Kill Pamela, that neither Mr. R——n or his accomplices might be guilty of Murdering Her'. Then they repay Richardson in rhetorical kind, and with added interest:

The Proprietors of Pamela's Conduct in High Life

Think fit, once for all, to give the following Answer to the Impertinent, Vain, Self-sufficient and Scurrilous *pretended* Author of *Pamela, or Virtue rewarded*, That they have already answered him, and in that Answer, to which they defy him to reply, justified their Proceeding; and as they have Signed it, look upon his Scandalous Advertisement as pointing them out for the Persons who are not (to use his own very improper Words) *above Scandal*, by which we suppose he means what he repeats, above *Scandalous Practices* and unworthy of Notice, they think this in a most flagrant Manner striking at, and endeavouring to Stain, their Characters, which stand *at least in as fa[i]r a light* as that pretended Author's; but they don't wonder at his being *so free with them*, since, in the Work he arrogates to himself, he has *burlesqued the Scriptures* and made *Time Servers, Fools, and Fidlers*, of the Reverend Clergy.[34]

By 13 August, Richardson was sufficiently rattled to advertise in the *Gazetteer* that his own third and fourth volumes ('BY The AUTHOR of the TWO FIRST') were '*in the PRESS, And will be Published with all convenient Speed'*. There was an element of truth in this (two printed sheets, or 48 pages of text, were circulating among Richardson's friends in Bath at the end of August),[35] but the letter to Leake makes clear that much of the continuation was still unwritten. Chandler remained well ahead, and was soon ready to advertise the second volume of 'PAMELA's CONDUCT in HIGH LIFE, to the Time of her Death. Publish'd from her original Papers. Interspers'd with several True, Moral and Entertaining Incidents and Characters' (*London Evening-Post*, 10–12 September 1741).

Stock of Chandler's opening volume was exhausted shortly afterwards, and on 3 October he announced a new edition in the *Craftsman*, with a rider informing the public that 'this genuine Edition was thought Necessary to be done by another Hand, and is not by the Author of Pamela, or Virtue Rewarded'. Further complicating the ever more dizzying notions of authenticity now in play was the new front opened a few days earlier by Mary Kingman, whose *Pamela in High Life* (a spurious version, in effect, of the spurious continuation, stealing the informal short title of Chandler's venture) was advertised on 29 September (*London Daily Post and General Advertiser*). Thereafter Richardson and Chandler vied indignantly between themselves for the language of genuineness, as in advertisements placed adjacently in the *London Evening-Post* of 8–10 October (figure 2.2). Richardson's forthcoming continuation would be published by Rivington and Osborn, 'whose Names only will be affix'd to the Genuine Editions'; Chandler's (with half an eye on Kingman) was '*the only Genuine Edition of the Continuation of Pamela*'. Only with the long-awaited publication of his authorized continuation in December does Richardson have his last, legalistic word. The second volume closes in an advertisement protesting, with obscure logic, that as 'some Imitators, who, supposing the Story of PAMELA a Fiction, have murder'd that excellent Lady . . . Persons may not be wanting, who will impose new Continuations upon the Publick'. If any genuine further volume appears, the notice insists, it will do so 'solely, at the Assignment of SAMUEL RICHARDSON of *Salisbury-Court, Fleetstreet*, the Editor of these Four Volumes of *PAMELA*; or, VIRTUE REWARDED' (IV, 472).

There was, however, no such volume. By the end of the year this particular phase of the controversy had played itself out, and the action had moved to the stage. Only *Joseph Andrews* remained, in February 1742, to draw a line under the whole affair, which Fielding must have followed with amusement. As the story of Pamela's supposed brother, and with a belated guest appearance by Pamela herself, Fielding's novel is itself a

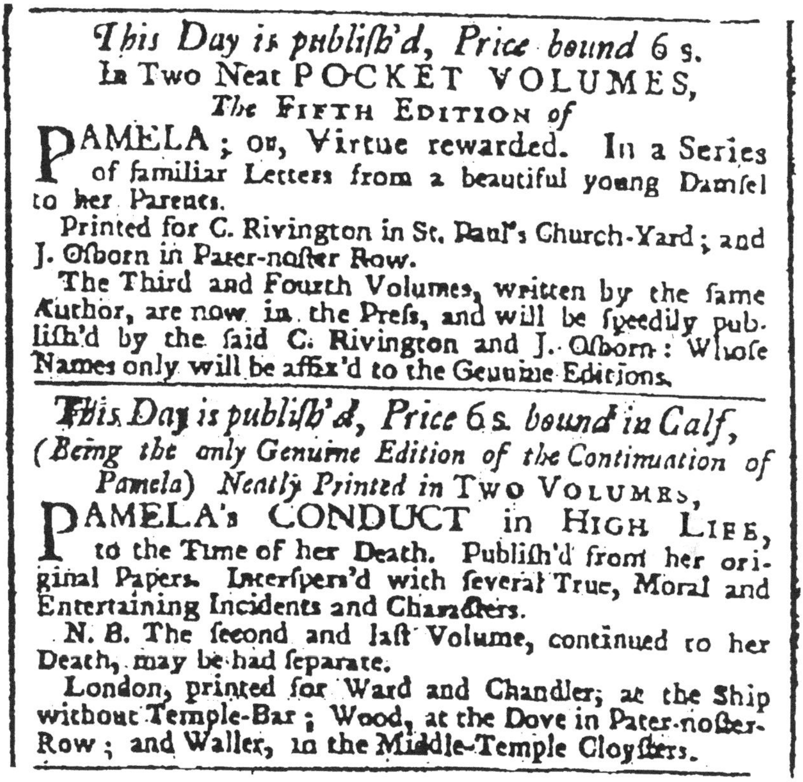

This Day is publifh'd, Price bound 6 s.
In Two Neat POCKET VOLUMES,
The FIFTH EDITION *of*
PAMELA ; or, Virtue rewarded. In a Series
of familiar Letters from a beautiful young Damfel
to her Parents.
Printed for C. Rivington in St. Paul's Church-Yard ; and
J. Ofborn in Pater-nofter Row.
The Third and Fourth Volumes, written by the fame
Author, are now in the Prefs, and will be fpeedily pub-
lifh'd by the faid C. Rivington and J. Ofborn : Whofe
Names only will be affix'd to the Genuine Editions.

This Day is publifh'd, Price 6 s. bound in Calf,
(*Being the only Genuine Edition of the Continuation of*
Pamela) *Neatly Printed in* TWO VOLUMES,
PAMELA's CONDUCT in HIGH LIFE,
to the Time of her Death. Publifh'd from her ori-
ginal Papers. Interfpers'd with feveral True, Moral and
Entertaining Incidents and Characters.
N. B. The fecond and laft Volume, continued to her
Death, may be had feparate.
London, printed for Ward and Chandler; at the Ship
without Temple-Bar ; Wood, at the Dove in Pater-nofter-
Row ; and Waller, in the Middle-Temple Cloyfters.

Figure 2.2. Competing advertisements for *Pamela* and *Pamela's Conduct in High Life*, *London Evening-Post*, 8–10 October 1741.

clever embellishment of the spurious continuation mode, and Richardson clearly saw it as an exercise of just this kind: 'a lewd and ungenerous engraftment', he later called it, resuming the terms of his attack on *Pamela's Conduct*.[36] In this context, Fielding's most brilliant touch comes in his closing sentence, which combines a mischievous allusion to Richardson's war against Chandler with a clever reversal of *Don Quixote* (Cervantes having closed his first part, as noted above, with a rash invitation to other pens). Joseph, we finally learn, will not 'be prevailed on by any Booksellers, or their Authors, to make his Appearance in *High-Life*'.[37] Nor was he, and Fielding thereby secures *Joseph Andrews* against the very kind of trespass his novel commits. Only later were the tables turned, when *Clarissa* received an alternative ending (by Lady Echlin) belatedly and in private, whereas *Tom Jones* promptly elicited *The History of Tom Jones the Foundling, in His Married State* (1749), which added insult to injury by disdaining to make the usual authenticity claim. As the preface arrogantly declares, 'the World should be satisfied that *Henry* FIELDING, Esq; is not the *Author* of this Book, nor in any Manner concerned in its Composition or Publication'.[38]

Many of the newspaper sources cited above are familiar from prior accounts; the unknown quantity to date has been the author of the disputed book, John Kelly. Richardson scholars have relied for their knowledge of Kelly on the angry insinuations of the letter to Leake: here *Pamela's Conduct* is the work of a failing hack who 'had several of his Performances refused by the Stage', and Richardson's mood had barely improved when he acidly revised this passage to read 'one Mr. Kelly, of the Temple, as he stiles himself'. There is rather more to Chandler's author, however, than Richardson's half-truths suggest. Several of Kelly's plays had been staged before the dispute about *Pamela's Conduct*, and all had done well enough to reach benefit nights (the third, on which authors were paid). In the same year, 1741, a further play was not so much refused by the stage as, rather more interestingly, banned by the censors. And while some of Kelly's title pages do pompously style him 'a Gentleman of the Temple' (rather than, as he was at other times, a gentleman of Newgate or the Fleet), this was a designation that both residence and education entitled him to use. It was only one, moreover, among a colourful repertoire of identities that Kelly juggled throughout his career, others being 'Menasseh ben Mirrash, Cook and Purveyor to the Sons of Parnassus', 'Timothy Scrubb, of Ragg-Fair, Esq.', and even, in a pleasing final twist, 'the Author of Pamela's Conduct in High Life'.[39] Though in some ways a representative Grubstreet nonentity, in others Kelly was a hack of a very unusual kind, and one all too capable (as he found to his cost) of making his mark. To reconstruct his life is not only to flesh out the painful, erratic lineaments of a Grubstreet career in the *Dunciad* era, and thus see, vividly personified, the social and professional milieu in which the *Pamela* controversy was manufactured. It is also to see this particular item in the controversy – one of the most influential – as springing from a rather more formidable source than Richardson admits.

Much of the newspaper quarrel turned, as noted above, on the relative qualifications of Richardson and Kelly to describe elite life. If Richardson could claim property rights over Pamela's story, then Kelly – or so went the impudent counter-claim from Chandler's camp – was better entitled to extend it into a realm where he, not Richardson, was the expert.

Modern readers have discounted this claim. 'Probably Kelly's knowledge of high life was as limited as Richardson's', write Eaves and Kimpel, and Richard Gooding finds in *Pamela's Conduct* 'a bland idealization of aristocratic existence that could only be the product of an outsider's imagination'.[40] Given his lowly position as a bookseller's hack (or, as Hammond has taught us to reevaluate this Scriblerian category, a 'professional imaginative writer'), these scholars seem on safe ground. Yet the truth is that Kelly's origins and education – in marked contrast to his later condition – were those of a wealthy patrician, and it was probably to this background that he owed the commission from Chandler. By the time of *Pamela's Conduct* he occupied a fascinatingly ambiguous and conflicted position, that of insider and outsider at once.

It seems almost certain (from the heading and signature on the holograph of Kelly's earliest known work, and from the wording of his record of entry to the Inner Temple)[41] that his family origins lay with the O'Kellys of Aughrim, one of the ancient landed families of County Galway. Aughrim is best known for the decisive victory of Williamite forces over the Jacobite army in July 1691, a year after the Battle of the Boyne, but by that time Kelly's nearest kin were a world away. His father, Smith Kelly, was a wealthy planter and merchant in Jamaica (where he seems to have named his estate after his ancestral home), and rose to become Provost Marshal of the island in November 1686.[42] Removed from office eighteen months later by the Governor, the Duke of Albemarle, he fled to England under threat of arrest, but was restored to his position during the Glorious Revolution.[43] He spent his final years in Jamaica, where his holdings were extensive. Large bequests of money, land and property (including slaves) are made in his will of September 1692, but these probably represent less than half his estate, the residue of which was left in the hands of executors on his son's behalf.[44] Among these executors, who were charged to bring up Kelly in the Anglican Church, was the fabulously wealthy Colonel Peter Beckford, Lieutenant Governor and President of Council on the island, and great-grandfather of the author of *Vathek*. By now the West Indies were a theatre of war, and Smith Kelly, probably sensing his insecure future, had already started to send large quantities of goods and gold to be sold on his behalf by merchants in London. The last shipment came only weeks before he was killed by French marauders in December 1693, at which time his wife and son were safely in England.[45]

Evidently, John Kelly was born with a silver spoon in his mouth – and one wonders what resonance Richardson's narrative of sudden, life-transforming enrichment can have had for a man who had plunged so far in the opposite direction. His place and date of birth remain uncertain, but he was probably born in Jamaica, either on the family's plantation or in Spanish Town or Port Royal, the administrative and trading capitals respectively, some time around 1684.[46] His upbringing was divided between Jamaica and London, where his mother married again in 1696,[47] and he may also have spent time on mainland Europe. He married young, in 1700, and seems to have returned to live in Port Royal for several years before settling again in London in 1710.[48] In December 1712 he was admitted to the Inner Temple, in which vicinity he resided intermittently for the rest of his life.

Though posthumously described in the *London Magazine* for July 1751 as 'an eminent counsellor, in the Temple', Kelly does not appear to have been called to the bar. He must have drawn, however, on his studies. Since 1697 his mother had been embroiled in Chancery proceedings against the London merchants commissioned to sell her husband's property a few years beforehand, alleging that they had conspired with his West Indian executors to defraud her and her son of £30,000.[49] By now most of the protagonists were dead or shortly to die (including the London merchants, Sir Bartholomew Gracedieu and John Heathcote, and all the executors), but Kelly doggedly pursued his case against their heirs. He met an unbeatable adversary in the governor of the Bank of England, Sir Gilbert Heathcote, said to be the richest commoner in the country, and also the most unyielding miser.[50] Kelly's entitlement to what remained of the estate after deduction of other legacies and costs was recognized by the court in 1710, but litigation ran on for a further eight years, by which time the residue had shrunk to nothing.[51] The whole process may even have left Kelly in deficit, and its failure condemned him to low life ever after.

Kelly's earliest known work, a manuscript comedy entitled 'The Islanders, or Mad Orphan', plainly encodes these struggles. Unctuously dedicated to the Princess of Wales (the future Queen Caroline), and datable to *c.* 1714–15 from topical references in the dedication, the play survives among the manuscripts presented by George IV to the British Museum. It has a bitterly personal edge, describing the return to Jamaica of an orphan named 'Infaustus' (or sometimes, more frankly, 'John') to confront the villainous guardian who has stolen his inheritance. The only justification available to this villain, 'Lucre' (perhaps the Port Royal merchant Charles Sadler, the most active of Smith Kelly's four executors),[52] is that he has given his ward a good education and enabled him to move in society in England. There are thinly veiled and mainly hostile representations of other prominent Jamaicans (though Beckford, as 'Colonel Blithe', gets off lightly), and the male elite in general are condemned as base, mercenary, and brutal to their slaves and wives. Various passing remarks (an ironic aside about the honesty of Chancery solicitors, a reference to the London merchant 'Sir Knavery') give further vent to Kelly's rage, and the tone is lifted only by a wishful conclusion in which Infaustus/John regains his fortune through the help of his father's book-keeper, 'Scrape' (probably Samuel Calthorpe, the family steward).

If Kelly was planning to repeat the success of Thomas Southerne's *Oroonoko* (based on Aphra Behn's novel of colonial corruption, and a repertory standby throughout the 1710s), he was in for a disappointment. There is no evidence that his play was ever staged,[53] nor that its stated 'design of exposing the vilainy of some West Indian Inhabitants towards Orphans'[54] received the attention of its royal dedicatee. Kelly was later to write of her with all the vitriol of an overlooked client.

In this decade Kelly and his wife were living in the parish of St James, Westminster, where several children were baptized and buried.[55] There are indications that in the 1720s he may have been trying to earn his living as a merchant,[56] but if so he had little success. The crisis came with his committal to the Fleet for debt in September 1727, and he was not discharged until the following May.[57] In this extremity he resumed his pen, turning in his earliest identifiable publication (from conviction, opportunism, or a combination of both) to the highly marketable business of seditious libel. First, in October, came his satire *The Hotch-Potch, or Favourite Fricassee'd, with a Ragout of Spiders, Cow-Heels and Old Hat*, swiftly followed by *The History of the Fall of Count Olivarez, Sole Minister to Philip IV, King of Spain*. That this second work was no exercise in neutral historiography is clear from further details on the title page, which unmistakably flag its anti-Walpole credentials: 'Wherein is set forth the Danger of entrusting to an overgrown Favourite, the Welfare and Liberties of a whole Nation . . . addressed to, and calculated for, a continual *Memento* to the Person to whom it can only belong.'[58] In the wake of *Gulliver's Travels*, the early *Craftsman*, and other items in the first great wave of anti-Walpole satire in 1726–7, the discourse here is familiar enough. In jumping so swiftly on the opposition bandwagon, Kelly was showing the nose for the newly fashionable that was to characterize his whole career. Both works attracted suspicious attention from Charles Delafaye, the official responsible for investigating antiministerial publications, who records that they were 'done by one Kelly in the Fleet – a West Indian who understands Spanish, Italian and French and gets his living by translating'.[59]

The earlier translations indicated by Delafaye's note remain unidentified, but Kelly was evidently touting various projects around the booksellers at this time. One idea, probably inspired by Eliza Haywood's *Love in Its Variety: Being a Collection of Select Novels; Written in Spanish by Signior Michael Bandello* (1727), was a further translation from Bandello that Kelly proposed in 1728 but seems never to have carried out. The source of this information is a letter from Kelly to the bookseller George Strahan, found in the pocket of a small-time printer who had been arrested in connection with the crypto-Jacobite newspaper *Mist's Weekly Journal*; later events suggest that Kelly may have shared this connection with *Mist's*, as Richardson certainly did at about the same time.[60] In June 1732, with a wild swing of the political needle, he began translating *The History of England* by Paul Rapin-Thoyras (the favourite historian of Fielding's Whiggish Aunt Western), in competition with the better-known version then being serialized by the Knapton brothers. He continued the work in fifty-three weekly numbers, completing a folio volume before handing on to another translator.[61] Other foreign-language undertakings include two primers, *French Idioms* (1736) and *A New, Plain and Useful Introduction to the Italian* (1739), and in 1740 he contributed to an expanded second edition in English of the Abbé Pluche's *Nature Delineated*.[62] He also wrote journalism in the immediate aftermath of his Fleet confinement, perhaps quietly on behalf of *Mist's* or its successor *Fog's*, and certainly for the *Universal Spectator*, an apolitical weekly launched by Defoe's son-in-law Henry Baker in 1728, to which he contributed at least twenty-four leaders in 1729–30.[63]

Kelly's most conspicuous role as his writing career took off (or, at any rate, flapped along) in the 1730s was as a playwright, and it is in this context that he appears in the only twentieth-century essay devoted to his work. ('This neglect is proper', concedes the author, Thomas Lockwood.)[64] In March–April 1732 his comedy *The Married Philosopher* had five performances at Lincoln's Inn Fields, reaping substantial benefit night receipts of £85 10s and promptly appearing in print.[65] A second edition came out the same year, and there was a one-night revival of the play at Covent Garden in 1733,[66] followed by (according to the Irish edition of 1734) a production at the Theatre Royal in Dublin. Based on Destouches's *Le Philosophe marié* (1727), this play has been credited with introducing the French *comédie larmoyante* to the English stage.[67] It was followed by a more modest success, *Timon in Love; or, The Innocent Theft* (again based on a French original, *Timon le misanthrope* (1722), by the Sieur de la

Drevetières de Lisle), which played at Drury Lane for three nights in December 1733. Kelly received twenty-five guineas for publication, which followed within the month.[68] The prologue ('By a Friend') was the work of Aaron Hill,[69] which raises an intriguing possible identity for the intermediary between Kelly and Richardson mentioned in Richardson's letter to Leake.

With its mild oppositional colouring, *Timon in Love* looks forward to the more strident antiministerial posture of Kelly's remaining plays. *The Plot* was a short ballad opera, voguishly advertised in the style of Gay and Fielding as 'A New Tragi-Comi-Farcical Operatical Grotesque Panto-mime', and performed three times as a Drury Lane afterpiece in January 1735. Publication was immediate, again.[70] More controversial was a later farce, *The Fall of Bob, Alias Gin*, which in January 1737 (as afterpiece to the anonymous *Defeat of Apollo; or, Harlequin Triumphant*) kicked off the politically audacious season at the Little Haymarket that was to culminate in the Stage Licensing Act.[71] Unusually, Kelly had already published this farce (as *The Fall of Bob; or, The Oracle of Gin, A Tragedy*) in October 1736, partly in burlesque of a Drury Lane hit of the previous spring (William Pritchard's *The Fall of Phaeton; or, Harlequin a Captive*; there may also be glances at the suppressed tragedy of 1731, *The Fall of Morti-mer*), and partly with reference to Walpole's recent Gin Act.[72] Never one to leave a good idea unmilked, Kelly had already brought out a verse satire on the same theme, *Desolation; or, The Fall of Gin*, as the Gin Act passed into law in May 1736.[73] He may also have written two advance puffs for the Little Haymarket venture, the second of which, in the *Daily Advertiser* of 7 January 1737, has been known to Fielding scholars for many years:

We are inform'd, that a certain Author, tir'd with the vain Attempts he has often made in the Political Way, has taken it into his Head . . . to explode the reigning Taste for dumb Shew and Machinery, and has declar'd open War against Harlequin, Punch, Pierot, and all the Modern Poets, viz. Joiners, Dancing-Masters, and Scene-Painters. 'Tis said . . . that he will open the Campaign next Week, having three new Pieces in Rehearsal on the Stage of the little Theatre in the Hay-Market.[74]

If Robert D. Hume is right that Fielding had not assumed control of the Little Haymarket by this point, and that the political author in question is Kelly,[75] it may well be that one or more of the new pieces involved (*The Defeat of Apollo*, *The Mirrour*, and *The Mob in Despair*, all performed in January but left unpublished) should be laid at Kelly's door. Further evidence is lacking, however, and Kelly seems to have been particularly wary of exposing himself at this time. The uncontroversial *French Idioms* was avowedly the work of 'John Kelly, of the Inner Temple, Esq.', but *Desolation* and *The Fall of Bob* were by 'Timothy Scrubb, of Ragg-Fair, Esq.' With this pseudonym, apparently purloined from its usual user, the vitriolic pamphleteer Eustace Budgell, Kelly deflects attention from himself and quietly implicates another: a gesture of authorial self-effacement and spurious association that looks forward to the *Pamela* affair.[76]

Some months later, as passage of the Licensing Act spelled the end of dramatic satire in this vein, Kelly contrived the biggest splash of his career. Hired to relaunch the flagging opposition periodical *Fog's Weekly Journal* from 4 June 1737, he began by professing impartiality, but then produced a series of spectacularly incendiary leaders that led to the journal's suppression after seven numbers. The seventh number (of 16 July) no longer survives, but its gist is clear from a gloating reference in the *Gentleman's Magazine*, which, having summarized the sixth number, adds that the author 'should have . . . kept within proper Bounds the Reflections he made on the History of the Emperor *Augustus* and his Empress (*Livia*) in his Paper of the ensuing Week; for which the Printer and Publisher were taken into Custody'.[77] Here was Kelly's belated revenge on Queen Caroline, the presumably indifferent dedicatee of 'The Islanders'. It took little time for the arrested printer, John Purser, to identify his author (adding that he had paid Kelly a guinea a week to edit the paper, plus a guinea each for several letters), and Kelly too was in Newgate by the end of the month.[78] A slur on the queen is unlikely to have been the most worrying feature of the newly extremist *Fog's* in ministerial eyes, but it gave officials the pretext they needed to nip the relaunch in the bud, while also punishing a writer who had been an irritant for a decade. A later memorandum by the Treasury Solicitor specifies Kelly's offence as 'writing Fog's Journal in which were some scandalous Insinuations relating to her late Majesty',[79] and Kelly was forced to petition the Secretary of State in abject terms. Confessing authorship, he swore 'that he had no design to give offence to the Government in the said Paper, but only to procure Subsistence for himself and family by writing the said Weekly Journal, being by reiterated misfortunes reduced to write for his Daily bread'. He also undertook 'never to write more upon any publick affairs, or upon any Subject that possibly can give offence'.[80] The petition seems to have helped Kelly escape the contemporaneous fate of the printer of the *Craftsman* (whose leader of 2 July brought him a year's imprisonment and a heavy fine), and he was released from Newgate on bail of £600.[81] Though relieved of the threat of prosecution, he was required to attend the King's Bench for four consecutive terms, until finally discharged in June 1738.[82]

Out of the frying pan, however, was into the fire. Within days Kelly was committed for debt to the Fleet again, where he remained until the following March.[83] Other traceable law-cases of the period (a suit against Kelly for £100 by a different creditor in 1738; a failed and obviously far-fetched attempt, in 1744–5, to claim half the estate of his first wife's grandfather) testify to his ongoing financial desperation.[84] By 1741, his nine-guinea advance for writing *Pamela's Conduct* must have seemed a mere drop in an ocean of need.

By now Kelly had a second wife, Mary Boucher, a widow, whom he married in 1735,[85] and possibly a second family. Deprived of his livelihood as an anti-Walpole polemicist and playwright, and ever alert to the newest areas of growth and opportunity, he began to look to the expanding market for prose fiction. (As in other respects, Kelly's career reads here like a low-level version of Fielding's, and reminds us that the Licensing Act, by removing both from the theatre, was a necessary condition for the *Pamela* controversy and its long-term generic effects.) Kelly had considered this route before with his unrealized Bandello proposal, and now sensed in particular the market that existed for sequels. Even before the opportunity presented by *Pamela*, he produced, in *The Third Volume of Peruvian Tales* (published July 1739),[86] his own continuation of fiction by another author: Thomas-Simon Gueullette's *Les mille et une Heures, contes péruviennes*, which had first been translated in a two-volume English edition of 1734. Kelly may also have done similar work for Chandler before *Pamela's Conduct*, perhaps as author of *The History and Adventures of Don Alphonso Blas de Lirias, Son of Gil Blas* (an anonymous extension of Le Sage's four-part novel) and/or as translator of *Persiles and Sigismunda* by Cervantes: both these works were published in April 1741 by Chandler and Ward. *Pamela's Conduct* was followed in December 1742 by a learnedly annotated translation of *Telemachus* (with different booksellers, a venture perhaps suggested by the prominence given to Fénelon's romance in *Joseph Andrews*), but not before Kelly had made an abortive attempt to return to the stage. As the long campaign against Walpole entered its endgame in November 1741, he published his last play, *The Levee*, defiantly advertised on its title page as having been 'accepted for Representation by the Master of the Old-House in Drury-Lane, but by the Inspector of Farces denied a Licence'.[87] With its exaggerated ridicule of the teetering Walpole (whose rituals for the reception of flattering suppliants were an instantly recognizable target), Kelly could hardly have expected his play to evade the new mechanisms of the Licensing Act. It gave gratifying scope, however, to his favourite theme of ungrateful patrons and overlooked merit (as the virtuous but unrewarded hero learns, 'Statesmen always write the Obligations they receive and the Promises they make on Sand'),[88] and the likelihood is that he intended *The Levee* as a reading play all along. Even after its satirical currency had been devalued by Walpole's fall, it was successful enough to generate a Dublin reprint of 1743 and a second London edition of 1744.

Little is otherwise discoverable about Kelly's output in the years after *Pamela's Conduct*, though he may have returned to journalism following Walpole's fall, and may even have been the author of a short dramatized resumption of the *Pamela* theme, 'Pamela the Second', which was serialized in one of his former vehicles, the *Universal Spectator*, in April–May 1742. Thereafter he seems to have been the author of an original novel, *The Memoirs of the Life of John Medley, Esq.; or, Fortune Reconcil'd to Merit*, dated 1748 and written 'by the Author of Pamela's Conduct in High Life'. The subtitle rings true as articulating a theme, evidently very personal in charge, that had pervaded Kelly's output since 'The Islanders', and his interests are also suggested by other features: an interpolated Italian tale; the story of a Bristol merchant with 'Black Domesticks'.[89] *John Medley* is a bloodless effort, however, quite without the topical energy of *Pamela's Conduct*. There is poetic justice in the possibility that this very mundane reprise of the 'virtue rewarded' theme was not Kelly's work at all, and that its attribution to 'the Author of Pamela's Conduct' was a nicely convoluted act of book-trade opportunism, grafting the novel illegitimately to what was itself an illegitimate (but evidently still celebrated) engraftment. The publication date for volume I is substantiated, and indeed slightly anticipated, by an entry in the *Gentleman's Magazine* register for November 1747 (p. 548), but the fact that volume II was not published until 1756 casts some doubt over Kelly's authorship of this second part, if not of the work as a whole. Whatever the truth, Kelly died five years before publication of this second volume, on 15 July 1751. He was buried at St Pancras on 21 July.[90]

Perhaps Thomas Lockwood was right to suggest that Kelly should stay forgotten. There is reason to pause, however, before writing him off. Simply as a case study in the economic and literary life of eighteenth-century Grubstreet (from which murky environment Kelly now emerges with a clarity unusual for a writer of his status in the trade), his career has much to tell us about the precarious emergence of professional writing in the expanding print culture of the *Pamela* moment. Opportunist and improvisatory, generically flexible and politically mobile, and above all keenly alert to whatever looked likely to sell, he provides in the shifting nature of his literary output a fine-tuned barometer of the marketplace for print in a period of change and growth. With his desperately juggled identities as a writer – the genteel and learned translator of Whig historiography and epic romance; the genial social satirist of the *Universal Spectator* and *The Married Philosopher*; the scurrilous seditious libeller of *Fog's* and *The Levee* – he does more than simply bring to life the frantic, pragmatic world of *The Author's Farce* or Hogarth's 'Distressed Poet'. He also embodies, within his sorry, struggling experience, a much larger process without. Having begun his career with a failed attempt to win high patronage by presenting a manuscript to royalty, and having ended it in adroit manipulation of the popular market for fiction, he nicely dramatizes the cultural shift to which Hammond applies the Bakhtinian term 'novelization':[91] a shift in the balance of literary power away from a traditional manuscript culture characterized by elite patronage, generic conservatism and classical erudition, and towards the vulgarly commercialized, market-led, innovative or hybridizing print culture of the modern age. Born to the first of these cultures, and plunged by personal misfortune into the second, Kelly survived, or just about: a resentful but resourceful foot soldier in the onward march of the moderns.

Comparing *Pamela's Conduct* to *Pamela* itself (and with a smugness hardly warranted by his own performance), the unknown author of *The Life of Pamela* calls Kelly 'an ingenious Writer at least, if we do not altogether allow of the Comparison that has been made between him and the Author of *Pamela*'s Letters, viz. That the last seem to be wrote by a Girl, but the other by a Man of Sense and Learning'.[92] This somewhat backhanded tribute has been interpreted to Kelly's disadvantage by modern critics. Kreissman writes that 'in saying this the author, whether he intended to or not, has applauded Richardson', and Eaves and Kimpel concur that 'if this comparison was meant to be uncomplimentary to Richardson, it also indicates his great strength: he was not a man of sense and learning, but, much more important for his purpose, he was able to write like a girl'. Gooding applies the point explicitly to *Pamela's Conduct*, in which the 'high-life banter' and 'bland stylistic homogeneity' of Kelly's characters effectively indicate social station, but at the expense of personality and voice: 'what is lost is Richardson's particularizing realism . . . what is gained is of more dubious value, a model of stylistic decorum based almost wholly on the rank of the speaker'.[93] Certain touches suggest greater subtlety on Kelly's part, and it would be possible to argue that he represents Pamela not simply as an elegant speaker, but instead as a speaker striving to be elegant, who sometimes misses her mark: in the passage exhibited in the *Gazetteer*, for example, when the befuddled heroine lapses into vulgar idioms like Eliza Doolittle in rewind, deft use is made of slippages in style and register to suggest the residual discomfort of her new station. But Kelly is no second Richardson, and there would be little mileage in trying to represent him as a creator of finely discriminated voices or complex inner lives. Nor is there evidence from surviving comments by early readers, for all the commercial impact of *Pamela's Conduct*, that much was thought of his artistry at the time. Characterization was too inconsistent, structure too digressive, plot too sensational. 'One great Beauty in Pamela is that the Characters are so admirably kept up; which ye other has no regard to', complained Mary Barber, and Elizabeth Teft applies this point to the erratic domestic government of Kelly's Mr B.: 'Like *Phaeton*, unskilful in Command, | Now gives a Loose, now keeps too strait a Hand'. For a third reader, Kelly's reliance on interpolated tales 'exposes the Imitator's Want of Skill to furnish proper Incidents for a Volume of his Heroine's Behaviour in High Life'. A fourth 'wept sorely' at the original, but found Kelly frivolous and fantastic: 'nothing can be more moving I think [than *Pamela*], we had read Pamela in High Life but did not like it, its all romantick improbabilities'.[94]

Whatever Kelly's shortcomings as a novelist, however, there are other good reasons for reading *Pamela's Conduct*. We may not agree with the blustering claims of its publisher, who boasted (as Richardson recalled) that it 'fell in nothing short of my two Volumes', but *Pamela's Conduct* remains of great interest when read as an interpretative foil to *Pamela* itself. It is worth remembering that when Richardson saw advance sheets of Kelly's material they struck him not only as theft but also as egregious misreading, and as subverting his enterprise so thoroughly as to compel reply: 'I saw . . . my whole Purpose inverted', as he told Leake. In this context, *Pamela's Conduct* demands analysis not as a faithful imitation of Richardsonian fiction, but as the opposite: as a work in which the assumptions and purposes of *Pamela* are so radically reversed as to expose in negative, and with all the sharpness and clarity of negative, the cherished priorities of the original text. Not only did *Pamela's Conduct* require Richardson to reassert his right of property over *Pamela's* world; it also required him to enter into interpretative battle over the novel's messages and meanings, and in this sense there is a dual aspect to Barbauld's celebrated judgment that Richardson's authorized sequel was 'less a

amazon.com

Returns Are Easy! Most items can be refunded, exchanged, or replaced when returned in original and unopened condition. Visit http://www.amazon.com/returns to start your return, or http://www.amazon.com/help for more information on return policies.

Your order of May 18, 2014 (Order ID 112-4630554-4161045)

Qty.	Item	Item Price	Total
1	'Pamela' in the Marketplace: Literary Controversy and Print Culture in Eighteenth-Century Britain and Ireland Keymer, Thomas --- Paperback (** P-1-Q37C123 **) 0521110181	$40.15	$40.15

	Subtotal	$40.15
	Tax Collected	$3.31
	Order Total	$43.46
	Paid via credit/debit	$43.46
	Balance due	$0.00

This shipment completes your order.

Have feedback on how we packaged your order? Tell us at www.amazon.com/packaging.

0/D0yktsLkk/-1 of 1-//CVG5/second/8510528/0519-02:00/0518-19:16   **B2B**

continuation than the author's defence of himself'.[95] Commercial and creative considerations were working as one, in mutual defence against Chandler's invasion on one front and Kelly's on the other. As a response to provocative misreading, indeed, Richardson's continuation is much more obviously marked by *Pamela's Conduct* than by the fugitive *Shamela*, which, as an easily available work by a canonical author, has probably assumed more importance in modern criticism than it had for Richardson himself.

There are many features of Kelly's text that Richardson must have seen as inverting his plan, not least the transformation of Pamela into an exemplar whose virtue emanates more from moral sense than religious piety. Some spirituality survives in *Pamela's Conduct*, but Kelly significantly secularizes the original emphasis, and Pamela now reads Marcus Aurelius as much as her Bible. Even more fundamental was Kelly's careful unravelling of Richardson's meritocratic (if not quite levelling) definition of virtue, in which true nobility is a property of individual souls, not inherited bloodlines. Here biography gives a useful lead, for to approach *Pamela's Conduct* in light of the vexed social position of its high-born, low-living author is to see it as recasting Richardson's themes of virtue, rank and upward mobility in ways loaded by private grievance. If Eagleton is right that '*Pamela* represents the comic moment of an aspiring class, buoyant, affirmative and . . . magically insulated from grave injury',[96] it is hard not to find in Kelly's continuation a resentful riposte from the sinking, the downwardly mobile, the traumatized *nouveau pauvre*. Not only in his personal history of childhood wealth and later dispossession, but also in his psychological inheritance as the scion of a leading Jacobite family broken by the Whig ascendancy, Kelly represents the loss of ancient privilege as surely as Richardson stands for the reverse. His situation is legible in his text. With his gentlemen robbers, masquerade scenes and interpolated tales of love across boundaries of rank, Kelly fully shares Richardson's interest in slippages and reversals of social identity. Where Richardson insists on Pamela's commonplace origins, however, Kelly provides her with an illustrious lineage beginning at the Norman conquest – thereby giving her a dynastic advantage over Mr B., whose family was first raised by 'a common Soldier in the Army of *Edward* the third' (1, 214). Paradoxically, the real upstart now is Mr B.'s titled sister, for "tis evident that *Pamela* . . . is a Gentlewoman, by many Kings Reigns of more ancient Descent, from more noble Blood, than *the imperious Lady Davers, the haughty Viscountess, the furious Peeress*, who disdain'd to own her Brother's Wife (her Superiour in Birth, and greatly, greatly so, in the Endowments of her Mind) for a Sister' (1, 215).

With this move, Kelly pointedly recuperates the novel for the ideology of rank it had seemed to erode, and severely attenuates Richardson's case for the spiritual equality of servant and princess. He does so at times with tongue in cheek: when Pamela boasts 'of being deriv'd from two such ancient and unblemish'd Families as that of *Andrews*, and that of *Jinks*' (I, 121), there is more than a touch of bathos in the second name, which sounds strangely like 'Jewkes', denotes a rowdy drinking game, and is otherwise used in the period for low-life buffoons.[97] But the underlying point is in real earnest, and Kelly's continuation as a whole is shot through with assumptions about the inseparability of virtue and breeding implacably at odds with Richardson's own. 'By raising Pamela's birth and thereby shifting the centre of value from the virtuous base-born to the genteel', Gooding writes, 'Kelly rejects Richardson's critique of hereditary honour and begins the process of reaffirming the aristocratic beliefs that the original *Pamela* attacks'. And when Gooding adds that 'reversion to the romance conventions of hidden genteel ancestry and innate class characteristics suggests . . . an attempt to appropriate Richardson's novel as an aristocratic text',[98] we may find the explanation in Kelly's life. Unmistakably, this is the work of a man for whom only the ancient codes and traditional assumptions of natural hierarchy – the assumption, in particular, that hereditary virtue clings to the blue-blooded, no matter how reduced their material condition – could give meaning to the miserably diminished position from which he wrote.

There is one respect, however, in which Gooding's description needs modification. Kelly eschews the most readily available romance device, that of abduction at birth from noble parents, and represents in Pamela instead a category of ancient gentry virtue more venerable in lineage than that of many peers and courtiers, and untainted by the pursuit of title and power. Plunged into poverty by family misfortune, dispossessed but uncorrupted, she boasts a superiority that is exactly his own. In Kelly's lexicon, indeed, aristocracy is as contaminated a category as for Fielding's Squire Western, and for much the same reason. Though conservative in theory, his recuperation of Richardson's plot for a traditional ideology of hereditary virtue is emphatically oppositional in practice, for the current establishment is itself a perversion of the ancient order. The high-political implications of this position are kept quiet, though Pamela is given one strident speech of pro-Stuart allegiance on the legitimate subject of Charles I (II, 43), and later recounts the tale of a virtuous nonjuror who 'proved a Gallant and Loyal Officer; but at the Revolution refused to continue in his Command' (II, 190). It is no doubt significant that she never returns to court after the Hanoverian accession.

Yet if *Pamela's Conduct*, in this and other points of bias and resistance, can clarify the contrasting priorities of the original text, it also demands to be read independently of *Pamela's* context, where Richardson's epithet 'spurious' will always blight it. Written at speed and for cash, it is the true summation of a hack career, and as such has an authenticity distinct from its fraudulence as a Richardsonian text. Indeed, it is in the very characteristic that Richardson critics have singled out for objection – its refusal to be unified – that *Pamela's Conduct* most eloquently expresses its alternative identity as the paradigmatic Grubstreet text. Driven by the pressing need to generate copy, Kelly falls back on the heterogeneous imaginative repertoire established by his life and writing, cutting and pasting the diverse modes of his earlier output with wild incongruity. Pragmatism and convenience are as important as conviction when he hurls together the Juvenalian clichés of antiministerial polemic ('some Men possibly have had a Ribbon given them for deserving a Halter' (I, 203)) with offcuts from his ongoing exercises in opposition satire, as when a time-serving clergyman in the novel 'frequents the Court, and never fails being at the Levee of a certain great Person' (I, 234). He unloads interpolated novellas in the style of Bandello (I, 161–80), flaunts his facility with French idioms ('he is, as the *French* say, *poli comme un cheval de carrosse*' (II, 170)), and punctuates the narrative with Spanish proverbs, usually of a cynical kind: '*Amigo de todos, amigo de ningunos*; who is a Friend to every Body, is (in Fact) a Friend to no-Body' (I, 195). The second volume draws extensively on personal memories of Queen Anne's court (and was recognized as introducing 'very exact Characters of several Persons . . . like one who was well acquainted with the Court at that Time').[99] Other parts of *Pamela's Conduct* are firmly rooted in the grim milieu of Grubstreet, however, even to the point of anticipating its publisher's fate. Of particular interest is Kelly's explanation of Mr Andrews's ruin, which begins in debts incurred by Pamela's brothers. His prose comes vividly to life in these narratives of dishonoured bonds and debtor's gaols, most of all in the case of the second brother, an improvident bookseller: 'he depending too much upon his own Judgment, ran into great Works, above what his Stock would bear, and thus was soon indebted to Stationers in considerable Sums; Copies for which he had given a great deal of Money, did not answer in the Sale, and his Creditors began to be clamorous' (I, 116). Bailed out of prison by his father, the bookseller dies soon afterwards, leaving Pamela's family with insuperable debts.

With all this diverse material, Kelly produces not a coherent Richardsonian novel but a swarming rag-bag of texts and discourses, directly derived and urgently repackaged from his past career. Eaves and Kimpel may well be right to say that the author 'seems more interested in his discussions' (interpolated moral and satirical essays reminiscent of – perhaps directly lifted from – his earlier work for the *Universal Spectator*), just as Gooding is right to note the incongruity of 'interpolated tales featuring such staples of romance as mysterious births and dramatic revelations of noble ancestry'.[100] From the Richardsonian point of view, these prominent features of Kelly's text are irrelevant, and discredit its status as even competent imitation; as an opportunistic conglomeration of just about everything that made Kelly the writer he was, however, they make perfect sense. In the sheer pragmatism of their use, they remind us that the *Pamela* controversy was always as much a mechanism for generating and selling copy as a struggle of literary interpretation.

During the parliamentary debate on the Licensing Act of 1737, which was to end Kelly's career in the theatre, the Earl of Chesterfield made his celebrated contention that 'wit . . . is a sort of property: it is the property of those who have it, and too often the only property they have to depend on'.[101] Having been the first journalist to print the speech (as he illegally did in *Fog's* on 2 July), Kelly knew Chesterfield's principle well. There is a sense, indeed, in which he lived his whole professional life by it ('It is indeed but a precarious dependence', as Chesterfield continues) while also, in his various thefts – of *Timon le Misanthrope*, of Eustace Budgell's pseudonym, of Richardson's fictional world – treating the property of wit as Moll Flanders treats bundles of linen. At once unique and thoroughly representative, Kelly is indeed (as Richardson characterized him) the archetypal bookseller's hack, but one who also shows us how vigorous and resourceful that category of writers could be. For all his hankerings for the hallowed courtyards of the Inner Temple, Grubstreet was his true milieu, and *Pamela's Conduct* is Grubstreet at its purest – which is to say, at its most chaotically and impudently hybrid.

The final irony in this history of imitation and theft is that Richardson may in the end have closed the intertextual loop by imitating his imitators, or stealing back from the thieves. Determined to produce his own continuation but devoid of material, he lamented the lack of scope for 'Plots, Stratagem and Intrigue' in married life, and hastily solicited advice and contributions over the summer, at least one example of which (Alexander Gordon's remarks on opera) he duly used.[102] In this process, *Pamela's Conduct* stood before him not only as a misreading to be contested but also as a fund of ideas to be reworked, including plot devices avoiding the lurid extremes proposed by friends such as Cheyne (who recommended plague, famine, and the 'sudden Conflagration' of Mr B.'s house).[103] The result is that Richardson's continuation lightly foreshadows the more intricate recyclings of *Tristram Shandy*, in which Sterne wittily plundered imitations and parodies of his first instalment to generate material for the next.[104]

When it came to refuting Kelly, Richardson took seriously the reader who advised him not to mention *Pamela's Conduct* beyond his paratextual matter: 'no Allusion, nor the most distant Hint relating to the Imitation, can be admitted in Pamela's story of herself, without being a Blemish . . . nothing shou'd be in the Body of the Work like the Reflection, which Cervantes cou'd not forbear upon the Imitation of his Don Quixote'.[105] The result is that Richardson's objections, though permeating his continuation, are never declared. Several pages are devoted to Pamela's pious forgiveness of Mrs Jewkes (III, 169ff.), in pointed contrast to her callous reflections in *Pamela's Conduct*: as Richardson's adviser noted, these reflections in Kelly's version 'give no advantageous idea of her Improvement in High Life, no Mark of a benign Temper, the true Spirit of Christian Charity'. Similarly, her bland acceptance of duelling in *Pamela's Conduct* (she sees nothing amiss when Mr B. refuses a handsome apology and shoots his adversary) is implicitly attacked when Richardson has her lament that 'Duels . . . so often happen in *London*, that those Enormities are heard of without the least Wonder or Surprize' (III, 142). At the same time, Richardson took the chance to respond to other continuations. When Mr B. withdraws his hostile opinion of Lord Davers, observing that 'now his Lordship improves upon me every time I see him' (IV, 413–14), he carefully defuses *The Life of Pamela*'s allegation that his original representation of Davers 'plainly betrays the Mechanick; for such, knowing nothing of the Behaviour and Conversation of the Nobility, imagine every *Lord* is a *Fool*'.[106] But no direct allusion is made to any rival continuation within the text, unless there is a wry glance at Kelly's background when, writing from Jamaica, Sally Godfrey tells Pamela of her keen admirers 'in this remote Part of the World' (IV, 287).

As the anonymous adviser added, however, there was nothing to stop Richardson turning the tables by reworking Kelly's ideas to his own advantage: 'I do not mean, that no Incident should have any resemblance; for thô like Incidents sometimes cause a Charge of Poverty in Invention, yet the Different Event of, or a shining instead of a barely unblameable Behaviour in a like Incident, may show superior Skill in ye Author.'

Richardson had completed his sequel by 8 October, less than a month after publication of Kelly's second volume, which includes a traumatic masquerade scene and an adulterous intrigue between a mysterious noblewoman and a finally penitent Mr B. Much of his writing was done in these crucial weeks, and it may well be to this material that he was indebted for comparable events, differently handled, in his own second volume. At the masquerade, for example, Kelly's Pamela expects 'to be entertained with some Wit from the Masks, but I found it lay mostly in the Dress: *I know you*, and *No but you don't*, was the general Accost and Answer' (IV, 198); Richardson's Pamela is likewise disappointed by the endless cries of '*I know you!* –Which is half the Wit of the Place' (IV, 91). The development of the episode is different, and Richardson does not follow Kelly in having Pamela abducted after a second masquerade (though he was to return to this device in *Grandison*). He may have been attracted, however, by his anonymous adviser's notion of a trumping exercise, in which he could reassert his own superior virtuosity as a novelist by conspicuously improving on an episode from Kelly. Parasitism could in the end be made to yield a kind of symbiosis; engraftment could nourish the root. In the form not only of spurious continuations but also of other novels more loosely based on Richardson's original, moreover, Grubstreet exploitations of *Pamela* could give significant impetus to a whole genre.

CHAPTER 3

Counter-fictions and novel production

Although five fictional responses to *Pamela* appeared in 1741, within a year of the first publication of the novel, only one, Fielding's *Shamela*, has yet received substantial critical attention. As the earliest and most dazzling of these counter-fictions – works that borrow from, comment on and pay homage to, but also often parody and subvert, their fictional precursors – *Shamela* exerted a strong influence on its successors, many of which, for example, took up Fielding's suggestion that Pamela's self-proclaimed obsession with 'virtue' might be read instead as a calculating exploitation of her 'vartue'. The first such work to follow *Shamela* was Eliza Haywood's *Anti-Pamela*, now belatedly recognized as one of the key publications in the *Pamela* controversy. The other counter-fictions of 1741 are James Parry's *The True Anti-Pamela*, published almost simultaneously with *Anti-Pamela* and linked through its title to Haywood's work; Charles Povey's *The Virgin in Eden*, which uses Bunyanesque modes and assumptions to deplore the corrupted modernity of Richardson's text; and the anonymous *Memoirs of the Life of Lady H-----*, loosely based on the life of Lady Hesilrige as well as on *Pamela*. These counter-fictions, together with the astonishingly popular *Pamela* itself and Richardson's own continuation, helped make 1741 a particularly fruitful year for the production of fiction, with the number of new novels attaining a peak not reached again until the late 1760s.[1] The link to *Pamela* in later novels such as *Virtue Triumphant and Pride Abated* (1752), *The Reward of Virtue; or, The History of Miss Polly Graham* (1769), and *The History of Miss Pamela Howard* (1773) went little further than the opportunist wording of these titles, but elsewhere Richardson's work continued to generate direct responses.

At the beginning of 1741, the once phenomenally productive Eliza Haywood seemed to be a spent force. Her latest novel, *The Adventures of Eovaai*, following a long string of popular successes in the 1720s and early 1730s, had appeared in 1736. Her account of British theatre, *The Dramatic Historiographer; or, The British Theatre Delineated* (1735), had been reprinted in 1740 but had not been succeeded by other critical or historical works. Her musical comedy, *The Opera of Operas*, co-authored with William Hatchett, had been a popular success in 1733, but no further stage plays had followed. And Haywood's career as an actress with Henry Fielding's Little Haymarket theatre company, in which she played leading roles on several occasions in 1736 and 1737, had come to an abrupt halt with the passage of the Licensing Act, which drove Fielding's company from the stage in May 1737.[2] In June 1741, however, Haywood's novel-writing career took off again, with the publication – anonymous, like almost all of the responses to *Pamela* – of *Anti-Pamela: Or, Feign'd Innocence Detected, In a Series of Syrena's Adventures*. It is among the most substantial of the *Pamela* counter-fictions and the only one in English known for certain to be by a woman writer.[3]

The publication of *Pamela* in November 1740 might in itself have been provocation enough to make Haywood resume her pen. Her own first novel, *Love in Excess* (1719–20), had achieved astonishing success on its initial publication, and the scores of amatory novels that she published over the next fifteen years were an important source for *Pamela*. Haywood had had a professional involvement with Richardson. New research has shown that he printed, in 1728, the first edition of Haywood's *The Agreeable Caledonian*; in 1732, the first and final volumes of the third edition of Haywood's four-volume collection, *Secret Histories, Novels, and Poems* (1724); and, in 1735, the third edition of her comedy *A Wife to be Lett* (1723).[4] Richardson's debt, in all of his novels, to amatory fiction of the kind he had printed in *Secret Histories* is obvious, yet it was a source he always refused to acknowledge. In his own accounts of *Pamela* – made in prefatory material to the novel, newspaper advertisements, and remarks to correspondents – Richardson took pains to promote his work as one of an entirely different order from the novels of his predecessors, including Haywood. In a letter to Aaron Hill, for example, written shortly after the publication of *Pamela*, Richardson expressed his wish that the book 'introduce a new species of writing, that might possibly turn young people into a course of reading different from the pomp and parade of romance-writing, and dismissing the improbable and marvellous, with which novels generally abound, might tend to promote the cause of religion and virtue'.[5] While refraining from naming any particular authors in his disparaging remarks on romances, Richardson reveals a considerable interest in and knowledge of such writing. To George Cheyne, similarly, writing in August 1741 of his plans for a continuation of *Pamela*, he declared that his aim was to 'decry such Novels and Romances, as have a Tendency to inflame and corrupt'.[6] Remarks such as these exemplify Richardson's fondness for dwelling on moral issues while also drawing deviously on amatory devices and tropes. On a later occasion, moreover, Richardson specifically mentions Haywood. In a letter to Sarah Chapone of December 1750, Richardson expresses his disgust with the memoirs of Laetitia Pilkington, Constantia Phillips, and Lady Vane, a 'Set of Wretches', he declares, 'to make the Behn's, the Manley's, and the Heywood's, look white'.[7]

After the second edition of *Pamela* appeared in February 1741, followed by Fielding's *Shamela* in April, Haywood had further compelling reasons to join the fray.[8] She had, from 1720 to 1725, been an inner member of the 'Hillarian Circle': the literary coterie assembled around Aaron Hill, author of most of the introductory material in the second edition of *Pamela*.[9] In his Introduction to the second edition, Richardson uses Aaron Hill's letters to draw attention to such models for *Pamela* as the Bible and Aesop, while suppressing any mention of English precursors such as Haywood. Haywood could well have discovered Hill's authorship of this material: his characteristically frenetic, hyperbolic style would alone have been enough to give him away. And having broken with Hill in the mid 1720s, Haywood might have found the Richardson–Hill combination at work in the second edition of *Pamela* an irresistible target.

Fielding's burlesque of *Pamela* in *Shamela* provided another reason for Haywood to write her own response. Haywood's dealings with Fielding – a complex mixture of collaboration, conflict and rivalry – date from 1730, when she was satirized as 'Mrs Novel' in Fielding's comedy *The Author's Farce*. Since a benefit performance of Fielding's *Historical Register* was held for Haywood on 23 May 1737,[10] the two authors seem to have drawn closer while she was acting in his plays. But a striking aside by Haywood in her later novel, *The History of Miss Betsy Thoughtless*, throws light on her changing attitude towards Fielding: a change apparently brought about by the closure of the theatres in 1737, for which Haywood held Fielding responsible. The Little Haymarket theatre, Haywood writes, was

then known by the name of F----g's scandal shop; because he frequently exhibited there certain drolls, or, more properly, invectives against the ministry: in doing which it appears extremely probable, that he had two views; the one to get money, which he very much wanted, from such as delighted in low humor, and could not distinguish true satire from scurrility; and the other, in the hope of having some post given him by those whom he had abused, in order to silence his dramatic talent.[11]

Not surprisingly, given the hostility manifested here, *Anti-Pamela* has *Shamela* firmly in its sights. Haywood's heroine, Syrena Tricksy, is a response to Fielding's Shamela Andrews, as well as to Richardson's Pamela. Like other authors engaged with *Pamela* in the 1740s, Haywood had to consider the prior claims made by *Shamela*, the earliest of all the transformations and continuations of Richardson's novel. But *Shamela*, like Fielding's stage comedies, was merely 'low humor' and 'scurrility'; *Anti-Pamela*, in contrast, exemplified Haywood's idea of 'true satire'.

Perhaps dazzled by the brilliance of *Shamela*, critics have been too ready to dismiss *Anti-Pamela* as a mere parasite: a *Pamela* without moral depth and a *Shamela* without wit. Eaves and Kimpel, for example, extend enthusiastic praise to *Shamela* but claim that Haywood's fiction was 'evidently trying to capitalize on *Pamela*'s popularity, since it has little connection beyond the title'.[12] Richard Gooding, while acknowledging that Haywood's novel does 'treat questions of sexual hypocrisy and the problem of being educated above one's degree', follows Eaves and Kimpel in stating that it 'bears only a tenuous connection to *Pamela*, since it presents a character unlike Richardson's'.[13] Haywood's title, however, like that of James Parry, does not necessarily advert to 'Antipamelist' sentiment (although it might include such sentiment), but rather to the narrative of an antitype to the virtuous Pamela prototype.

In rewriting *Pamela*, Fielding gave his heroine a strikingly demotic vitality. Shamela, despite the urgings of her calculating mother, Henrietta Maria Honoria Andrews, is as interested in the pleasures of the flesh as in the rewards of upward class mobility. Consider the following conversation, in which Squire Booby, Fielding's blundering reworking of Mr B., finds Shamela reading, as he supposes, Rochester's poems:

No, forsooth, says I, as pertly as I could; why how now Saucy Chops, Boldface, says he – Mighty pretty Words, says I, pert again. – Yes (says he) you are a d—d, impudent, stinking, cursed, confounded Jade, and I have a great Mind to kick your A—. You, kiss — says I. A-gad, says he, and so I will. (p. 317)

Shamela's primary emotion, here and elsewhere in her dealings with Booby, is sexual frustration; his oafish form of lovemaking is not intimidating, like Mr B.'s, but simply repulsive. As Shamela later writes to her mother, contrasting her new husband Booby with her lover Parson Williams, '*O! what a devilish Thing it is, for a Woman to be obliged to go to Bed to a spindle-shanked young Squire, she doth not like, when there is a jolly Parson in the same House she is fond of*' (p. 340).

Pamela, with its lowly heroine winning the hand of a highly eligible country squire, is a frame-breaking work: the extraordinary controversy it generated was in part, at least, a response to the new social paradigm it had presented. *Shamela* also breaks the frames of its cultural moment: overturning conventional assumptions about female delicacy by making its heroine, though not its hero, a fully sexualized being. *Anti-Pamela*, in turn, rewrites these precursor texts without returning to existing frames of representation. Haywood fragments Richardson's predatory hero, Mr B., into a series of much smaller male roles, and transforms his inexperienced, tremulous heroine into the far more active, if depraved, Syrena Tricksy. But Haywood does not necessarily satisfy the expectations of modern readers. The primary distinction between *Pamela* and *Anti-Pamela* is that in Richardson's novel the heroine is repeatedly endangered by others, both male and female, whereas in Haywood's response it is the heroine herself who poses constant dangers to her fellows: Syrena is predator rather than prey. Unlike Shamela, however, she finds all of her suitors sexually repulsive; she seeks to marry upwards not, like Shamela, in order to combine a wife's respectability with a mistress's sexual pleasure, but rather to enjoy the wealth and power that only a suitable union could provide.

A telling contemporary analysis of *Anti-Pamela* is provided in a hitherto neglected document: the preface to the 1743 French edition by its translator, Éléazar de Mauvillon.[14] That de Mauvillon recommends *Anti-Pamela* at the expense of Richardson's novel is not surprising, but the justification he provides for doing so is of considerable interest. Of *Anti-Pamela* he declares, 'les régles de la vraisemblance y sont beaucoup mieux observées que dans la PAMELA de Mr Richardson'. Richardson's novel, he complains, is a compound of confusion; its heroine 'une Fille qui a un attachement presqu'inouï pour la Vertu, & qui néanmoins est la plus grande grimaciére & la plus ambitieuse personne du monde . . . c'est un caractére si compliqué, qu'à chaque feuille du Livre, on croit voir une autre Héroïne'. Haywood's Syrena, in contrast, is a character 'soutenu du commencement jusqu'à la fin; c'est toujours une Coquette, qui ignore tout, excepté l'art de tromper, dans lequel elle excelle', and 'on voit même son habileté croître par degrés avec son âge; & . . . son goût pour la débauche augmente à mesure qu'elle a plus d'habitude avec les Hommes'. Syrena's character develops plausibly during the novel but remains consistent and thus convincing; Pamela, with all her conflicting qualities, is merely a fantasy figure. In a final thrust at Richardson, de Mauvillon declares, 'c'est toujours lui qui parle, & jamais une Fille',[15] an especially wounding criticism of an author who prided himself on his skill in ventriloquism, in allowing his characters to speak without heterodiegetic intervention.[16] For de Mauvillon, Haywood succeeds where Richardson fails: she creates a fully developed female character who is not a personification of virtues that women might hope to possess, but rather a persuasive representation of an individual endowed with vicious qualities that some women do possess.

Another useful point of departure in considering the assumptions and aims of *Anti-Pamela* is its elaborate title page, closely modelled on that of Richardson's novel. *Pamela*'s subtitle, 'Virtue Rewarded. In a Series of Familiar Letters from a Beautiful Young Damsel, to her Parents', is transformed into 'Feign'd Innocence detected; In a Series of *Syrena*'s Adventures'.[17] The masculine construction of female virtue in *Pamela* foregrounds 'a Beautiful Young Damsel'; the feminine construction of female hypocrisy in *Anti-Pamela* foregrounds 'Adventures', a term that male novelists would seldom associate with their heroines. *Pamela*, according to its title page, was published 'in order to cultivate the Principles of Virtue and Religion in the Minds of the Youth of Both Sexes'; *Anti-Pamela*, 'as a necessary Caution to all Young Gentlemen'. Richardson's putative readership is mixed; Haywood, in contrast, addresses her novel specifically to men. In a phrase removed from some of the later editions, the title page of *Pamela* also proclaims that the novel 'is intirely divested of all those Images, which, in too many Pieces calculated for Amusement only, tend to *inflame* the Minds they should *instruct*'.[18] Haywood's title page makes no such defensive claims for the novel's purity. On the contrary, *Anti-Pamela* will deal explicitly with the perils of sexual licence, arming male readers 'against a partial Credulity, by shewing the Mischiefs that frequently arise from a too sudden Admiration' and thus spoofing the moral claims of Richardson's paratexts, as Fielding had done.

Haywood's way of dealing with the elaborate introductory material in the second edition of *Pamela* is quite different from that of Fielding in *Shamela*. Instead of taking issue with Hill's hyperbolic claims for the novel, as did Fielding and many of *Pamela*'s other antagonists, Haywood simply ignores them. *Anti-Pamela* opens with the narrator's description of Syrena, rather than with any puffing of the novel by a friend of the author; Hill is thus written out of Haywood's work altogether. Given the prominent role that Hill had played in Haywood's fiction of the mid 1720s, as Beauclair in *The Injur'd Husband* (1723) and as the exemplary Lauranus in *Memoirs of a Certain Island Adjacent to the Kingdom of Utopia* (1725), as well as in poems published in the second volume of *Secret Histories*, [19] Haywood's silent treatment of her former mentor here is striking. And her silence is still more resonant in light of the possibility that Hill is specifically alluding to Haywood in a passage printed in the introductory matter to *Pamela*, in which he declares that he is 'inextricably in *Love* with this delightful Defect . . . *Excess*' (p. 507). As Kate Williams suggests, Hill here 'furnished a studied clue to the name of the novel, printed by Richardson, that informed his interpretation of *Pamela* as supplying "*livelier Rapture, than the Loose can* dream"'.[20] Richardson, moreover, might have chosen to reproduce Hill's letters in *Pamela* partly because of Hill's connection with Haywoodian fiction, implying continuity between his novel and amatory fiction and thus appealing to Haywood's old market. Hill's letters, after all, manage to insist on both the edifying qualities of *Pamela* and the intense pleasures it holds for its readers, who will enjoy Richardson virtuously as much as they ever enjoyed Haywood illicitly.

Although the plot of *Anti-Pamela* differs markedly from that of *Pamela*, it contains numerous telling allusions to scenes and incidents from the earlier work; much of the pleasure of reading Haywood's novel derives from her skilful re-presenting of such episodes to her own ends. As the wildly varying responses among its readers testify, *Pamela* is a highly complex fiction. Even its opening sentence, in which Pamela writes to her parents, 'I have great Trouble, and some Comfort, to acquaint you with' (p. 10), is ambivalent: will this be a success story about its lowly heroine's triumphs, or a harrowing tale of her distresses? Mr and Mrs Andrews themselves at first have strong misgivings about their daughter's innocence, and although they are soon persuaded of her virtue, a series of charges is brought against her both by Mr B., her would-be seducer, and by other characters in the novel. Richardson thus encourages alternative interpretations of his heroine's actions; when Mr B. accuses her of being an 'artful young Baggage' or denounces her 'lucky Knack at falling into Fits, when she pleases' (pp. 28, 65), some readers of the novel share his point of view, while others, the Pamelist party, are quick to defend the beleaguered heroine. Haywood, in contrast, eschews such ambiguities. Complementing the elaborate title page, a further subtitle on the first page, 'Mock-Modesty Display'd and Punish'd' (p. 53), clarifies once again just what kind of a heroine we are about to encounter. Unlike *Pamela* too, *Anti-Pamela* features an obtrusive narrator who, in the opening paragraph, describes Syrena's youthful beauty and appearance of innocence, despite her being 'guilty of Things, which one would think should have given her the boldest and most audacious Air'. Her mother, similarly, is described at the outset as 'one of the most subtil Mistresses in the Art of Decoying that ever was', with a pupil in Syrena who 'knew not only how to observe, but also to improve' (p. 53). The question here is not whether Syrena will be virtuous or vicious, but rather what means she will undertake to promote her own interests at the expense of others.

On several occasions, Syrena is placed in situations resembling those that Pamela experiences, but almost always playing an active rather than a passive role. In *Pamela*, for example, Mr B. early on presents his young maid with a gift of clothing belonging to his late mother, including 'Four Pair of fine white Cotton Stockens'. Her embarrassment at such an intimate gift, and at Mr B.'s remark that he knows 'pretty Maids wear Shoes and Stockens', makes her 'so confounded', she declares, 'you might have beat me down with a Feather . . . So, like a Fool, I was ready to cry; and went away curcheeing and blushing' (p. 19). *Anti-Pamela* also features a gift of stockings from Syrena's first suitor, Lieutenant Vardine, and she too is reluctant to accept them, but in this case, as she tells her readers, 'tho' I did not repent my having refused the Stockings (tho' indeed they were very pretty) yet I did, that I had not done it with more Complaisance' (p. 62). Here and throughout the novel, Syrena is acting a part; rejecting the stockings, if the refusal is properly calculated, will further provoke Vardine's passions, but rejecting them too abruptly will merely offend and discourage him.

Among the most notorious of the 'warm' scenes in *Pamela*, which Richardson subsequently took endless pains to justify, is that in which Mr B. emerges from his hiding-place in Pamela's closet to join her in bed, where she seeks the protection of her fellow-servant Mrs Jervis. At this delicate conjuncture, Pamela subsequently writes to her parents, 'I found his Hand in my Bosom, and when my Fright let me know it, I was ready to die; and I sighed, and scream'd, and fainted away. And still he had his Arms about my Neck; and Mrs. *Jervis* was about my Feet, and upon my Coat. And all in a cold, clammy Sweat was I . . . one Fit following another, till about three Hours after' (p. 63). Playing on her readers' knowledge of this episode, Haywood has one of Syrena's suitors, Mr L., likewise emerge from a closet, but to far less dramatic effect; the heroine calmly warns him that she is expected by a fellow-servant below, 'on which he gave her two or three hearty Curses' (p. 99). When Mr L. subsequently comes closer to physical intimacy with Syrena, she understands that by seeming to resist his approaches she can substantially raise her market value: 'so feigned to be in a great Confusion – trembled – set my Breasts a heaving . . . counterfeited Faintings, fell dying on the Floor, and between every pretended Agony, lifting up my Eyes, cry'd, O! Sir, you have kill'd me—but, I forgive you' (p. 106). Her actions closely mimic those of her precursor and have a similar effect on her lover, but here the heroine is in complete control.

In her dealings with many other lovers, Syrena stages variant versions of this scene. A nameless elderly gentleman, for example, overcome with desire by her charms, exclaims 'Good God! what a Neck, what Breasts are here! . . . putting my Handkerchief back with one Hand, and laying the other upon my Breast'. Syrena's mild resistance, combined with her sorrowful words, 'I am unhappy, it is true; but I am virtuous, and will be always so' (p. 179), has the requisite effect, with her lover reduced to stammering expressions of eternal devotion. A parallel passage in *Shamela* reveals the disparity between Fielding's and Haywood's responses to *Pamela*. Unlike Syrena, Shamela is not only an opportunist, out to trap a wealthy man into marriage; she possesses an earthy physicality alien to Haywood's heroine. The figure in *Shamela* most involved with her breasts and their flimsy covering is not Squire Booby but Mrs Jervis: 'Come, says she, my dear Honey-suckle, I have one Game to play for you; he shall see you in Bed; he shall, my little Rose-bud, he shall see those pretty, little, white, round, panting——and offer'd to pull off my Handkerchief' (p. 317).[21] Significantly, Shamela blushes in earnest, for the only time in the parody, at Mrs Jervis's lesbian overtures. Such queering of the sexual dynamics would be unthinkable in *Anti-Pamela*, which is designed not to complicate the gender relations of Richardson's novel but to simplify them. No woman ever wants to gaze beneath Syrena's handkerchief, and her blushes are never involuntary.

Pamela's fortunes reach their lowest point when, a prisoner at Mr B.'s Lincolnshire house, she contemplates suicide by drowning herself in his ornamental pond. Before rejecting the idea as the promptings of Satan, she dwells with relish on the thought of her newly repentant persecutors: 'when they see the dead Corpse of the unhappy *Pamela* dragg'd out to these slopy Banks, and lying breathless at their Feet, they will find that Remorse to wring their obdurate Hearts, which now has no Place there!' (p. 172). Richardson conveys with brilliant effect the struggle in Pamela's mind as the immediate consolation of revenge on her tormentors slowly gives way to considerations of Christian ethics and filial responsibility. In Haywood's reworking of this scene, such complexities are cast aside. Syrena, rather than meditating in isolation on suicide, uses it as a simple means of blackmail in her negotiations with Mr D.:

Thus, added the young Dissembler, I am abandon'd to the World. – Destitute of Friends, of Lodging, or any Means of supporting a wretched Life; and what encreases my Misfortune, I fear I am with Child? – What then can I do but die? And die I will. The Minute I go from you, I will seek out some private Stairs that lead to the *Thames*, and throw myself in (p. 137)

Significantly too, Syrena imagines herself not as a romantically deceased heroine in a country estate, but rather as part of the vile flotsam and jetsam of the Thames in London, from which decaying corpses were routinely retrieved.

For all of her guile, Syrena ultimately fails to become the wife of any of the men who pursue her. While Pamela's virtue is indeed triumphant, allowing her to move up several steps in the social structure in marrying a landowner with two substantial country estates, we see Syrena, in the final sentence, exiled from metropolitan pleasures and 'sent under the Conduct of an old Servant of one of her Kinsmen to *Wales*' (p. 227). That she should be banished from polite society in this fashion is essential. *Shamela* concludes on an ambiguous note, with Parson Tickletext telling Parson Oliver, in a hasty postscript, that 'Mr. *Booby* hath caught his Wife in bed with *Williams*; hath turned her off, and is prosecuting him in the spiritual Court' (p. 344). Yet Shamela still has her lover; and she has, after all, been 'turned off' by her boobyish husband from the outset. Syrena, in contrast, ends up without husband, lover, wealth or reputation.

The first edition of *Anti-Pamela*, modestly priced at two shillings stitched or two shillings and sixpence bound (compared to six shillings bound for *Pamela*), was published on 16 June 1741 by J. Huggonson. It was followed by what purported to be a second edition, published on 29 October 1741 but dated 1742. As Sale notes, this was in fact 'a second issue of the sheets of the first edition with a new title-page', published by Francis Cogan who had apparently taken over Huggonson's unsold stock.[22] Well before Cogan's reissue appeared, *Anti-Pamela* had attracted the attention of 'A. Merryman', probably a pseudonym for Abraham Ilive, who had published George Bennet's aborted poem *Pamela Versified* and was the proprietor of a daily paper, *All-Alive and Merry; or, The London Morning Post*.[23] Consisting of a single half-sheet and costing only a farthing, *All-Alive and Merry* specialized in the serialization of books, reprinting an instalment from a chosen work in at least one of its six daily columns. *Anti-Pamela* was the seventh of eleven works reprinted by Ilive in this form: others included *Robinson Crusoe* (1740) and *Joseph Andrews* (1743). The title given to *Anti-Pamela* in *All-Alive and Merry* was 'Familiar Letters, from a Beautiful Young Damsel to her Parents' – the subtitle of

Pamela itself. This was apparently an attempt to profit from the continuing fame of *Pamela* while furnishing readers of the newspaper with the text of a recently published Antipamela: the original novel and the response all in one.

Anti-Pamela was surprisingly popular in Europe, with French and Dutch translations appearing in 1743, and a German translation in 1743–4 which went into a second edition in 1746.[24] In addition, an anonymous French novel, *Anti-Pamela ou Mémoires de M. D. ***, possibly by Claude Villaret, appeared in 1742, ostensibly published in London but actually in Paris. Claiming falsely to be a translation of James Parry's *The True Anti-Pamela*, it has no connection with Haywood's *Anti-Pamela* but merely capitalizes on the title. Perhaps because of the prominence it gained through these translations and imitations, *Anti-Pamela* achieved a rare distinction. In a decree of 15 April 1744 both *Pamela* and *Anti-Pamela* were placed on the Vatican's Index of Prohibited Books, and a decree of 22 May 1745 added the respective French translations. Together with the French translation of Swift's *A Tale of a Tub* (a generically marginal case) these were the only works of English fiction placed on the Index in the eighteenth century, with Sterne's *A Sentimental Journey* following in nineteenth-century listings. None of Fielding's, Smollett's, or even Cleland's novels received similar attention.[25]

In England, in contrast, despite the *All-Alive and Merry* serialization, sales of *Anti-Pamela* were sluggish. An advertisement in Haywood's *The Virtuous Villager*, published in March 1742, noted that two more of her publications were available at her bookselling outlet, the 'Sign of Fame': *The Busy-Body; or, Successful Spy* (1741), a translation from a French novel, and *Anti-Pamela*.[26] Little is known about this short-lived bookselling venture, which, Catherine Ingrassia suggests, was perhaps an attempt to 'control the means of her own production and to make a profit, or at least to support herself with something other than her writing alone'.[27] The Sign of Fame, however, seems to have had little success in disposing of *Anti-Pamela*, of which no further editions appeared. In September 1745, Francis Cogan tried, unsuccessfully, to sell the copyright to the novel. In a second attempt, on 10 July 1746, Cogan did sell it (with two others) to John Nourse, Fielding's bookseller, for the nominal sum of ten shillings and sixpence.[28] By then, five years after its first publication, the book was out of print.[29] Nourse presumably had hopes of a future revival of interest in *Anti-Pamela*, but no further editions would appear. And the disappointing sales of *Anti-Pamela* thwarted Haywood's plan to produce a continuation mooted at the end of the novel, where she declares that 'what befel' Syrena after her banishment to Wales 'must be the Subject of future Entertainment' (p. 285).

Haywood continued her argument with *Pamela* in several subsequent publications, including *The Virtuous Villager, or Virgin's Victory*.[30] The novel is a translation and adaptation of Charles de Mouhy's *La Paysanne parvenue* (1735–7). In *Pamela Censured*, published in April 1741, one of the anonymous author's objections to Richardson's novel was its inferiority to de Mouhy's earlier work: 'Was no Romance or Novel ever published with a Design to recommend moral Virtue? – Is *Pamela* the First of that Kind! No surely; as to your Title, *La Paysanne parvenue* now translated into *English*, a little *French* Novel, is something more modest, and as much calculated for the Encouragement of Virtue.' (pp. 6–7). The reference here is to an English adaptation of *La Paysanne parvenue* published a year before Haywood's, *The Fortunate Country Maid*. As Charles Batten, Jr notes, this translation 'bears a striking resemblance to *Pamela*: in both works the heroines, almost identical in social position, face similar trials and ultimately are rewarded in the same fashion'.[31] In the preface to her own version of de Mouhy's novel, Haywood claims that she will 'rescue' the characters from their treatment in the rival translation, in which their 'Elegance of Stile, as well as Sentiments, Wit and Spirit, are most miserably impaired throughout'.[32] *The Virtuous Villager*, in distinguishing itself from *The Fortunate Country Maid*, also sought to distance itself from *Pamela*. Its title page refers to the 'Calamities' suffered by 'credulous believing Woman', and its heroine depicts her own account as 'a kind of Mirror, wherein my Sex might view themselves, and perceive by what swift Degrees Errors, if not timely repelled, gain Entrance into the Heart' (p. 5). Haywood thus implies that Richardson's heroine was among the ranks of credulous women, unaware, like her author, of her own frailty.

In June 1743, two years after *Anti-Pamela*, Haywood addressed her treatise *A Present for a Servant-Maid* specifically to female servants. Among some forty categories under which typical servant misconduct is considered are several alluding to scenes from *Pamela*. These headings include 'Telling the Affairs of the Family', as Mr B. repeatedly objects is the case with Pamela; 'Listening to Fortune-tellers', a central episode during Pamela's Lincolnshire captivity; 'Giving pert or saucy Answers', which Pamela herself concedes she is quick to do; 'Apeing the Fashion', 'Hearing any Thing said against your Master or Mistress', and 'Giving your Opinion too freely' – all part of the charges brought against Richardson's heroine; and, most obviously, 'Temptations from your Master'. In addressing this issue, Haywood is clear about what virtuous servants should do: 'if he persists in his Importunities, and you have reason to fear he will make Use of other Means than Persuasions to satisfy his brutal Appetite . . . you have nothing to do, but, on the first Symptom that appears of such a Design, to go directly out of his House'.[33] That, of course, is exactly what Pamela does not do. Instead, she tells her parents, she must first finish embroidering Mr B.'s waistcoat, 'after which, I have only some Linen to get up, and do something to, and shall then let you know how I shall contrive as to my Passage; for the heavy Rains will make it sad travelling on Foot' (p. 54).

In her most ambitious novel, *The History of Miss Betsy Thoughtless* (1751), Haywood returns to *Pamela* once again. In a conversation with her unpleasant husband Mr Munden, Betsy tells him 'that she found he was fashionable enough to suffer virtue to be its own reward' (p. 539), alluding, of course, to the subtitle of Richardson's novel. And in the final sentence of *Betsy Thoughtless*, the narrator declares: 'Thus were the virtues of our heroine (those follies that had defaced them being fully corrected) at length rewarded with a happiness, retarded only till she had render'd herself wholly worthy of receiving it' (p. 634). Referring to this comment, Christine Blouch states that Betsy has learned 'that the most essential virtue is appearing to be virtuous',[34] suggesting that Betsy is merely an improved version of Syrena. But to be Thoughtless is not to be Tricksy: Haywood makes a clear distinction between improvidence and hypocrisy. Far from objecting to virtue being rewarded, Haywood created, in Betsy Thoughtless, an alternative to Richardson's heroine: one whose virtue had to be purged of the follies that threatened to deface it, and whose rewards were earned with severe pains. Haywood resisted, while internalizing, Richardson's novel because his heroine seemed to her guilty of hypocrisy, the quality that most fully characterizes Syrena Tricksy, but of which Betsy Thoughtless, for all her follies, is never culpable.

In her final novel, *The History of Jemmy and Jenny Jessamy* (1753), Haywood was still brooding over *Pamela*. Here, in the third volume, a woman who has narrowly escaped seduction recounts the story of a meeting with her would-be seducer, Mr Welby, and the proposal of marriage that ensues. Chaperoned by her aunt, she has taken a coach with him to Ranelagh: 'my aunt was so much in his interest, or rather mine, that she gave him all the opportunities the place would admit of to declare his passion to me, which he did in the most pathetic terms, while looking on the story of Pamela, painted on the walls' (III, 299). Francis Hayman is known to have executed at least two paintings of scenes from *Pamela* for the supper-boxes at Vauxhall Gardens in 1742 (see chapter 5 below), but Haywood is the only source for this report of a Ranelagh series, 'painted on the walls' by an unnamed artist. Ranelagh was formally opened by George II on 24 May 1742 as a rival to Vauxhall,[35] and (unless Haywood was getting her pleasure gardens muddled) depicting scenes from *Pamela* seems to have been among the areas in which Ranelagh and Vauxhall competed. The passage in *Jemmy and Jenny Jessamy* underlines the parallel between Mr Welby and Mr B., and between the would-be victim who becomes his wife and Pamela. Like Pamela, Mrs Welby refrains from treating her suitor with 'severity', but the word emphasizes the quality that Haywood finds lacking in Richardson's novel: an outright condemnation of men such as Mr B. who make attempts on women through force or through fraud.

Haywood probably borrowed the title of *Anti-Pamela* from an autobiographical work by James Parry, who on 26 May 1741 advertised his forthcoming *Memoirs of the Life of Mr. James Parry . . . being the Anti-Pamela of Monmouthshire*. On 12 June, another advertisement listed Parry's impending book as *Anti-Pamela; Or, Memoirs of Mr. James Parry*, trading, as Sale notes, 'more directly upon the reputation of *Pamela*'.[36] When Haywood's novel was published before his, Parry changed his title yet again, this time alluding to both Richardson's and Haywood's works. *The True Anti-Pamela; or, Memoirs of Mr. James Parry* appeared on 27 June, eleven days after *Anti-Pamela*, selling for sixpence more, at three shillings bound. Its title caught the eye of Lord Hervey, who sent it to Lady Mary Wortley Montagu, then residing in Italy, on 16 July, less than three weeks after its first publication. Lady Mary had requested copies of *Pamela* and *Pamela*-related material, but sending her *The True Anti-Pamela*, 'a Book you did not desire, which is the Memoirs of an Organist of Ross', was Hervey's idea.[37] The first edition of Parry's *Memoirs* was followed by a pirated London reprint of 1741 and by a pirated Dublin reprint; a second London edition appeared in October 1741 (1742 on the title page), and in 1770 an expanded third edition was published.[38] Parry's bid to exploit the popularity of *Pamela* was thus at least partly successful: the four later editions might not have appeared without the glamour of Richardson's title to increase sales.

Dismissing *The True Anti-Pamela* in a brief paragraph, Eaves and Kimpel follow McKillop, who finds the work 'interesting only for its title'.[39] In McKillop's view, the connection between *Pamela* and *The True Anti-Pamela* is fully explained by a passage in Parry's preface: 'If *Pamela* is a virtuous Character, I think *Anti-Pamela* (alias *Parthenissa*) the Reverse.

For *Pamela*, a poor innocent Virgin, withstood all the Attacks of Person of Fortune; the reverse, *Anti-Pamela*, is rich, and kept me for her Pleasure several Years, still leading me on with the Thoughts of marrying me, till I was almost ruined, and then she jilted me' (p. v). Parthenissa, the name chosen by Parry for his wealthy former mistress, Mary Powell, alludes to the heroine of the romance *Parthenissa* (1654–65) by Roger Boyle, earl of Orerry, and adroitly highlights the fact that Pamela is also a romance name. As Terri Nickel observes, however, the central character in the memoirs is not Parthenissa but rather Parry himself, who thus 'begins to seem more and more like the original Pamela – poor, almost ruined, and clearly the victim of someone his social superior'.[40] Parthenissa, conversely, acts in the same lordly manner as Richardson's Mr B.: opening Parry's letters behind his back, for instance, and having him arrested on false charges, as Mr B. does with Parson Williams (pp. 48, 218). Parry exploits the resemblance ingeniously by abusing his Parthenissa at one point as 'You B—': both 'bitch' and 'Mr B.' (p. 257).[41]

Like Eliza Haywood in her *Anti-Pamela*, Parry leaves a door ajar to continuation at the end of the memoir, announcing his 'hope to give my Friends, &c. a farther Account of myself' (p. 316).[42] Such an account does appear in the expanded 1770 edition of *The True Anti-Pamela*, but it is by another, anonymous hand, recording Parry's exploits in 1741 on board the privateer *The Revenge*, and ending with his death (he is 'shot through the heart' by a Spanish sailor) and burial at sea. The original work concludes as Parry is about to embark as Master of Arms on the *Revenge*, and, as Moira Dearnley notes, this makes a particularly 'fitting ending to his own revenge tragedy'.[43] It is striking too that *Pamela*, with its emphasis on female reputation and definitions of virtue, could be appropriated and used to facilitate the prosecution of a private gender war, such as that between Parry and Mary Powell.

In both the original and the 1770 edition of *The True Anti-Pamela*, the memoir proper is followed by an appendix containing fifty-eight letters by Parry, Parthenissa, and other correspondents.[44] Here too Parry's appropriation for his own purposes of the epistolary form made famous by *Pamela* is notable. His collection is prefixed by an editorial comment that four kinds of letters are distinguished through alphabetical notes: those 'written in Characters', 'written backwards', 'written in Lemon Juice', and 'written in Urine'. There are also occasional editorial comments on the letters, of the kind that Richardson made in a bridging passage in *Pamela*. Mr B.'s machinations, Richardson tells his readers, 'will shew the base Arts of designing Men to gain their wicked Ends' (p. 92); Parthenissa's schemes, in one of Parry's coarser editorial interventions, made 'most People . . . of Opinion she's a W----' (p. 410).

Another early Antipamela, *The Virgin in Eden; or, the State of Innocency* (1741) is among the oddest of the responses to Richardson. Its author, Charles Povey, then aged ninety, would live until 1743.[45] A piece of vanity publishing, *The Virgin in Eden* was adorned with Povey's coat of arms and 'sold . . . at the Author's House, No. 3, in *Little Ailie-Street*'. A catalogue at the end of the tract lists forty projected works, with resonant titles such as *A Dispute in order to shew which Sex is most guilty of Incontinency* and *The Compositions of licentious Authors justly censured*, and Povey's actual publications date back over sixty years. Born in *c.* 1651 at the very height of the Cromwellian era, he writes with biblical cadences and a godly enthusiasm that mark him, in the latitudinarian climate of the 1740s, as an exotic, zealous blast from the Puritan past. One of the ironies of *The Virgin in Eden*, and a sign of its extremism, is that Povey chose as the target of his strictures a writer, in Richardson, who considered himself an upholder of old-style religious rigour in degenerate times.[46]

The crowded title page of *The Virgin in Eden* begins in Bunyanesque fashion, referring to 'A *Nobleman*, a *Student*, and *Heiress*, on their progress from *Sodom* to *Canaan*', and to the parable of a shepherd and his wife 'who dwelt in thatched Tenements, secluded from Noise and Snares. Their holy Living and Dying'. In 1741, however, the book of the moment was not *Pilgrim's Progress* or Jeremy Taylor's *Holy Living* and *Holy Dying* but *Pamela*, and Povey's title page finds room for Richardson too. 'PAMELA's Letters', it proclaims, are 'proved to be immodest Romances painted in Images of Virtue: Masquerades in Disguise, that receiv'd Birth now Vice reigns in Triumph, and swells in Streams even to a Deluge'. In the opening paragraphs of the Preface, *Pamela* finds a more prominent place: 'Good God! what can Youths and Virgins learn from *Pamela's* Letters, more than Lessons to tempt their Chastity; those Epistles are only Scenes of Immodesty, painted in Images of Virtue; Disguises in Masquerade, as I shall prove, both from Truth and Reason, in the Conclusion of this my Work' (p. [i]). *The Virgin in Eden*, Povey continues, was written specifically in opposition to *Pamela*: 'by this every Speech and Language may vote, which of the two Essays they recommend to succeeding Ages, as most worthy and useful to cultivate Virtue in the Minds of Youth'.

When Povey turns from his own allegory of a virtuous virgin to an onslaught on *Pamela*, he seizes on its weakest link: the introductory material added to the second edition. The letters and verses 'directed to the Editor in Commendation of those volumes', declares Povey, 'at first

Sight gave me pleasing Ideas of finding Lessons of Education for Youth'. But the letters belied the lewdness of the work, which will deprave rather than edify its young readers: 'Good God! Can amorous Embraces delineated in these Images, tend to inculcate Religion in the Minds of Youth, when the Blood is hot, and runs quick in every Vein? Are these Lights to direct the Soul to a crucify'd Jesus?' Inadvertently anticipating the comic premise of *Joseph Andrews*, he protests that Pamela is depicted in ways 'that cannot but raise vain Desires even in men as chaste as *Joseph* when tempted by his Mistress' (pp. 68, 69). Like Fielding in *Shamela*, Povey reworks particular passages from Richardson's promotional front matter: thus where Aaron Hill thinks Pamela 'a salutary *Angel*, in *Sodom*' (*Pamela*, p. 507), Povey likens her 'to one of the fair Apples of *Sodom*' (p. 70). He also heavily mimics Richardson by assembling a series of promotional letters of his own, all of which predictably commend *The Virgin in Eden* while endorsing its revisionist reading of *Pamela*. Two are from a 'young Nobleman' and 'a young Lady'; the other three construct an ecumenical front against *Pamela* in letters from an Anglican divine, a dissenting minister, and a Quaker. All five letters are dated, and if genuine (which should not, of course, be assumed) would indicate that Povey was circulating his work in manuscript before early August 1741. His correspondents expand Povey's critique of *Pamela* in various ways. The nobleman, for example, reveals that he had previously been naive, taking Richardson at face value, but that he now sees how the novel corrupts its readers: 'Undefiled Virtue never treats with Vice: she immediately takes Wing, as timorous Lark pursued by the devouring Hawk. *Pamela*, had she been as chaste as represented, would have run to her Father's Cottage, as to an Ark of Security. Chaste Virgins never parly twice with wanton Rakes' (p. 77). Eliza Haywood, as noted above, also alludes to Pamela's dallying at Mr B.'s Bedfordshire house in her treatise *A Present for a Servant-Maid* (1743).

Just as Povey's eponymous virgin was intended to replace Pamela as a model of virtue, so his book was designed to displace *Pamela* as a bestseller and reach the widest possible readership. One of his correspondents, the young lady, claims that she will present each of the royal princes with a copy of *The Virgin in Eden*, 'deliver'd from my own Hand' (p. 78). Country-dwellers and foreigners would also be reached. The title page emphasizes that a previous tract by Povey, *The Torments after Death* (1740), had been sold in 'vast Numbers', with purchasers buying 'Four, Seven, and in some Houses Twenty' copies, 'to send into the Country and beyond the Seas'. Despite his efforts in marketing, however, unsold copies of *The Virgin in Eden* must have cluttered Povey's house for the last two years of his life. Four further 'editions' dated 1741 all appear to be simple reissues of the first, with fresh title pages added to create a false impression of rapid sales. At least 200 copies were still hanging fire in January 1743, when Povey put a clause in his will arranging for them to be distributed to 200 impoverished widows.[47] Years later, an enterprising publisher thought *The Virgin in Eden* worth reviving – first with a revised title more fully indicating its Bunyanesque credentials, *The Virgin in Eden; or, Pilgrim's Progress* (1767), and then in the style of a sentimental novel as *The Fair Wanderer; or, The Triumph of Virtue* (1770) – but it seems unlikely ever to have been sold in large numbers. Its interest lies not in its popularity or influence but in its representation of the outer limits of Antipamelist diatribe.

Like all those involved in the *Pamela* controversy, Povey had to compete for public attention not only with Richardson but with a host of rival Pamelist and Antipamelist writers. Less than two weeks after *The Virgin in Eden*, *Memoirs of the Life of Lady H------, The Celebrated Pamela. From her Birth to the present Time* was published anonymously, on 4 December 1741. This was also the day on which Richardson's continuation of *Pamela*, advertised since August, was registered at the Stationers' Company. The publisher was Thomas Cooper, a well-established seller of pamphlets, who had various business dealings with Richardson from 1732 to 1741.[48] The author must have hoped to profit from the continuing public interest in the novel by answering a question posed by many readers: was there a real-life model for Pamela? Richardson drew attention to the issue himself in the first edition of *Pamela* (1740). An undated letter from Jean Baptiste de Freval to Richardson here notes that 'it will appear from several Things mentioned in the Letters, that the Story must have happened within these Thirty Years past' and claims that Richardson had been obliged 'to disguise a few of the Circumstances, in order to avoid giving Offence to some Persons, who would not chuse to be pointed out too plainly in it' (p. 6). In a letter to Richardson of 15 January 1741, Aaron Hill attempted to find out more about the identity of these persons, inquiring, with characteristically egregious flattery, 'whether there was any Original Groundwork, of Fact, for the general Foundation of the Story? . . . Have you not felt it a Curiosity to see some authentic Account of the Birth, and first Stages towards his present Perfection of Glory, of that Conqueror of ye East, Koulican?'[49]

Richardson's responses to Hill's inquiry took several forms. In a reply to the letter, he provided a lengthy account of having heard from an anonymous gentleman, now deceased, with whom he had been intimately acquainted 'such a story as that of Pamela'. This informant had been told about Pamela's prototype, also a fifteen-year-old servant girl who married a young gentleman, 'about twenty-five years ago' (in about 1715) and had met the married couple himself.[50] When, twelve years later, the Dutch translator of *Clarissa*, Johannes Stinstra, asked Richardson about the sources of *Pamela*, he provided a similar account but set the events some ten years closer to the present, in 1725: 'I my self knew no more of the Story, than what I recollected a Gentleman told me of it Fifteen Years before I sat down to write it; and as it was related to him by an Innkeeper in the Neighbourhood of the happy Pair; and which Gentleman had been at the Time, several Years dead.'[51] Further letters by Richardson – to Aaron Hill, Lady Bradshaigh and Thomas Edwards – also deal with the subject. To Hill he remarked that he had proposed the story of *Pamela* for twenty years 'to different Persons (who thought the Subject too humble for them)', and also claimed that an anonymous 'Gentleman' was 'in my Eye' when he created both Mr B. and Lovelace: 'the best of him' for Mr B.; 'the worst of him for Lovelace'. To Lady Bradshaigh he wrote that 'the Stories of Pamela and Clarissa were laid 15 or 20 Years before their respective Publication'.[52] With Thomas Edwards, however, Richardson took a quite different line. In response to a letter from Edwards recounting the story of a girl who resembled his heroine, Richardson replied, in a clear instance of mock-modesty displayed, 'I am charmed, my dear Mr Edwards, with your sweet Story of a Second Pamela. Had I drawn mine from the very Life, I should have made a much more perfect Piece of my first Favourite.'[53]

Richardson also considered the issue in print, primarily as a strategy for refuting the claims to authenticity made in spurious continuations to his novel, but also with reference to the private and public attempts to identify a true-life prototype of his heroine. In the preface to the first edition of his continuation of *Pamela*, published only three days after *Memoirs of the Life of Lady H------* on 7 December 1741, Richardson refers to 'Importunities and Conjectures in relation to the Person and Family of the incomparable Lady, who is the Subject of these Volumes'. He provides little information about her, but states that 'the most material Incidents (as will be collected from several Passages in the Letters) happen'd between the Years *1717* and *1730*', adding that 'there was a Necessity, for obvious Reasons, to vary and disguise some Facts and Circumstances, as also the Names of Persons, Places, &c'.[54] Pamela's wedding in the original novel would thus have taken place a year after the death of Mr B.'s mother, in 1718. In a dedication designed for the octavo edition of *Pamela* (1742) but not published (see chapter 1 above), Richardson addresses 'the truly admirable Lady' whose 'Picture is attempted to be drawn and Excellencies delineated, in Numberless Places in the Work'. He does not provide a date for her wedding on this occasion, but claims that 'the Lady is living' and has inspired him with 'a Veneration that begun in the same Hour that I was first admitted into your Presence'.[55] This claim to a personal acquaintance is perhaps a rhetorical device; Richardson's letters to Hill and Stinstra both suggest that he has heard about but never met his model for Pamela.

In proposing an original for the heroine of *Pamela*, the author of *Memoirs of the Life of Lady H------* made an astute choice. 'Lady H------' is a transparent abbreviation of Lady Hesilrige, née Hannah Sturges (1709–65); her suitor, 'Sir A— H—', is Sir Arthur Hesilrige (1705–63), seventh Baronet, of Northampton. Hannah Sturges, a coachman's daughter, was sixteen, the same age as Pamela, when she married Sir Arthur; at twenty, he was five years younger than Mr B. In 1738, their portraits were painted by Philip Mercier, who a few years later would also paint portraits of the fictional Pamela (see chapter 5 below).[56] The Hesilriges were alive in 1742, when Richardson wrote the dedication intended for the octavo edition of *Pamela*, and both outlived him.[57] Their wedding date (1725) fits with the account in Richardson's letters to Lady Bradshaigh and to Stinstra, although not with those in de Freval's introductory letter to *Pamela* (after 1710), Richardson's letters to Hill (1715 and 1720) or the preface to the continuation, *Pamela II* (1717). Richardson could have read the condescending notice of their marriage in *Mist's Weekly Journal* for 14 August 1725; as Eaves and Kimpel note, he had published a series of advertisements in the *Journal* in the previous year, and perhaps printed an issue in 1728.[58]

Despite the similarities, to term Lady Hesilrige 'the Celebrated Pamela', as the author does on the title page, is an obvious piece of opportunism. Several other possible models – labouring-class women who married high-born men between 1710 and 1725 – can be readily identified.[59] The essay on Richardson published in the *Universal Magazine* for 1786, probably by Frances Brooke, declares confidently that 'the master of Pamela was the father of the present Earl of Gainsborough, who rewarded the inflexible virtue of Elizabeth Chapman, his game-keeper's daughter, by exalting her to the rank of Countess'.[60] Literary parallels are likewise commonplace. Richardson could have read a sketch by John Hughes in the *Spectator* for 10 May 1715 with a plot similar to that of

Pamela, and part of Marivaux's *Marianne*, also featuring a persecuted, low-born heroine, had been available in English translation since 1737.[61] *Memoirs of the Life of Lady H------* avoids the problem of rival claimants by simply turning its heroine into Pamela, and presenting itself as the authentic version of her story. Allusions to the 'Reward of Virtue' and to 'HIGH or LOW LIFE' in the brief preface suggest that readers will here gain access to *Pamela* itself, at a twelfth of the cost and a fraction of the length of Richardson's four volumes. There is also a hit at *Pamela*'s introductory letters: in this version, 'the usual Formalities of a dull and tedious Preface, or an unprofitable Introduction, shall be omitted' (pp. 1–2).

In order to compress *Pamela* into a mere fifty-nine pages,[62] *Memoirs of the Life of Lady H------* omits most of Richardson's characters: Mrs Jewkes, Mrs Jervis, Lady Davers, Jackey, and Colbrand are all deleted. A large role, conversely, is given to Sir A—'s mother, who does her best to separate the couple after their marriage. As Moyra Haslett notes, the anti-hierarchical implications of *Pamela* are muted here by having 'statements concerning the inherent dignity of the lower-class servant . . . articulated by Sir Arthur, not by his lowly born wife'.[63] One eighteenth-century reader, perhaps led by the title to expect something closer to Richardson's novel, wrote, on the first page, 'Read Dec. 1775 very different'.[64] But this is to ignore some significant points of contact. Ian Watt famously suggests that *Pamela* gratified 'the reading public with the combined attractions of a sermon and a striptease';[65] *Memoirs of the Life of Lady H------* fastens on both aspects of the novel.

Readers seeking striptease in the *Memoirs* would have found it early in the book. Sir A—, who has just left university and returned to his country seat, first sees Pamela as she is washing dishes in the scullery: 'the Weather being very hot, her Bosom was naked; for she imagined no body saw her but the Cook-maid. Sir *A*— could not help taking notice of the Beauties he there espied; which suddenly inflamed his Imagination, and caused a Tumult in his Spirits' (p. 13). There is also a risqué remark by Sir A—'s sharp-tongued mother: 'I'll engage she was not ignorant of the Means to make such a young Spark as you believe her a Maid' (pp. 36–7). Like Cleland's Fanny Hill, the heroine of another fictional *Memoirs*, published seven years later, Pamela is apparently supposed to be adept in the use of a blood-filled vaginal sponge to simulate virginity.[66] For the more didactically minded, the last fifteen pages of *Memoirs of the Life of Lady H------* summarize Pamela's exemplary marital life. Most of the characteristics ascribed to her here are taken from Richardson's novel, and readers are assured knowingly that '*Pamela*'s Virtue may justly be said to have met with its due Reward' (p. 52).

At least two of Richardson's correspondents were intrigued enough by *Memoirs of the Life of Lady H------* to ask him whether Lady Hesilrige was in fact his model for Pamela. In a letter of early 1742, a group of 'Six Reading Ladies' (possibly pseudonymous, and playing wittily on 'reading') remarked that both Lady Gainsborough and Lady Hesilrige 'are exemplary Ladies, but can't find their Story in your Account'. Richardson drafted a reply but did not address the issue.[67] In 1751, Sarah Chapone inquired about the originals of both Pamela and *Clarissa*'s Anna Howe, mentioning Richardson's putative use of Lady Hesilrige. Richardson responded to the letter but acknowledged no models for his characters, declaring simply that 'Miss Howe as well as Pamela was intirely the Creature of my Fancy'.[68] For Richardson to hint at a 'Groundwork' for *Pamela* as a marketing device for the novel was one thing. But when pressed about parallels between his heroine and particular individuals, such as Lady Hesilrige, he was quick to emphasize the originality of his fiction. Correspondents such as Thomas Edwards might tell a 'sweet Story' with echoes of Richardson's heroine, but *Pamela* itself was *sui generis*, not to be confused with a mere 'engraftment'[69] such as *Anti-Pamela* or *Memoirs of the Life of Lady H------*.

Of all the works participating in the *Pamela* controversy, the most commercially successful has been John Cleland's notorious erotic novel, *Memoirs of a Woman of Pleasure* (1748–9), the sales of which (largely underground until the 1960s) have over the centuries almost certainly exceeded those of *Pamela* itself. Like *Pamela* it went through numerous English editions, and like *Pamela* it was translated into many European languages.[70] There are striking parallels between the two novels, and Cleland is far from hostile to Richardson.[71] Cleland clearly had an eye on *Shamela* in writing his work, but his heroine, Fanny Hill, is in many ways the antithesis of Fielding's, and her views on love and fidelity are closer to those of the heroine of *Pamela*. Richardson, Fielding and Cleland also have in common a link to the French book illustrator, Hubert Gravelot. After providing the majority of the twenty-nine illustrations for the 1742 octavo edition of *Pamela* (see chapter 5 below), Gravelot went on to design sixteen plates for the 1749 French translation of *Tom Jones*.[72] Then, in 1766, he furnished a London edition of *Memoirs of a Woman of Pleasure* with a remarkable thirty-two illustrations.[73] Some of the wealthier readers for whom the octavo *Pamela* was primarily intended would presumably also have savoured Gravelot's erotically charged prints for the *Memoirs*, as well as his much more decorous work for *Tom Jones*.

Cleland alludes to *Shamela* on several occasions in the *Memoirs*. Early in the novel, Fanny's girlhood friend Esther Davies tells her 'as how several maids out of the country had made themselves and all their kin for ever, that by preserving their VARTUE, some had taken so with their masters, that they had married them, and kept them coaches, and lived vastly grand and happy' (p. 3). This is often taken as an Antipamelist jibe, but the echo of *Shamela*'s distorted spelling of 'Vartue' is, significantly, ascribed not to Fanny but to her false friend, who drops her as soon as the two girls arrive in London, expressing the hope that 'I should always have the grace to keep myself honest, and not bring a disgrace on my parentage' (p. 5). 'Honest' for both Esther and Shamela means undetected in misdeeds, and each intends to make her fortune through hypocrisy and deceit. When Fanny, employed as a prostitute by Mrs Cole, is called on to fake a virginity that she has long since lost, she too adopts Shamela's intonations. Her would-be deflowerer, Mr Norbert, is equipped with a 'machine, which was one of those sizes that slip in and out without being minded' (p. 133). Fanny protests 'that I was afraid it would kill me – Lard! – I would not be serv'd so.—I was never so us'd in all my born days.'

Fanny Hill, however, plays the role of Shamela with some reluctance, and in general she resembles Richardson's heroine more closely than Fielding's. When Pamela stumbles during an escape attempt, she falls unconscious: 'In this dreadful way, flat upon the Ground, lay poor I, for I believe five or six Minutes' (p. 171). So too does Fanny, when, in a notorious scene, she attempts to summon help after spying on two homosexuals. Jumping down from a chair, she does so 'with such an unlucky impetuosity, that . . . I fell senseless on the ground, and must have lain there some time e'er any one came to my relief' (p. 159). Shamela too faints during one of Booby's blundering sallies, but her swooning is a counterfeit, resolutely maintained 'for a full half Hour' (p. 319). Fanny is even capable of adopting Richardson's 'writing to the moment' technique, using it to describe the moment of penetration after her reunion with Charles at the end of the novel: 'I see! I feel! the delicious velvet tip! – he enters might and main with – oh! – my pen drops from me here in the extasy now present to my faithful memory!' (p. 183). When Shamela, in contrast, mimics the convention, she does so in a *reductio ad absurdum* account of Booby's entrance into her bedroom: 'Odsbobs! I hear him just coming in at the Door. You see I write in the present Tense, as Parson *Williams* says' (p. 318).

Fifteen years after publishing *Memoirs of a Woman of Pleasure*, Cleland returned to *Pamela* in 'The Romance of a Morning', one of four short

novels collected together as *The Surprises of Love* (1764).[74] Here the hero,
Mr Vincent, the second son of a 'gentleman of a very large fortune', falls
in love with Isabella, the virtuous ward of an impoverished farmer and his
wife. In the characteristically knotted style of his later fiction, Cleland
now enters into Vincent's consciousness and depicts his 'inward conflict
of thoughts':

> Superior as he was to any vulgar prejudices about differences of condition,
> respects of fortune, or of rank, had never had but a very moderate place in his
> estimates of the fair-sex, and now they began to have less influence than ever.
> The ridicule of falling in love with a Pamela would, it is true, have nearly
> appeared as much a ridicule to him as to any one: But such is the nature of the
> Passions, while they trample on Reason, to keep, however, all the measures they
> can with her. (p. 178)

Vincent is as sensitive to ridicule over a misalliance as Mr B., but Isabella,
although employed as a lady's maid, is in fact the estranged granddaughter of a wealthy steward who has been made a lord. At the end of the novel
she is reunited with her grandfather, Lord Firenew, who gives her the bulk
of his 'great fortune' when she marries Vincent. In a final allusion to
Pamela, Cleland claims that Isabella has 'reaped the rewards of her pious
gratitude to the guardians, which Providence had raised for her in the
days of her orphanship and desertion of friends' (p. 203). In practice,
however, Isabella has reaped the rewards of her noble ancestry, while
Vincent can give free rein to his passions without deposing his reason.
Turning his back on the disruptive social implications of *Pamela*, in 'The
Romance of a Morning' Cleland presents a deeply conservative counter-
fiction. Ann Louise Kibbie remarks astutely that in *Memoirs of a Woman
of Pleasure*, Cleland's project 'is to reconcile the sentimental and the
mercenary'.[75] In 'The Romance of the Morning', however, as in most of
Cleland's later fiction, the mercenary takes control.

Like *Pamela*, in which Mr B. dresses up as the maid Nan to gain access
to Pamela's bed, *Memoirs of a Woman of Pleasure* features a cross-dressing
scene: one of the heroine's fellow-prostitutes attends a masquerade as a
'smock-fac'd boy' (p. 154) and attracts the attentions of a man who
mistakes the appearance for the reality. *The Female Soldier; or, The
Surprising Life and Adventures of Hannah Snell*, published in June 1750,
a year after the second volume of Cleland's novel, has a cross-dresser as its
heroine. This anonymous popular biography, published in both a 46-page
octavo and a 187-page longer version, with engravings,[76] recounts the
dashing exploits of Hannah Snell, who under the name of James Gray

served in the army and the navy from 1745 to 1750. In a concluding summary of her career, the author declares, in the short version of the text, that his heroine, 'in the midst of thousands of the Martial Gentry, preserved her Chastity by the most virtuous Stratagems that could be devised'. Hannah Snell 'is a real *Pamella*; the other a counterfeit; this *Pamella* is real Flesh and Blood, the other is no more than a Shadow' (pp. 40–1). Commenting on this passage, Dianne Dugaw contends that 'Hannah's story is not really Pamela's at all – the narrator's Richardsonian projections notwithstanding' (p. ix). But the longer version of the text makes clear in what sense Hannah Snell replaces 'the late famous *Pamela*, who for some Time alarmed the Town with her extraordinary Virtues'. Richardson, the author declares, has fabricated the heroine of his 'fabulous Story', 'whereas the Virtue and Chastity in particular of our Heroine, who is no Shadow, but true Flesh and Blood, have been amply displayed in one of the remotest Corners of the World; and doubtless will now be displayed all over *Europe* with equal Lustre' (pp. 166–7). Unlike *Pamela* and *Memoirs of a Woman of Pleasure, The Female Soldier* had limited success in Europe, appearing only in a Dutch translation. But Hannah Snell played herself on the London stage, in performances at Sadlers Wells, and chapbook versions of her story were published in London (1756), York (1809), and Northampton, Massachusetts (1809).[77]

Joseph Spence, who described Richardson in 1748 as 'one of the most worthy hearted men, that ever I knew in my life' and who considered writing a memoir of the novelist after his death,[78] wrote two miniature epistolary fictions suggesting alternative plot developments for *Pamela*. The first, a series of letters exchanged 'between a Mother, and her Daughter lately gone to Service', appeared in a collection entitled *Moralities: Or, Essays, Letters, Fables; and Translations*, published in April 1753 under the pseudonym 'Sir Harry Beaumont'. Two letters by Jenny, describing the household of her master, Mr Johnson, occupy only three of the twenty pages. The principal character here is her mother, who expands the occasional homilies of Richardson's Mrs Andrews into a formidably didactic epistolary *vade mecum*. Mr Johnson, we hear from Jenny, is sixty-five: he 'has always an easy, smiling Look; and is very good to all his Servants' (p. 57). Her mother, however, advises her that 'all young Women shou'd look on the Men in general, as a Sort of Beasts of Prey', and urges her to be especially wary of 'those, who are the most vehement in their Praises of you' (pp. 69, 73). Jenny has neither the special virtues of Pamela nor the vices of Shamela and Syrena: she is simply a conventional servant-maid, who, her mother hopes, might make a match with an 'honest Lover', such as Thomas the coachman (p. 71). Her master, Mr Johnson, is neither a predator nor a potential husband.

Spence also wrote the unpublished 'Letters from a Maid-Servant Lately Come to Town, To Her Relations in Hamshire', in which an ingénue, Mary Adams, records her impressions of London: 'The young fellows, in town, are ten times more impudent, than ours in the Country. My Old friend Tom us'd to think it a mighty matter, if he cou'd steal half a kiss from one, whilst one was a Milking; but the Rakes here – Lord have mercy upon us!'[79] Her master is the exemplary figure that Richardson came to wish he had created in Mr B., and his 'kind Advice to Maid Servants', transcribed in the final letter, defines the terms of the ideal master–servant relationship. Mary's failure to make any impression on his heart is less a parody of Pamela's success than an acknowledgment of her uniqueness. While taking up elements from Haywood's *A Present for a Servant-Maid* (1743), the piece also alludes to Aaron Hill's prefatory assertion in *Pamela* that 'the *moral Meaning* of PAMELA's Good-fortune' is 'far from tempting young Gentlemen to marry *such* Maids as are found in their Families' (p. 517).

Also above the need to write for publication was Lady Mary Wortley Montagu, whose personal freedom from the Grubstreet marketplace coexisted with a voracious appetite for its productions. Parry's *True Anti-Pamela* was just one item among many large consignments of the new prose fiction and related material that Montagu had sent to her on the continent after leaving England in 1739. On this occasion she had requested *Shamela*'s key intertexts (*Pamela* itself, Cibber's *Apology*, and Middleton's *Life of Cicero*), and her addiction to popular print – 'binge reading' is Isobel Grundy's term for her habits of consumption – was to hit its extreme eleven years later, in 1751, when Montagu read twenty-seven volumes of fiction, including *Clarissa*, within a fortnight.[80] Richardson commanded her strong but reluctant absorption throughout this period, and her sardonic remarks on the challenge to hierarchy implied by Pamela's elevation are well known: 'the Joy of the Chambermaids of all Nations', she loftily calls Richardson's novel in a letter of 1750, and later scoffs at a levelling marriage in Italy as 'exactly ressembling and, I beleive, copy'd from Pamela'.[81]

Less often noted is the extent to which Montagu's fascination with, and resistance to, Richardson's work informs her unpublished romances. Her earliest surviving narrative, 'Indamora to Lindamira', is a direct response to one of the most prominent novels of her youth, the anonymous

Adventures of Lindamira (1702), and in later romances she resumes the habit of reworking and contesting published fiction. Only rarely does this intertextual dimension break the surface, as when we learn of the virtuous heroine in 'Princess Docile I' that 'Her Governess had already given her *Pamela*, to form her Heart'.[82] Montagu's challenge to Richardson's tale of virtue rewarded, however, is no less real for remaining implicit. It is above all an aristocratic challenge, in which Montagu reasserts the style and values of heroic romance with all the conservatism of an aging, isolated exile, though also with a distinctive twist of feminist complaint. The complex shape of her engagement is at its clearest in her second court tale, 'Louisa' (written some time after 1742), which Grundy introduces as 'surely reflect[ing] Delarivier Manley's seduction fictions on one hand and Richardson's *Pamela* on the other' (p. xviii). Narrated in a detached voice that holds the tale's emotional content at arm's length, 'Louisa' exemplifies the disdain expressed in Montagu's letters for the enabling vulgarities of Richardsonian realism: its indecorous self-revelations ('Fig leaves are as necessary for our Minds as our Bodies', as she protests of *Grandison*); its immersion in low particulars ('I will not imitate R[ichardson] by giving a long detail of triffles').[83] Although the pull of Richardsonian inwardness is felt at several points, not least in the passionate letters that punctuate the narrative, Montagu's fascination with 'the whole state of [Louisa's] heart' (p. 60) is for the most part restricted to hyperbolic third-person telling, not dramatic first-person showing.

In thematic terms, Montagu uses 'Louisa' to contest *Pamela*'s definition of virtue as a matter of piety and spiritual election, and in this sense follows the public lead of her cousin Henry Fielding. Where Fielding proposes charity and benevolence as the core values of *Joseph Andrews*, however, Montagu looks back instead to romance ideology and classical republican ethics, crediting her heroine with 'a sense of Honnour and innate Virtue more rigid than that of the Catos and Scipio's of Rome' (p. 43). Like Pamela, Louisa is a low-born beauty who marries into the social elite, but Montagu pointedly presents this marriage not as the reward of virtue, but rather as the self-denying choice that virtue makes in preference to loss of honour. Seduced in all but the act by a philandering royal, Louisa sacrifices herself in marriage to a grotesque minor aristocrat (her Mr B. is named the Count de Belforrest), and finds herself miserably yoked to a man 'who had a Serpent in his Breast that turn'd all things to poison' (p. 74). Unable to emulate the classical Lucretia, Louisa foresees the miseries her marriage will entail, 'and it had been a thousand times easyer for her to put an end to her Cares, by the Poison, or the

Dagger, but her Religion forbid her to think that way, and she could not otherways live and preserve her Virtue' (p. 69). Here is an understanding of female virtue as a form of heroic endurance that can only be fulfilled in adversity, and an understanding of marriage that emphatically rejects the comic escapism of Richardson's text. In the governing image of Montagu's grim and punitive revision, Louisa escapes the crime of self-poisoning by marrying an aristocrat, but in so doing embraces the poison, metaphorically or even literally, at the hands of her lordly spouse: 'She knew very well the Severe temper of the Count; she had heard how he had poison'd his first Wife, and she did not doubt if he marry'd her, it was to make her a Prisoner for the rest of her Life' (p. 68). It is a gloomy fable of entrapment, transposing *Pamela* to a romance sphere in which the only scope for female virtue lies in renunciation or self-mortification.

Even Montagu's voracious reading of *Pamela* counter-fictions did not extend as far as *The Life of Miss Fanny Brown*, a semi-autobiographical novel by John Alcock (1715–1806), for which subscription proposals were published, in January 1756, in the *London Evening Post*.[84] Alcock, the organist at Lichfield Cathedral, clearly found it hard to attract subscribers: the novel, published under the pseudonym John Piper, appeared only in March 1761 (though dated 1760).[85] In an obvious attempt to drum up customers, a proposal for printing the work of February 1759 gave the novel the sub-title 'The Second Pamela'.[86] The title page of the published novel, however, bears a different sub-title, with no mention of *Pamela*, and Alcock makes only a perfunctory reference to Richardson's work, declaring in his preface (p. xxxi) that his own reading of novels has been confined to just two books: 'the two first volumes of *Pamela*' and Smollett's *Roderick Random* (1748). Naming two works that had been attacked for their immorality is another transparent ploy to attract readers, rather than an actual engagement with Richardson's novel.[87] Alcock might have borrowed his pairing of Richardson's and Smollett's first novels from John Kidgell's experimental novel *The Card* (1755), which concludes with a metafictional ball in which one dancing couple is formed by 'Roderick Random, Esq., with Mrs. *Booby*, late Miss *Pamela Andrews*' (II, 294).[88]

The anonymous author of *The Theatre of Love* (1758), a collection of twelve short fictions, draws on *Pamela* in two of the stories. The first, 'Innocence in Distress: Or, Virtue Triumphant', signals its use of Richardson in its sub-title. The heroine, Sophia Meanwell, flees from her licentious employer Bellario, taking refuge with her brother in London where she marries a wealthy tradesman. Sophia's virtue is thus rewarded in a manner more conventional than that of Pamela; both heroines have fortunate marriages, but Sophia's affluent husband is a man of her own class.

'Jenny: Or, the Female Fortune Hunter', the final item in *The Theatre of Love*, is a more complex and thoughtful response to *Pamela*. Its heroine is a farmer's daughter who is 'immoderately fond of Reading' (p. 232). Among the books she devours are *The Fortunate Country Maid* and *Pamela*, as well as 'a great many others; which say, *as how*, from the lowest State of Poverty, *Virtue* will bring *Servant-Girls*, and Folks of *low Degree*, to ride in their *Coaches and Six*, and marry their Masters; with other equally surprizing Things' (p. 233). Jenny seems also to have read *Shamela*, since she envisages her fortune 'if she was *vartuous*, and rejected the illicit Amours of the People of Fashion that she expected would pay their Court to her' (p. 234). But *Pamela* is her principal guide: 'A second perusal . . . created some new Thoughts in her Head. She thought, that to put herself in Fortune's Way, she must go to *Service*; and then undoubtedly, if she persevered in the Road of Virtue, as *Pamela* did, she should meet with the same Fortune' (p. 235). Jenny goes to London with her head full of Richardson's novel. The coachman has told her of a tradesman in need of a servant, 'but a Tradesman would not suit *Jenny*. *Pamela's* Husband was a *Squire*, and worth a great deal of Money; and therefore she thought, that by a similar behaviour, *she* ought not to marry any one under that Degree, and was as well entitled to such a one as *Pamela* was; because she was as handsome as *Pamela* is described, and was determined to act as virtuous' (p. 237). Returning briefly to her parents in the country after her first venture in London fails, she takes up *The Fortunate Country Maid* and *Pamela* once again. With their help, her fantasies grow stronger: 'she now indulged herself in acting the Prude with one, the Coquet with another; and the 'Squire, her Master, after having in vain attempted her Virtue and Innocence, now breathing an honourable Passion, she was marry'd to him, and tasted some of the supremest Pleasures IMAGINABLE' (p. 240). After enjoying these flights of imagination, however, Jenny makes a second visit to London, which proves equally disappointing. She fails to attract either her new employer, an elderly baronet, or his eligible nephew, and a last returns to the country for good, where she is then married to Ralph, son and heir of Farmer Hodges. No blame, however, is levelled at Richardson for leading Jenny astray. The fault, we are told, is that of Jenny herself, whom the author locates finally in the tradition of Charlotte Lennox's Arabella: '*Jenny* has now quite forsaken her *Quixotism*, wonders at her mistaking the *true End and Design* of those excellent Books, before mention'd; and makes as good a Wife as any Woman in the Parish, and *Ralph* is as good a Husband' (p. 248). Like Spence, the author insists that Pamela is a special case; Richardson cannot be held responsible for those who wilfully misread his novel.

Misreading *Pamela* is also a feature of the anonymous *The Feelings of the Heart; or, The History of a Country Girl* (1772). Here the naive young heroine, Sophia, is given a copy of *Pamela* by her mother, who hopes that the novel will warn her of the perils of love: '"This", said she "is perhaps a dangerous instructor, but dangerous distempers require dangerous remedies. Read this, Sophia," continued she, "and learn from it to guard against the artful snares of men"' (1, 36). Sophia opens the book 'with indifference', but is soon captivated: 'I sat up most of the night, and finished the volume. I now saw my late imprudence in the strongest light. I imagined myself the suffering, humble Pamela, and the amiable Lord Edmond was converted into the intriguing Mr. B—' (1, 37). Sophia, however, has been misled. Lord Edmond, whom she will eventually marry, proves to be virtuous, while other men intrigue against her. At first identifying only with Pamela's 'distress', in which she 'soon lost the remembrance' of her own (1, 57), Sophia comes to see that her mother's warnings were well intended but misdirected.

In the later 1770s, with the cult of sensibility, the sentimental, and the feeling heart in full flower, *Pamela* was more likely to be depicted as a pernicious force. In Henry Brooke's *Juliet Grenville: or, The History of the Human Heart* (1774), the heroine has been reading *Pamela*, 'which already had made some noise in the world', not privately but aloud, to the Countess of Cranfield. Asked by the Countess for her views on the novel, Juliet responds with remarkable eloquence. Although she admires Richardson's ability to touch the passions, she blushes 'at the manner in which he undresses our sex'. His ideas are 'much too frequently and unnecessarily wanton' and she also disapproves of the novel's title:

can virtue be rewarded, by being united to vice? Her master was a ravisher, a tyrant, a dissolute, a barbarian in manners and principle. I admit it, the author may say; but then he was superior in riches and station. Indeed, Mr Richardson never fails in due respect to such matters; he always gives the full value to title and fortune. (111, 91–2)

Juliet, in contrast, who through a series of startling plot reversals will prove to be of nobler descent than her beloved, marries him not for 'title and fortune' but only for love.

Pamela also plays a significant part in *The Sylph* (1779), probably by the Duchess of Devonshire.[89] Here a father recounts a story about his daughter Nancy, betrayed by a seemingly friendly female neighbour. The woman in question, who has in fact been employed by the libertine Colonel Montague to act as his bawd, 'continually was introducing instances of handsome girls who had made their fortunes merely from that circumstance'. Telling Nancy 'what a fine opportunity it would be, to raise her family, like *Pamela Andrews*', she gives her a copy of 'those pernicious volumes'. Reading Richardson's novel persuades Nancy to discard her previous suitor, who has none of the Colonel's glamour: 'his language was insipid, after the luscious speeches, and ardent but dishonorable warmth of Mr B—'. Nancy, who narrowly escapes becoming a cast-off mistress, has been corrupted by a novel that taught her to 'disrelish the honest, artless effusions of her first lover's heart' (pp. 136–7).

As novels such as *Juliet Grenville* and *The Sylph* reveal, the old charge against Pamela of hypocrisy and cunning manipulation in 'bringing a Man to her Lure'[90] was being expanded by novelists of the 1770s, who capitalized on the enduring popularity of Richardson's novel while depicting its heroine as a dangerous personification of the artful, unfeeling heart. Critics such as Gerard Barker, Isobel Grundy, Jerry Beasley and Joseph Bartolomeo have noted the centrality of *Clarissa* and *Sir Charles Grandison* as dominant models for novelists of the next generation,[91] but *Pamela* too continued to inspire and provoke. And for dramatists, as the next chapter shows, *Pamela* was by far the most important of Richardson's novels, generating theatrical and operatic adaptations until the final decades of the century.

CHAPTER 4

Domestic servitude and the licensed stage

In his first major poem, *London,* published two years before *Pamela* in 1738, Samuel Johnson warned of the public damage done by the Licensing Act of 1737:

> With warbling Eunuchs fill a licens'd Stage,
> And lull to Servitude a thoughtless Age.
>
> (ll. 59–60)

In the following decades, however, a new generation of actors, dramatists and managers – figures such as David Garrick, Isaac Bickerstaff and Samuel Foote – emerged to revive theatrical culture, and Richardson's tale of private servitude was among the resources that enabled them to do so. There was a need for a new type of comedy, politically untendentious but with other tensions to make up for the lack of partisan charge, and *Pamela* supplied dramatists with just this kind of material. A fashionable work, it became an apt vehicle for fashionable actors, the perfect play to promote the culture of theatrical celebrity that developed after the Licensing Act. Its richness as a resource is also shown by exploitations in the very different circumstances of France and Italy. This chapter, while concentrating on English adaptations and on those translated into English by Voltaire and Goldoni, will also briefly consider the earliest French dramatic versions of *Pamela,* closely involved as they were with the *Pamela* controversy in England and with the novel's French translation, published in London with Richardson's cooperation.

In June 1741, seven months after the first publication of *Pamela,* Henry Giffard (1694–1772), manager of the Goodman's Fields Theatre, London, took a small group of actors to present a summer season at the Tankard Street Theatre, Ipswich. Goodman's Fields had opened as an unlicensed playhouse in 1729, and had been under Giffard's management since 1731. Among his touring company at Ipswich was a fledgling actor of twenty-four, David Garrick, who played a variety of comic and tragic parts under the pseudonym of 'Mr. Lyddall'.[1] In October of that year, Giffard entrusted his brilliant protégé with the title role in Colley Cibber's adaptation of *Richard III* at Goodman's Fields. Garrick's debut on the London stage on 19 October was a sensational success, comparable to that of Richardson's first novel. The conjuncture of the Garrick and *Pamela* crazes was noted by Joseph Warton in a satiric poem of 1742, *Fashion*, which contains an account of a fop:

> With him the Fair, enraptur'd with a Rattle,
> Of *Vauxhall, Garrick*, or *Pamela* prattle.[2]

Painters too were turning to Garrick and *Pamela* as subjects at about the same time. Thomas Bardwell and Bartholomew Dandridge both depicted Garrick as Richard III in late 1741 or 1742, while Francis Hayman and Hubert Gravelot were creating paintings from at least three of their engravings of scenes from *Pamela*.[3] Like the author of *Pamela*, Garrick maintained his anonymity for as long as possible, thus heightening popular interest in his identity. He had appeared on *Richard III* playbills as 'a Gentleman', and his name remained concealed (or at least undeclared) through several further productions.[4]

While Garrick was embarking on his acting career, Giffard was capitalizing on *Pamela* fever by turning the novel into a stage comedy. According to Joseph Dorman, who claimed that 'the Theatres have been oblig'd to him for several polite Pieces', Giffard had already composed or adapted some works for the stage.[5] One such is his adaptation of Dryden's *King Arthur*, performed at Goodman's Fields for six weeks from 17 December 1735. At about this time, Giffard could have discovered Richardson's authorship of *A Seasonable Examination of the Pleas and Pretensions of the Proprietors of, and Subscribers to, Play-houses, Erected in Defiance of Royal License* (1735).[6] In this anti-theatrical pamphlet, Richardson strongly endorses a parliamentary bill, introduced in March 1735 by the Opposition Whig Sir John Barnard, designed to close down Goodman's Fields on social and moral grounds. Richardson refers to Giffard by name throughout the pamphlet, and though the bill was voted down, Giffard might later have savoured the prospect of exploiting the fame of a novel by his old antagonist. The Stage Licensing Act brought about a three-year suspension of activities at Goodman's Fields, but in autumn 1740 the theatre re-opened, and was allowed to operate for two more seasons, until 1742.[7] In *A Seasonable Examination*, Richardson, fearing for the welfare of his apprentices, complains that theatres '*amuse* the *Eye* and the *Ear*, and intoxicate, thro' them, the *Understanding* (p. 11). Now he was threatened not only with renewed theatrical activity, but, ironically, with risqué dramatic productions that his own novel had generated. One of the poems he received after the first publication of *Pamela*, by the pseud-onymous 'Philo-Paideias', complains that 'Too long have Tales obscene defil'd the Stage'.[8] The writer perhaps envisaged a new, moralized drama being ushered in by *Pamela*, but Giffard's somewhat salacious adaptation was not of this improving kind.

Rehearsals of Giffard's *Pamela* began on 22 September 1741; according to a newspaper advertisement, 'several Gentlemen were present, who were extremely pleased with the performance'.[9] The leading roles were taken by Giffard himself as Belvile, his version of Mr B., with his wife, Anna, as Pamela. The Giffards, aged forty-seven and thirty-four respectively, were some twenty years older than Richardson's youthful couple: Mr B., when the novel opens, is a young man of twenty-five, and Pamela merely fifteen.[10] Henry Giffard was regarded more highly as a manager than as an actor: one of his contemporaries, the actor Benjamin Griffin, com-plained about his 'dismal voice'.[11] Fortunately, the part of Jack Smatter, Giffard's version of *Pamela*'s Jackey, nephew of Lady Davers, was taken by Garrick. The comedy opened on 9 November 1741, within three weeks of Garrick's triumphant *Richard III*. Billed as the 'Gentleman who acted King Richard', Garrick was performing his first newly written role on stage.

Given the continuing popularity of *Pamela* a year after its initial publication, Giffard's decision to dramatize it was a shrewd one.[12] The fifth edition of the novel appeared on the same day that rehearsals began, and in the six weeks before the premiere the first part of a spurious continuation, a French translation, and second editions of both Haywood's *Anti-Pamela* and Parry's *The True Anti-Pamela* were all published in London.[13] *Pamela* fever was still at its height, and Giffard's comedy proved to be among the most frequently acted plays of the 1741–2 Goodman's Fields season. Between 9 November and 18 December it went through seventeen performances, with a final performance on 26 February 1742.[14] Giffard dramatized scenes in the novel that would best suit his comic purposes and added some amusing stage business of his own.

A letter from Garrick to his brother Peter shows that he was better pleased with his own acting than with the quality of the play:

Pamela is wrote by Mr Giffard himself. I had no hand in it at all excepting writing ye French Letter wch was vastly lik'd, & tagging ye fourth Act — It is very hungry [unsatisfactory] & was chiefly lik'd by ye Middling & low Kind of Spectators. You may Assure Anybody It is not of my writing.[15]

Richardson, who remarked in a letter of 1748 that he had never seen Garrick on the stage, must have stayed away from the production, although in *Clarissa* he praised Garrick publicly.[16] The cast-list of Giffard's comedy suggests some of the ways in which the 'Middling & low' theatre-goers would have been entertained. The part of Colebrand (thus spelled in Giffard's play), much expanded from his small role in Richardson's novel, was played by Charles Blakes, an actor specializing in comic foreigners.[17] Richardson's Colbrand, a huge, taciturn Swiss, is here transformed into an ebullient, scheming Frenchman, with a ludicrously thick stage accent. Another of Giffard's novelties was having Mr B.'s Lincolnshire housekeeper, Mrs Jewkes, played by Richard Yates, with Yates's wife Elizabeth taking the part of the Bedfordshire housekeeper, Mrs Jervis. Richardson's novel emphasizes Jewkes's alarmingly mannish physique and her sexual interest in Pamela, who complains of her advances: 'once she offer'd to kiss me. But I said, I don't like this Sort of Carriage, Mrs. *Jewkes*; it is not like two Persons of one Sex' (p. 108).[18] By having a male actor, rather than a woman, make advances to Pamela on stage, Giffard at once exaggerates and attenuates the novel's sexual tensions: the sexuality becomes more overt, but a man in drag, for an eighteenth-century audience, was less threatening than the figure of the predatory lesbian.[19]

Garrick, the newly celebrated star actor, was Giffard's trump-card, and the seasoned theatre manager exploited his appeal to the full. As the speaker of the 35-line Prologue, Garrick held the stage alone at the outset of the play. The prologue creates an ingenious link among Giffard, the 'Author-Errant of to-Night'; the 'Gentleman' speaking the lines, embarking on his first season on the London stage; and Pamela, the patroness of these two knights-in-arms:

> Sacred to Her, the Champion Pen he draws,
> Enough rewarded — to support her Cause.
> (p. [v])

The play begins not with the events preceding Pamela's dismissal from Belvile's household, but with a group of servants discussing the turmoil caused by the impending discharge of both Pamela and Mrs Jervis. In this way Giffard accelerates the action of the novel, and allows for the arrival of Lady Davers, accompanied by Garrick as Jack Smatter, as early as the second act.

Giffard makes deft use of Smatter as a foil for Pamela, contrasting her insistent piety with his rakish fopperies. There is an amusing shift in

linguistic registers as his address to 'my little *Pammy!*' and his scorn for
her 'old Daddy's thatch'd Hovel, and the comfortable Diet of brown
Bread and rusty Bacon' is followed by her unctuous reply: 'My Pleasures,
Sir, thank Heaven, have turn'd more upon the Improvement and Correction of my Mind, than the Gratifications of my Appetite' (p. 23). To his
own role of Belvile, Giffard gave a measure of dignity and polish lacking
in Richardson's Mr B.[20] All but one of B.'s physical assaults on Pamela are
removed from the play, and his attempted rape in the fourth act ('*Laying
hold of her*' and '*Struggling with her*' in the stage directions, p. 47) is
rapidly thwarted by the intervention of Parson Williams, who takes a
much more active role than in the novel. Since Williams was played by
Giffard's son William, the Goodman's Fields audience could enjoy the
spectacle of a family struggle for power at this critical moment: Giffard *fils*
protecting his mother from the villainous attempts of his father. Thanks
to Williams's intervention Belvile is wholly reformed by the end of the
fourth act, as he reveals in the 'tag' composed by Garrick:

> In lawless Pleasures sunk, to Virtue blind,
> Thy friendly Care has rais'd my sinking Mind . . .
> By gentle Gales, my calmer Passions move,
> My Pilot, Thou; my Harbour, virtuous Love.
> (p. 53)

With the complications of the main plot resolved and his hero and
heroine safely married, Giffard could devote the final act of his play to
broad comedy. Lady Davers and Jack Smatter make a repeat appearance,
taunting Pamela with coarse insults until they too come to appreciate her
virtue. Garrick's finest moment as Smatter, however, is his reading of a
letter from Colebrand to Mrs Jewkes, whom Colebrand has tricked into a
bigamous marriage. Having secured Mrs Jewkes's modest fortune, Colebrand has decamped to France, where he has a wife and 'tirteen little
pretty Enfans, all like myself, which your good Guinea sal make alive fort
bien' (p. 67). The letter, composed by Garrick himself, allowed full scope
to his virtuoso skills: the impecunious product of Lichfield grammar
school playing a wealthy, aristocratic fop, who in turn is imitating a
coarse, scheming, Frenchman, speaking broken English and denouncing
Mrs Jewkes as 'a damn'd heretique old Vitch . . . more proper for
Monsieur de Devil, dan for Your tres humble Serviteur, at a Distance'.
Giffard's decision to make Colebrand a comic Frenchman, rather than a
menacing Swiss, is probably related to a rise in popular Francophobia in
1741, following the outset of the War of Austrian Succession in December

1740. Richardson's Colbrand, presumably Swiss-German rather than Swiss-French, derives from the chivalric romance *Guy of Warwick*, in which the Giant Colbrand is a Danish champion opposing the hero.[21] Giffard's distinctly unchivalrous Colebrand, in contrast, does battle not on behalf of but with a woman.

The epilogue to *Pamela*, spoken by Anna Giffard, is poised between sexual innuendo and didacticism. At the outset, Mrs Giffard depicts herself as a confirmed Antipamelist:

> Was ever such another Blockhead seen!
> To choose a Servant for his Heroine!

Amusingly, she envisages the love-life of the newly married couple:

> Besides, a Girl, so over-fond of Grace,
> Might be devout in an improper Place;
> And pour forth Sermons from her fervent Mind,
> When the poor Man's quite otherwise inclin'd.

The closing lines of the epilogue, however, invite the audience to take a Pamelist stand. Like Belvile we should be responsive to the virtue that Pamela personifies, allowing 'humble Truth and Innocence' to move us 'to reward and love'. The author's supposedly lofty intentions are likewise lauded:

> He knew his Judges, and he wish'd to find
> A Theme might justly please a British Mind.
>
> (p. [69])

Appropriately, this sympathetic account of Giffard's motives in writing, producing and acting in the comedy is spoken by his wife. The play's dedication to Princess Amelia, enlisting the royal family in the pro-Pamela cause, is still more high-minded: Amelia is depicted as 'Protectress in the Cause of Virtue' (pp. [iii–iv]) and thus, by implication, as a champion of Richardson's lowly heroine.

The first edition of Giffard's *Pamela*, with its somewhat impudent, unauthorized dedication, was published on 17 November by the bookseller Jacob Robinson. He had first announced the impending publication on 9 November, the day of the play's first performance, but on 16 November another bookseller, Samuel Lyne, advertised the sale of a rival dramatic version, *Pamela; or, Virtue Triumphant*, said to be 'the original *Pamela*' and described on its title page as a comedy 'intended to be Acted at the Theatre Royal in *Drury-Lane*'.[22] Whatever the author's intentions may have been, no performance of this play at Drury Lane is known to have taken place. A newspaper advertisement for Giffard's comedy described it as 'the genuine comedy of Pamela', warning readers against confusing the play with its upstart competitor, 'under a like Title, pretending to be a Thing *design'd* to be acted at Drury-Lane, but which is quite different from this Comedy, tho' many have been imposed upon to buy it for the same'.[23] It is possible that *Pamela; or, Virtue Triumphant* was an otherwise unidentified *Pamela* play performed, together with Robert Dodsley's *Sir John Cockle at Court* (1738), between the two halves of a concert at the French Theatre in the Haymarket on 28 December 1741.[24]

Robinson's *Pamela*, although published on 17 November, bore a date of 1742: common practice for a book published in the last two months of the year, and one followed by Richardson for both the first edition of *Pamela*, published in November 1740 but dated 1741, and the first edition of *Pamela in her Exalted Condition*, published in December 1741 but dated 1742. Confusingly (and perhaps deliberately), Lyne's *Pamela*, published only one day before Robinson's, was dated 1741, making it seem the earlier of the two works. Lyne also undercut Robinson's price by a third, charging a shilling (twelve pence), compared to Robinson's eighteen pence.[25]

Giffard's *Pamela*, however, proved to be much the more popular of the plays. Two pirated editions were swiftly published, both dated 1741 and thus appearing within a few weeks of Robinson's edition. In a newspaper advertisement, Robinson described the second of these piracies, published by H. Hubbard, as 'a spurious mangled Piece, hawk'd about under the Title of this Play, at the Price of Six Pence'.[26] A third pirated edition appeared in Dublin in December 1741 (see chapter 6 below). A year later, in November 1742, there was still sufficient interest in Giffard's play for Robinson to publish an authorized second edition, this time priced at a shilling and thus matching the cost of the *Pamela* play published by Samuel Lyne.[27] The play was also promoted in *The History of the Stage* (1742), an anonymous, opportunist compilation drawing heavily on Colley Cibber's *An Apology for the Life of Mr. Colley Cibber* (1740), in which the author justifies its inclusion by emphasizing its fame: 'We come now to give our Readers the celebrated Comedy of Pamela, which, tho' it may seem to some to be foreign to our purpose, yet as it certainly relates to the Stage, we don't doubt of its being agreeable to all Persons.' Intriguingly, matters have been 'so contrived, that it may be stitched up by itself, without interfering with our History'.[28] The play thus seems to have been issued together with *The History of the Stage* in yet another pirated edition; readers of the *History* could, in theory, choose whether to bind the play with their copies or to have it 'stitched up' separately. In practice, as the cynical compiler of the *History* doubtless realized, most readers would have valued the play more than the hack compilation and would have had no reason to keep the two bound together.[29]

Giffard continued to vaunt both his comedy and the talents of Garrick as late as 1753, when he published a two-volume epistolary novel, *Memoirs of Sir Charles Goodville and his Family, in a Series of Letters to a Friend*. The work has been known to Richardson scholars since 1936, when both Sale and McKillop noted Richardson's concern that it might be mistaken for the forthcoming *Sir Charles Grandison*, long awaited by his numerous admirers.[30] The author of *Sir Charles Goodville* has now been identified, on solid external evidence, as Giffard,[31] whose leech-like attachment to Richardson thus proves to be still more tenacious than hitherto suspected. One of the letters in *Sir Charles Goodville*, set in the early 1740s, contains a panegyric on Garrick's performances of Richard III at Goodman's Fields. Garrick also, the letter-writer continues, played 'a pert, flashy Character, in a Play, wrote upon the Novel called *Pamela*; in which he discharged himself, with great Life, and Smartness, suitable to what, I conceive, the Author intended'. Since the writer of the play was Giffard himself, this insight into the author's intentions is hardly remarkable. Like Garrick, who claimed that the letter by Colebrand that he contributed to *Pamela* was 'vastly lik'd', Giffard singles out this part of the performance for special praise: 'in the last Act, he read a Letter, wrote by a *French* Valet de Chambre, little acquainted with *English*, in the drollest Manner, and with as high Marks of Comic Humor, as ever I saw executed' (1, 261). Giffard's concern, of course, is not with 'the novel called *Pamela*', which he passes over hastily, but rather with his own appropriation of the novel as a comic drama and with his success as a theatre manager in selecting the right actor to play the comic lead. Garrick and Giffard are linked together by the phrase 'great Life, and Smartness'; Richardson is left on the sidelines.

Unlike Giffard's *Pamela*, with its authorship established by Garrick's letter and its documented stage history, *Pamela; or, Virtue Triumphant* remains clouded in obscurity. Sale has attributed it tentatively to the actor James Dance, who would later use the stage name of James Love. Sale's grounds for doing so were that in 1782, Isaac Reed had credited Love with the authorship of Giffard's *Pamela*. Here Reed was clearly mistaken, as Garrick's testimony indicates, but Sale conjectures that Reed had simply confused the two similarly titled comedies; *Pamela; or, Virtue Triumphant* could thus be attributed to Dance 'without doing violence to the known facts'.[32] As Sale's cautious phrase suggests, the case for Dance's authorship is highly speculative. In autumn 1741, when both comedies were being written, Dance was only twenty. He published a long heroic poem on cricket in 1744 and wrote several plays in the 1760s; the records of his acting career begin in 1745, when he is known to have played at Goodman's Fields. As a precocious young man about town, Dance could have been commissioned by Lyne to work up a dramatization of *Pamela*, but it is equally possible that Sale's guess about his authorship is erroneous.[33]

Another of Sale's conjectures, that 'Lyne's publication was a bookseller's scheme, designed to make profit at the expense of both Richardson and Robinson',[34] is more persuasive. The book is unattractive, and was obviously printed in haste.[35] Lyne also found an inexpensive way to furnish his edition with a frontispiece: simply lifting, without acknowledgment of course, the frontispiece to the anonymous *Pamela in High Life* (see chapter 5 below). Pamela here is wearing her country clothing, in preparation for her journey home: described in the play as 'a home spun Stuff Gown and Petticoat, a neat round ear'd Cap and a green Knot, a plain muslin Tucker, and a clean Straw-Hat in her Hand' (p. 37). Appropriate stage directions were written by Lyne's dramatist to accompany the design: '*The Squire sitting, Mrs.* Jervis *and* Pamela *enter, he rises, and takes her by the Hand*' (p. 39).

Unlike Giffard, who made substantial alterations to the plot and structure of *Pamela* for his production, the author of *Pamela; or, Virtue Triumphant* followed Richardson's text with few significant changes. Since the play, despite the claims of its title page, seems not to have been written with a view to performance, it could ignore stage practicalities and represent even the most theatrically problematic scenes. Thus we are shown Pamela by the pond, throwing her clothes into the water, and even clambering over the garden wall, with a stage direction sure to alarm both actresses and set designers: '*she tries to get over the Wall, and just as she gets hold of the Top the Bricks give way, she falls, and some Bricks . . . are supposed to hurt her very much*' (p. 67). The length of the play is also excessive: extensive cuts would have been made had it ever been performed in a theatre.

In one respect, *Pamela; or, Virtue Triumphant* does diverge from its source, turning away from the novel's transgressive social implications: the challenge to hierarchies of rank entailed in the marriage between master and servant, wealthy country squire and impoverished lady's maid. Giffard's play, much like Richardson's own continuation of the novel, deflects the potential subversiveness of the marriage by making Pamela a model of dignity and piety: despite her lowly birth, theatre-goers could have readily accepted her as a suitable partner for Belvile. In *Pamela; or, Virtue Triumphant* the heroine is more given to self-abasement, and after the marriage she becomes an excessively humble wife, overwhelmed with gratitude towards Beaulove for his benevolence in marrying her. In the final moments of the play, the Squire is busy providing Pamela with 'a few Rules'. This scene in the novel is followed by over a hundred pages of marital developments, but here it becomes the dramatic climax. To each of Beaulove's rules Pamela responds with histrionic delight, and her final words are to request further commands from her husband: 'Oh dearest Sir! Have you no more of your sweet Injunctions to honour me with, they oblige and improve me at the same Time' (p. 92). In this version of the *Pamela* story, the servant remains a servant while the master, 'dearest Sir', remains firmly in charge.

The two *Pamela* plays of 1741 were followed in 1742 by two ballad operas, neither of which is known to have been performed on stage. One of these, 'Pamela the Second', misleadingly described by Eaves and Kimpel as 'a dramatic poem',[36] was serialized across three weekly numbers of the *Universal Spectator, or Weekly Journal* (24 April–8 May 1742). Cast in the form of a ballad opera, it is evidently the work of a frustrated playwright, and is introduced as 'a Kind of a Parallel Case' to *Pamela* that has recently occurred in Buckinghamshire, where 'a Gentleman in that Country has flung the Story into Dramatick Scenery' (p. [i]). As it develops, however, 'Pamela the Second' takes a rather different turn from Richardson's novel, with Pamela successfully repelling her master's advances until (as though in some wry reworking of the Pamela–Williams relationship in *Pamela* itself) she is reunited with 'William', a lover of her own social level. The piece is an intelligent reworking of the novel's debates about virtue and class, and rather literary in flavour. Strewn with quotations (some flagged, others buried), it shows particular familiarity with the dramatic repertoire of the day, as well as a taste for seventeenth-century verse.

Given that one of the leading contributors to the *Universal Spectator* was John Kelly (who supplied at least twenty-four articles in the early years of the journal, and later received credit for the collected reprint of 1747),[37] it is tempting to speculate that this piece may mark a return to the *Pamela* theme, a year later, by the author of *Pamela's Conduct in High Life*. Whoever wrote 'Pamela the Second', it is interesting to note that at a time when the fortunes of the *Universal Spectator* were flagging badly (between 1737 and 1742, a one-twelfth share in the journal had slumped in value from £23 to £2 2s),[38] the invocation of Richardson's novel still seemed a viable strategy for reviving sales.

A more substantial ballad opera, *Pamela: Or, Virtue Rewarded. An Opera*, appeared at about the same time as 'Pamela the Second'. It was advertised, in an anonymous collection of political satires entitled *No Screen! Or, the Masque Remov'd* (1742), as forthcoming in a new series of plays to be issued weekly as *The Beauty of the Muses: or, the Universal Entertainer, and Companion to the Theatre*, of which the first number would be published on 3 April.[39] Whether or not the serial materialized (no copy has been found), the opera was published separately that year by the Newcastle bookseller John White, who had also advertised *The Beauty of the Muses*. No performances of the opera have been recorded,[40] and, until recently, its authorship was obscure, nothing being known of its ostensible author, 'Mr. Edge'. In an article of 1989, however, Victor Link drew attention to the statement on the title page that Edge was also the author of *The Woman of Taste* and of *The Female Rake; or, Modern Fine Lady*.[41] The latter work, a ballad opera, was performed by Fielding's company at the Haymarket in 1736; *The Woman of Taste* is a revised version, first published in 1738. These operas are traditionally attributed to Joseph Dorman, who can thus be assumed to have written the *Pamela* ballad opera, his choice of the pseudonym 'Edge' remaining unexplained.

As the title page of Dorman's opera reveals, it is not based directly on Richardson's novel but (in yet another instance of the intricate web of cross-borrowings and thefts that characterizes the *Pamela* vogue) is 'alter'd from the Comedy, call'd PAMELA'. It provides a revised and abridged version of Giffard's text, interspersed with numerous songs. With remarkable effrontery, Dorman attacks his immediate source in a preface, complaining that Giffard's Belvile is neither 'a Gentleman, or Lover, though he ought to have shone in both'; that Jack Smatter is 'introduc'd to serve no Purpose at all'; and that he cannot recall in the history of the English stage 'a worse Performance than the Comedy of PAMELA'. Dorman attributes the poverty of Giffard's play to the haste of its composition, 'for, to my Knowledge, several different Persons were writing on that Subject at the same Time; and happy was he who could draw the Scene first' (pp. vi–vii). Two of these 'several different Persons' are Giffard and the author of *Pamela; or, Virtue Triumphant*; a third may be the author of 'Pamela the Second', also in ballad opera form, but hardly long enough, at three broadsheet pages, for even a brief afterpiece.

Although Dorman's preface criticizes Giffard's lack of taste and judgment, the adaptation is in fact much coarser than its source. In the opening scene, for example, the ballad opera interjects some broad humour with Isaac's interruption of his fellow-servant's tedious speech, 'Got drunk every Day': the author is obviously playing for laughs. When Belvile laments the absence of Pamela in song, it is hard to recognize him as Richardson's wealthy landowner:

> How tedious the Minutes have past,
> > Depriv'd of the Sight of that Fair;
> No Comfort from others I taste,
> > I'm sad, if my *Pammy's* not there.
> > > (p. 42)

Pamela's songs are no less risible; a series of feminine rhymes, on one occasion, makes her a figure of fun, rather than a model of virtue:

> No stately Grandeur shall entice,
> > Nor tempt me to do Ill-a;
> I'll shun the Great, and hate their Vice,
> > To live in Cottage still-a.
> > > (p. 45)

As James Turner has noted, the author of the ballad opera also 'adds extra bawdy details to Giffard's text, having Mr. Andrews arrive while the newlyweds are actually doing "a Job" together in bed, and faint on hearing this news'.[42] The part of Colbrand, however, is omitted entirely, and thus the amusing subplot created by Giffard involving the jilting of Mrs Jewkes by the scheming Frenchman is lost.

In avoiding the issue of class-crossing raised by Richardson's novel, Dorman follows Giffard's lead. As his respectably married heroine assures her father in the final scene, her virtue has bought her wealth and social standing: ''Tis made the *Purchase*, not the *Exchange*' (p. 63). The opera concludes with 'a little musical Entertainment' furnished by Parson Williams. After Belvile and Pamela dance together, he sings a song comparing the 'hidden Fire' and 'intrinsic Worth' of a prized diamond to the 'latent Beauties' of his wife, her lowly origins all but forgotten (p. 64).

After 1742 English playwrights continued to adapt *Pamela* but without making use of its title, which was becoming less of a drawing card. In some cases they drew on elements of the plot; in others, a character's knowledge of *Pamela* provides insights into his or her values and taste. In James Miller's comedy *The Picture*, for example, based on Molière's *Sganarelle* (1660), which opened at Drury Lane in February 1745, the heroine, Celia, is accused by her choleric father, Mr Per-Cent, of being corrupted by modern novels: 'These confounded Romances have been the

Ruin of thee; I warrant thou canst say more of *Pamela*, or *Joseph Andrews*, than thy Catechism' (pp. 9–10). Celia, however, has not been corrupted but enlightened by reading Richardson and Fielding; instead of marrying for money, she wishes to follow the dictates of her conscience and her heart. It is striking that Miller depicts both *Pamela* and *Joseph Andrews* in a positive light, contrasting them with the spiritual autobiographies, such as George Whitefield's *A Short Account of God's Dealings with the Reverend Mr George Whitefield*, that are among Fielding's targets in *Shamela* and *Joseph Andrews* but which Mr Per-Cent endorses: 'Read these, read these, and learn Obedience better.'

Edward Moore's *The Foundling*, which opened at Drury Lane on 13 February 1748 with an all-star cast, makes much fuller use of Richardson's novel. In the first act the rakish Belmont, played by Garrick, is urged by his friend Colonel Raymond to marry the lovely Fidelia, played by Susanna Cibber:

Col. Come, come, *Charles*, if she is as well born as you pretend, what hinders you from cherishing these Qualities in a Wife, which you wou'd ruin in a Mistress? – Marry her, marry her.

Bel. And hang my self in her Garters next Morning, to give her Virtues the Reward of Widowhood! – Faith, I must read *Pamela* twice over first – But suppose her not born as I pretend; but the Out-cast of a Beggar, and oblig'd to Chance for a little Education.[43]

The Colonel, in response to Belmont's class-bound objections, contends that in marrying Fidelia, his friend 'will have the Merit of raising her to a Rank which she was meant to adorn – And where's the mighty Matter in all this!' Belmont, however, is intent on making Fidelia his mistress, not his wife. The tensions are ultimately resolved when the foundling Fidelia is revealed to be the long-lost daughter of Sir Charles Raymond, the Colonel's father. Class conflicts and the prospect of a misalliance are thus eliminated at a stroke, and in a wonderfully overblown finale the former Fidelia, now Harriet Raymond, finds herself at the heart of an extended family. Belmont's sister Rosetta, her bosom friend, at last agrees to marry her suitor, Colonel Raymond. Harriet thus acquires a new father, brother, fiancé and father-in-law, while also gaining Rosetta as a sister-in-law in two ways: through her brother the Colonel and through Harriet's husband-to-be Belmont.

Belmont, Moore's reformed rake, derives from two literary precursors: the Bevil of Richard Steele's *The Conscious Lovers* (1722) and the Mr B. of *Pamela*. Anthony Amberg, Moore's modern editor, contends that 'though

Moore was certainly influenced by the example of Richardson's Mr. B—, the differences between the novel and the play in both characters and plot are much more conspicuous than the similarities' (p. 46). Frank Ellis, in contrast, believes that the plots of the two works, 'viewed at a sufficient distance . . . are identical', and that 'besides a common infrastructure the two works share a number of themes and motifs'.[44] Moore was certainly conscious of the parallels himself. In addition to Belmont's declaring his unwillingness to become a second Mr B., another character, Faddle (played by Charles Macklin in the 1748 production), reveals his knowledge of both *Pamela* and the *Pamela* vogue. He has, he declares, been with a group of friends, 'toasting a Round of Beauties'. When it comes to Fidelia's turn, 'what think you, says Billy, of keeping her in a Show-glass, by Way of – Gentlemen & Ladies, walk in & see the Curiosity of Curiosities – the perfect Pamela in high Life! – Observe, Gentlemen, the Blushing of her Cheeks, the turning up of her Eyes, & her Tongue, that says nothing but Fie! Fie!' (p. 275). The allusion is to a waxworks display, representing scenes from the continuation of *Pamela*, that had been exhibited in London from 19 November 1745 to 13 August 1746 and advertised as 'a Curious Representation of PAMELA in High Life' (see chapter 5 below). Moore picks up the wording and provides an imitation of the unknown waxworks proprietor with Faddle's 'Gentlemen & Ladies, walk in & see the Curiosity of Curiosities' (p. 48).

The Foundling had a successful first run of eleven nights, and played on fifteen occasions in all in its first season. During Moore's lifetime it received further productions at Drury Lane in 1749 and 1750, in various English provincial theatres, and in Edinburgh and Dublin. It also went through four published editions, in which, despite its topicality, Moore retained the allusion to the waxworks exhibition of *Pamela*, removing it only in 1756 when *The Foundling* was reprinted in his collected works, *Poems, Fables, and Plays*, published by subscription a year before his death.[45]

Richardson seems to have found Moore's treatment of *Pamela* and his boosting one of the numerous spin-offs from the novel unexceptionable. In September 1748, seven months after the first performance of *The Foundling*, he sent Moore a pre-publication copy of the fifth volume of *Clarissa*. And in responding to Moore's detailed commentary, Richardson expressed the hope, with obvious mock-modesty, that 'the poor Clarissa may be admitted to fill a Gap in the Reading World, while Mr Moore and Mr Fielding are . . . reposing their Understandings'.[46] Moore also contemplated writing a tragedy based on *Clarissa*, but had abandoned the project by April 1751. According to Richardson, Lovelace was to have been played by Garrick:[47] a part that would surely have given greater scope to his talents than either the Jack Smatter of Giffard's *Pamela* or the Belmont of Moore's *The Foundling*.

Another dramatic work with close links to *Pamela*, Isaac Bickerstaff's sentimental comic opera *The Maid of the Mill*, opened at Covent Garden on 31 January 1765. Bickerstaff's preface, which pays a remarkably full acknowledgment of his debt to the novel, shows that four years after Richardson's death the *Pamela* vogue was still far from *passé*. Bickerstaff first notes the ubiquity of dramatic adaptations of the novel: 'There is scarce a language in Europe, in which there is not a play taken from our romance of Pamela; in Italian and French, particularly, several writers of the first eminence, have chosen it for the subject of different dramas.' In his own play, 'almost every circumstance' derives from Richardson's novel:

the courtship of Parson Williams – the Squire's jealousy and behaviour in consequence of it, and the difficulty he had to prevail with himself to marry the girl, notwithstanding his passion for her – the miller is a close copy of Goodman Andrews – Ralph is imagined, from the wild son which he is mentioned to have had – Theodosia, from the young lady of quality, with whom Mr B. through his sister's persuasion is said to have been in treaty before his marriage with Pamela – even the gipsies, are borrowed from a trifling incident in the latter part of the work.[48]

The preface encouraged contemporary reviewers to make comparisons, favourable or unfavourable, between the comic opera and *Pamela*, focusing on Bickerstaff's recasting of the heroine and Mr B. as Patty and Lord Aimworth. The *Gentleman's Magazine*, which seldom took note of new plays, did review *The Maid of the Mill* and found that Bickerstaff had understated its originality: 'tho' the circumstances or incidents of his piece may have been suggested by those of *Pamela*, they are notwithstanding very different, and upon the whole it seems to have as good a claim to originality as most other performances of the kind even where no imitation is acknowledged'. The reviewer also contends that the opera is more palatable than its source, since 'the greater part of the incidents in *Pamela* are produced by the attempts of Mr B. to obtain her upon dishonourable terms; but in this performance Lord *Aimworth* is a better character, and has never made such an attempt, nor intended it, upon *Patty*'.[49] The *Monthly Review*, in contrast, suggested that the opera was still more dangerous than the novel in its effects on society:

To encourage young people of family and fortune to marry so very disproportionately, as, in the present instance, Lord Aimworth with a miller's daughter, is even worse than the story of Mr. B. and Pamela, on which this opera is founded; and very little better than Lady —'s running away with her footman. – Ought such gross indiscretions to be *countenanced* on the public stage?[50]

For the first reviewer, Lord Aimworth's chaste character makes the play more commendable than the novel; for the second, his being a lord makes the misalliance still more objectionable than that in *Pamela*, where Mr B., for all his wealth and power, is still an untitled country squire.

Bickerstaff's prefatory remark that Patty's brother Ralph is modelled on Goodman Andrews's 'wild son' shows his familiarity with *Pamela II*, as well as the original novel; Pamela's father writes to her about his 'unhappy' son and his unfortunate grandsons for the first time at the outset of Richardson's continuation.[51] Lord Aimworth also has much more in common with the morally reformed and generous Mr B. of the latter part of *Pamela* and of the continuation than with the blundering sexual predator we first encounter. Patty's declaration in *The Maid of the Mill* – 'Alas! who could live in the house with lord Aimworth, see him, converse with him, and not love him?' (1, 10) – echoes numerous such remarks by Pamela about her husband in Richardson's continuation but would seem perverse in the early part of the novel, when her primary goal is to avoid Mr B.'s unwelcome sexual advances. Aimworth's repeated commendations of Patty's extraordinary merits and beauty – 'has she not all the graces that education can give her sex, improved by a genius seldom found among the highest?' (1, 19) – likewise resemble Mr B.'s panegyrics on his bride, rather than the coarse abuse of the servant-maid ('saucebox', 'boldface', etc.) that Fielding mocks so effectively in *Shamela*. Bickerstaff deftly raises Patty's social standing by distinguishing her clearly both from her scapegrace brother Ralph and from her loutish suitor, farmer Giles. When Lord Aimworth terms Giles an 'ill bred illiterate booby' (1, 27), the effect is again to distance himself from Fielding's parodic version of Mr B.: the booby here is not the squire but his rival the farmer, a far less sympathetic character than his counterpart, Parson Williams, in *Pamela*. Bickerstaff also makes ingenious use of the febrile scene in which Pamela contemplates suicide beside the pond at Mr B.'s Lincolnshire estate. In *The Maid of the Mill*, Lord Aimworth's friend Sir Harry Sycamore tells him that 'despair . . . makes girls do terrible things. 'Twas but the Wednesday before we left London, that I saw, taken out of Rosamond's pond in Saint James's Park, as likely a young woman as ever you would desire to set your eyes on; in a new calamancoe petticoat, and a pair of silver buckles in her shoes' (I, 54). The items of clothing – calamancoe petticoat and silver shoe-buckles – are taken directly from *Pamela* (pp. 19, 78). Pamela's culpable flirtation with suicide is thus deftly transformed to the drowned young woman of the play, and removed from the more high-minded and resolute Patty.[52]

Both in published form and on stage, *The Maid of the Mill* attained a popularity in the late eighteenth and early nineteenth century rivalling that of *Pamela* itself. Within ten years of its first publication in 1765, an astonishing 20,000 copies of the opera had been sold. On the London stage, it went through twenty-nine performances in its first season and over a hundred by 1775.[53] It continued to be produced, with revisions by John O'Keeffe and others, until at least the 1830s, and its fame spread beyond England, with performances recorded in Dublin, St Petersburg, New York, Philadelphia, and Kingston, Jamaica. On 14 November 1792, George Washington himself was present when *The Maid of the Mill* was performed in Philadelphia, and according to a reporter for the *Federal Gazette*, the President was seen to shed 'the tribute of a tear' at the most affecting parts.[54] As Victor Link suggests, its success helped to provoke operatic adaptations of novels by Fielding and Smollett, including Joseph Reed's *Tom Jones, a Comic Opera* (1769) and William Ryley's *Roderick Random* (1790).[55] It also paved the way for another comic opera partly based on *Pamela*, William Shield's *Rosina*, with a libretto by Frances Brooke, written in 1771–2 but first performed only ten years later, on 31 December 1782.

In *Rosina*, Mr B. is divided into two characters, the virtuous Mr Belville and his dissolute brother, Captain Belville: an adroit move that takes account of the dual nature of Richardson's initially repellent but later repentant hero. Rosina, the counterpart to Pamela, is a young orphan who has been brought up on Mr Belville's estate. After being rescued from Captain Belville, who attempts to abduct her, Rosina is found to be the daughter of Mr Belville's old friend Colonel Martin and the granddaughter of Squire Welford. She is thus a suitable match for Mr Belville, and the opera naturally concludes with her accepting his hand in marriage. Brooke's Advertisement to *Rosina* deflects attention away from *Pamela* by claiming that 'the fable of this piece [is] taken from the book of Ruth',[56] but the work clearly draws on both Richardson's novel and Bickerstaff's previous operatic version.

Brooke, who wrote a biographical essay on Richardson in 1779 and knew his son-in-law Edward Bridgen,[57] also alludes to *Pamela* in her novel *The Excursion* (1777). Here, in a passage conflating scenes from *Pamela* and *Clarissa*, the heroine is warned by her uncle of the real dangers of 'worthless acquaintances', rather than 'against the giants of the modern novel, who carry off young ladies by force in post-chaises and six with the blinds up, and confine free-born English women in their country houses, under the guardianship of monsters in the shape of fat housekeepers'.[58] While the novel met with only limited success, reaching a second edition in 1785, Brooke's operatic response to *Pamela* was astonishingly popular. *Rosina* went through 39 performances in its first season at Covent Garden and was performed over 200 times before 1800.[59]

The Maid of the Mill also inspired another reading of Richardson's novel: Samuel Foote's one-act, anti-sentimental Antipamela, *Piety in Pattens, or The Handsome Housemaid*. In this puppet-show farce, first performed at the Haymarket on 15 February 1773 as part of his *Primitive Puppet-Shew*, Foote reduced the cast of *The Maid of the Mill* to a mere four characters: Squire Turniptop, his housekeeper Mrs Candy, Polly Pattens his maid, and Thomas the Butler, who vies with the Squire for Polly's hand. While Bickerstaff's Patty, his counterpart to Pamela, is a model of propriety and eloquence, Foote's Polly is as ill-spoken and coarse as Fielding's Shamela. And like Fielding, Foote ridicules the Richardsonian term 'virtue' by repeatedly deforming it as 'vartue'. In her opening soliloquy, Polly declares that 'to part with my vartue, and become what I trembles to think of, — no, that I never can — For why, as Mrs. Candy often has said, says she, Vartue, Polly, upon two legs, is more better than vice, tho' drawn in a Coach with Six horses.'[60] The word is then held up to inspection and further mocked in a dialogue between Polly and the Squire:

Pol. I hope you don't think I'll part with my vartue.

Sq. Pho, child! that's an old-fashion'd word never mentioned within the Bills of Mortality; part with it? no, no, you may leave it behind you in the Country, for you will have no use for it where you are going. (p. 44)

Turniptop's project, dimly understood by Polly, is to install her as his mistress in London. Polly, instead, like Pamela, determines to return to her parents, and like her precursor she dresses down accordingly, 'equipt with her Bonnet and Bundle' (p. 46; *Pamela*, pp. 78–9). Like Mr B., but much more rapidly, Turniptop comes to see the error of his libertine ways and proposes marriage to Polly. Momentarily, the farce seems to be heading for a class-crossing, Richardsonian conclusion, as the heroine asks herself 'is it possible Polly Pattens shall become the wife of a Squire? and shall Vartue be rewarded at last?' (p. 49). Instead, Foote packs a series of reversals into his compressed finale. Imitating Lord Aimworth in *The Maid of the Mill*, the Squire offers to give up Polly in favour of Thomas the Butler: 'I will stock Nettle-bed Farm which is Ten pounds a Year, and settle it on you for both your lives.' Polly, however, unable to choose between her two devoted suitors, decides to take neither and return to her 'favorite Mops and Brooms' (p. 50). She is not the first of the heroines modelled on Pamela to remain single, but she is surely the first to do so voluntarily.

Although *Piety in Pattens* was ill received on its first performance, it was successfully revived three weeks later and was produced frequently both before Foote's death in 1777 and for the remainder of the century: close to a hundred performances took place, some with puppets and some with actors.[61] In June 1777, Frances Burney's sister Charlotte saw the farce, 'most wretchedly written and acted', accompanied by Garrick, who 'laughed as much as he could have done at the most excellent piece in the world'.[62] It was too slight a work for Foote to publish, but its popularity on stage is indicative of the triumph of the new laughing comedy over works such as *The Maid of the Mill*. *Piety in Pattens* preceded Goldsmith's *She Stoops to Conquer* by a month; one of the less predictable effects of *Pamela* was that it should inspire a puppet-show farce that in turn was at the vanguard of the late-eighteenth-century vogue for anti-sentimental drama.[63]

The wave of plays and ballad operas based on *Pamela* published and performed in England in 1741–2 was soon followed by a similar vogue in France. The task of the adapters was facilitated by the publication, in October 1741, of the French translation of *Pamela*, published in London. These plays, in turn, would help to make *Pamela* a European as well as a merely British and Irish phenomenon, and thus attract new purchasers for further English editions of the novel. Despite his occasional world-weary protests about the proliferating adaptations of *Pamela*, Richardson must have recognized that in augmenting the novel's fame they would increase both his celebrity and his profits.

Also paving the way for the French adaptations were various critical essays and pamphlets, such as a fervently Pamelist piece by Desfontaines in *Observations sur les écrits modernes* (29, June 1742, 193–214); a hostile pamphlet response, entitled *Lettre à Monsieur l'Abbé Des Fontaines sur Pamela* (August 1742); and *Lettre sur Pamela* (1742), a sardonic commentary on the novel bearing the probably false imprint 'Londres'. Although the author of the *Lettre* dismisses the French translation as 'une assez mauvaise traduction d'un Original singulier' (p. 3), and claims to discuss the novel in its authentically (though lamentably) Anglo-Saxon form, coincidences of wording make it clear that he was using the translated text.[64] The author goes on to describe his mingled admiration and disdain for the original version: 'malgré la negligence du style, je l'ai dévoré, & je ne rougirai point de dire qu'il m'a touché & même attendri' (p. 4). In London the novel has become 'le meuble à la mode', and in France, even if it is the product of a maladroit, half-witted neighbour (and one with which France was currently at war), it fascinates 'tous les Lecteurs de profession que le tumulte des armes a laissés dans Paris' (pp. 2, 3). Unsophisticated in its literary style, and resembling in this the uncouth nation it depicts, it has a few raw merits in which even the civilized can find pleasure. Beneath these and other sallies of Gallic charm, the author of *Lettre sur Pamela* shows himself a remarkably shrewd reader of Richardson's text. Though offered in a spirit of mild Antipamelist mockery, his comments on various peculiarities of Pamela's conduct and motives draw out the complexity of her representation with a subtlety unusual in early criticism. With his incredulous repetition of the phrase 'une veste à broder' (pp. 16–17), the author is one of many critics to note the suspect nature of Pamela's explanation for remaining in her persecutor's house. Charles Povey's *The Virgin in Eden* anticipates the point in clumsier form with his observation that had Pamela been truly chaste she 'would have run to her Father's Cottage, as to an Ark of Security' (p. 77). Richardson himself, always sensitive to such criticisms, added a passage to later editions of the novel explaining that Mrs Jervis, not Pamela, was eager for the waistcoat embroidery to be completed.[65] The author of *Lettre sur Pamela* also wittily notes the oddity of Pamela's choice of a youthful parson for her protector ('c'est proprement donner son bien à garder aux voleurs'), and nicely catches the presumptuousness of her rewritten psalms ('Mademoiselle Andrews s'amuse à parodier David', pp. 20, 22).

The middle way between Pamelist effusion and Antipamelist outrage that characterizes *Lettre sur Pamela* is also that taken by three *Pamela* comedies produced in Paris in 1743. The first, Louis de Boissy's three-act *Paméla en France, ou la vertu mieux éprouvée*, opened at the Théâtre Italien on 4 March and lasted for thirteen performances.[66] The heroine is delivered from her captivity in Mr B.'s Lincolnshire house by a French countess, who takes her to France. There, at the countess's manor house, Pamela's virtue will be better tested ('mieux éprouvée', as the subtitle indicates) than in the original novel. The supposed countess is revealed to be an amorous marquis, whose refined attempts at seducing Pamela come much closer to succeeding than do the blundering efforts of the English squire. De Boissy takes up the idea of cross-dressing the marquis from the notorious scene in *Pamela* in which Mr B. disguises himself as the maid Nan, feigning a drunken stupor in order to gain access to her bedroom, watch her undressing, and then attempt to rape her in her bed. De Boissy's Pamela, who quickly adapts to French polite society, is a far more genteel figure than Richardson's rustic servant-maid. And as James Turner suggests, the probable casting of Marie-Jeanne Riccoboni, then the company's star actress, in the leading role would have given the heroine further dignity and weight.[67] De Boissy also finds an ingenious way of avoiding the class-crossing marriage that a French audience would have found rebarbative. At the end of his play, hero and heroine are transformed into allegorical, operatic figures, 'Le Plaisir' and 'La Sagesse', and join in a dance with 'La Décence' and 'La Volupté'. The marquis does agree to marry Pamela, but a wedding between two such intangible personifications could pose no threat to the social order.

A disastrous five-act verse dramatization of *Pamela* by Nivelle de La Chaussée, performed nine months later, on 6 December 1743, at the Comédie française, did not survive beyond its opening night.[68] Its short-comings were mocked in a parody by Claude Godard d'Aucour, *La Déroute des Paméla* (1744), performed at the Théâtre Italien on 23 December. Here, the original English Pamela arrives in France, looking for 'la Paméla Française' of La Chaussée, and 'la Paméla Italienne' of de Boissy (as played at the Théâtre Italien). Echoing Richardson's own complaints about his novel having been traduced, the English Pamela rebukes these two would-be daughters for falsely assuming her name. First, she addresses the Italian Pamela, telling her that she has deceived the public into thinking of her as the original:

> Pour elle on vous prend chaque jour,
> Quoique vous n'en soyez qu'une fade Copie.
> Certain petit Marquis a pour vous de l'amour;
> Vous voulez jouer la Cruelle,
> Afin d'imiter Paméla.
>
> (pp. 12–13)

Next, she tells the French claimant that if she wishes to pass herself off as Pamela's daughter she must disguise herself more thoroughly:

Si vous vouliez que pour elle on vous prît,
Il falloit emprunter ses traits, son caractère,
Mais vous n'en avez que l'habit.

(p. 24)

The mock-indignation here resembles that of the booksellers Richard Chandler and Caesar Ward, who used newspaper advertisements in summer 1741 to declare the superior authenticity of their own continuation in comparison with Richardson's original. Godard d'Aucour's fascination with the two previous French *Pamela* plays is also revealed in a series of authorial notes attached to the published text, in which allusions to de Boissy and La Chaussée are glossed with quotations and mocking commentaries.

Although La Chaussée's dramatization received the most hostile reception of the three French *Pamela* plays of 1743, its long-term effect was much the most important, since it helped impel Voltaire to write his own adaptation of *Pamela*, *Nanine*. Voltaire's fascination with *Pamela* has been the subject of much critical discussion. Thanks to the researches of André Magnan and others, it is known that a series of forty-two letters from Voltaire to his niece Mme Denis, written between July 1750 and December 1753 during his stay at the Prussian court of Frederick II, was heavily revised to form an epistolary fiction that Voltaire referred to on several occasions as *Paméla*. These letters have now been collected and published separately, so that the work can be read as an entity.[69] Jonathan Mallinson points out various suggestive links between Richardson's epistolary novel and Voltaire's epistles, including a parallel between Mr B. and the King of Prussia (persistently implied by Voltaire's term of 'maître' to describe his royal patron) and the captivity that both Pamela and Voltaire were forced to endure.[70]

Shortly before turning to his epistolary *Pamela*, Voltaire adapted the novel as a three-act comedy, *Nanine, ou le préjugé vaincu*, in 1749. In a letter of 24 July 1749, a month after the premiere of *Nanine* at the Comédie française on 16 June, Voltaire contemplated extending his work into a five-act play, which would contrast with the vapidity of La Chaussée's comedy: 'Savez vous bien que je pourois en faire cinq actes? Le sujet le comporte. La Chaussée avoit bien fait cinq actes de sa Paméla, dans laquelle il n'y avoit pas un scène.'[71] Elsewhere, Voltaire mocks La Chaussée's project in the persona of an imaginary actress, Mlle de la Motte, who complains of the difficulty of learning the lines of so unmemorable and unprofitable a play: 'Sa Paméla, que nous eûmes tant de

peine à apprendre, et que le public eut si peu à oublier, sa Paméla qui
mourut le jour de sa naissance, fut sur le point de nous faire mourir de
faim tout un hiver.'[72]

In La Chaussée's *Pamela*, Milord B. is literally dying of love for the
heroine during much of the play, and his death is averted only by
Pamela's finally agreeing, with the reluctant consent of Miledi Davers,
to marry him. In *Nanine*, the comte d'Olban, Voltaire's counterpart to
Mr B., is a much more rational being, intrigued by the orphaned servant
Nanine but far from being hopelessly enamoured of her. He comes
dangerously close to marrying his relative, the Baronne de l'Orme, and
only when it is obvious that Nanine has no interest in any other man, and
that her father is a worthy old soldier, Philippe Hombert, can a wedding
between the count and his former servant take place. Early in the play, the
count has lent Nanine an English book, unnamed but clearly a copy of
Pamela, on which she is quizzed both by her rival the Baronne and by the
count himself. To the Baronne, Nanine declares:

> L'auteur prétend que les hommes sont frères
> Nés tous égaux; mais ce sont des chimères;
> Je ne puis croire à cette égalité.
>
> (p. 93)

To the count, Nanine's objections to the dangerously egalitarian tendencies of *Pamela* are still more emphatic. Far from making her change her
mind, she tells him, it has confirmed her belief in the necessity of a social
hierarchy:

> Il ne m'a point du tout persuadée:
> Plus que jamais, monsieur, j'ai dans l'idée,
> Qu'il est des coeurs si grands, si généreux,
> Que tout le reste est bien vil auprès d'eux.
>
> (p. 103)

Ironically, of course, Nanine will ultimately marry up in much the same
fashion as her precursor; the English intertext, as Peter Hynes remarks, is
'obviously and indeed explicitly relevant to her own story'.[73] But like his
heroine, Voltaire was reluctant to give Richardson's novel too much
credit. Its title is absent both from the title of his play and from its text,
in which we hear only of an anonymous 'livre anglais'.

The initial reception of *Nanine* at the Comédie française in June 1749
was disappointing, and the production closed after twelve performances.[74]
In the opening words of his preface to the play, Voltaire terms it a
'bagatelle' (p. 65) and he repeatedly disparaged it in his correspondence,

telling Frederick II, for example, that 'une petite fille que son maître épouse ne valait pas trop la peine de vous être présentée'.[75] His mockery of *Nanine* resembles his acerbic comments on its source. 'Les longs et insupportables romans de Paméla et de Clarice', he declared, 'ont réussi parce qu'ils ont excité la curiosité du lecteur, à travers un fatras d'inutilités, mais si l'auteur avait été assez malavisé pour annoncer dès le commencement que Clarice et Paméla aimaient leurs persécuteurs, tout était perdu, le lecteur aurait jeté le livre'.[76] Voltaire's recognition, however, that Richardson's art depends on the reader's implication and involvement shows the depth of his appreciation of the novelist. And in the long term, his *Pamela* play, *Nanine*, became the most popular of his comedies, both in France and abroad, and itself became the subject of a parody, *Nanine, soeur de lait de la reine de Golconde* (1768), attributed to Pierre-Thomas Gondot and François-Georges Desfontaines.[77] Translations, in several competing versions, appeared in German, Dutch, Russian, Danish and Italian. In English, prose translations appeared as part of two collected editions of Voltaire's dramatic works, the first in 1761–3, the second, by David Williams, in 1781. Neither was performed on stage, but Charles Macklin's *The True-Born Scotchman* (1764), a comedy very loosely based on *Nanine*, was a popular success in London and in Dublin, both in its original version and in its later revised and expanded version as *The Man of the World* (1785).[78]

Less than a year after *Nanine*'s premiere in Paris, Goldoni's adaptation of *Pamela* opened in Mantua, in spring 1750. It then became part of Goldoni's famous season, in Venice, of sixteen new comedies, all produced in 1750–1.[79] It was first published in Italian in editions by two different publishers in 1753, and reprinted on numerous occasions during Goldoni's lifetime.[80] An extensive review of 1755 in the Paris journal, *Le Journal étranger*, compares Goldoni's comedy favourably with those by de Boissy, La Chaussée and Voltaire. Unlike the French dramatists, the reviewer declares, Goldoni has distanced himself sufficiently from Richardson to make his play palatable to French taste. In particular, 'il ne donne point, dans son dénoûement, l'exemple d'une honteuse mésalliance, pour relever la vertu de son Héroïne'.[81] From January to August 1755 the *Journal* was edited by Prévost, translator of *Clarissa* and *Sir Charles Grandison*, as well as an important novelist in his own right, who might have written the review himself.

In his *Memoirs,* written in French in 1784–7, some thirty-five years after the first performance of *Pamela*, Goldoni describes it as the most popular of his plays to that date.[82] Subsequently, Goldoni provided both a sequel to the comedy, *Pamela maritata* (1760), and librettos for two operatic versions with music by Piccini, *La buona figliuola* (1760) and *La buona figliuola maritata* (1761).[83] Goldoni's various adaptations of *Pamela* inspired a host of translations and re-adaptations. In Italy, dramatists such as Pietro Chiari, Lonfranchi Rossi, and Francesco Cerlone produced their own *Pamela* comedies. French works based on Goldoni's original play include an unpublished comedy of 1759 by Voltaire's niece, Mme Denis; Voltaire's own comedy *l'Écossaise* (1760); and a comedy by François de Neufchâteau, *Pamela, ou la vertu récompensée*, first performed in Paris in 1793.[84] And yet more adaptations of Goldoni's *Pamela* appeared in Germany, Austria and Spain.[85]

The English translation of Goldoni's original *Pamela* was published by John Nourse in 1756 in a bilingual edition, with Italian and English on alternating pages. In addition to *Pamela*, the volume contains a bilingual edition of Goldoni's *The Father of a Family*.[86] The book was advertised primarily as a way of mastering Italian (much as Richardson had originally sought to promote his French-language edition of the novel), and a list of Nourse's publications appended to the *Pamela* translation is headed by *A New Method of Learning the Italian Tongue*. Nourse, however, had already been involved with several Richardson translations and adaptations, and his choice of *Pamela* as one of two Goldoni plays to be included in the volume is hardly accidental. In 1746, Nourse had bought the copyright to Eliza Haywood's *Anti-Pamela* (see chapter 3 above). In 1751, his name appeared on the title page of Prévost's translation of *Clarissa* as the London publisher, although the work was printed in France. And in April 1757, Richardson wrote to a correspondent of having received 'thro' Mr Nourse's Hands' twelve sets of the French translation of *Sir Charles Grandison* by Gaspard-Joël Monod.[87] Richardson might also have received from Nourse, at about the same time, a copy of the English–Italian edition of Goldoni's *Pamela*, although no relevant document has been found.

The translation was positively reviewed in the *Monthly Review* by James Grainger, who contends that Goldoni's alterations to the plot and characterization of *Pamela* make his play superior to the novel. Grainger has 'never had that very high opinion of Pamela's virtue, which many of Mr. Richardson's female partizans entertained. It is plain she had address enough to see, that if she persisted in her denial, Mr. B.'s love for her would triumph over the pride of family.' In Goldoni's play, in contrast, 'the passion of love is painted with no less truth than delicacy', although readers would appreciate 'a little more gaiety, and less pathos; more humour, and less argumentation'.[88]

Nourse's bilingual editions were intended for individual readers, not for the stage; this perhaps explains why in the English version the play's location, appended to the 'Dramatis Personae', lacks the phrase 'in una camera con varie porte' (in a room with several doors), and why part of the first stage direction, '*Pamela a sedere a un piccolo tavolino*' (Pamela is to sit at a small table), is missing (pp. 2–3). No performance in English of Goldoni's *Pamela* took place in the eighteenth century, but both of Goldoni's *Pamela* operas were produced in London: *La buona figliuola* receiving eighty-three performances in Italian at the King's Theatre between 1766 and 1775, and its sequel, *La buona figliuola maritata*, thirteen performances between 1766 and 1771. An English version of *La buona figliuola* by Edward Toms, *The Accomplished Maid*, was less successful: produced nine times at Covent Garden in December 1766, it was never revived.[89]

Goldoni was an acutely self-conscious dramatist, and his observations on the relationship between his play and Richardson's novel are of considerable interest. In both his preface to the play, first published in 1753, and his much later *Memoirs*, Goldoni explains the central problem that he faced in dramatizing *Pamela*. Despite the novel's popularity in Italy, to depict a cross-class marriage on stage would offend his audience: 'le but moral de l'Auteur Anglois ne convenoit pas aux moeurs et aux lois de mon pays' (p. 277). In the preface, Goldoni voices his approval of Lady Davers's objections to the marriage, and suggests that Richardson '*either ought not to have raised any difficulty, upon such a circumstance, or he ought to have solved it, in a manner more becoming the honour of his country*' (p. vii). No such criticism of Richardson is made in the *Memoirs*, in which Goldoni contrasts English and Italian laws in order to explain his need to alter the plot of the novel: 'A Londres un Lord ne déroge pas à la noblesse en épousant une paysanne; à Venise un patricien qui épouse une plébéienne, prive ses enfans de la noblesse patricienne, et ils perdent leurs droits à la souveraineté' (p. 277). In the preface, Goldoni also compares his adaptation of *Pamela* with that of the 'celebrated M. Voltaire' in *Nanine*. Voltaire's strategy was to preserve the cross-class marriage but to set the play in France; Goldoni, however, was '*too much pleased with the beauty of the English characters*' to remove them from '*that illustrious nation*' (p. xi).

Goldoni's solution to the problem of the misalliance is to make Pamela a nobleman's daughter.[90] Mr Andrews, it transpires, is in fact the Earl of Auspng, a Scottish Jacobite forced into hiding after the failed Rebellion of 1715. Perhaps with an eye on the presence in Italy of the Jacobite court in exile (originally, in 1717–18, at Urbino), Goldoni has thus made

Pamela's father not only an aristocrat but, as an adherent of an ancient legitimacy, an aristocrat of the purest and oldest lineage. His hero, Lord Bonfil, is also no mere country squire but a member of the nobility, and the play is set in London; no mention is made of Bedfordshire or Lincolnshire estates. Bonfil's friends too are noblemen: replacing the uncouth rural visitors who descend on Mr B. in Richardson's novel are two urbane figures, Lord Arthur and Lord Coubrech. Lord Arthur, moreover, turns out to be the son of the Earl of Ausping's oldest friend, who had, just before his death, secured the Earl a royal pardon. Thus the marriage of Bonfil and Pamela comes to seem the most logical of unions: they are equals in rank, they have friends in common, and of course they are in love.

Goldoni further distances his play from the low-life elements in Richardson's *Pamela* through its dedication to 'his Excellency the Marquis of Ginori'. The dedication is replete with flattery for this 'magnanimous, great, and respectable patron', who is 'great by birth, by the antiquity of his family, and by his wealth'. Far from upholding the anti-hierarchical, democratizing tendencies of the novel, Goldoni buttresses his play with a thoroughly class-bound appeal to the Marquis, as from servant to master: 'I, among the adorers of your name, I, with my Pamela in my arms, approach you with humility and confidence' (pp. iii, v). It is tempting to suppose that Goldoni, or at least his English translator, had tongue in cheek in this portrait of the author enfolding the book, much as Mr B. repeatedly enfolds the heroine.

In adapting *Pamela* for the Italian stage, Goldoni made sweeping changes to both plot and characterization. Most of the novel's servants disappear: Mrs Jervis is retained as Lord Bonfil's London housekeeper, but Mrs Jewkes, Nan and Colbrand are removed, as is Parson Williams. Lady Davers's nephew Jackey becomes Sir John Arnold, newly returned from the Grand Tour. In his *Memoirs*, Goldoni draws attention to Sir John as a character 'qui égaye infiniment le sérieux de la Piece' (p. 279), having acquired on his travels all the absurdities of the countries he has visited. *Pamela* was the first of Goldoni's comedies to eschew entirely the use of masks. Applauding the 'merry, sprightly comedies' of Italy, with their traditional harlequins, and regretting that 'in London you will not suffer any masks on the stage' (p. 55), Sir John is used to win the audience's support for the new kind of play. If so rebarbative a character is enamoured of the old-style harlequinades, the claims of sentimental comedy seem more compelling.

Goldoni's hero Bonfil is a more attractive figure than Mr B. Instead of grappling physically with Pamela, he is made to struggle with his own conscience. The internal conflicts he experiences between his love for Pamela and his knowledge that to marry her would disgrace his family name paralyze his power to act and bring him close to nervous collapse. As Ted Emery observes, Goldoni's alterations 'change Richardson's focus considerably, transforming the original conflict of virtue and vice into one between *reason* and *passion*'.[91] Bonfil's violence, at one point, is directed not at Pamela but at Lady Davers's nephew, Sir John Arnold, who has insulted her; a stage direction tells us that he '*runs like a madman to his sword, and drawing it, goes towards the door*' (p. 131). Here Goldoni makes ingenious use of an incident reported by Mr B. in Richardson's *Pamela*: during his Grand Tour, he had been involved in a duel with 'a Man of Title in *Italy*, who, like many other Persons of Title, had no Honour' (p. 432). In Goldoni's dramatization Bonfil too confronts a 'Person of Title' with no honour, but he does so in defence of Pamela's reputation, and in the play, unlike the novel, no blood is spilled on either side.

Goldoni's Pamela is also a more dignified figure than Richardson's humble heroine. Unlike her precursor she acknowledges her love for Lord Bonfil from the outset, but until the secret of her noble birth is revealed, she has no aspirations to marriage. Instead she acts as Bonfil's counsellor, warning him that 'every bad action reflects dishonour on a gentleman; and there cannot be a baser nor blacker act than that of betraying an innocent maid' (p. 23). Lady Davers at first resembles Richardson's homicidal, dagger-wielding Lady Olivia in *Sir Charles Grandison*, declaring to her brother 'if I had the least notion, that this hussy was ever to bring such disgrace upon our family, I would throttle her with my own hands' (p. 29).[92] At the end of the play it is not Pamela's virtue that has converted her new sister-in-law but her birth; as the heroine herself acknowledges, 'the low born Pamela might lessen the honour of your noble family; Pamela in a better condition may expect your favour' (p. 173). Lord Arthur, who had warned Bonfil that 'violent love, that blind passion which makes the object appear beautiful, does not last long', and that 'the indulging of our irregular appetites is succeeded by maturer thoughts' (p. 77), is shown to be right: it is neither blind passion nor irregular appetites but mature judgment that brings the reformed hero and virtuous heroine together here.

Before the secret of Pamela's birth is revealed, two of Goldoni's characters attack the prejudices of their class-bound society. The first, Sir John Arnold, urges Bonfil to ignore objections to the misalliance, of which he has seen many examples on his travels: 'The world indeed laughs at them; parents make a noise; but you know the proverb, it is only a three day's wonder' (p. 129). In giving these sentiments to the foppish and foolish Sir John, Goldoni sabotages their force. The second, Mrs Jervis, declares in a memorable speech that 'the world would be much better than it is, if it had not been spoiled by mankind, whose pride has subverted the beautiful order of nature' (p. 137). In Richardson's novel, and in Giffard's play, we see Pamela herself taking a similar stand. But in Goldoni's comedy, such levelling sentiments can be voiced only by a minor character, whose belief in the equality of high and low is a sign not of her innate goodness but of her limited understanding. The true counterpart to Richardson's Pamela in Goldoni's comedy is not the aristocratic heroine but the irreverent Mrs Jervis, whose status as a servant remains unchanged at the end of the play and whose views are unheeded by all.

It would take well over 200 years for Goldoni's adaptation of *Pamela* to reach the English stage. Its first, fleeting appearance was as part of a new play, Fidelis Morgan and Giles Havergal's *Pamela or the Reform of a Rake*, performed in London by Shared Experience from January to April 1985. As the authors note, their adaptation draws on Giffard's *Pamela*, Voltaire's *Nanine*, and Goldoni's *Pamela nubile*, as well as on Richardson's novel; an early scene between Lady Davers, Pamela and Belville is taken directly from Goldoni.[93] Then, on the bicentenary of his death, the English translation of Goldoni's first *Pamela* play at last received its premiere: in summer 1993, an adaptation by Paola Polesso was produced in Cambridge, London and Dublin.[94] Fittingly, both Morgan–Havergal and Polesso are as cavalier with Goldoni's play as he had been with Richardson's novel: transforming a transformation as had so many of their predecessors in the protracted *Pamela* controversy, including the artists who form the subject of the next chapter.

CHAPTER 5

Pamela *illustrations and the visual culture of the novel*

In April 1741, scenes from *Pamela* were engraved on a ladies' fan by some anonymous artists: the first of countless illustrations of Richardson's novel. Some of these illustrations, such as the twenty-nine engravings by Hubert Gravelot and Francis Hayman commissioned by Richardson for the 1742 octavo edition and Joseph Highmore's twelve paintings of the novel, engraved by Antoine Benoist and Louis Truchy, are relatively well known. Other visual renderings, however, have been entirely ignored. Of particular interest are ten plates engraved by John Carwitham for *The Life of Pamela* (1741), five naive, anonymous engravings in a piracy of *Pamela* published in instalments by Mary Kingman (1741), and a hitherto un-known frontispiece to the anonymous *Pamela in High Life*, also published by Kingman in instalments in late 1741. These engravings all predate those by Richardson's officially commissioned illustrators, Gravelot and Hayman, and provide an important context for their work. They show that the force driving visual depictions of *Pamela* came from below. Richardson did not, as is often supposed, approach Gravelot and Hayman in a void, but as a response to the various piracies and adaptations of his novel that had already introduced illustration as a selling point. And collectively, they suggest the extent to which *Pamela*, in its various manifestations, was responsible for an early emergence of English novel illustration, predating by two decades the sustained development of such illustration in the 1760s.

Among the merchandise which, in the opportunistic consumer culture of the day, grew up around *Pamela* was the fashionable item described in an advertisement in the *Daily Advertiser* for 28 April 1741:

This Day is publish'd

For the Entertainment of the Ladies, more especially those who have the Book, PAMELA, a new Fan, representing the principal Adventures of her Life, in Servitude, Love, and Marriage. Design'd and engraven by the best Masters.

The fan was 'Sold by M. Gamble, at her Warehouse, No. 19, in Plough-Court, Fetter-Lane; and at all the Fan-Shops and China-Shops in and about London'. No copy is known to have survived (presumably they were all fluttered to bits), though several Gamble fans and fan-leaves are now in the collection of the Fan Museum in London, together with a fan of 1796 illustrating *A Sentimental Journey*.[1] The *Pamela* fan must have seemed a doubly voguish accessory. London printers began producing cheap paper fans from about 1720 to compete with French and Chinese imports, and their wares were regulated by Act of Parliament in 1735. Other fans inspired by novels followed later, and in 1749 the theft of a *Tom Jones* fan at a Norwich assembly and the distress of its owner ('She lov'd the Toy, because she lov'd the Tale') became the subject of a whole mock-heroic poem, in imitation of *The Rape of the Lock*. No *Tom Jones* fan is known to have been produced, but the author of the poem appealed to 'some ingenious Artist' to take up the hint: there was 'a rich Fund, for the Pencil', in the 'Scenes of *Tom Jones*', and these scenes would 'still please, tho' stript of Words'.[2]

Previous commentators on the *Pamela* controversy have assumed that in the absence of a copy of the 1741 fan, the subjects of its engravings 'by the best Masters' must remain unknown. A brief description does, however, survive, in a letter from Elizabeth Postlethwaite to her married sister, Barbara Kerrich. Elizabeth, living with her parents in the rectory at Denton, Norfolk, had been given the fan by her stepmother Matilda, who bought it for her in Norwich: a town in which fans seem to have found special favour. On 4 September 1741, Matilda wrote to Barbara Kerrich that Elizabeth 'likes it so well that she will get one for you, if you have not seen any'.[3] Elizabeth may have liked her *Pamela* fan, but rather than buying another for her sister she gave away her own, sending it across Norfolk, from southerly Denton to Barbara's home in Dersingham on the northwestern side. In a letter of 29 September, Elizabeth, perhaps prompted by Matilda Postlethwaite, wrote to Barbara that 'I believe I didn't tell you my Mother gave me the Pamela fan I sent you': in this family of limited means, credit had to be given where it was due. Previously, on 13 September, Elizabeth had described to her sister the item she was about to receive: 'I have sent you a Pamela Fan. I wish they had made her look better where she is getting out at the window, she cut a sad figure. They have drawn Mother Jewkes well, she looks like what she is, she have a fine broad face.'[4] For the fan to represent Pamela 'in Servitude, Love, and Marriage', there must have been at least three illustrations,[5] of which Elizabeth here describes one, Pamela in marriage.

The scene is probably that in which Pamela is escaping through a parlour window from Lady Davers and Jackey: 'I got upon the Seat, and whipt out in a Minute' (p. 398).[6] The illustrator would know that just before the escape, Pamela has used a fan of her own expressively: 'I was so vex'd, I bit a Piece of my Fan out, not knowing what I did, but still I said nothing, and did nothing but flutter it, and fan myself' (p. 388). The remark that Mrs Jewkes 'looks like what she is' implies that she has been depicted as a caricatured mannish lesbian, the 'fine broad face' indicating her menacing, predatory appearance.

Despite this knowing comment, Elizabeth Postlethwaite, daughter of a clergyman, writing to her sister Barbara, a clergyman's wife, has nothing to say about the illustrations showing Pamela in love. A magazine poem of 1740, however, entitled 'On the New Fashioned Fans with Motto's', published just months before the *Pamela* fan was on sale, suggests that these illustrations might not have met with clerical approval:

> New schemes of dress, intrigue, and play,
> Want new expressions every day:
> And doubly blest! must be that mortal man,
> Who may *converse* with *Sylvia* and her FAN.[7]

Here the rather blatant concluding innuendo is a reminder that fans were not necessarily a badge of exemplary domestic virtue, and that the whole story might not be told by Stephanie Fysh's analysis of the signifying potential of Mrs Gamble's product. 'In the fans, *Pamela* becomes a means to make a statement', as Fysh writes: 'its narrative, packaged into a single object, becomes a sign of the virtue of the fan's holder, who herself is asked by the advertiser to turn it back on herself, and view "Virtue's Reward" in her *Pamela* fan'.[8] With its illustration of a highly charged seduction narrative, and its declaration of the bearer as a paid-up fashion victim, the fan may well have lent itself to more coquettish uses. Perhaps it could even have displayed the bearer's availability for the kind of recreation offered by Shamela's mother (in Fielding's version of the same bawdy pun) 'at her Lodgings at the *Fan* and *Pepper-Box* in *Drury-Lane*' (p. 314).

The *Pamela* fan was advertised as an accompaniment, not a replacement, for *Pamela*: its owners would derive more 'Entertainment' from its depictions of the novel if they already owned the book. When Elizabeth Postlethwaite received her copy of the fan in September 1741, she had not yet read *Pamela* and did not possess a copy. In January 1742, however, she and her stepmother were immersed in the novel and wetting its pages with their tears, as Matilda tells Barbara Kerrich: 'yr sister & I wept sorely nothing can be more moving I think'.[9] By March 1742, Elizabeth had 'resolv'd to buy it', and two years later she at last received a copy, of the third duodecimo edition, as a present from her father. She was, as she told Barbara, 'in love with Pamela. I never read anything pleas'd me better.'[10] For Richardson, of course, this was the ideal outcome; the merchandise, at once appropriating and promoting his text, had led to a purchase of the novel itself. The numerous illustrations engendered by *Pamela* in the wake of the fan were largely beyond Richardson's control – with the obvious exception of those he commissioned himself – but they worked to his advantage in making his novel an ever more popular and desirable item.

On 24 July 1741, three months after the Gamble fan was first advertised, a new *Pamela* poem was announced in the *Daily Advertiser*. *Pamela Versified* was to be issued in fifteen numbers, 'adorn'd with Copper-Plate Cuts' (see chapter 1 above). In the event, only two numbers of the poem seem to have been published, presumably with the promised illustrations, and none is known to have survived. The engravings would, however, have been seen by the early participants in the *Pamela* controversy, including Richardson himself, and it is possible that, like the designs on the lost *Pamela* fan, they exerted some influence on the novel's subsequent illustrators.

Among the first illustrations of *Pamela* published after 'Pamela Versified' are those in *The Life of Pamela*, published serially in twenty-one instalments in 1741. Priced at four shillings, the work was something of a bargain, providing 500 pages of text, as well as 9 engravings and a frontispiece.[11] The presence of illustrations is used as a selling-point on the title page, which draws attention to the 'great Number of COPPER-PLATES describing her in the different Stations of Life'. The frontispiece and illustrations indicate the name of the engraver, John Carwitham, who may also have been responsible for designing the plates. Hanns Hammelmann and T. S. R. Boase, although unaware of his *Pamela* engravings, note that Carwitham's 'one contribution to decorative art . . . shows an original and inventive talent for illustration'.[12] The expense of a more prestigious artist would have been too great for the downmarket *Life of Pamela*, but Carwitham's illustrations are surprisingly effective. Although most of them depict scenes from Richardson's *Pamela*, two represent incidents created by the author of the *Life*.

The title page of *The Life of Pamela* emphasizes the social distance that the heroine travels, 'from the lowest Degree of Rural Life' to becoming 'Mistress of a most splendid House and Fortune'. Carwitham's

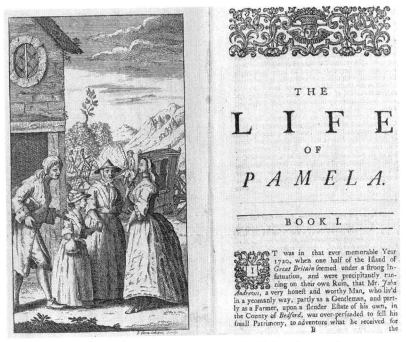

THE

L I F E

OF

P A M E L A.

BOOK I.

T was in that ever memorable Year 1720, when one half of the Island of *Great Britain* seemed under a strong Infatuation, and were precipitantly running on their own Ruin, that Mr. *John Andrews*, a very honest and worthy Man, who liv'd in a yeomanly way, partly as a Gentleman, and partly as a Farmer, upon a slender Estate of his own, in the County of *Bedford*, was over-perfuaded to sell his small Patrimony, to adventure what he received for

Figure 5.1. John Carwitham. Engraving of a fabricated scene, from
The Life of Pamela, 1741.

frontispiece portrays a stately, elaborately dressed and coiffed Pamela, in full possession of her new wealth. The next illustration, in contrast, shows her as a child, being delivered by her parents to the care of her new employer: a scene invented by the author of the *Life* (figure 5.1). By placing the countrywoman Mrs Andrews and the estate-owner, Mr B.'s mother, beside each other, Carwitham effectively represents the gulf that Pamela will traverse, from cottage to country-house.

Carwitham's remaining engravings, illustrating several of the best-known scenes in *Pamela*, are aimed at a wide variety of readers. The sentimentally inclined will be taken by Pamela weeping into a handkerchief outside the summer-house, while a smirking Mr B. looks on. A more dynamic engraving shows the assembled servants bewailing what they suppose to be Pamela's drowning in the pond, with Mrs Jewkes wringing her hands in distress and the colossal Colbrand peering at Pamela's clothes floating in the murky water. In the background, Nan can be seen searching the woodshed, in which the prostrate heroine is concealed.

With salacious male readers in mind, Carwitham furnishes an engraving of Pamela undressing for bed, her right breast completely exposed and illuminated by a conveniently placed candle. Mr B., disguised as the maid Nan, with an apron thrown over his head, can see nothing, but Mrs Jewkes observes her charge with apparent interest. Other plates in the series bring out the novel's conflicts of class and rank. An illustration of Pamela kneeling beside her father, with an overturned card-table strategically placed between them and a row of Mr B.'s acquaintances, stiffly trying to keep their composure, is especially attractive, as is that of a light-footed Pamela about to make her exit through a window, taking advantage of Lady Davers's having turned her back while cooling herself with a fan. This illustration alludes wittily to the earlier fan illustration, both through the choice of scene and through Lady Davers's prominently displayed accessory. And some of Carwitham's earlier illustrations might likewise have been prompted by scenes depicted on the fan or in *Pamela Versified*: the summer-house scene, for example, would have been an obvious choice for both of Carwitham's predecessors.

At about the same time as serial publication of *The Life of Pamela* began, the first of twenty instalments of a piracy of *Pamela* was published by Mary Kingman (see chapter 2 above), illustrated with five naive, anonymous engravings. Janet Aikins, the first critic to take notice of these illustrations, states that four of the five 'feature scenes or situations similar to those' that Hayman and Gravelot would depict, but in fact only two of their illustrations have the same subject. This undermines her claim that the 'creators of the piracy' may have had 'information about Richardson's project'.[13] Kingman's piracy was probably published in all three parts before Gravelot and Hayman had even been commissioned, and in any case she is unlikely to have had knowledge of their dealings with Richardson. The influence, if any, was in the other direction: both Richardson and his chosen illustrators had ample time to look at the engravings in Kingman's volume, and to decide which of the scenes they would portray in the octavo edition.

The Life of Pamela and Kingman's *Pamela* piracy were apparently rival productions: appearing in a similar number of parts, both containing illustrations, and both adding new material to Richardson's novel. Like *The Life of Pamela*, the virtually unknown piracy is of considerable interest. It begins by reprinting the Preface and Introduction to *Pamela*, from Richardson's fourth-edition text. Appended to this material, and printed as though it were also part of Richardson's novel, is a seven-page section, entitled 'The Parentage of Pamela', accounting for her parents' poverty (they have been ruined by a profligate son, Robert), and describing the circumstances of Pamela's employment by Mr B.'s mother. This passage is illustrated by a plate, with the caption 'Pamela going to Service Attended by her Father & Mother'. The engraving resembles the one created for *The Life of Pamela* but without the presence of Mrs B. and with the addition of an exterior view of an imposing B. Hall, a large, somewhat prison-like structure with a roof topped by outsized statues.

The other engravings in the pirated *Pamela*, none with captions but all paginated for the binder, are based on scenes from Richardson's novel. The first, depicting Pamela in her round-eared cap and country garb, talking to an astonished Mrs Jervis while Mr B. makes his entrance, illustrates a passage just before one chosen by Carwitham for *The Life of Pamela*, in which Mr B. is examining the heroine in her rustic disguise. The second, in which Pamela steps into a chariot while Mr B. looks on through a window (figure 5.2), has no counterpart in Carwitham, but would later be painted by Joseph Highmore (see below). The third, Pamela by the pond contemplating suicide, again illustrates a scene just before that chosen by Carwitham. The 'pond' here, with Pamela's garments floating on the surface, is a diminutive ornamental pool, quite unlike the novel's 'so large a Piece of Water' (p. 174). The final engraving is of Pamela overturning a card-table as she kneels, arms outstretched, before her father, a scene also depicted by Carwitham.

In the absence of firm publication dates for the multiple parts of either *The Life of Pamela* or the pirated *Pamela*, it is unclear whether Carwitham was indebted to the anonymous engraver, whether the piracy drew on the *Life*, or whether the influence worked in both directions. It is, however, obvious that the *Pamela* illustrators were conscious of one another's work, and that in many cases the subject and form of an engraving were determined more by the existence of a precursor than by the details of Richardson's text. Exemplifying such artistic interchanges is a newly discovered frontispiece to *Pamela in High Life* (figure 5.3), of which the first of three instalments was published on 29 September 1741.[14] This unsigned engraving is closely modelled on Carwitham's illustration in *The Life of Pamela* of Pamela in country dress standing beside Mrs Jervis, while a seated Mr B. poses questions to the supposed newcomer. All three figures are based on those in Carwitham's engraving, as are several of the gestures, such as Mr B.'s supporting his right elbow on a small table. The unsigned engraving was then in turn used as the frontispiece for the comedy *Pamela; or, Virtue Triumphant*, published in November 1741, the only change being that the design was reversed in the re-engraving

Figure 5.2. Engraving of Pamela stepping into the chariot, from the pirated edition of *Pamela*, 1741.

Figure 5.3. Frontispiece engraving of Pamela in country dress, with Mrs Jervis and
Mr B., from *Pamela in High Life*, 1741.

process. Just as the authors of *Pamela* verses, counter-fictions, dramatic adaptations, etc., were vying with and lifting material from one another, so too were *Pamela*'s illustrators.

Richardson's own illustrated edition of *Pamela* did not appear until May 1742, over a year after the Gamble fan and about six months after the illustrations in *The Life of Pamela* and the *Pamela* piracy. He had, however, been thinking of the novel in visual terms since December 1740, within a month of its first publication. *Pamela* was selling rapidly, and adding engravings, as well as new introductory material, to the second edition would invest the book with greater dignity. Richardson's edition of *Aesop's Fables*, published a year earlier in November 1739, contained an illustrated title page, signed by John Clark, a plate illustrating the life of Aesop, and twenty-four engravings, each with ten diminutive illustrations.[15] The title page boasted of the book's 'Containing Two Hundred and Forty Fables, with a Cut Engrav'd on Copper to each Fable': for this children's book, quantity not quality was the watchword. John Clark's name would do nothing for sales, and the 240 crowded illustrations (probably his work) are unsigned, but what the edition lacked in elegance it made up for in bulk. In his preface to the *Fables*, Richardson noted the 'alluring Force which Cuts or Pictures, suited to the respective Subjects, have on the Minds of Children', and expressed the hope that the plates, engraved 'at no small Expence', would 'excite their Curiosity, and stimulate their Attention'.[16] One child known to have enjoyed these illustrations is Harry Campbell, a seven-year-old boy living in Aaron Hill's home. After reading Hill's account of Harry weeping over the scene of Pamela's meditations on suicide, Richardson sent the boy a copy of the *Fables*; Hill records his charge's delight in the book.[17]

For *Pamela*, in contrast, Richardson adopted a minimalist strategy, proposing not a throng of anonymous illustrations but two high-quality engravings, to which the utmost care would be devoted.[18] The second edition of the novel, first advertised on 27 January 1741 and published on 14 February, was to feature frontispieces to the two volumes, designed by William Hogarth. The first surviving report of the project occurs in a letter of 29 December 1740 to Richardson from Aaron Hill, who remarks: 'The designs you have taken for frontispieces, seem to have been very judiciously chosen; upon pre-supposition that Mr. Hogarth is able (and if any-body is, it is he), to teach pictures to speak and to think.'[19] In a missing letter, Richardson had apparently told Hill what the subjects of these frontispieces would be and whom he had commissioned, or hoped to commission, to design them. Richardson had earlier expressed his admiration for Hogarth in *The Apprentice's Vade Mecum* (1734), in which he concludes a satirical portrait of a fop with the wish that 'to complete the Ridicule, and shame such Foplings into Reformation, the ingenious Mr. *Hogarth* would finish the Portrait' (p. 35). Hogarth had already achieved fame as a book illustrator with his designs for an edition (1726) of Samuel Butler's *Hudibras*, and given Richardson's ambitions for his novel it is not surprising that he wished to collaborate with the most celebrated English artist of his time.[20]

Early in 1741, something obviously went wrong with Richardson's project. The evidence is again found in a letter from Aaron Hill: 'I am glad your designer falls to work on the *bundles*; because there is something too intensively reflective in the passions, at the *pond*, that would make such significant calls for expression and attitude, as not to allow the due pardon, for those negligent *shadows of form*, which we commonly find, in a frontispiece.'[21] In a missing letter to which Hill is replying, Richardson must have told him about a change of plans. Pamela's contemplated suicide at the pond had been intended to serve as the frontispiece to the first volume. This scene was now being replaced with a lighter, earlier one: Pamela dividing her clothes into three bundles. The phrase 'your designer' suggests that a new, less glamorous artist had been appointed instead of Hogarth. Hill supplies no information about the second frontispiece, but presumably the unnamed 'designer' would turn to it once the bundles scene had been completed.

When the second edition of *Pamela* was published on 14 February, however, no frontispieces were provided. At the end of his Introduction to the edition, Richardson explained their absence:

it was intended to prefix two neat *Frontispieces* to this Edition, (and to present them to the Purchasers of the first) and one was actually finished for that Purpose; but there not being Time for the other, from the Demand for the new Impression; and the Engraving Part of that which was done (tho' no Expence was spared) having fallen very short of the Spirit of the Passages they were intended to represent, the Proprietors were advised to lay them aside. And were the rather induced to do so, from the following Observation of a most ingenious Gentleman, in a Letter to the Editor. 'I am so jealous, *says he*, in Behalf of our *inward* Idea of PAMELA's *Person*, that I dread *any* figur'd Pretence to Resemblance.' (pp. 517–18)[22]

From this it appears that the bundles scene, the subject of the first frontispiece, had been completed and engraved, but that the results pleased neither Richardson nor his fellow 'Proprietors' in the novel, the booksellers John Osborn and Charles Rivington. The second frontispiece seems never to have been finished or engraved and its subject remains unknown, as do the identities of the designer and of the engraver for whom 'no Expence was spared'.

In view of the well-established affinities between Hogarth and Fielding, it is tempting to hypothesize that Richardson belatedly realized he had chosen the wrong illustrator for his novel. Eaves, for example, speculates that 'Richardson did not like the interpretation Hogarth gave his novel', and that 'Hogarth, seeing Pamela with the eyes of a Fielding, confronted Richardson with a graphic "Shamela".'[23] Marcia Allentuck wonders whether 'Hogarth's gift for highlighting incongruities, which perhaps revealed itself . . . in his preliminary designs for Richardson, caused Richardson's condemnation of them'.[24] Ronald Paulson, similarly, suggests that Richardson 'found Hogarth's illustration insufficiently spiritual in its representation of his heroine', and that Hill's letter of 9 February 'could be describing dissatisfaction with the application of Hogarthian forms and a recognizable likeness to the ineffable Pamela'.[25] The problem with such conjectures is that they go well beyond the meagre historical record. The only evidence for Hogarth's having any part in the abortive project is in Hill's letter of 29 December. It is possible that Hogarth declined a request from Richardson at about this time; that he accepted and then changed his mind, without beginning the work; that he drew the scene of Pamela's meditations on suicide by the pond before withdrawing or being dismissed; or even that he drew both the pond scene and the bundles illustration that was to replace it. Unless further evidence emerges, the extent of his involvement, if any, cannot be determined.

Whatever the reasons for Hogarth's refusal, resignation or dismissal, Richardson abandoned his plan for frontispieces to *Pamela*. Before publication of the third duodecimo edition in March 1741, the fourth edition in May, and the fifth edition in September, there was ample time for both designs to be completed and, if necessary, re-engraved, but Hill's 'dread' of '*any* figur'd Pretence to Resemblance' seems, for the time being, to have carried the day. Richardson did, however, determine to include engravings in the deluxe, octavo edition of *Pamela*, which he conceived as the definitive version of the novel. That the original plan for two frontispieces was now being replaced by one for a far larger number of illustrations is a sign of Richardson's increasing ambitions for *Pamela* and the need to outdo his competitors: his illustrations would be both more plentiful and of higher quality than theirs.[26] Richardson first mentions his plans for the edition in a letter of 8 October 1741 to Ralph Allen. Here he refers to 'an Octavo Edition I am Printing, which is to have Cuts to it, done by the

Best Hands', and states that he hopes 'to publish by the latter End of November: The Copy is all finish'd; but the Number Printed, being large, makes it tedious at the Press'.[27] Richardson's estimate was out by over five months: the edition was finally published on 8 May 1742. It contained seven 'Cuts' in each of the first three volumes and eight in the fourth: 'an unusually large number for any English literary work of the period, and an extraordinary number for prose fiction', as Eaves observes.[28] The time needed for these illustrations to be designed and engraved might account for the delay in publication.

No records of Richardson's dealings with his illustrators, Hubert Gravelot and Francis Hayman, are known, and since they are not named in his letter to Allen, it is not certain that they had been commissioned at this stage.[29] When their services were secured, Richardson could boast with some justice of having found the 'Best Hands' to illustrate *Pamela*. Gravelot, who had been living in England since 1732, was the foremost book illustrator of the day, his recent work including illustrations for the second series of Gay's *Fables* (1738) and the second edition of Theobald's *Works of Shakespeare* (1740). Brian Allen, discussing the rage for French art in England in the early 1740s, notes that 'Gravelot played a major rôle by injecting a distinct note of French elegance into the shaky tradition of English draughtsmanship. The Frenchman's characteristically sinuous, spidery line could enliven even the most mundane subject matter.'[30] Hayman was still at an early stage of a career that would continue for over thirty years, but he had already collaborated with Gravelot in 1737 and 1738 on vignettes and decorations for the popular Vauxhall song-sheets.[31] Allentuck describes the pair as 'fashionable, experienced, and somewhat toney artists',[32] an apt description of Gravelot but not of the junior partner, Hayman, who would become fashionable only after his work on *Pamela*. Although he supplied fewer of the designs (twelve to Gravelot's seventeen) and did none of the engraving, Hayman's name is listed before Gravelot's on Richardson's title page, perhaps for patriotic reasons.

Gravelot and Hayman were doubtless consulted, but the choice of scenes to be represented for the octavo edition of *Pamela* is thoroughly Richardsonian. The even-handedness of supplying seven illustrations for each of the first three volumes is an attempt to assert that the continuation has as much incident and significance as the original novel; giving an extra, eighth engraving to the final volume is to take this assertion one step further. The exclusion of all of the much-criticized 'warm' scenes is also a sign of Richardson's guiding hand; prurient readers will search in vain for representations of Pamela in a state of undress, or being fondled or assaulted by Mr B. The bundles scene is illustrated, perhaps with sufficient pathos to overcome Hill's misgivings about conveying 'our *inward* Idea of PAMELA's *Person*'. Richardson probably prescribed that his heroine should be portrayed first as a virtuous maiden and then as a dignified, capable wife and mother, instead of the scheming hypocrite seen by Fielding, Haywood, and other Antipamelists; that Mr B. should be represented as the mature figure that he becomes in the continuation of the novel, rather than the blundering country squire of the first two volumes; and that illustrations of the married couple should demonstrate the harmony of their union, contradicting the scepticism of readers offended by the misalliance. In the continuation of *Pamela* Richardson furnished a verbal portrait of his heroine, providing several details, such as her slender neck and serious expression, which his illustrators would follow.[33] He also ensured that the engravings would be bound at the appropriate place in the volumes by having the relevant page number printed in each case. The images were, of course, to be seen in conjunction with the text, not viewed as a replacement for it.

Eaves's contention that the Gravelot–Hayman illustrations are 'as excellent as even fastidious Richardson could have desired'[34] has been challenged in articles by Allentuck and Stephen Raynie. Allentuck contends that 'there is a curious alienation between text and illustration in almost every instance. The illustrations rarely address themselves to the emotive unities of the text.'[35] For Allentuck, Gravelot and Hayman's designs are austere and simplistic, detached from the teasing ambiguities of the novel. Stephen Raynie, citing Allentuck, takes a quite different approach. Where she finds stasis and frigidity, he sees the illustrations as offering a series of subversive readings of the text, making 'it more likely that anti-*Pamela* interpretations would emerge in opposition to the author's purported moral purpose'.[36]

Allentuck's objections are based on only two of the twenty-nine plates (both by Hayman): the first showing Mr B. reading one of Pamela's letters to her parents and the second depicting Pamela angling for carp, a reclining Mrs Jewkes beside her. Both neutralize the textual dynamics, as Allentuck suggests, but many of the other engravings are livelier. Among the more expressive of the illustrations are Hayman's depiction of Mr Andrews pleading with Mr B. for his daughter's return; Gravelot's first contribution to the series, showing a gipsy fortune-teller reading Pamela's palm, with Nan and Mrs Jewkes as onlookers; Gravelot's rendition of Pamela kneeling at her father's feet, beside the overturned card-table; and

Hayman's drawing of Pamela fleeing from Lady Davers, with the gigantic Colbrand blocking the path of any pursuer. In Raynie's feverishly Freudian reading, nothing is what it seems. Mr B., for example, is supposed, in his confrontation with Goodman Andrews, to sport 'an odd vulval-looking fold in the crotch of his trousers'; in an illustration by Gravelot of Lady Davers berating the newly married Pamela and Mr B. in their bedroom, 'the arm that Pamela stretches towards Lady Davers seems about to fondle Mr. B.'s crotch'; and in the angling scene, Pamela is grasping 'an obvious phallic symbol'.[37] Sometimes a fishing-rod is just a fishing-rod.

Although the Gravelot–Hayman engravings have been the subject of much critical discussion, the parallels between their designs for the first two volumes and those by the previous *Pamela* illustrators, especially Carwitham, have been largely ignored. An intriguing example, in the first volume, of a Hayman illustration responding to one by Carwitham is his depiction of the problematic pond-side scene, which Hill had earlier advised Richardson would be unsuitable for a frontispiece. Hayman has ingeniously reversed the perspective of Carwitham's engraving. In Carwitham's illustration, Pamela's pursuers loom large in the foreground, while the heroine, cowering in the woodshed, is scarcely visible. Hayman, in contrast, makes the shed and its woodpile a major part of his design; the heroine occupies centre stage, while the servants are given a subordinate role in the background. In the second volume, two of Gravelot's designs are related to Carwitham's. Like his predecessor, Gravelot illustrates Pamela's dramatic reunion with her father: 'I knew the Voice, and lifting up my Eyes, and seeing my Father, gave a Spring, overturn'd the Table, without Regard to the Company, and threw myself at his Feet' (p. 294). Both illustrators depict the overturned table and startled onlookers, but while Carwitham has Pamela kneeling before Mr Andrews, Gravelot's more reserved heroine stays upright. In his illustration of Pamela's wedding (figure 5.4), Gravelot also draws on Carwitham's engraving: the same six figures are present in both designs, including Nan slipping in through the door, and both artists show Mr B. about to place a wedding ring on Pamela's finger. Hayman's portrayal of Pamela's escape from Lady Davers, his only contribution to the second volume, illustrates a scene chosen both by Carwitham and by the anonymous fan engravers. Unlike Carwitham, however, Hayman sets his scene outdoors. A striking feature of his engraving is the black pine-tree, its spiky foliage reaching out towards the fleeing Pamela, mirroring her outstretched arm and pointing fingers.

Figure 5.4. Hubert Gravelot. Original drawing for his engraving of Pamela's wedding in the octavo edition of *Pamela*, vol. II, 1742.

In their illustrations for the third and fourth volumes of the octavo *Pamela*, Gravelot and Hayman had few precursors. The anonymous fan engravers had devoted at least one design to the married Pamela, but Carwitham and the illustrator of the pirated *Pamela* were concerned only with the original novel. Richardson himself emphasized that his continuation of the novel was 'to be more calm, serene, and instructive, and such as should be Exemplary, as I may say',[38] suggesting that his illustrators might have been directed to place particular emphasis on the heroine's dignity and maternal qualities here.[39] These later illustrations are also enlivened by the occasional *jeu d'esprit*, such as Hayman's engraving of the tyrannical Sir Simon Darnford throwing a book at his daughter (figure 5.5). It is a rare moment of slapstick humour in the continuation, and Hayman makes the most of his licence for comedy, emphasizing Sir Simon's swollen, gouty leg, his nightcap, and his heavy crutch, as well as Polly's uplifted hand with which she tries to protect her face. The portrait on the wall is of a stout patriarch with a long cane: an amusing parody of its owner.

Ten of Gravelot's seventeen original drawings for the octavo *Pamela*, as well as one by Hayman, are known to be extant.[40] Richardson was fortunate in his final choice of engraver: the plates are remarkably faithful to the originals. On at least one occasion Gravelot does modify the original design: in the drawing of Pamela's reunion with her father, Goodman Andrews's appearance is more urbane than in the engraving, and he wields a straight walking cane, rather than a knotty, twisted piece of wood. Charles Grignion, Gravelot's pupil, declared that he was 'a designer but could not engrave. He etched a great deal in what is called the manner of Painters etchings, but did not know how to handle the graver.'[41] But this was a purist's view; Grignion worked exclusively as an engraver, whereas Gravelot engaged in a wide range of artistic activities. Hammelmann and Boase note that Gravelot 'ceased engraving altogether after his return to France', but contend that 'his minute technique, which he passed on to Grignion and other pupils, was far in advance of the careless practice then customary in England'.[42]

At about the time that Hayman was designing his illustrations for *Pamela*, in late 1741 and early 1742, he was commissioned by Jonathan Tyers, the proprietor of Vauxhall Gardens, to execute a series of paintings for the supper-boxes. Among the numerous canvases painted or supervised by Hayman were two adapted from his work on the octavo *Pamela*: Pamela with her bundles, a painting now lost; and Pamela fleeing from Lady Davers, now at Sizergh Castle (figure 5.6). For this painting,

Figure 5.5. Francis Hayman. Engraving of Sir Simon Darnford throwing a book at his daughter, from the octavo edition of *Pamela*, vol. III, 1742.

Figure 5.6. Francis Hayman. Painting of Pamela fleeing from Lady Davers, from his design for the octavo edition of *Pamela*, 1742.

Hayman changed the composition to an oblong shape to fit the requirements of the supper-boxes, and made several other alterations: Colbrand, for example, looms still larger than in the plate, and the more distant of Lady Davers's two male footmen is older, stouter, and more impassive.[43] Gravelot also reworked his engraving of Pamela and the fortune-teller as a painting, now at Chatsworth.[44] The engraving shows Pamela closely guarded by Mrs Jewkes and Nan. In the painting Gravelot, like Hayman, turns the design into an oblong, extending the scene to the right by adding another female servant, who has no counterpart in the novel.

In a petition of 7 January 1742, Richardson, together with the booksellers Rivington and Osborn, applied for a Royal Licence for the octavo *Pamela* (see chapter 1 above).[45] Believing that the work 'may be of great Service to the Publick', they were 'desirous of reaping the Fruits of their great Expence and Labour, and of enjoying the full Profit and Benefit that may arise from Printing and Vending the same, without any other Person interfering in their just Property'. Among the largest of the costs would have been payment to Gravelot and Hayman, which may have approached the sum they were paid by Sir Thomas Hanmer in 1741–3 for producing thirty-six designs for a quarto edition of Shakespeare: £300 for Gravelot and £150 for Hayman.[46] Although the Royal Licence was granted one week later, Richardson's hope of 'enjoying the full Profit and Benefit' was not to be realized, for despite its splendid appearance the octavo edition attracted few purchasers. All other editions of *Pamela* published between 1740 and 1761, the year of Richardson's death, sold at 6s for two or 12s for four volumes;[47] at £1 4s the price of the octavo edition must have seemed inflated.

Those who received presentation copies of the octavo *Pamela* appreciated its elegance. Even the cantankerous George Cheyne, who had complained of the small type and 'bad Paper' of the first edition, refers approvingly to his pre-publication copy as 'your fine Present of the fine new Edition of Pamela'.[48] Two later recipients of the octavo volumes were equally enthusiastic. William Warburton thanks Richardson for 'a very kind and valuable present of a fine edition of your excellent work, which no one can set a higher rate upon'.[49] And Edward Young, in 1746, informs Richardson that his stepdaughter Caroline Lee 'has just now read you over in your new and splendid suit, (with which you was so kind as to present her;) and she is too much a woman not to like you still better for being so well dressed'.[50] But for all the compliments they elicited, such gifts did nothing for sales. In a letter to Thomas Osborne, Jr of 1759, Richardson added a postscript thanking the bookseller 'for your promised settlement of Pamela octavo'.[51] The letter is in the hand of an amanuensis, with the exception of the word 'promised' inserted by Richardson. When it came, the settlement must have been a small one, for in 1772 remaining sheets of the edition were reissued, with new title pages but with none of the illustrations to which so much care had been devoted.[52] Richardson's 'great Expence and Labour' seem to have been in vain. None of the editions of *Pamela* that he published after 1742 was illustrated; nor would he commission illustrations for either *Clarissa* or *Sir Charles Grandison*.[53]

The Gravelot–Hayman designs were reproduced in Europe, initially in a four-volume French edition published in Amsterdam in 1743–4, in which Jan Punt and Pierre Yver re-engraved all twenty-nine of the original illustrations.[54] This edition also contains an allegorical frontispiece by Yver, used in each volume, depicting Pamela spurning Cupidity, a woman holding an overflowing bag of coins, but touching a statue of Virtue. As an elaborate caption explains, 'Pamela embrasse la Vertu, & méprise les offres de la Cupidité, représentée par une vieille Séductrice. Derrière Paméla est son Père qui bénit le Ciel de sa sagesse, & son Ament qui la considère du côté de sa vertu, sous l'ombre de laquelle il cherche le repos.'[55] Richardson, however, made nothing from this Amsterdam edition: the powers of the Royal Licence did not extend beyond the Channel. Ten years after his death, in 1771, a three-volume abridged French translation of the first part of the novel was published in Frankfurt, Leipzig and the Hague, 'traduit de l'anglais de Mr. Grandisson'. This odd version, which begins with Pamela leaving the Lincolnshire house before she returns on hearing of Mr B.'s illness, contains re-engravings of eight of the Gravelot–Hayman illustrations, all but one unsigned, and, as in the Amsterdam edition, with no indication that the designs have an English origin.[56]

By mid 1742, several illustrated versions of *Pamela* were available from London booksellers, and Hayman's two paintings from his designs were on display at Vauxhall. Given the intense popular interest in the novel, as well as the artistic activity it had already inspired, it is not surprising that, at about this time, another prominent artist, Joseph Highmore, conceived the plan of painting a series of scenes from the novel, with prints being sold to subscribers. Highmore was a friend of Gravelot and had painted his portrait.[57] Another friend of Highmore, Hogarth (who probably had his own inside knowledge of Richardson's visual conception of *Pamela*), had recently begun work on a new series of six paintings, *Marriage A-La-mode*, of which the prints were advertised for subscription in April 1743. Highmore's *Pamela* paintings constitute the first sequence based on an English novel, but Hogarth's major narrative series, including *A Harlot's Progress* (1732) and *A Rake's Progress* (1735), provided Highmore with suggestive models for his work.[58]

Unlike Hogarth's progress paintings, however, which tell their own original story, Highmore's series had to follow Richardson's plot. And in contrast to Hogarth, Highmore is not primarily a satirist. Several of his *Pamela* paintings can best be described as conversation pieces. The term, first used in the early eighteenth century, denotes informal, small-scale portraits, with groups of figures depicted in a relaxed manner, at home in what are obviously familiar surroundings.[59] Highmore's *Pamela* paintings are small, each one measuring about 25 × 30 inches, and all but the first contain at least three figures in domestic surroundings. The influence of French rococo style is also clearly apparent in Highmore's series, at times creating sentimental effects quite different from those of Hogarth's more powerful and intricate compositions.

Highmore had completed ten of his twelve paintings by early 1744. In February he placed a series of eight newspaper announcements, inviting subscriptions for

Twelve Prints, by the best French Engravers, after his own Paintings, representing the most remarkable Adventures of *Pamela*. In which he has endeavour'd to comprehend her whole Story as well as to preserve a Connexion between the several Pictures; which follow each other as Parts successive, and dependent, so as to compleat the Subject. This is more distinctly illustrated in a printed Sheet given to the Subscribers, wherein all the Twelve Pictures are described, and their respective Connexions shewn.[60]

Subscribers, who would pay a guinea down and another on delivery, a saving of half a guinea on the post-subscription price, could see the ten completed paintings at Highmore's house in Lincoln's Inn Fields. The advertisement was repeated on 10 May, this time announcing that all twelve paintings had been completed and that 'Several of the Plates are Engraving, one of which is already finished.'[61] In the event, the prints were not sold until July 1745, two months after Hogarth's *Marriage-A-La-mode* series was issued.[62] The sheet describing the prints and their 'respective Connexions', a bonus for Highmore's subscribers, is not known to have survived: a regrettable loss, since it must have contained clues to Highmore's own interpretation of his work.

The engravings made from Highmore's paintings contain detailed captions in English and French, showing that Highmore was aiming at a continental as well as an English clientele. The prints were made by two French artists living in London, Antoine Benoist and Louis Truchy, both capable but by no means the 'best French Engravers', as Highmore's advertisement conventionally claimed.[63] The prints follow the original paintings with only minor variations, although all but the first and ninth were reversed in the engraving process.[64]

Working independently of Richardson, whom he first met only after completing the *Pamela* series, Highmore could paint whatever aspects of the novel appealed to his commercial instincts and his artistic imagination. Although seven of his twelve paintings have counterparts among the Gravelot–Hayman illustrations, the structure of his series is quite different from theirs. With no brief to give equal attention to the continuation of *Pamela*, Highmore devoted only a single painting to each of the last two volumes. Between these two images, Pamela advances from being still childless (though pregnant) to being the mother of six young children: the ending of the sequence is drastically foreshortened. The caption to the final engraving works overtime to abstract about a thousand pages of fictional developments in a single sentence: 'This last Piece leaves her in full possession of the peaceable fruits of her Virtue long after having surmounted all the difficulties It had been exposed to.' Seven of

Figure 5.7. Joseph Highmore. Engraving by Louis Truchy, from his painting of Pamela and Mr B. in the summer house, 1745.

Highmore's paintings are devoted to Richardson's first volume and another three to the second, creating a pictorial version of the novel in which Pamela's trials as a virginal maidservant are of far more importance than her social life as mistress of a country house.

Critics such as Warren Mild and Louise Miller have studied the links between Highmore's paintings and the Gravelot–Hayman engravings.[65] But that Highmore was also responding to the earlier *Pamela* illustrations by Carwitham and others has been entirely overlooked. The second of his paintings, for example, depicts, according to the caption to Truchy's engraving, 'Mr B. expostulating with Pamela in the Summer house after some liberties taken, Mrs. Jervis (who is seen through the Window) having just before left her' (figure 5.7). Although there is no counterpart to this painting in the octavo edition, Carwitham had previously chosen the same scene. Highmore's painting, however, is a far more complex design. One witty touch is provided by two chairs with heart-shaped backs, hinting at Mr B.'s now overtly amorous intentions. Pamela's needlework has fallen to the floor in disarray and is placed to the side. Mr B., with his brightly decorated coat and striking red trousers, occupies the centre of the painting, just as he is coming to dominate Pamela's life. His housekeeper Mrs Jervis, in contrast, is reduced to Lilliputian size in the background, and is hurrying away from the summer house; she can clearly afford Pamela no protection here. The portico and stately trees also seen through the window emphasize the magnificence of Mr B.'s ancestral home, as do the coats of arms on the backs of the chairs.

Among the most successful of Highmore's paintings is his depiction of Pamela being dismissed from Mr B.'s service. The caption to Benoist's engraving sets the scene: 'Pamela setting out in the traveling Chariot (for her Father's, as she is made to believe) takes her farewell of Mrs. Jervis, and the other servants; Mr. B. observing her from the window; by whose private orders she is carried into Lincolnshire'. The central figure here is Robin the coachman, with his splendid blue coat set against the red wheels and shaft of the carriage. As an emblem of his treachery, his face is turned towards the house, so that the weeping Mrs Jervis and other servants, but not the viewer of the painting, can see his expression. The carriage, with Mr B.'s coat of arms embossed on the door, is being pulled around in an arc towards the viewer; Highmore conveys the sense of motion here brilliantly. Pamela averts her gaze from the house she must leave, while Mr B., a tiny figure in an upstairs window, likewise ignores the dramatic scene he has arranged. In thus separating the characters' lines of vision, Highmore creates a discordant effect appropriate to the un-happy conclusion of Pamela's residence at the Bedfordshire house. High-more's painting is far more successful than the engraving of this scene in the pirated *Pamela*, in which the household servants are stiffly posed and unexpressive, but the ingenious idea of a diminutive Mr B. looking on from a window originates there.

Atypically for an uninvited participant in the *Pamela* controversy, High-more became a close friend of Richardson. Although his interpretation of the novel is much bolder than that of the official illustrators, Gravelot and Hayman, Richardson must have admired his work. Highmore went on to paint several portraits of Richardson and his wife, two paintings of scenes from *Clarissa*, of which one is known today, and a lost painting of the mentally disordered Clementina della Porretta, the Italian heroine of *Sir Charles Grandison*.[66] But sales of the *Pamela* engravings, of which the number issued is unknown, seem to have been as sluggish as those of the octavo edition of the novel. A second issue of 1762, sold at the drastically reduced price of twelve shillings, was still available from the publisher Boydell in 1803.[67] In 1750, however, one of Highmore's engravings attracted the attention of the anonymous designer of a broadsheet depicting the celebrated gentleman highwayman, James Maclean, in his prison cell.[68] Maclean's figure, in a pleasing irony, is copied from that of Mr B. at his wedding, with the addition of heavy fetters shackling his legs. His cell is equipped with a writing-desk strewn with manuscripts: a deft allusion to the ever-scribbling Pamela. Each of the seven other characters in the broadsheet, who are visiting Maclean before his execution, also has an original in Highmore's series. For the broadsheet artist, Highmore's figures must have personified gentility; Maclean's reputation was such that only fashionable members of society would be shown being received as the great man's guests.

In April 1745, a year after Highmore's *Pamela* series was first advertised but three months before the prints were completed, an anonymous artist created a waxworks display of scenes from the novel and exhibited it in London at Shoe Lane, just steps away from Richardson's printing-office at Salisbury Court. The opening of the exhibition was heralded by a suitably tub-thumping newspaper advertisement:

> *This is to acquaint all Gentlemen and Ladies,*
>
> That there is to be seen, without Loss of Time, at the Corner of Shoe-Lane, facing Salisbury-Court, Fleet-Street,
>
> PAMELA; or, Virtue Rewarded.
>
> Being a curious Piece of Wax-Work, representing the Life of that fortunate Maid, from the Lady's first taking her to her Marriage; also Mr B. her Lady's Son, and several Passages after; with the Hardships she suffered in Lincolnshire, where her Master sent her, and the grand Appearance they made when they came back to Bedfordshire. The whole containing above a hundred Figures in Miniature, richly dress'd, suitable to their Characters, in Rooms and Gardens, as the Circumstances require, adorn'd with Fruit and Flowers, as natural as if growing. Price Sixpence each.
>
> This Piece of Work is recommended by all that have seen it to be the most curious Thing of the Kind that ever was seen, and is now shewn by the Person that made it.[69]

Like the fan, the waxworks were a fugitive commodity, but the full text of this surviving advertisement (abbreviated in previous transcriptions) yields more information than might be supposed about the disposition of the show and its relation to earlier illustrations.[70] The first scene rendered in wax was apparently the one created for both the pirated *Pamela* and *The Life of Pamela* but not present in Richardson's novel: Pamela being handed over by her parents to her new mistress. Other scenes have counterparts among Highmore's paintings, such as 'the Hardships she suffered in Lincolnshire' and her wedding. The mention of 'a hundred Figures' suggests the exhibition's surprisingly large scale, as does the remark that both indoor and outdoor scenes are depicted, 'with Fruit and Flowers, as natural as if growing'. Among the flowers must have been the sunflower, also represented by Highmore, near which Pamela plans to hide her clandestine correspondence with Mr Williams. Fysh conjectures that other scenes might have included Pamela with her bundles of clothing, watched by Mrs Jervis and the closeted Mr B.; Pamela getting into bed with Mrs Jewkes, with B. disguised as Nan; and Pamela over-turning the card-table as she greets her father: all the subjects of paintings by Highmore.[71]

The advertisement's warning about the need to see the exhibition promptly proved to be unnecessary, since unlike other such displays it remained in place for well over a year. The admission price of sixpence must have made it far more accessible than either the expensive octavo *Pamela* or Highmore's even dearer prints. In November 1745, seven months after the display opened, a continuation was announced. The advertisement for this sequel provides still more details than its predecessor, perhaps because the second part of the novel was less well known. The show, again 'to be Seen without Loss of Time' and also costing sixpence, constituted

A Curious Representation of PAMELA in High Life, in particular the receiving her Father and Mother, the Discovery of her Family at Sir Simon Andrews's [*sic*], the grand Figure they made at Tunbridge with Lord and Lady Davers, a view of Pamela in her Sitting-up-Room, receiving Company, and in her Nursery with her Children; the whole being finish'd in a genteel Taste, and the Figures richly drest, and larger than the first Piece of Wax-Work of this Kind, which was call'd the Low Life of Pamela, which is also shewn with this new Addition.[72]

The concluding scene, Pamela 'in her Nursery with her Children', is also the last that Highmore painted for his series, but unlike Highmore the waxwork artist gave Richardson's continuation as much attention as the original novel. The new advertisement, moreover, emphasizing the 'gen-teel Taste', 'richly drest' figures, and larger size of the second display, seems to be aimed at a more upmarket audience. The original exhibition is disparagingly renamed 'the Low Life of Pamela'; the cognoscenti will be better entertained by 'PAMELA in High Life'. From 9 January to 13

August 1746, however, the two parts of the exhibition were displayed together, as the 'whole Life of PAMELA, both in high and low Life', together with another waxwork entitled 'BRITANNIA triumphant'.[73] At the height of the war against France and Spain, the domestic virtue of Richardson's heroine and the naval prowess of George Anson's fleet combined in patriotic celebration.

While Highmore was overseeing the engravings of his paintings and the waxworks artist was preparing his show, Robert Feke, a portraitist working in Newport, Rhode Island, was painting his own representation of Pamela. Feke could have read the novel within a few years of its first publication, since copies were quick to arrive in America.[74] His portrait, entitled *Pamela Andrews*, depicts a straight-backed, serious young woman. The oval frame, shapely figure, carefully arranged cap (with two dainty points), white ruffles, and gloved arms all convey an effect of graceful elegance. Feke's heroine is demure and dignified; it is difficult to envisage her as the sharp-tongued servant-maid of volume 1, or being tormented by aggressors such as Mr B., Mrs Jewkes, Lady Davers and Jackey. Other than its title, which could have been a later addition, nothing in the painting specifically connects the subject with Richardson's novel: this is not so much Pamela in High Life as Pamela with no life.

The most lubricious representations of *Pamela* are those undertaken by the French painter Philip Mercier, who lived in England from about 1716 until his death in 1760. His paintings of Pamela were probably undertaken shortly after those of Highmore. Their subject, not an episode in the novel, is Pamela rising from her bed (figure 5.8).[75] The bed curtain, thrust aside by her left hand, hangs parallel to her nightgown, pulled aside to expose her left breast. The lower part of this gown rides up over one thigh, while Pamela's disarmingly open gaze invites us to admire the voluptuous display of flesh. The letter on the writing-desk beside the bed, written to her 'dear Father', is signed 'your dutiful and ever-chaste Daughter Pamela'. Mercier's Pamela thus resembles parodic versions of Richardson's heroine, such as Fielding's Shamela; she is, we might imagine, planning to become Mr B.'s mistress (or already so installed), while assuring her anxious parents of her virtue. The books and writing implements here echo their counterparts in the first of Highmore's paintings; Mercier's Pamela keeps up the appearance of being a studious reader and writer. Mercier painted at least three other versions of this painting, with various details altered and Pamela's nightgown pulled still further aside.[76] In the largest of these versions, the inscription on Pamela's letter is

Figure 5.8. Philip Mercier. Painting of Pamela rising from her bed, *c.* 1745.

changed slightly, to read 'Your faithful Ever chaste Daughter Pamela'.[77] For another version, much smaller than the others, Mercier painted a companion piece of identical size, showing a bare-breasted Pamela pulling on a stocking.[78] Here the writing-desk with its candlestick has been moved to the left of the bed and the letter replaced with an open book, but Pamela is glancing sideways in the opposite direction, as if expecting a visitor.[79]

In depicting Pamela in this manner, Mercier was responding to several earlier commentators on *Pamela*, as well as to previous illustrators of the novel. A bare-breasted heroine had appeared in *Memoirs of the Life of Lady H------* (1741), in which Pamela, implausibly, undertakes topless dish-washing (see chapter 3 above). Earlier still, John Carwitham's engraving of Pamela undressing for bed, and also exposing a breast, provided a version of the heroine very different from that of Gravelot and Hayman. And even the normally decorous Highmore had painted two of the novel's 'warm scenes', including one in which Pamela is disrobing with her dress raised above her knees. James Turner's remark that Highmore here selects 'the most voyeuristic station and moment'[80] for his composition applies equally to Mercier's paintings.

In September 1750, purchasers could obtain for two shillings, from a Fleet Street printshop, an engraving of one of Mercier's paintings: 'a Beautiful Print, seventeen Inches by fifteen, of PAMELA rising from her Bed, from an original Painting of Merciers, in the Possession of the Hon. Arthur Hill, Esq; engrav'd by THOMAS CHAMBERS'. Also available at the shop was the painting, 'framed and glazed in the neatest manner'.[81] The print by Chambers (or Chambars), who would later work for Horace Walpole, was one of two made from Mercier's painting; the other was by the French engraver Jean Heudelot.[82] Richardson, by now, was immersed in writing his final novel, *Sir Charles Grandison*. The sale of representations of Pamela that he would have considered grossly indecent, at a printshop almost as close to his premises as the 1745 waxworks exhibition, must have served as an uncomfortable reminder that *Pamela* was firmly established as part of English (and European) popular culture, and that the torrent of responses to his novel was beyond his control.

In 1750, a decade after its first publication, *Pamela* prints, as well as poems and plays, were still being produced, and attracting more spectators and readers than the novel that had engendered them. Between 1751 and 1768, however, as Eaves has noted, no new pictorial representations of the novel are recorded.[83] Amateur artists, of course, were drawn to Richardson's novel. One such was a young woman in Diss, Norfolk, who at an unknown date painted a portrait of Pamela 'giving her commands in the nursery with her children about her': a scene previously illustrated by Gravelot, as the final engraving for the 1742 edition, by Highmore as the last of his twelve *Pamela* paintings, and by the waxworks modeller. The portrait is said to be a 'very agreeable one' by the pseudonymous 'Philo-Naturae', who contributed a letter, dated 10 July 1756, to the *London Magazine*, in praise of the 'Natural Genius *to be observed in* Children'.[84] The unnamed artist, daughter of a Norfolk attorney, had studied colouring in London 'about two years ago', in 1754, but her painting of Pamela in the nursery had been undertaken earlier. Although her admirer believes that her work 'will reflect no small lustre upon the *English school of painters*', regretably her *Pamela* painting, like the rest of her productions, is not known to be extant.

When professional artists engaged with *Pamela* in the later eighteenth century, their choices of subject were, with one exception, heavily indebted to those of their predecessors. Among the least distinguished of the later illustrated editions is an abridgment of *Pamela* published by Francis Newbery, the son of John Newbery, in 1769, containing six lifeless prints designed and engraved by John Lodge.[85] Five of his subjects are found in the Gravelot–Hayman engravings, as well as in the other illustrations of the early 1740s and in Highmore's paintings. There is also a frontispiece, portraying Pamela in country garb outside a farmhouse or cottage, but this too lacks any vitality.

A more original selection of subjects is found in the six woodcuts illustrating another later abridgment of *Pamela*, published by Thomas Saint, tentatively attributed by Eaves to Thomas Bewick and dating from about 1779.[86] Three of the woodcuts depict scenes that none of the previous illustrators had chosen: Mrs Jewkes introducing Pamela to Colbrand; Mr B. making offensive remarks to Pamela, in the company of Mrs Jewkes; and Colbrand giving Pamela a letter written by Mr B. All of these illustrations place Pamela in unpleasant situations, as do the others that echo scenes represented by previous artists. The effect on the juvenile readers for whom this abridgment was intended must have been disheartening. Richardson's subtitle, 'Virtue Rewarded', is retained on the title page, but the woodcuts afford no sign of Pamela's virtue receiving rewards of any kind.

Not until 1785–6, when *Pamela* appeared in James Harrison's *Novelist's Magazine*, did a significant artist, Edward Burney, produce a series of engravings, sixteen in all, to rival those of Gravelot and Hayman. Founded in 1779, the *Novelist's Magazine* appeared weekly in sixpenny instalments until its demise in 1789. It reprinted prose fiction, making popular English novels and novels in English translation widely available in cheap but attractive form.[87] Among the more than sixty works that it reprinted (almost all from before the 1770s because of copyright restrictions) were Richardson's three novels. *Sir Charles Grandison* appeared in 1782–3 (volumes 10–11), *Clarissa* in 1783–4 (volumes 14–15), and *Pamela* in 1785–6 (volume 20). Each novel reprinted in the *Novelist's Magazine* was embellished with original engravings by prominent illustrators, a feature that helped to increase the magazine's sales. At the height of its popularity, some 12,000 copies of each weekly number were sold: a far larger number of readers thus had access to the *Novelist's Magazine* reprint of *Pamela* than to any of the editions published in Richardson's lifetime.

Harrison's principal illustrator, Thomas Stothard, provided the twenty-eight designs for *Sir Charles Grandison* and the thirty-four designs for *Clarissa*. In a magazine poem of 1833, Charles Lamb recalled his youthful delight in the 'pictured wonders' that Stothard had created for the magazine:

Clarissa mournful, and prim Grandison!
All Fielding's, Smollett's heroes, rose to view;
I saw, and I believed the phantoms true.[88]

For *Pamela*, however, Harrison appointed not Stothard but the younger and much less experienced Edward Francesco Burney. In 1780, at the age of nineteen, Burney had made an early bid for fame, displaying three watercolours of his cousin Frances Burney's best-selling novel *Evelina* (1778) at the Royal Academy, and winning the praise of Joshua Reynolds.[89] He began working as a book-illustrator in 1784, drawing four large designs for his uncle Charles Burney's volume on the Westminster Abbey Handel commemoration. Shortly afterwards, in 1785, he joined the stable of *Novelist's Magazine* illustrators, providing designs for the *Arabian Nights* (volume 18) and *Humphry Clinker* (volume 19), but his engravings for *Pamela* were the most extensive and innovative of his undertakings for Harrison.[90] All sixteen of the *Pamela* engravings, dated between 8 October 1785 and 21 January 1786, bear his name as designer, together with that of one of the four engravers employed on the project: James Heath, Angus, William Walker, and Birrell.

Some of Burney's plates depict well-worn subjects, but even in these he generally succeeds in emphasizing a detail ignored by previous illustrators and thus bringing new life to the scene. In his first illustration, for example, showing Pamela wearing her country garb while Mrs Jervis looks at her in astonishment, the housekeeper's spectacles play a central part in the design (figure 5.9). In the much cruder illustration of this scene by the anonymous illustrator of Mary Kingman's pirated *Pamela* (1741), Mrs Jervis's spectacles are also displayed, but there they are merely an accessory; Burney, in contrast, uses them to emphasize Pamela's ability to astonish her fellow-servants, as well as her employer. Burney's third engraving, of Pamela cowering in the woodshed after her failed escape attempt (figure 5.10), also depicts a familiar scene, but he is the first of the illustrators to take up a striking detail in the text. Nan, the servant who discovers Pamela, 'was sadly frighted, but was taking up a Billet to knock me on the Head, believing I was some Thief, as she said' (p. 109). In Burney's design, the 'Billet' is a hefty log, held aloft by a muscular Nan, and Pamela seems in greater danger of being bludgeoned to death than she had of being drowned in the ornamental pond.

Burney also illustrated several passages that previous artists had ignored. A lively engraving in volume I represents, for the first time, Parson Williams being cudgelled by two supposed robbers, actually in the employ of Mr B. Williams also features in another engraving, walking

Figure 5.9. Edward Francesco Burney. Engraving of Pamela in country dress, with Mrs Jervis, from the *Novelist's Magazine* edition of *Pamela*, 1785.

Figure 5.10. Edward Franceso Burney. Engraving of Pamela in the woodshed, with Nan, from the *Novelist's Magazine* edition of *Pamela*, 1786.

with a book in hand and being accosted by Mr B. In the text, the squire remarks superciliously: 'I thought the Man would have jumped into the Brook, he gave such a Start at hearing my Voice, and seeing me' (p. 281). Burney represents Williams's confusion, with the startled clergyman raising his hand, as if to ward off more assailants. Other innovative designs by Burney include a sentimental set-piece from the continuation of *Pamela*, in which Mr Andrews tells his wife and young daughter of the family's sudden financial ruin, and one of Lord H. writing his ill-spelled letter to his uncle, Lord Davers, furrowing his brow as he wields a pen with obvious difficulty. Burney was able to look at a familiar text with a fresh gaze. His reputation today derives primarily from his various paintings of his cousin Frances, the best known of which is that depicting her in a huge Lunardi bonnet, reproduced in numerous studies of the novelist and in editions of her works. This painting was probably executed in about 1785, when Burney was turning his attention to *Pamela*.[91] It is appropriate that the artist who created a memorable portrait of the author of *Evelina*, the most celebrated English epistolary novel to follow *Pamela*, *Clarissa* and *Sir Charles Grandison*, should also have produced much the best illustrations of *Pamela* in the second half of the eighteenth century.

CHAPTER 6

Commercial morality, colonial nationalism, and Pamela's Irish reception

In Richardson's continuation, Pamela recounts the cautionary tale of Coquetilla, the disgraced daughter of an English baronet, who 'was forced to pass over Sea, to *Ireland*, where nobody knew her, and to bury herself in a dull Obscurity . . . and dy'd unpity'd and unlamented, among Strangers' (IV, 458). Ireland offered not only provincial remoteness, however, but also the cultural bustle of a metropolis second only to London in the Atlantic world; and when Pamela arrived there herself she did so in triumph, and among friends. Public enthusiasm was fostered but also complicated by competition between Richardson and Irish booksellers that heralds the furore over *Grandison* in 1753–4, and thereafter *Pamela*'s reception in Ireland becomes marked, perhaps partly as a result of the dispute, by a satirical and sceptical cast. Several London-based participants in the vogue, from John Kelly to Isaac Bickerstaff, were Irish in immediate or more distant origin, but national identity is a special factor in the case of writers based wholly or recurrently in Dublin, a city whose tangled affinities and antagonisms with Richardson's London exerted a distinctive pull on their readings. The major Irish responses are J----W----'s *Pamela; or, The Fair Impostor*, a mock-heroic poem of 1743; *The Fair Moralist* (1745) by Charlotte McCarthy, a Dubliner who wrote and published the novel in London before returning to Ireland the following decade; and *A Dramatic Burlesque of Two Acts, Call'd Mock-Pamela*, an anonymous farce staged at Thomas Sheridan's Smock-Alley Theatre in 1750. In this chapter, these works are read in light of other evidence of the Dublin vogue, and of significant Irish anticipations of Richardson's theme in the anonymous novel *Vertue Rewarded; or, The Irish Princess* (1692) and Charles Shadwell's comedy *Irish Hospitality; or, Virtue Rewarded* (1717).

The first copies of *Pamela* to enter Ireland were probably gifts sent personally by Richardson to established contacts in Dublin, including Patrick Delany (*c.* 1685–1768), for whom he had already printed several works, and Mary Barber (*c.* 1685–1755), whose *Poems on Several Occasions* (1735) he supported as printer and subscriber. Beyond their existing links with Richardson, both these friends had backgrounds predisposing them in favour of *Pamela*'s social agenda. An ambitious academic and cleric, Delany had risen from humble origins (his father, once a servant, was a small-scale farmer), and he owed much of his substantial income, which he profligately outspent, to having married an English widow of superior rank.[1] Though a staunch upholder of the Protestant ascendancy, Delany had little time for the aristocratic froth of its highest echelons (where he was regarded, like his friend Swift, as a suspect Tory), and in his fashionable sermons he rejected as 'foolish and ill founded' all notions of inherited nobility. 'Nothing but a man's own merit, can intitle him to any degree of distinction and regard', he insisted, locating virtue and piety primarily in 'the middle state'.[2] Delany also ran one of Dublin's foremost literary salons at his suburban retreat of Delville in the village of Glasnevin, and it was here, as well as in Delany's city lodgings, that Swift would preside over a poetry-writing circle – 'a *Senatus Consultum*', as Swift called it – whose members included Barber, William Dunkin, Constantia Grierson and Thomas Sheridan the Elder.[3] By sending the novel so promptly to Delany, Richardson may even have hoped to bring it to Swift's attention, much as he contrived to reach Pope via friends in Bath. Swift was now a recluse, and in terminal decline, but Delany's reply suggests that he shared the novel with other members of his Delville set. 'We are all in high Delight with the noble Sentiments, and fine Precepts for the Conduct of Life, with which that work abounds', Delany writes of the opening volumes in January 1741. A year later, he repeats the inclusive plural with reference to the continuation: 'we are all highly delighted, and, I hope, improved'.[4]

Mary Barber was also of modest background, and struck Swift as 'better cultivated than could well be expected . . . from . . . the Scene she hath acted in, as the Wife of a Citizen'. The fecklessness of her husband, an improvident clothier, left her dependent on writing to support her children, and although she secured extensive patronage from the elite – Adam Budd calculates that one third of the British nobility and baronetage is represented on her subscription list – Barber was not afraid to satirize privilege when it neglected the traditions of Tory paternalism. In one poem, the pampered Castalio enjoys an annual income of £10,000 while hypocritically whining that he lacks 'the Pow'r to bless, | And raise up Merit in Distress'.[5]

Barber took longer than Delany to record her enthusiasm for Richardson's own tale of merit blessed, but the lapse of time makes her a valuable witness of public reception. The first Irish reprint had not quite appeared when Delany wrote in thanks, but by the time of Barber's letter the following summer two Dublin editions were in circulation, and *Shamela* and *Pamela's Conduct* had also both been reprinted in Dublin.[6] Indeed, Barber may unwittingly have contributed to a book-trade dispute that ominously heralded Richardson's later struggle with George Faulkner (1699–1775), the leading Dublin printer and bookseller, over copyright to *Grandison*. She had not read far in *Pamela*, Barber tells Richardson, 'before I sent to my Friend Faulkner, and advised him to advertise, that he wou'd print it, but he happened to have got one at the same time'.[7]

The Copyright Act of 1710 did not extend to Ireland, where literary property remained unprotected for the rest of the century, and Faulkner was known in the Dublin trade for his '*great diligence* in London'[8] – in other words, for identifying the hottest new literary commodities and producing discounted editions for the Irish market, usually without payment or authorization. With his fellow bookseller George Ewing, Faulkner advertised a Dublin reprint of *Pamela* for sale in late January, undercutting Richardson's edition at a price of 5s 5d while deftly encouraging impatient readers to pay the full six shillings. Copies could be reserved by gentry prosperous enough to forfeit their Irish discount, the advertisement continues: 'as the Demand for this Book is expected to be very great, it is hoped Gentlemen will be pleased to send Silver, as it will be very difficult to provide Change'.[9] Trade was indeed brisk – by 14 March Faulkner and Ewing were advertising their second edition – but there was also a sly subtextual aspect to this reference to coinage. In alluding to the scarcity of coppers in circulation, Faulkner may also have been invoking the old *cause célèbre* of 'Wood's halfpence', and behind it the larger issue of commercial inequalities and financial disputes between Britain and Ireland. As the occasion for Swift's *Drapier's Letters* of 1724, this attempt by Walpole's ministry to impose debased coin on Ireland inspired a discourse of national solidarity and resistance on which Faulkner was later to draw in the *Grandison* dispute, when pre-publication sheets were stolen in London and published in Dublin, with much noisy indignation ensuing on both sides.[10] Here was an authentic home-grown edition, Faulkner seems to suggest, to be paid for in authentic currency that would not be exported – a patriotic message that obscures the profit Faulkner stood to reap personally by appropriating Richardson's text.

On this occasion, Richardson reacted quietly and pragmatically to Faulkner's manoeuvres, perhaps reassured by the domestic protection newly afforded by the Importation Act (1739), which closed a loophole in copyright law by prohibiting the importation of piracies printed abroad.[11] Problems returned, however, when Richardson's two-volume continuation appeared. Less than three weeks after London publication, on Christmas Day, Faulkner and Ewing, together with William Smith, were selling their own reprint in Dublin, again discounted at 5s 5d, and advertising that 'such Persons as have the former Volumes, and are willing to compleat their Sets, are desired to send one of their Books . . . that their Binding may match'.[12] This time Richardson had contracted with a minor Dublin bookseller, Thomas Bacon, to send sheets of the sequel directly from London for Bacon to reprint, and had good reason to feel that he had made this arrangement with due deference to protectionist sentiment in Dublin. As he later recalled, Bacon 'set up entirely on the Irish footing, and purposed to employ Irish Printers, to buy his paper of Irish Stationers, and to avail himself, as other Irish Printers and Booksellers made it their endeavour to do, of such copies of books published in London as he could procure early, and *fairly, by consent of the Proprietors*'.[13] However, Faulkner's conger successfully bribed someone (probably one of Richardson's journeymen) to procure the same sheets clandestinely, thereby forestalling Bacon's edition and enabling them to bring out their own with minimal delay. Richardson responded by rushing 250 copies of his London edition to Dublin for Bacon to sell, but Faulkner (one of whose allies later claimed that Richardson had sent 1,500 copies) was only inspired to raise the competitive stakes. A few months later, in April 1742, Faulkner advertised the Irish edition as a set in 'four neat pocket volumes' for 10s 10d, continuing to undercut Richardson's duodecimo price while also pre-empting his octavo edition of both parts (which was the first authorized simultaneous publication of all four volumes, and an edition rendered immune to piracy throughout the entire Hanoverian realm – in Ireland and America, that is, as well as Britain – by the Royal Licence that Richardson had procured).[14] Meanwhile, the unfortunate Bacon was frozen out of business by his Dublin brethren, apparently in retaliation for his dealings with Richardson and for his role in a separate dispute of 1742 surrounding a Prévost novel. He ended his days as an ordained minister in Maryland, 'publishing his sermons and exercising his musical talents in performance and composition as "Signior Lardini"'.[15]

The result of this fierce book-trade competition was that *Pamela* soon moved beyond the rarefied elite of Delville, and became widely dispersed through all strata of the Dublin reading public. As in London, reception began with polite and gratifying praise emanating from sympathetic literary circles, but grew more open, unpredictable and disorderly as it rippled outwards. In her letter to Richardson, Barber speaks first of 'the Universal Applause *Pamela* met with, which it so justly merited', making clear that Richardson's novel had caught the public mood in Ireland quite as comprehensively as at home. Limits soon emerge, however, to the 'universe' that Barber has in mind:

> every body in this Kingdom whose Approbation was worth regarding, that I have met with or heard of, was highly delighted with it. The only objection I have heard made by the best judges, that is, by People of Taste and Virtue was, that y^e Scene where y^e Master and M$^{rs.}$ Jewkes had her in Bed between them, was a little too strongly painted.[16]

So much for those whose approbation was worth regarding, the best judges, the people of taste and virtue – people, in short, of a kind to recoil from steamy three-in-a-bed scenes. Dublin was no more entirely composed than London of respectable readers and authors, however, and as time wore on would also yield up more rowdy and subversive responses.

Nor was Dublin simply a smaller London, of course, and the distinctiveness of its literary culture does much to explain the slant of its response to *Pamela*. Culturally as well as politically, Dublin lived in London's shadow, and whether slavishly adopting or pointedly eschewing imported trends could not escape the anxieties and aspirations of colonial dependence. For the young Edmund Burke, Dubliners were stupefied by indiscriminate consumption of English literature, especially drama, and Burke railed against 'the senseless Encouragement we give their wretched Productions; so plentifully do they supply, and so greedily do we swallow that Tide of fulsom *Plays, Novels*, and *Poems* which they pour on us, that they seem . . . to have associated for the Destruction of Wit and Sense'.[17] Yet Dublin was also a dynamic metropolis with a complex identity of its own, assured in its primacy not only across Ireland but also (as Toby Barnard notes of Dublin's magnetism for the gentry of Wales and western England) 'as the dominant city in a region which straddled the Irish sea'.[18] This cross-channel aspect is worth stressing, for Dublin in the second quarter of the eighteenth century was far from reflecting the demographic, social and cultural balance of Ireland beyond the Pale. The indigenous population, Catholic in religion and Gaelic in speech, was on the rise (a trend documented with memorable paranoia by Swift), but Protestants accounted for two-thirds of the recorded population of the city in 1732, and were still in the majority at mid century.[19] Unlike the Protestant counties of Ulster, moreover, with their seventeenth-century influxes of Scots Presbyterians, these Protestants were overwhelmingly Anglican and Anglophone. They dominated even more as a proportion of the book-buying and theatre-going population, and in cultural terms informal spaces such as Faulkner's bookshop in Essex Street or Sheridan's theatre of Smock-Alley were no less important than St Patrick's Cathedral or Trinity College as engines of the Protestant interest. Here was the stronghold of a community that would come to be termed Anglo-Irish, descended in the main from waves of English colonizers from the twelfth century onwards, and scornfully aloof in the collective identity it fashioned for itself from the colonized, subaltern natives of Gaelic Ireland.

That is not to say, however, that the Dublin culture in which *Pamela* was received stood towards England in a relationship of cosy harmony or cringing deference. J. C. Beckett writes of Protestant Ireland that 'its culture was essentially an English culture, modified by local circumstances, not an Irish culture that had been partly anglicised', but the modification is as important here as the dependence.[20] As Burke's tirade shows, conscious and vigorous moves were afoot to shape a literary culture uniquely Dublin's own, and these moves followed broader trends that had gained momentum since the Williamite war of 1689–91. In the words of the historian Nicholas Canny, Ireland makes unusually clear 'the process by which colonizing groups come to perceive themselves as a people distinct both from those resident in their country of origin and from those indigenous to their place of settlement', and in this period settler identity took shape through a kind of triangulation in which English England became little less 'other' than Irish Ireland.[21] Politically, alienation from Britain was intensified by economic disputes arising from trade restrictions, constitutional clashes concerning parliamentary jurisdiction, and local resentments surrounding preferment in church and state, and in the Walpole years this process was compounded by growing perceptions of English culture as vitiated by court degeneracy and city corruption. For Canny, the characteristic self-image of Protestant Ireland as a locus of moral integrity and rigour was forged in conscious rejection of English decadence as much as of native barbarism, and it was consolidated in an ongoing sense of embattled opposition to both perceived alternatives. The 'colonial nationalism' of eighteenth-century Ireland was quite without the decolonizing strain of protest to be heard in Gaelic verse of the period, and its principal forum, the Irish Parliament, was as much an instrument for curtailing the rights of Catholic Ireland as for asserting its own against Westminster. Yet the characteristic discourse of colonial nationalism was also shot through with adversarial tension towards Britain, the many ties of affinity and interest notwithstanding, and would eventually mutate into the full-blown, inclusive nationalism that begins with Wolfe Tone.[22]

This stance was more ambivalent and fluid at mid century, but the steady assimilation of Catholic families into the Protestant elite (Delany and Sheridan were among the beneficiaries of this cross-generational trend) was one of several factors consolidating, while also complicating, a sense of cultural distinctness that was slowly maturing. Throughout the century, Protestants appropriated the label 'Irish' to identify themselves (as in Swift's notorious use of the term 'whole people of Ireland' to denote Protestants of the established church),[23] and although at one level this strategy worked to erase the prior claims of native Ireland, it also marked an eloquent renunciation of residual Englishness. Vexed negotiations of national identity pervade the literature of the period, a body of writing that richly illustrates the postcolonial insight, as Thomas McLoughlin puts it, 'that the interaction between coloniser and colonised generates not just a shifting and unstable relationship but also recurring problems of allegiance and self-definition'.[24] It is in this context – a context of identity formation in which Englishness is characteristically disparaged and blamed – that the *Pamela* controversy in Dublin is best understood.

Some sense of what might have been at stake in *Pamela* for Irish readers can be gauged from two literary works of the previous half-century which, in pioneering Richardson's theme of virtue rewarded, also used this theme to address the contested issue of national identity. Their plots of social mobility take on particular resonance in the fluid context of post-Cromwellian, post-Williamite Ireland, when ancient bloodlines did not protect Stuart adherents from massive confiscation of estates, and pro-Hanoverian arrivistes could spring from nowhere into landed eminence. The first of these works is *Virtue Rewarded; or, the Irish Princess* (1693), an anonymous novel set during the defining moment of the Williamite war, and identifiable from its ideological slant and local knowledge, as Hubert McDermott writes, as 'almost certainly written by a member of the Irish planter community *about* that community'.[25] It is hard to accept McDermott's case for *Virtue Rewarded* as a source for *Pamela* (after its one edition it sank without trace, and its most memorable part, a lurid interpolated tale of Peruvian cannibalism, looks forward if anything to Swift), but the novel does anticipate Richardson by narrating the attempted seduction of a low-born girl by a suitor of eminent rank, and their eventual marriage. The interesting aspect of this plot in *Vertue Rewarded* is that it becomes an occasion to contest Spenserian stereotypes of the indigenous Irish – 'how barbarous soever the partial Chronicles of other Nations report 'em' (p. 29) – while also, and much more emphatically, making special claims for the superiority and uniqueness of Protestant Ireland. As Canny notes, the subtitle illustrates the extent to which the Protestant settler community was already appropriating the term 'Irish' for itself, the heroine Marinda being unequivocally of planter stock, and in the text this version of Irishness is promoted in contradistinction to both native barbarity and English decadence. At one point the superior civility of a Dublin Protestant distinguishes him so sharply from other characters 'that they did look like our Wild *Irish* to him' (p. 20), while Marinda's status as the primary embodiment of settler virtue is encapsulated in her introduction as 'an Innocent Country Virgin, ignorant of the Intrigues and Tricks of the Court Ladies' (p. 1) – a line Canny cites to illustrate 'the tendency of Irish Protestants to depict themselves as honest country folk free from the corruption of metropolitan society'.[26] In her concluding marriage to a foreign prince in William's army, Marinda achieves not only 'the reward of her invincible Vertue' (p. 102) but also the symbolic affirmation of a moral superiority belonging to her community at large.

Charles Shadwell's farce of a generation later, *Irish Hospitality; or, Virtue Rewarded* (1717), has also been cited as an early instance of national self-fashioning, this time on the Smock-Alley stage. Born and raised in England, and a staunch Whig like his father (the Williamite poet laureate Thomas Shadwell), Charles Shadwell quickly adapted to local conditions after migrating to Dublin in 1713, and was a prominent supporter of Swift's *Drapier's Letters* campaign. In the prologue to his historical tragedy *Rotherick O'Connor, King of Connaught* (1720), Shadwell laments a theatrical culture in which 'Forreign Stories do our Stage Adorn', and in *Irish Hospitality*, writes Christopher Morash, he gives comic expression to 'a developing pride in anything that might mark out the Anglo-Irish from their English contemporaries'.[27] Morash points to a fox-hunting baronet in the play, Sir Jowler Kennel, who is little more than Squire Western with a brogue, and is ridiculed by other characters for his rustic coarseness. Elsewhere, however, Shadwell shares the more ideologically loaded interest of *Vertue Rewarded* in identifying innocence, straightforwardness and honesty as the defining virtues of Irishness, and even takes the step of embodying them in a heroine, Winnifred, whose mother, Shela Dermott, is unmistakably of native stock. As Winnifred is reminded by her benevolent landlord Sir Patrick Worthy, 'thy Family have been Tennants to our Estate above these hundred Years, and always have been Honest; and assure thy self thy Vertue shall be rewarded'.[28] By contrast, the play's most suspect characters are also the most anglicized, notably Sir Patrick's dissolute son Charles, who returns from his studies at Brasenose College in Oxford – 'we call it *Brazen-face*, for shortness' (p. 274) – intending to trick Winnifred into bed by a sham marriage.

The anticipation of *Pamela* here is unremarkable, but in developing this scenario Shadwell also shares the intimation that would give rise to *Shamela* – that 'Virtue and Honour, are words us'd often to put on ill Designs' (p. 207) – and goes to great lengths to acquit his heroine of suspect motivation. Where Pamela's virtue consists in repelling Mr B. until marriage is offered, Winnifred's persists further: though in love with Charles, she selflessly turns him down in order to protect her patron's dynastic interests. 'Powerful Love, and vile Ambition intice me to go on, and my sordid Interest prompts me to it', as she soliloquizes in her hour of temptation, 'whilst Justice, Honour, and all that's Vertuous, shows me my false, ungrateful Heart in all its Baseness' (p. 268). Only when Charles craftily threatens suicide does she fall for his plan, but the situation is redeemed when Sir Patrick comes to terms with the misalliance, forces Charles into a genuine ceremony, and recognizes honest Winnifred 'as the richest Jewel in our Family, for her Vertue is of Inestimable Value' (p. 302). With this conclusion, Shadwell stages a euphoric unification of competing national identities, and in the marriage of Charles and Winnifred the settler gentry is symbolically restored by, and hybridized with, indigenous Irish merit: 'thou hast a World of Vertue, and of Goodness too, my Title will make thee a Lady, and in return all our Children shall inherit thy Vertues' (pp. 300–1).

The Fair Quaker of Deal (1710) was Shadwell's one success on the London stage, and *Irish Hospitality* is no more likely than *Virtue Rewarded* to have been known to Richardson. Setting aside the coincidence of titles and subtitles, similarities between *Pamela* and both these works involve formulaic elements that recur in countless other amatory fictions or sentimental comedies of the day. If Richardson was unaware that his subtitle had been used before, however, the same would not have been true of his Irish audience, or some of its members; and to such readers Faulkner's edition of *Pamela* may have seemed to be more an act of retrieval than an act of theft. By pirating *Pamela*, Faulkner was merely reappropriating for the literary economy of Dublin, and as an Irish manufacture, a production that from this perspective had first been purloined from Ireland and rebranded as English.

For *Pamela* not only retells the same basic story as *Vertue Rewarded* and *Irish Hospitality*. It also defines as quintessentially English the simple virtues that Shadwell and his anonymous precursor had earlier claimed, in strenuous colonial-nationalist terms, as peculiarly Irish. Messages of this kind are most overt in the commendations of Webster and de Freval, which invoke national stereotypes to elevate *Pamela*'s moral and mimetic rigour by contrast with romance. This is not French froth but '*English* Solidity' (p. 9); it is not French dross – the trope of good and bad coinage again – but '*English* Bullion' (p. 6). Here Webster and de Freval take their cues from the text itself, which in the continuation culminates with Pamela's boast that her travels abroad have failed to corrupt 'an Heart as intirely English, as ever' (IV, 400). Such declarations support the argument of Ewha Chung (who cites Gerald Newman's account of English nationalism in the 1740s as a nativist reaction against 'French' sophistication, intensified by the context of war) that Pamela is 'a paragon for a Protestant English nation'. Pamela's characteristics closely match 'Newman's assessment of what constitutes "English" virtue: sincerity, honesty, purity (innocence), frankness, and moral independence', and sometimes Richardson makes the link with national identity explicit.[29] He does so less intensively than Chung suggests, but as the novel progresses, and especially in the continuation, explicit patriotic excursuses are clearly heard. As 'an *English* Game in its Original', whist tempts Mr B. into a Whiggish eulogy of the British constitution as guaranteeing the rule of law (p. 405), and Mr B. is himself compared by Lady Davers, in his domestic management, to 'a true *British* Monarch, [who] delights to reign in a free, rather than in an abject Mind' (III, 105). Not only does Pamela's undesigning honesty express the characteristic virtues of her nation, it now seems. Her free and prosperous condition also epitomizes the political benefits of the present settlement – though Richardson may also be hinting here, in Pamela's various conflicts with Mr B., at the need to stay vigilant against threats of infringement.

In this context, the sceptical and satirical cast to *Pamela*'s Irish reception, notably after publication of Richardson's continuation, assumes a larger significance. By gently mocking or crudely ridiculing Pamela's claims to honesty and innocence, Irish writers were not merely echoing *Shamela*. Nor were they merely exercising the taste for burlesque that still pervaded the literary culture of Dublin after Swift fell silent, though this was certainly a factor. If Pamela was an English icon, it is specifically as such that she was a source of both trouble and fun for Irish writers, and by debunking her claims to virtue they resisted any suggestion that this virtue was the property of England. It is hard to imagine, moreover, any great enthusiasm even among elite Irish circles for *Pamela*'s celebratory asides about Britain as a beacon of liberty following the Williamite settlement. Ascendancy writers drew on the same constitutional rhetoric themselves, without deeply probing the contradictions of Lockean contract theory in a colony based on dispossession and exclusion. But they did so not to celebrate a state of liberty they derived from Britain, using it instead to challenge British encroachments on the sovereignty of the Dublin parliament. Constitutional issues were never explicit in Irish responses to *Pamela*, which played the controversy for laughs rather than protest, and which like British responses had more to do with commercial opportunism than ideological resistance. Nevertheless, they contributed to a climate of mistrust concerning political, commercial and cultural relations with Britain in which a conspicuous English literary import (and one proclaiming its Englishness) was as likely to be suspected as embraced.

If Ireland was indeed moving at mid century from uncritical replication of English taste towards assertions of literary independence, the reception of *Pamela* throughout the 1740s demonstrates the phenomenon in microcosm. Two features of the Dublin vogue show how closely early reception followed the English model. As in England, top racehorses began to be named or renamed after Richardson's heroine, the main difference lying in the sectarian atmosphere that surrounded Irish racing: meetings were popular at all social levels, sometimes riotously so, but penal legislation enacted by the Dublin parliament in the 1690s prohibited Catholics from owning horses worth more than £5. We may be sure, then, of the confessional allegiance of Crosdall Miller, whose chestnut mare Pamela finished among the places at Castlebar and Ballinasloe in the 1742 season, and in 1744 'Mr. *Dillon*'s Ches. M. *Pamela*' came second at Galway. Later in the decade, Miller entered another Pamela, a grey mare, at Ballinasloe and Aughrim. She won at Cashill in 1748, but at the Curragh she came in a distant fifth to the patriotically named Irish Lass. On this last occasion the runner-up was Clarissa, a mare owned by Sir Edward O'Brien of Dromoland, an avid patron of the turf with a taste for tragedy and a genius for naming: he also owned a Calista, and when laying out a course on his own estate he gave the name Newmarket-on-Fergus to a nearby village.[30]

A more solid indicator of the Irish vogue is the early appearance of *Pamela* on the Dublin stage, which came in the shape of Henry Giffard's *Pamela. A Comedy*, the play first performed on 9 November 1741 at

Goodman's Fields, London. As John C. Greene and Gladys Clark note in their calendar of the Dublin stage, it was also performed twice at the Smock-Alley Theatre, on 7 and 10 December 1741. Somewhat exaggerating the intensity of English demand for the play (which, though certainly a hit, was discontinuously staged, and did not reach its eighteenth night until February), advertisements in the *Dublin News Letter* claimed that the comedy 'has been performed 18 Nights successively in London, and still continues to be acted there with universal Applause'.[31] Two Irish performances look thin by comparison, but the smaller size of Dublin's theatre-going public, compounded by competition from the rival theatre in Aungier Street after 1734, made it impossible for any work to be sustained for long at Smock-Alley, where plays would often open, close, and have benefits in a single night.[32] In this case, the benefit was on the second night, and was paid to William Rufus Chetwood, who had spent the previous two decades as prompter at Drury Lane and an occasional playwright, and was billed in advertisements for Giffard's play as 'an utter Stranger in the Country'. Chetwood had struggled in London, and was confined for debt in the spring of 1741; he revived his fortunes in Dublin by importing not only fashionable new plays but also the latest staging techniques. As he later reported of his innovations at Smock-Alley, 'when I came first from England, in the Year 1741, I brought over an experience'd Machinist, who alter'd the Stage after the Manner of the Theatres in France and England, and formed a Machine to move the Scenes regularly all together'.[33] As Chetwood's first benefit in Dublin, *Pamela. A Comedy* may well have marked the launch of these innovations, which drew Smock-Alley closer to London theatre norms in technique as well as repertoire.

Unknown to Greene and Clark and not recorded elsewhere, a Dublin edition of Giffard's play was also published, and at least one copy survives (listed for sale in 2000 by Dramatis Personae Booksellers). This edition, issued in December 1741 but bearing a date of 1742, was published by Oliver Nelson, a prominent figure in the Dublin vogue who had already marketed his reprint of Robert Dodsley's *The Blind Beggar of Bethnal-Green* as 'Wrote on the same plan with Pamela, viz. Virtue attack'd and triumphant',[34] and also published editions of *Shamela* and *Pamela's Conduct*. Nelson's edition also contains a cast-list, which reveals that Dublin theatre-goers could see many of the principal Smock-Alley actors in the production, including Thomas Este as Belvile, Robert Wetherilt in Garrick's role of Jack Smatter, and Fanny Furnival as Pamela.

In addition to the Dublin appearance of an English *Pamela* play, evidence of a home-grown Irish dramatization, predating Giffard's version, has come to light. Greene and Clark reprint an intriguing letter written on 24 December 1741 to Faulkner in his capacity as editor of the *Dublin Journal*, and published in the number for 22–6 December. The letter is from H. Eyre, a minor actor who had performed at Smock-Alley in the 1738–9 season, but who was anxious to dissociate himself from the recent staging of Giffard's play, which, he insisted, 'is not that written by me, therefore I do not hold myself anyway accountable for its Faults'. Instead Eyre reminds Faulkner that 'last spring I showed you the manuscript of one written on the same subject by me which was read and approved of by the Gentlemen the Proprietors of the Theatre Royal in Aungier-Street, and by them ordered into Rehearsal and you advertised it to be played'. In June 1741, it turns out, the *Dublin Journal* had indeed announced that a comedy based on *Pamela* would be played on the 18th of the month, although no performance then took place. Eyre attributes the cancellation to the recent arrival of celebrated actors from London, including James Quin and Catherine Clive, who performed to packed houses in Dublin during the summer of 1741. Had his play been performed as scheduled, it would have predated the first London performance of Giffard's *Pamela* comedy by almost five months. Eyre adds that the proprietors of the Theatre Royal had now agreed that his comedy would 'be acted some nights in February, for my sole and entire benefit', but no subsequent record of performances of this play at Aungier Street can be discovered, and neither the manuscript nor a printed version is known to be extant.

Thereafter, *Pamela* entered the general currency of the Dublin theatre, much as it had done in London. A revealing instance comes in an early farce by Thomas Sheridan the Younger (1719–88), actor-manager at Smock-Alley from 1743 to 1754, and linchpin of a literary dynasty whose members included his father Dr Thomas Sheridan, the friend and biographer of Swift; his son Richard Brinsley Sheridan, who dominated London theatre in the 1770s; and his wife Frances Sheridan, whose most successful work, *Memoirs of Miss Sidney Bidulph* (1761), was dedicated to Richardson (with whom the couple became friendly in the mid 1750s). Controversy regularly surrounded Sheridan's management at a time when theatre in Dublin, as in London before Walpole's Licensing Act, was a prominent and often riotous forum for the venting of opposition sentiment – 'the very Place where the People have distinguished their Patriot Spirit . . . to shew their Sense of whatever Grievance or Oppression they have laboured under', as 'Libertus' wrote in 1754.[35] Sheridan's refusal to appear in Addison's *Cato* in July 1743 was widely misread as indicating Jacobite disaffection, and in December 1744 he provocatively restaged one of the plays that had provoked the Licensing Act, Henry Brooke's *Gustavus Vasa*, renaming it *The Patriot*. To put on a play prohibited in Britain was implicitly to challenge the Declaratory Act of 1720, which notoriously asserted the right of Westminster to make laws binding in Ireland, and Sheridan briefly became a colonial-nationalist hero. Two years later, however, he squandered the goodwill of Trinity College, a key constituency of Protestant Dublin, by beating up a drunken undergraduate who had left the pit and groped an actress, noisily claiming from the stage (while still in costume as Vanbrugh's Aesop) to be 'as good a Gentleman as any in the House'.[36] Riots followed for a week, together with a pamphlet war between 'gentlemen' and 'players' that was shot through with something of the tension between social ranks that pervades *Pamela* itself. Thereafter Sheridan worked hard to entrench a middle-class sense of decorum in his theatre, but severe disturbances returned in 1754, when the political atmosphere was charged by the Money Bill crisis, the greatest trial of strength between Dublin and Westminster since Wood's halfpence. When an actor in Voltaire's *Mahomet* was rapturously applauded for a speech about ancient rights, but then refused, apparently on Sheridan's instructions, to give an encore, the theatre was gutted by rioters, while the military and constabulary made themselves scarce for several hours. Sheridan promptly left Ireland to work in London, returning for an unsuccessful second stint at Smock-Alley in 1756–8 while also planning to launch a 'Hibernian Academy' in Dublin on new educational principles. By this time, his enthusiasm for Richardson's novels was a matter of notoriety, and provoked one satirist to propose, with mocking innuendo, a sister academy in which young noblewomen would study 'the Works of *Crebillon* and other Authors of equal Purity':

And as she hears that the young Gentlemen of the [Hibernian] Academy are to be taught Morality from *Pamela*, Sir *Charles Grandison*, *Clarissa Harlow*, and other Novels, she presumes the same Course of Morality will be highly proper for her female Students; she likewise hopes that both Sexes, as they read the same Books, may study them together, by which many concealed Beauties may be discovered, and Friendships contracted to the mutual Satisfaction and Emolument of all Parties.[37]

Sheridan's acquaintance with *Pamela* had begun early, and Esther Sheldon gives relevant information about his two-act afterpiece *Captain*

O'Blunder, a play first staged at Smock-Alley in February 1743 just days after Sheridan's debut as an actor, though Sheldon believes it to have been written in 1741. It was later performed and published under the title *The Brave Irishman* (?1746). The play derives remotely from Molière by way of the collaborative English farce of 1704, *Squire Trelooby*, and perhaps also by way of Shadwell's *Plotting Lovers* (1720), which turns the Cornish hero of *Squire Trelooby* into an Irishman, but otherwise closely follows the English text. Sheridan's version is more original, and in building on *Squire Trelooby* he takes the opportunity to stress themes of a kind made fashionable by the *Pamela* vogue, rewriting *Pamela*'s valorization of innate merit over technical rank in a resonant Irish key. Although O'Blunder speaks like a stage Irish servant, as Morash notes, 'he shows through his actions . . . that he is more of a gentleman than the English and French grandees who mock him'.[38] O'Blunder's English rival, on the other hand, fleetingly contemplates marrying into the Irish peasantry in the shape of a character like Shadwell's Winnifred, and invokes *Pamela* as sanctioning the idea. In the surviving manuscript of the play, though not in the published version of 1754, this high-born character is drawn to the heroine's servant-maid Betty, declaring in a soliloquy that 'the admirers of Pamela will never think the worse of me for it. I'll have some poor Author to write a second Part of Pamela upon my Story, & crowd all the female Virtues that can be assembled into my Spouse that is to be.' Noting that this passage is marked for excision in the manuscript, Sheldon suggests that 'Richardson had outdated it by publishing his own sequel in 1741.'[39] A more likely explanation is that *Captain O'Blunder* included the explicit allusion to *Pamela* in its earliest performances, when the controversy in Dublin was live, and that the cut was made at the time of publication a decade later. The likelihood is that Sheridan wrote the play not before but after the Dublin publication of Kelly's continuation (June 1741) and perhaps also after Richardson's own (December); he was not predicting a 'second Part of Pamela', as Sheldon believes, but reacting to it. In so doing, he identifies the English rival of his play as a version of Mr B. (though more of a phoney: he is an Irishman in disguise, it turns out). O'Blunder himself is an honestly Irish alternative, framed by Sheridan as a counterweight to the usual fortune-hunting stereotype of comic drama, uninterested in the servant-maid and intent on her wealthy mistress.

Only after this farce did the most direct and substantial Irish interventions in the *Pamela* controversy begin to appear, the foremost being J----W----'s mock-heroic poem *Pamela; or, The Fair Impostor. A Poem. In Five*

Cantos. Uncertainty surrounds the exact origin of the poem, but it is certainly Irish. Published in London on 5 January 1744 by Edward Bevins, it was sold by James Roberts, a prominent pamphlet-shop proprietor with whom Richardson often dealt. The rarer Dublin edition, dated 1743 and lacking a bookseller's name on the title page, has the appearance of a later piracy disguised by a false date, and McKillop assumes as much from the later appearance of an advertisement for the poem in the Dublin *Flying Post* for 31 March 1744.[40] Sale takes the Dublin title page at face value, however, while D. F. Foxon hedges his bets with reference to conflicting bibliographical clues. As Foxon notes, the regular collation of the Dublin version 'suggests that this is the later edition despite the date, but it is unusual to find a Dublin reprint with more pages than the original'.[41] It now appears, from an earlier advertisement in Faulkner's *Dublin Journal* for 13–17 December 1743 announcing publication of the poem 'next Wednesday', that the Irish edition is indeed the original. On this occasion, London was following Dublin.

Internal evidence supports the assumption of Irish authorship. Spoken accents are meticulously distinguished in the poem, which retains the English setting of Richardson's novel while clearly giving the narrator an Irish voice. The characters' voices veer, by contrast, between Lady Bracknell and Eliza Doolittle. The Mr B. figure (Sir Blunder, whose name thus nods towards Sheridan's farce) speaks in clipped tones that caricature English gentility. When he exclaims 'Dem me,—I love you, Mem' (i. 40), his accent is indicated by a phonetic spelling frequently used by Irish playwrights from George Farquhar to John O'Keeffe to mark elite affectation. Pamela, by contrast, speaks at times in over-corrected cockney, so that her favourite work of pornography, *Aristotle's Masterpiece*, is rendered as '*Harrystottle*' (iii. 86). All the while, J---- W----'s narrator signals his amused detachment from the world of the poem with Swiftian rhymes which, though true homophones in eighteenth-century Dublin, would have been off-rhymes to English ears. By invoking a pattern of articulation distinct from Richardson's setting, and audibly Irish, J---- W---- imbues the whole with an aura of national satire. Nowhere is the effect more pointed than when he employs one of Swift's most characteristic Irish rhymes: 'Not more the Wretch who haunts a Court in vain, | The Country Curate, or the City Dean.' (iii. 121–2).[42] It is possible that the author was a minor member of the Delville circle named John Winstanley (1677–1750), who lived in Glasnevin for much of his life and brought out a volume of occasional poems in 1742, including laudatory epigrams to Delany and Swift, who both subscribed (Delany for six copies). This volume includes a mock epicedium on the death of a pet in which a nubile Pamela also features,[43] and boasts among its subscribers not only the Dublin elite but also such English luminaries as Pope and Cibber. If John Winstanley was indeed the real J---- W----, he seems to have been caught between competing impulses of disclosure and concealment, revealing initials he can have shared with few other realistic candidates for authorship, but retaining the opportunity to disavow a poem that would certainly have offended Delany.

In plot and interpretation, *The Fair Impostor* is essentially a versification of *Shamela*, and heavily indebted to Fielding's re-reading. Here again we have a subversive narrative of plebeian hypocrisy and manipulation, in which a wily chambermaid ensnares her master while copulating cheerfully with Parson Williams and smugly proclaiming her 'Vartue' (ii. 140). Where Shamela's depravity is inherited from her orange-selling mother, however, that of J---- W----'s heroine is all her own. In a passage closely modelled on Pope's eulogy to his incorruptible father in the *Epistle to Arbuthnot*, Pamela's parents are cast as contented paragons of honest industry – as 'Strangers to Frauds and Flatteries of Courts, | To Rumours, Lies, and busy Fame's Reports' (i. 67–8). Fielding's Shamela is innately corrupt, albeit rather winning in her exuberant dedication to the art of thriving; J---- W----'s Pamela is gradually corrupted by the luxury about her, and in the mock-heroic idiom of the poem always retains a vestige of pastoral allure, casting sunbeams or blooming like a rose as she glides serenely by. This modification suggests a touch of novelistic subtlety on J---- W----'s part, and he elsewhere shows alertness to hints in Richardson's original such as the lesbianism of Jewkes, who upbraids Sir Blunder in the bedroom scene 'for not having done, | What she'd have wish'd, had been the Case her own' (v. 82–3). The poem also sinks recurrently into crude misogyny, not least in the Swiftian recoil from female voraciousness implied by an early reference to Pamela's 'wide Extremity below' (i. 150) – a sneer repeated when on his wedding night Sir Blunder, ignorant of the Williams affair, finds himself 'perplext a wide Extreme to meet' (v. 188). Claude Rawson has noted J----W----'s scabrous evocations 'of several of Swift's downbeat renderings of female sexuality', while finding in the anaemic Sir Blunder an echo of Rochester's 'Disabled Debauchee'. He judges the poem overall 'a not ineffective rewriting, heavy-jowled and somewhat thuggish, with something of the relation to its prototypes that Fielding's *Jonathan Wild* (published earlier the same year, and whose initials the anonymous poet oddly shared) bore to Gay's *Beggar's Opera*'.[44]

If any larger claim is to be made for *The Fair Impostor*, it must be with reference to the depth of this intertextual layering, which enriches the bludgeoning coarseness that Rawson describes. With its mock-heroic elaboration 'In Five Cantos', the poem sustains the characteristic tonal complexity of burlesque, indulging its author's taste for chaos and misrule – for 'vast Confusion', 'wild Confusion' (ii. 158; iv. 98) – with the erudition, if not quite the stylistic panache, of a well-versed connoisseur. In so doing, *The Fair Impostor* not only drags *Pamela*'s euphoric tale of gentrification back into realms of squalor, but also derides its claims to significance through a jeering series of botched analogies with classical myth. As Terry Eagleton writes of the burlesque mode of William Dunkin (another Glasnevin poet), 'there is something about its mock-seriousness which might be said to speak specifically to Irish conditions . . . A rhythm of inflation and deflation, of edifying discourse and crude debunkery, seems peculiarly suited to a society in which a lineage of high learning sits cheek-by-jowl with the dinginess of everyday life.'[45] Applied to the English setting of J---- W----'s poem, moreover, mock heroic also lends itself to the project of undercutting Pamela's role as exemplar of English virtue. The poem's heroic couplets set up expectations of grand analogy, and these expectations are jarringly fulfilled in allusions that link Pamela and Sir Blunder with Tarquin and Lucretia (ii. 57), Paris and Venus (ii. 105), Alcides and Deianira (iv. 58). Martial imagery further inflates Richardson's tale, before relentlessly puncturing it, in a context of heroic conflict. In the epic simile that opens the fourth canto, Pamela and Sir Blunder circle one another with tactical circumspection. 'As skilful Generals, with watchful Eyes, | Concert an Ambush, or avoid Surprize, | Feign fearful Flights, yet no Advantage lose, | And sometimes this, and sometimes that pursues', so Pamela and her antagonist 'Contend for Conquest, and disdain to yield; | While one great End alike directs them all, | The Hero's Ruin, or the Virgin's Fall' (iv. 1–12).[46] It is in keeping with this mock-epic tone that Pamela becomes 'this heroic Maid' (i. 120), while the rank of Mr B. is raised by a notch to cast him as simply 'the Knight'.

Pamela's combat with Sir Blunder plays out, moreover, at supernatural as well as human levels. Avoiding the Christian machinery of Richardson's text, in which Pamela lays claim to the aid of a just and active Providence, J---- W---- turns to pagan forces. Blessed by Venus and cursed by Juno, his heroine finds the vigilant chastity on which her schemes depend alternately protected and jeopardized by minions of these goddesses, whose names confirm the overarching intertextual connection already implied by the poem's five-canto form. Where in Pope's *Rape of the Lock* 'The graver Prude sinks downward to a *Gnome*, | In search of Mischief still on Earth to roam', so in *The Fair Impostor* Juno assails the heroine with 'malignant Spirits at her Birth, | Obnoxious GNOMES, and mischievous on Earth' (i. 131–2). Where in Pope 'The light Coquettes in *Sylphs* aloft repair, | And sport and flutter in the Fields of Air',[47] in J---- W---- Venus 'meditates the future Maid, | And summons SYLPHS and SYLPHIDS to her Aid' (i. 141–2). It is clear at such moments that J---- W----'s poem is as much a pastiche of *The Rape of the Lock* as a travesty of *Pamela*; and in case his form and borrowed machinery are not enough to signal the fact, he also engineers several yet more ostentatious echoes of Pope. In the second canto, as Sir Blunder plots his nocturnal foray into Pamela's bed, Venus's servant Ariel marshals the defence,

> And warns his little Legions of the Air,
> To guard PAMELA with redoubled Care.
> 'Some heavy Cloud, which yet the Fates decree,
> She may with Care avoid, (he cry'd) I see,
> Impends ere Day o'er fair PAMELA's Head,
> Before she rises from her downy Bed;
> Or if a Lover by Appointment meets,
> To gain a Kiss, or slip between the Sheets;
> Or if to steal some precious private Thing—
> A secret Lock to beautify a Ring—
> Her Top-knot, Snuff-box, Girdle, or her Shoes,
> Or some more trifling Toy a Maid may loose:
> Of these be diligent, be these your Care;
> I'll be myself the Guardian of the Hair,
> That on her Head, and that which grows elsewhere.'
>   (ii. 73–87)

It is hard to miss the directness with which these lines draw on a parallel moment in *The Rape of the Lock*, where Pope's Ariel issues a similar warning to the sylphs while similarly refusing to distinguish between trivial and serious losses:

> This Day, black Omens threat the brightest Fair
> That e'er deserv'd a watchful Spirit's Care;
> Some dire Disaster, or by Force, or Slight,
> But what, or where, the Fates have wrapt in Night.
> Whether the Nymph shall break *Diana's* Law,
> Or some frail *China* Jar receive a Flaw,
> Or stain her Honour, or her new Brocade.
>   (ii. 101–7)

It is not only this celebrated passage, however, that J---- W---- invokes, for he also concentrates in Ariel's speech a number of further echoes. The 'trifling Toy a Maid may lose' recalls Pope's 'moving Toyshop of their Heart' (i. 100); Pamela's 'Top-knot, Snuff-box, Girdle' recall the fashionable ephemera of Belinda's toilet (i. 138) and the foppery of Sir Plume (iv. 123–30); the hair 'which grows elsewhere' makes blatant the innuendo in Belinda's famous 'Hairs less in sight, or any Hairs but these!' (iv. 176). In Sir Blunder's acquisitive fascination with Pamela's 'secret Lock', moreover, J---- W---- brings clearly into play the stolen prize, the 'ravish'd Hair' (iv. 10), on which Pope's great poem of sexual warfare turns.

The Fair Impostor is not only a cynical burlesque of Richardson's novel, then, but also a bawdy elaboration of Pope's poem. It sharpens its revision of *Pamela* through appropriations from *The Rape of the Lock*, subjecting the novel to an effect of mock mock-heroic, as it were, in which the noble feats of Homeric epic and the debased courtliness of Pope's satire come into play as simultaneous points of belittling contrast or unflattering likeness. A range of earlier parodies – not only *Shamela* but also such poems as Giles Jacob's obscene *Rape of the Smock* (1717) – enabled this move on J---- W----'s part, but his fusion of all these precursors was wholly new. By combining Richardson's plot with Pope's machinery, *Pamela*'s matter with *The Rape of the Lock*'s manner, moreover, he detects and exploits an affinity between his primary sources that goes beyond gender politics and the theme of displaced rape. *The Fair Impostor* takes from *The Rape of the Lock* and applies to Richardson's novel two particular satirical gambits that had been used by Pope to voice marked (if elsewhere mitigated) hostility to the world he describes. The most familiar is Pope's wry misapplication of forms and conventions traditionally used to celebrate epic endeavour, thereby highlighting a disparity between heroic form and post-heroic content in which the empty frivolity to which court society has now decayed is clearly exposed. 'There Heroes' Wits are kept in pondrous Vases, | And Beaus' in *Snuff-boxes* and *Tweezer-Cases*' (v. 115–16): such contrasts ridicule a debased courtliness, measuring the trivial sexual warfare of Hampton Court against the truly heroic feats of a chivalric past. J---- W---- points just such disparities between epic language and foppish action to achieve his own ridicule of Sir Blunder's world, but he also draws on the more specifically topical scope of *The Rape of the Lock*, and on those memorable moments where Pope looks beyond the vile bodies of Belinda and her set to take in the larger structures of injustice and oppression on which their privilege rests. 'The hungry Judges soon the Sentence sign, | And Wretches hang that Jury-men may Dine'

(iii. 21–2): this celebrated couplet, in which Pope looks past the leisurely high jinks of Hampton Court to the brutal reality beyond, is not an irrelevant digression, nor is it simply a point about lax legal process. Wretches hang not only that judge and jury may end their sitting and get to dinner; wretches hang as a matter of policy and public example, that the propertied elite may dine on the fruits of enclosure safe in the knowledge that coercive legislation (the game laws) could be called on, and conspicuously enforced, to keep the feast from the dispossessed poor.

In J---- W----'s hands, this intermittent strain of sociopolitical innuendo in *The Rape of the Lock* works intriguing effects on *Pamela*. The inherent satirical tendencies of Pope's form enable him to rewrite the novel as a mock-heroic exposure of a world increasingly close to that of Pope's poem – a debased, frivolous and self-gratifying world of titled oafs and social climbers. The elevation of Mr B. to the rank of 'Sir BLUNDER, proud of an illustrious Line' (i. 37) intensifies the novel's critique of elite degeneracy, and this point is reiterated as the knightly trials and quests that the poem affects to celebrate are revealed as no more than a sequence of clumsy gropings. With his 'Dem me's' and 'Mems', Pamela's persecutor sounds like no one so much as Sir Plume. Pamela, for her part, is closer to her namesake in another poem by Pope than to Richardson's paragon – to the Pamela of Pope's 'Epistle to Miss Blount, with the Works of Voiture', who, as though in some bizarre anticipation of Antipamelist satire, is rendered paradoxically miserable, 'A vain, unquiet, glitt'ring, wretched Thing', by the prestigious marriage she achieves. The height of her ambition is represented in the kind of gaudy paraphernalia derided in both the 'Epistle' and *The Rape of the Lock*, as she and her master become locked in a mutually devious struggle of varying lusts, hers for his gold and his for her flesh:

> With deep Designs he acts a double Part,
> To win, and to betray PAMELA's Heart . . .
> With vary'd Art she plays the subtle Game,
> And ev'n her Frowns but fan the rising Flame.
> The future Prospect of a happy Life,
> Of rumbling Coaches, and an honour'd Wife;
> Of Flambeaux, Titles, Equipage, and Noise,
> And a long Series of protracted Joys;
> Of Courts, Plays, Operas, Assemblies, Beaux,
> Of Lap-dogs, Parrots, Masquerades, and Shews,
> The chief Ambition of the Female Kind,
> Like flowing Tides come rushing on her Mind.
> (ii. 32–3, 42–51)

Here Pamela's struggles with her master come close to those of Pope's
Belinda and the Baron, whose real-life counterparts were embroiled
in games of courtship where, for all the superficial frivolity of the
manoeuvres, matters of dynastic and personal seriousness were at stake.[48]

J---- W---- also takes from Pope his broader sense that these struggles
somehow typify, indeed symbolize, the shallow and devious acquisitiveness
of a whole culture shot through with corruption. Where Pope links 'the
long Labours of the *Toilette*' with the similarly calculating machinations of
judges and stockjobbers (*RL*, iii. 21–4), or where he builds a picture of
global hypocrisy from 'The Courtier's Promises, and Sick Man's Pray'rs, |
The Smiles of Harlots, and the Tears of Heirs' (*RL*, v. 119–20), J---- W----
follows suit. Finding in Pamela and Sir Blunder the true exemplars of moral
and social corrosion, he repeatedly links their conduct with wider targets:

> Not more the Wretch who haunts a Court in vain,
> The Country Curate, or the City Dean,
> The Half-pay Hero, long disus'd to fight,
> The voting Burgess, or the cringing Knight,
> Sighs for Preferment, than Sir BLUNDER sighs,
> To make the fair PAMELA's Heart his Prize.
> Not more a broken Gamester longs to play,
> Or the high Pensioner for Quarter-Day;
> Not more a Lady longs new Modes to try,
> Or the young Heir to see his Father die,
> Than he to bribe PAMELA to his Will,
> And yet keep free from galling Wedlock still!
>
> (iii. 121–32)

An earlier passage is similarly indebted to the equivalent moment in Pope
(the opening of canto iii) for its survey of the noon-day nation:

> Now pleading Counsels were by Fools retain'd,
> And ruin'd Clients of their Money drain'd.
> Now the new Bridegroom long had left his Bride,
> And Judges, brib'd, had set Decrees aside.
> BETTY had stolen from her Master's Room,
> And trembling Criminals attend their Doom.
> Now busy Footmen brush th'unpaid-for Cloaths;
> And the stiff Dunn to's Lordship's Levee goes.
> The greasy Duchess, at her Toilet, now
> Repairs the wrinkled Face, and grizly Brow.
> PHOEBUS had half the teeming Earth survey'd,
> Ere yet his Beams awak'd the lovely Maid.
>
> (iii. 1–12)

Yet there are two linked paradoxes here. The first is that in using Pope to rewrite *Pamela* as a satire on high-life degeneracy, and more generally on the corrupted culture for which it stands, J---- W---- was not grafting something alien to Richardson's novel but making evident a subtext that was always inherent. In important respects, the heroine's Englishness expresses the oppositional idealism described in Christine Gerrard's account of the Patriot case against Walpole,[49] and the novel as a whole, though without the unequivocal commitment of the later Pope, bears distinct traces of the final stage of the anti-Walpole campaign. With its conspicuous valorization of country virtue over court vice, and its parallel insistence that worth depends on conduct not rank, *Pamela* displays the depredations and corruptions of the ruling oligarchy in the unreformed Mr B. – a JP and an MP, and one rumoured to be in line for the ennoblement with which Walpole characteristically rewarded political service. The novel's game of whist, in which 'the Knave . . . signified always the prime Minister' (p. 404), is one point where this reading moves close to the surface. In this sense, the oppositional character of J---- W----'s satire is already inherent in the satirized original, and in its Irish dimension needed only a hostile tweak to messages about national character that Richardson had established. The second paradox, more simply, is that by using Pope as a means of administering this tweak, J---- W---- was further reliant on English self-criticism for the groundwork of his satire on the English. For all its intertextual virtuosity, J---- W----'s poem is profoundly indebted to English satire for its critique of English society.

Some of the suspicions that animate *The Fair Impostor* are also to be detected in Charlotte McCarthy's *The Fair Moralist; or, Love and Virtue, A Novel* (1745). This is a work in which, as Jerry C. Beasley writes, 'the plot line more than faintly echoes *Pamela*, suggesting the impact of Richardson's famous work upon the most minor of minor novelists'.[50] McCarthy (fl. 1745–68) is indeed obscure, though not entirely without interest. Born and raised in Protestant Dublin, where her father 'had served the government justly, near fifty years',[51] she balanced an obsessive fear of Catholic treachery (later attributing her damaged health to a Jesuit plot to poison her) with religious writings sympathetic to Catholicism and hostile to the emphasis on faith over works of the Methodist movement – a movement with which Richardson's novel was sometimes confused. The poems published by McCarthy with *The Fair Moralist* reveal a staunch colonial patriot for whom no discernible gap existed between Irish and British interests, though she was also alert to the complications and tensions of Irish identity. In an epigraph 'Written *extempore* under a

Bunch of Shamarocks (otherwise call'd, *Three Faces under a Hood*) on St. *Patrick's* Day', she finds in the plant the appropriate Janus-faced emblem of a diverse nation: 'hence know, *Hibernia's* kind, | Has several Faces to one Body join'd'.[52]

In the mid 1740s McCarthy was living in England, where she supported herself by writing and theatrical agency: newspaper advertisements of 1749 for summer performances in the fashionable suburbs of Richmond and Twickenham specify her lodgings near the playhouse as the point for ticket sales. Her novel was duly published in London (with an expanded second edition of 1746), but reappeared in Dublin in 1747, where it was emphatically presented by its Irish publisher, William Ranson, as *Pamela* rewritten for Ireland. Adjusting the original title to *The Fair Moralist; or, Love and Duty*, Ranson cheekily lifts the promotional wording of Richardson's title page and pastes it to McCarthy's, almost verbatim: 'A NARRATIVE, which has its Foundation in Truth and Nature . . . Now first Published in order to cultivate the Principles of RELIGION and VIRTUE, in the Minds of the Youth of both Sexes.' Now that this genuinely Irish novel existed to perform the functions advertised by Richardson, the implication was, *Pamela* could be cast aside, and McCarthy read instead. *The Fair Moralist* had always implicitly indicated an Irish setting, and on two occasions, when the roaming heroine fears becoming 'to hungry Savages a Prey', McCarthy even throws in the notorious Spenserian stereotype of native cannibalism.[53]

In her advertisement to the second edition, McCarthy expresses surprise at the success of a novel that had been printed at first, she modestly claims, for distribution to friends. Doubtless she now exaggerates 'the extraordinary Desires of the Publick to see it again in Print' (pp. iii–iv), and it is hard to dismiss Beasley's alternative view of McCarthy's narrator, 'whose insistent pomposity of manner and turgidity of language sorely try the reader's endurance'.[54] That said, it is also clear that appreciable numbers of readers felt inclined to persist, perhaps encouraged by aspects of the novel outgrowing its didactic surface. 'A pastoral romance with romantic passions, seduction, betrayal, reversals, and discoveries', as Betty Rizzo characterizes the work, 'the novel is moralistic but includes illicit affairs, the rehabilitation of a fallen woman, and a lively, indecorous, Boccaccio-like episode'.[55] At one point the early plot of *Joseph Andrews* is recast with a lesbian twist, when the heroine, cross-dressed as a servant boy, is propositioned by her grotesque mistress – an impulse McCarthy attributes with nice detachment to 'the Father of Mischief, whose peculiar Study is to torment the Minds of the Virtuous' (p. 65). Flirtations with amatory scandal remain at the margins, however, and the main appeal of *The Fair Moralist* stems from the clarity with which McCarthy resumes, while significantly adjusting, *Pamela*'s themes of social mobility and virtue rewarded. Richardsonian echoes are everywhere, and McCarthy enthusiastically embraces *Pamela*'s provocative distinction between merit and rank. Though of genteel birth (and certainly not, like Shadwell's Winnifred, of native stock), the heroine Emilia is the impoverished orphan of virtuous parents, and moves through the novel as an exemplar of 'plain Honesty . . . dress'd in home-spun Gray' (p. 11). Pursued by a rakish aristocrat named Philander, whom she resists and at last reforms, Emilia angrily rejects the jewels he uses to tempt her, insisting all the time on 'Honesty and Innocence; Things which are seldom found in Palaces, yet yield more secret Pleasure to the Mind, than Crouds of glittering Courtiers in a Ring' (p. 35).

While drawn to *Pamela*'s characteristic contrast between virtuous austerity and elite corruption, however, McCarthy has evident reservations about Richardson's ending, which happily assimilates Pamela into the elite herself. Reflecting Antipamelist suspicions about the nature of a virtue that proves so materially enriching, McCarthy writes in her preface that 'Virtue would be seldom pretended to, were it not the best Cloak to conceal Vice' (p. v), and goes to great lengths to protect Emilia from suspicions of this kind. As in *Pamela*, the rake reforms and proposes marriage, but McCarthy then introduces a twist recalling Shadwell's play. Emilia selflessly refuses Philander's offer, insisting instead that he marry a woman he has previously seduced – almost as though Pamela had renounced her claim on Mr B.'s hand in favour of Sally Godfrey. Beasley is right to find here not only a departure from *Pamela* but also a direct response: troubled by the seeming worldliness in Pamela's virtue, McCarthy looks forward instead to the emphasis on self-denial that Richardson, no doubt influenced by the recurrence of this Antipamelist objection, would later make in *Clarissa*. Conveniently, another suitor then emerges to end *The Fair Moralist* in a double marriage, thereby allowing the narrator to conclude from the examples of both couples that 'Virtue, and Love, must meet their just Reward' (p. 105). In studiously refusing to associate Emilia's virtue with material reward, however, McCarthy balances this Richardsonian wording with implicit acknowledgment of the objection that more aggressively characterizes other Irish responses: that the moral rigour of Richardson's English heroine is in fact a strategy for acquiring wealth and power.

This allegation returns with full satirical force in a Smock-Alley farce of 1750, *A Dramatic Burlesque of Two Acts, Call'd Mock-Pamela: or, A Kind*

Caution to Country Coxcombs. The recent discovery of this play indicates the remarkable longevity of the *Pamela* vogue not only in Ireland, where responses remained satirical in emphasis to the last, but also in Europe in general. It was in the same year, after all, that Lady Mary Wortley Montagu wrote from Italy that the novel 'is still the Joy of the Chambermaids of all Nations', and after its first performance in Dublin *Mock-Pamela* proved marketable enough to be imported to the English theatre. Perhaps through McCarthy's influence, it was staged at Richmond on 4 August 1750 as an afterpiece to the popular Vanbrugh–Cibber collaboration, *The Provok'd Husband.*[56] The Dublin performance had been at Sheridan's Smock-Alley on 14 May 1750, with *Henry IV, Part 2* as mainpiece. A benefit for Theophilus Cibber, who took the part of Squire Gudgeon, a burlesque caricature of Richardson's Mr B., this performance also featured an epilogue 'on the modern Flashes and Fribbles' by Theophilus's aging father, Colley Cibber, which was 'to be spoken (in the character of a Beau) by Mrs. Bland'.[57] Esther Bland, who took no part in the play itself, was Smock-Alley's leading actress, and her cross-dressing epilogue, in the guise of one of the 'Flashes and Fribbles' being satirized, was presumably a highlight of the evening.

In her biography of Thomas Sheridan, Esther Sheldon notes the productions at Smock-Alley and Richmond, but not the publication of the play. *Mock-Pamela* was advertised in the *Dublin Journal* for 12 May 1750 by its publisher, Edward Bate, who stated that it would be 'printed a few days before the Representation, and sold at the Theatre'. Poorly printed, cheaply produced, and unnoticed by previous scholars, it now survives in a single known copy in the library at Trinity College, Dublin. Cibber's epilogue was not included in Bate's edition, however, and seems to have disappeared, together with the musical settings for songs in the comedy by the German-born composer, John Frederick Lampe. A concluding note in the text states that Lampe's music 'will be publish'd by him with all convenient speed',[58] but no copies – if this publication ever materialized – have been found.

No great critical claim can be made for *Mock-Pamela*, but it is a deft enough satire, and retains something of the wit and ingenuity of its most obvious model, *Shamela*. This debt is immediately acknowledged. Holding a copy of *Pamela* in her opening speech, the servant Blossom praises Richardson's novel for teaching her how much better she might do than become the mistress of Squire Gudgeon, her young master: 'Thou ravishing, charming, sweet, wonderful, pretty, dear, dear little *Pamela*, let me kiss thee' (p. 3), she announces, her gushing adjectives recalling not only Parson Tickletext on 'sweet, dear, pretty *Pamela*' but also the 'pretty, little, white, round, panting' breasts that transfix Fielding's Mrs Jervis.[59] Like Shamela, Blossom then deploys a variety of schemes to lure Gudgeon into marriage. She responds to one of his bumbling advances, '*halling her about and kissing her*' in the stage directions, as though battling homicide and arson: 'Oh, oh, murder, fire, murder, help, help!' (p. 11). She is equally adept at feigning tragic distress: 'O! what ails me? where am I? O! I faint, I die! (*Sinking into the Chair.*)' (p. 19). Gudgeon, in turn, is oafish, callow and self-important, blustering to his mother about having 'come to the age of discretion, to an estate of two thousand a year, to the best kennel of hounds in *Glostershire*, and to the honour of being prick'd down at Court, for high sheriff o'the county' (p. 11). Like a juvenile Squire Western, he is inseparable from his dogs, and 'can eat, drink, sleep, and make a noise indeed like them, but he has not half their sagacity, or good breeding' (p. 17).

A copy of *Pamela* accompanies Blossom around the stage for much of the play, and she reads the novel shamelessly as a manual of husband-hunting. As she says in a typical aside, adroitly feigning a bout of tearful contrition, 'thank *Pamela* for that' (p. 19). Her fondness for the pen ultimately foils her plans for marriage, when Gudgeon becomes aware of her incriminating letter to a scheming aunt who is, we learn, 'tire-woman to the play-house in *Good-mans-Fields*' (p. 6) – a detail that nicely combines the profession of Shamela's mother with the venue of the first *Pamela* play. Thwarted in her ambition of attaining 'the antient and honourable title of Madam *Gudgeon*' (p. 4), Blossom nevertheless secures her fortune when Gudgeon is forced to buy her off. Subtitled a 'Kind Caution to Country Coxcombs', the play concludes with Gudgeon blaming himself for following 'rebel passions' rather than 'reason's rule'. Blossom has merely followed 'nature – pure nature!' in 'endeavouring to get so good a husband'; Gudgeon, in contrast, is punished for ignoring the stratifications of rank, and thus incurs his mother's patrician scorn: 'thou booby, thou monster, thou idiot! would'st thou go and take thy own footman's harlot to be thy wife? the base born brat of thy own steward and house-keeper too' (p. 30). 'Booby', of course, is Fielding's name for the hapless hero of *Shamela*, and *Mock-Pamela* operates with assumptions similar to Fielding's own: only a fool of a squire would take an interest in a servant, and only a hypocrite of a servant would feign romantic interest in a man who had wanted her for his mistress.

In characterizing Squire Gudgeon, the anonymous author adds a new twist to Fielding, drawing on a comic tradition that includes among its products Sir Gudgeon Credulous in John Wilson's *The Projectors* (1665) and Sir Andrew Gudgeon in Susannah Centlivre's *The Artifice* (1723). Proverbially greedy and gullible, and likely to bite unguardedly at any bait, the gudgeon of this piscatory *Pamela* proves true to his name. Where in the original novel the heroine likens herself to 'a poor Carp . . . betrayed by false Baits' (p. 131), *Mock-Pamela* turns the tables to have her exult that 'the *Gudgeon*'s fairly hook'd and let me alone to hold him fast' (p. 31). The England of the play is a place of greedy fools and acquisitive hunters, and here again a discreet but discernible national edge is on show in this Smock-Alley satire. In the Irish ur-*Pamelas* of 1693 and 1717, *The Irish Princess* and *Irish Hospitality*, ancient bloodlines are rejuvenated and reformed through marriage with exemplars of virtue deemed innately Irish, but *Mock-Pamela* conspicuously denies a reading of this kind to Richardson's novel. As though satirically endorsing a colonial-nationalist ideology in which English moral integrity has declined at home and survives only as transplanted in Ireland, the play represents Squire Gudgeon as a decadent shadow of his 'antient and honourable' line, while wealth is grasped in the mercenary hands of Fieldingesque schemers and thrivers. The English myth of native virtue is roundly debunked; the Irish myth – which Richardson, unwittingly, had seemed to steal – survives intact.

As ever throughout the tortuous history of the *Pamela* vogue, however, ideological considerations pale before those of commerce, and there is no reason to think that Richardson would have been greatly distressed by this play. As a businessman, and indeed as a father, he objected vehemently to Irish reprintings of his work, which would deprive his family of revenues rightfully theirs. Yet stage adaptations, including the Irish dramatizations, were another matter. There is no firm record of Richardson's ever seeing a dramatic version of *Pamela*, but he must have known of their existence, and must have realized, too, that their performance would do nothing but good for his sales. He is likely to have heard from his friend Cibber about the *Provok'd Husband–Mock-Pamela* double-bill at Richmond in 1750, a few miles from his summer home in Fulham, and there is a tantalizing possibility that he may even have seen it. Just two days after the Richmond performance, on 6 August, Richardson wrote a letter reworking the piscatory metaphor that was central to the Irish play. Forward girls such as the ambitious Gunning sisters, he tells Sarah

Wescomb, 'seem too much in haste to make their Fortunes, to catch their Fish. When Women turn *Seekers*, it will not do. Gudgeons may bite; but not even then but by Accident, and thro' Inexperience of the Wiles of Anglers.'[60] If 'Gudgeons' is prompted here by *Mock-Pamela* (and Richardson can be found using the word on only one other occasion, when he carries it across from L'Estrange's edition of Aesop[61]), it seems likely that Richardson was including the play in the counts he produced to estimate, with evident pride, that 'the History of Pamela gave Birth to no less than 16 Pieces'.[62] A decade after *Pamela* had appeared, Richardson was continuing to monitor its effects, and apparently without rancour.

Afterword

In January–February 1786, a dispute between two women writers over the merits of *Pamela* enlivened the pages of the *Gentleman's Magazine*. It was provoked by the publication of Clara Reeve's *The Progress of Romance* (1785), a study of the rise of the novel, in which *Pamela* is described as Richardson's masterpiece: 'The Originality, the beautiful simplicity of the manners and language of the charming maid, are interesting past expression; and find a short way to the heart.'[1] In a stinging letter to the editor, Anna Seward declared that 'no person endowed with any refinement of perception, any accuracy of judgment, can think *Pamela* superior to *Grandison*, and *Clarissa*'. Reeve had, according to Seward, lavished excessive praise on Richardson's 'perishable *Pamela*', a 'withering branch on a tree of aramanth', in order to boost the reputation of her own *The Old English Baron*, which could stand comparison with Richardson's first novel, but not with his masterpiece *Clarissa*. A month later, the *Gentleman's Magazine* printed a wounded reply from Reeve, denying the charge of disingenuousness and stating that her friend Martha Bridgen, Richardson's daughter, had approved her remarks in *The Progress of Romance* before their publication.[2] Reeve had the last word in this brief skirmish, but these were clearly less hospitable times for *Pamela* than 1741, when, under Edward Cave's genial proprietorship, the *Gentleman's Magazine* pronounced it a flagrant 'Want of Curiosity not to have read *Pamela*' (see chapter 1 above).

When Catharine Macaulay published her *Letters on Education* in 1790, with two chapters devoted to the 'Literary Education of young Persons', the tide seemed to have turned against *Pamela* for good. In the second of these chapters, Macaulay considers the 'formidable body of novel writers' (p. 142), whom she regards as a thoroughly pernicious influence on youthful readers. Among the few novels she condones are *Don Quixote*, which 'may be read at every period of life', and *Joseph Andrews*, which 'may be read with safety, and even with improvement by youth' (pp. 144–5). Richardson, however, though 'regarded as the most moral novel writer of the class', is a more difficult case, and *Pamela* is especially problematic: it 'exhibits a pattern of chastity in low life', but 'conducted in such a manner as to render it totally unfit for the perusal of youth'. All of Richardson's novels, she contends, have their merits, but should be read at 'an age when the judgment is sufficiently ripe to separate the wheat from the chaff' (p. 147). First the poet Seward, the Swan of Lichfield, and now the radical historian and polemicist Macaulay had joined the Anti-pamelist ranks.[3]

Macaulay's suspicion of Richardson, and of *Pamela* in particular, was commonplace among radically minded women in the 1790s. Elizabeth Inchbald, for example, in her comedy *Next Door Neighbours* (1791), makes use of Richardson's novel but is careful to suppress its name. Inchbald's play, as Angela J. Smallwood observes, is based on two earlier, unrelated French comedies: *Le Dissipateur* (1736), by Philippe Néricault (Destouches), and *L'Indigent* (1782), by Louis-Sébastien Mercier.[4] In Mercier's play, the wealthy De Lys, a counterpart to Mr B., is bent on seducing the innocent Charlotte. At one point he compares her to Pamela and is not surprised to hear that she too has read Richardson's novel: 'Vous avez donc été formée par des livres' (II, v). Charlotte admires *Pamela* but notes that 'le malheur' has been a still stronger force in her life ('plus instructif encore'). In Inchbald's version, a parallel conversation takes place between the rakish Sir George Splendorville and his intended prey, Eleanor:

SIR GEORGE. Nay, listen to me. Your sentiments, I make no doubt, are formed from books.

ELEANOR. No, from misfortunes—yet more instructive. (II, i)

Inchbald, while drawn to a play that draws on *Pamela*, has removed the novel from the dialogue; Eleanor has not formed her sentiments from Richardson's, or any other, novel. She is, as Smallwood aptly terms her, a '1790s version of Pamela', but one with no ostensible knowledge of her precursor.

Another radical woman writer to question the value of Richardson's novels was Mary Hays. Her *Letters and Essays, Moral and Miscellaneous* (1793) contains a panegyric on *Clarissa*, 'a book, which I would recommend to the attention of any young persons under my care' (p. 95). But four years later, in her essay 'On Novel Writing' (1797), Hays damns Richardson with faint praise, terming him the 'incomparable' author of 'the exquisite novel of Clarissa', while deploring the 'false and pernicious principles, the violations of truth and nature, the absurd superstitions and

ludicrous prejudices . . . with which it abounds'.[5] Two years later, Mary
Robinson, an admirer of both Hays and Mary Wollstonecraft, took a
sideswipe at *Pamela* in her novel *The Natural Daughter* (1799). Here a
servant sent by her mistress to a bookseller, Mr Index, requests a half-
remembered title, 'something about Virtue Rewarded'. Index, however,
advises her to choose some more fashionable reading: '"O, child! that is a
work of such gothic antiquity, that we have not had one copy in our shop
these twenty years. Nobody would think of dosing over such dull
lessons."'[6]

Conservative writers in the 'war of ideas' (Marilyn Butler's apt term for
the charged ideological atmosphere of fiction in the 1790s) were more
likely to take a sympathetic attitude towards Richardson.[7] In *Rosina*
(1793), by the Minerva Press novelist Miss Pilkington,[8] the heroine
engages in a long debate on the merits of reading with her philistine
neighbour, Mrs Lewis. After deploring historical writing and Pope's *Rape
of the Lock* – 'what a deal of stuff he spins you out of a mere nothing' –
Mrs Lewis turns her attentions to *Pamela*:

However, though these poetry books are foolish enough, they are not half so bad
as your romance books, like Pamela there, shewing how low creatures may be
married to great lords, and men of fortune; and if it should come in your way, I
charge you not to read it: there's no answering for what strange vagaries it might
put into your head.

Pilkington is clearly satirizing Mrs Lewis, although she notes that Rosina
too 'was no violent admirer of Richardson's first heroine' (III, 40–1). The
main point though is not the merit, or otherwise, of Richardson's novel,
but its remarkable currency: in 1793, *Pamela* was still a test-case in a
discussion of suitable reading material for young women.

Pilkington's attention might have been drawn to *Pamela* by an essay on
the novel in the *Lady's Magazine* for April 1793. While acknowledging
Clarissa to be Richardson's masterpiece, the anonymous author also
admires its predecessor, describing the reading experience in terms strikingly similar to those lavished on it in the 1740s. Like Aaron Hill, the
critic emphasizes the novel's hold on its readers' imaginations: 'the tender
tale so winds about our hearts, that we think we are conversing with
the amiable heroine; and it is but upon reflection, we can be persuaded
we are only reading a fiction'.[9] This critic also notes that unlike *Clarissa*
and *Sir Charles Grandison*, *Pamela* is still widely read; for all their
merits, the sheer size of Richardson's later novels deters 'the generality
of readers'.

Probably inspired by this tribute, a rival of the *Lady's Magazine* took advantage of the continuing popularity of *Pamela* in an attempt to boost its flagging sales. The *New Lady's Magazine* had been founded by Alexander Hogg in 1786 in imitation of the popular *Lady's Magazine*. By 1794, however, the upstart *New Lady's* was struggling to attract both contributors and readers. In January it announced that henceforward it would be accompanied by a supplement, *Hogg's New Novelist's Magazine*, which would reprint classic novels, beginning with *Pamela*, to be followed by *Sir Charles Grandison* and *Clarissa* (in that order), and then by *Don Quixote* and Smollett's translation of *Gil Blas*.[10] In July, however, a change of strategy took place. The weekly instalments of *Pamela* had apparently been selling sluggishly. Hogg therefore inserted the first forty pages of his edition into the *New Lady's Magazine* itself, numbering the pages separately. A prefatory announcement noted that subsequent issues would publish the remainder of Richardson's work, which was 'the most valuable and entertaining Novel ever written' (9, 298).[11] In October, Hogg claimed that 'the Introduction of Richardson's excellent Novel of Pamela has contributed much to the Advantage of our Magazine' (9, 346) by increasing the number of subscribers.[12] In November 1795, the final instalment appeared at last, allowing Hogg to promise readers of the December issue that with 'the Completion of that elegant Work' (10, 178), his magazine would now have room for more new contributions. Hogg's readers must have deserted him, however; the *New Lady's Magazine* ceased publication for good with its issue of May 1797.

Whether its reprinting of *Pamela* speeded or retarded the demise of the *New Lady's Magazine*, in the mid 1790s, and well into the nineteenth century, Richardson's novel remained the subject of controversy. In 1796, William Beckford published his satirical novel *Modern Novel Writing, or the Elegant Enthusiast*, under the pseudonym of Lady Harriet Marlow, followed a year later by *Azemia. A Descriptive and Sentimental Novel*, this time dedicated to Lady Harriet under the pseudonym of Jacquetta Agneta Mariana Jenks. *Modern Novel Writing* parodies a wide range of sentimental and Gothic fiction, including *Louisa; or the Reward of an Affectionate Daughter* (1790) by Beckford's half-sister, Elizabeth Hervey. But the work most closely involved with *Modern Novel Writing* is *Pamela*, which provides Beckford with an amusing chapter, 'The Struggles of Virtue Prevail'. Here the heroine, Arabella, receives a letter from a friend, 'the valuable suffering Amelia', recounting her attempted seduction by Lord Mahogany and his accomplice, the 'wicked Marchioness' (1, 120). The letter is, as Frank Gees Black was the first to note, 'an almost literal transcript of Pamela's famous account of the attempted rape',[13] with the Marchioness taking over the role of Mrs Jewkes and Mahogany that of Mr B. Beckford deftly perverts the already fervid eroticism of Richardson's notorious scene by making the marchioness an enthusiastic collaborator in the would-be rape, rather than a servant in her master's pay. Beckford also heightens the disparity in rank between Pamela and Mr B. by giving titles to both of Amelia's persecutors. His ingenious adaptation assumes a close familiarity with *Pamela*, which was still a favourite among novel readers. *Azemia* also features a heroine whose virtue is under assault, but this Turkish-born counterpart to Pamela is ignorant of English fiction, showing 'how damsels have been spirited off, and shut up by sundry evil-disposed gentlemen – a circumstance which is hardly omitted in any novel since the confinement of Pamela at Mr B----'s house in Lincolnshire, and the *enlevement* of Miss Byron by Sir Hargrave Pollexfen' (11, 186–7). Azemia is clearly exceptional; an English heroine, in contrast, would be expected to be intimately familiar with Pamela's trials, as well as with those of Harriet Byron in *Sir Charles Grandison*.

Although several participants in the Jacobin–Antijacobin debate took a stand on the merits of *Pamela*, few were as strident as an anonymous reviewer of Isaac Bickerstaff's *The Maid of the Mill* (see chapter 4 above). Writing in an Irish magazine in May 1793, he termed the play 'one of those delusions which frequently destroy the proper subordinations of society'.[14] In France, where two dramatic adaptations of the novel played active roles in the cultural politics of the Terror, the stakes were higher. Voltaire's *Nanine*, which unlike Goldoni's *Pamela nubile* had not trans-formed Richardson's heroine into a daughter of an aristocrat but pre-served her low social rank, found favour on the revolutionary stage. In 1789–99 it played in Paris on 136 occasions (second only to *Brutus*, with its obvious revolutionary potential, among Voltaire's plays), while in the Girondist stronghold of Bordeaux, with 45 performances, it was the most popular Voltaire play of all.[15] The play's modern editors, Labriolle and Duckworth, note that its egalitarian sentiments corresponded with those of the period, while R. S. Ridgway goes further, declaring that it 'un-doubtedly helped to create the state of mind which led . . . to the "nuit du quatre août", when the French nobility renounced its privileges in an effusion of sensibility'.[16]

The success of *Nanine* in the 1790s was in marked contrast to the alarmingly hostile reception of a more recent dramatic adaptation, Fran-çois de Neufchâteau's *Paméla, ou la vertu récompensée*, written in 1788 and first performed at the Comédie française in August 1793.[17] In its original

form, the comedy was closely modelled on *Pamela nubile*. Neufchâteau
had read his play to the aged Goldoni in June 1788, and announced his
fidelity to the Italian *Pamela* in prefatory verses comparing *Pamela nubile*
favourably with the various other adaptations. Had Neufchâteau's *Pamela*
been performed at the time of its composition, in *ancien régime* France, it
would have been considered a radically minded work. But by the time
that it opened in August 1793, the Terror was under way, and after
repeated attacks in the press, the production was shut down within a
month by the Committee of Public Safety. Neufchâteau made various
changes to satisfy the Committee, including the restoration of Pamela's
lowly descent; the play then reopened on 2 September. On this occasion,
however, a soldier, Jullien de Carentan, took offence at a speech in praise
of religious tolerance, concluding with the lines:

> Ah! Les persécutors sont les seuls condamnables
> Et les plus tolérants sont les plus raisonables!
> (IV, xii)

Carentan's memorable outburst – 'Point de tolérance politique! c'est un
crime!' – caused the play to be removed from the stage again; Neufchâteau
and the actors were imprisoned, and the Comédie française closed.[18] In
danger of being guillotined, Neufchâteau survived by mounting a lengthy
published defence of his work, refuting charges that it was counter-
revolutionary.[19] His appeal eventually succeeded, and a year after the fall
of Robespierre, on 22 July 1795, the play was performed again at the
Feydeau Theatre. The fortunes and misfortunes of *Paméla, ou la vertu
récompensée* in the early 1790s form a nightmarish counterpart to those of
Richardson's novel in the early 1740s. Both Richardson and Neufchâteau
took on the task of defending their work against their critics, one contending that his novel would not undermine the established social order,
the other that his play upheld liberty and fraternity. As Lynn Festa
concludes, *Pamela* had gone, in fifty years, from 'upsetting the aristocracy
with its celebration of a servant's ascent through superior virtue to
scandalizing revolutionaries'.[20]

By the early nineteenth century, English critics, as well as French
Jacobins, were more likely to criticize Richardson for upholding the social
hierarchy than to condemn him for challenging it. Epitomizing this
change is Anna Laetitia Barbauld's remarkable 200-page biographical
and critical essay of 1804, prefixed to her six-volume selection of
Richardson's correspondence. In a judicious assessment of the strengths
and weaknesses of *Pamela*, Barbauld contends that among its faults is

its moral, 'more dubious than, in his life time, the author's friends were willing to allow'. A milder English counterpart to the fulminating revolutionary Carentan, Barbauld sagely suggests that the 'excessive humility and gratitude' displayed by Pamela and her parents towards Mr B. show 'a regard to rank and riches beyond the just measure of an independent mind'. She also objects, like so many of the Antipamelists, to the 'indelicate scenes in the novel', which 'have been justly found fault with, and are, indeed, totally indefensible'. As for the second part of *Pamela*, it is, she declares, 'like most second parts, greatly inferior to the first'.[21]

Barbauld's edition received extensive reviews in the literary magazines, and her discussion of Richardson's novels attracted as much attention as her editing of the correspondence. Some reviewers felt that she had been unduly generous to *Pamela*: the *Critical Review*, for instance, claimed that 'of the rising generation few have heard of *Pamela*', and that its continuation was 'a tax on the reader and purchaser'. Christopher Moody in the *Monthly Review*, similarly, expressed surprise that 'after so long a repose, we should now conjure up [Richardson's] ghost'. A reviewer in *The Sentinel*, in contrast, claimed that Barbauld 'does the grossest injustice' to Richardson, 'that illustrious and immortal author', and deplored her criticisms of his style and characterization. Francis Jeffrey, taking a middle path in the *Edinburgh Review*, felt that Barbauld's critique of *Pamela* was replete with 'good sense and propriety' and quotes from it at length.[22] No consensus had formed on the merits of Richardson's first novel. The reviewers agreed with Barbauld that *Clarissa* was Richardson's masterpiece, but *Pamela* was as disruptive a force as ever, dividing nineteenth-century reviewers into Pamelist and Antipamelist camps as it had its first readers.

Pamela remained a remarkably popular novel at the turn of the century. When the bookseller James Lackington published his memoirs in 1791, he marvelled at the recent growth of the reading public, conjecturing that 'more than four times the number of books are sold now than were sold twenty years since'. Among his examples of best-sellers are four novels of the 1740s and 1750s – Fielding's *Tom Jones*, Smollett's *Roderick Random* and *Peregrine Pickle*, and *Pamela*: 'when *Dolly* is sent to market to sell her eggs, she is commissioned to purchase "The History of Pamela Andrews"'.[23] The *Pamela* purchased at a market stall might well have been an abridgment. Between 1769 and 1808, at least seven shortened versions of the novel appeared: two in London and five in America.[24] A little later, an abridged Welsh translation took the form of a third-person narrative, divided into seven sections, each with a brief summary prefixed.[25] In 1801,

Richardson's own final revision of both parts of *Pamela* was published, with a prefatory note by the publishers explaining that the text, in its 'altered and improved form', was furnished by Richardson's surviving daughter Anne.[26] Shortly afterwards, in 1810, another drastically altered and abridged edition of both parts of *Pamela* appeared: published by Charles Cooke in his inexpensive 'Select Novels' series. This provided the text for at least ten further editions before 1838, and thus became the most widely read version of *Pamela* in the first half of the nineteenth century.[27] Cooke's edition also, inadvertently, became a standard text for much of the twentieth century, when Everyman reprinted it in London in 1914, thus imposing on numerous unwitting readers a heavily revised abridgment of *Pamela* for which Richardson was in no way responsible.[28]

In his Ravenna Journal for 4 January 1821, Byron recorded a newspaper account of a gypsy woman accused of murder, who had bought bacon and other items from a Tunbridge grocer. On his counter, the grocer had 'a *book*, the Life of *Pamela*, which he was *tearing* for *waste* paper, &c.', with 'a *leaf* of *Pamela wrapt round the bacon*'.[29] The time was indeed now come, as Swift had written a century beforehand, 'when a *Book* that misses its Tide, shall be neglected . . . like Mackarel a Week after the Season'.[30] Byron's bacon (with Lackington's eggs) points up the nature of *Pamela*, and of novels in general, as a perishable marketable commodity, a breakfast that will not keep. Intent on ridiculing Richardson, Byron gave no consideration to what edition of *Pamela* the grocer was recycling. Judging from the book's short title, it might well have been a 36-page chapbook, *The Life and Extraordinary Adventures of Pamela, daughter of Goodman Andrews, a labourer*.[31] Undated, it was published by William Mason of Clerkenwell Green, active from 1817 to 1829. Both its price, sixpence, and its brevity would have made it attractive to the busy grocer, for whom it could serve double duty: first as reading matter and then as wrapping paper. The chapbook contains a hand-coloured frontispiece (figure A1), of a clumsiness unparalleled among the novel's numerous illustrations. With her dress open and one breast entirely exposed, as she is assaulted by a predatory Mr B., Pamela here is a crude counterpart to the similarly bare-breasted figure depicted by Carwitham in *The Life of Pamela* (1741) – a work that the anonymous author of the chapbook might have drawn on for his own compilation.

But *Pamela*, for all Byron's lordly disdain, attracted wealthy purchasers too. One such was the owner of a copy of the four-volume 1810 edition, advertised by the publishers as the definitive version of Richardson's final revision of *Pamela*. Possessing what could be regarded as the standard

Figure A1. Frontispiece to *The Life and Extraordinary Adventures of Pamela, c.* 1817–29.

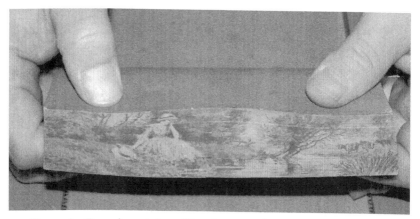

Figure A2. Fore-edge painting of Pamela contemplating suicide by the pond, *c.* 1810–20, from a copy of the 1810 edition of *Pamela.*

edition of a classic novel, the owner then customized it to his taste.[32] At an unknown date, probably at about the time that Mason issued his sixpenny chapbook, an artist was commissioned to furnish each volume with a delicately rendered fore-edge painting. Among the passages illustrated (figure A2) is that of *Pamela* contemplating suicide by the pond. The anonymous painter has made the novel's ornamental pond into something more like a river, redolent of the Lincolnshire fenland in which the scene is set. The pastoral tranquillity of this illustration, with Pamela in little danger of drowning, is a far cry from the coarseness of the *Life and Extraordinary Adventures* frontispiece. Together these two illustrations, executed some eighty years after the novel's first publication, suggest the breadth of creative responses to *Pamela*, its openness to multiple renderings, and the polyvalence of its appeal in the marketplace.

A chronology of publications, performances and related events to 1750

Publication dates derive from the earliest known newspaper advertisement or magazine listing for each work, and in some cases predate those recorded in William M. Sale, Jr, *Samuel Richardson: A Bibliographical Record* (New Haven: Yale University Press, 1936) and/or the Riverside edition of *Pamela* by T. C. Duncan Eaves and Ben D. Kimpel (Boston: Houghton Mifflin, 1971). Performance dates are from Arthur H. Scouten (ed.), *The London Stage, 1660–1800, Part 3, 1729–1747*, 2 vols (Carbondale: Southern Illinois University Press, 1961), John C. Greene and Gladys L. H. Clark, *The Dublin Stage, 1720–1745: A Calendar of Plays, Entertainments, and Afterpieces* (Bethlehem, PA: Lehigh University Press, 1993), and original newspaper sources. Further detail is given in notes to the chapters, which also document many other relevant publications (this chronology being confined to works in which connections to *Pamela* are overt and sustained).

1739–40

Nov.–Jan. *Pamela* drafted: 'I began it Nov. 10 1739, and finished it Jan. 10 1739–40' (SR to Aaron Hill, *c.* 1 Feb. 1741).

1740

11 Oct. Open letter 'To my worthy Friend, the Author of *Pamela*' published in *Weekly Miscellany*, 'in hopes by this Means to quicken the Publication of it'.

4 Nov. *Pamela* registered at Stationers' Company in names of SR and his booksellers Charles Rivington and John Osborn.

6 Nov. *Pamela* published anonymously by Rivington and Osborn in two 12° volumes, dated 1741.

20 Nov.   SR advertises in *Daily Gazetteer* for further correspondence ('under what Restrictions he pleases') with author of a manuscript critique of *Pamela* sent anonymously to Rivington on 15 Nov.

Nov.–Dec.   *Pamela* recommended by Revd Benjamin Slocock from pulpit of St Saviour's, Southwark (Hill to SR, 6 Jan. 1741).

13 Dec.   *Weekly Miscellany* reprints SR's preface and conclusion to *Pamela*.

late Dec.   *Pamela* reviewed in Dec. number of *History of the Works of the Learned*.

1741

27 Jan.   Forthcoming 2nd edn of *Pamela* announced in *Daily Gazetteer*.

31 Jan.   1st Dublin edn of *Pamela* published by George Faulkner and George Ewing.

late Jan.   *Gentleman's Magazine* announces receipt, too late for insertion, of 'several Encomiums' on *Pamela*, and puffs forthcoming 2nd edn.

12 Feb.   Alexander Pope's 'Approbation and Pleasure' on reading *Pamela* is conveyed to SR from Bath by George Cheyne, and widely reported.

14 Feb.   2nd edn of *Pamela* published, 'a large Impression having been carried off in less than Three Months', with new paratextual material, much of it by Hill.

23 Feb.   London correspondent of *Göttingische Zeitungen* reviews *Pamela*.

28 Feb.   *Weekly Miscellany* reprints letter and verses by Hill from 2nd edn.

12 Mar.   3rd edn of *Pamela* published.

14 Mar.   2nd Dublin edn of *Pamela* published.

27 Mar.   French translation advertised in *Daily Post* as 'in the Press, and speedily will be published'.

c. Mar.–Apr. *Robinson Crusoe's London Daily Evening Post* begins serializing *Pamela*, as indicated by surviving number of 20 May; serialization completed after 21 Sept. 1742 and before 12 Nov. 1742.

2 Apr. Fielding's *Shamela* published; 2nd issue follows *c.* 3 Nov.

7 Apr. Verse epigraph in *Daily Advertiser*, 'Advice to Booksellers, (After reading *Pamela*)', implicitly identifies SR as author; reprinted in *Gentleman's Magazine* for April.

15 Apr. *Shamela* published in Dublin by Oliver Nelson.

mid Apr. SR starts writing his authorized continuation, having heard that a rival sequel is 'in great Forwardness' (SR to James Leake, Aug. 1741).

25 Apr. *Pamela Censured* published by James Roberts.

28 Apr. Fan representing scenes from *Pamela* advertised for purchase 'at all the Fan-Shops and China-Shops in and about London'.

5 May 4th edn of *Pamela* published; SR appends note to advertisements attacking the forthcoming 'spurious Continuation' and announcing that he 'is actually continuing the Work himself' (*Daily Gazetteer*, 7 May).

c. May–Sept. London piracy of *Pamela* published by Mary Kingman in 3 instalments, based on SR's 4th-edn text.

28 May 1st volume of John Kelly's *Pamela's Conduct in High Life* published by Richard Chandler and Caesar Ward; SR places advertisements 'to assert his Right to his *own Plan*, and to prevent such an *Imposition* on the Publick' (*Daily Gazetteer*, 30 May), and an advertising war ensues.

late May Sarcastic verse commendation ('Remarks on *Pamela*. By a Prude') published in *London Magazine*, reprinted in *Scots Magazine* for July.

10 June SR mockingly reprints and distributes gratis a specimen of *Pamela's Conduct*, which he also inserts in newspapers 'to convince the Publick how well the Volume call'd *Pamela in High-Life*, deserves *that* Title' (*Daily Gazetteer*, 4 June).

16 June   Publication of Eliza Haywood's *Anti-Pamela*; reissued on 29 Oct., by which time an unauthorized serialization is well advanced in surviving numbers (20 Oct. 1741 – 2 Jan. 1742) of *All-Alive and Merry*.

18 June   Comedy based on *Pamela* by H. Eyre scheduled for performance at Theatre Royal, Aungier-Street, Dublin, but cancelled.

22 June   Dublin edn of *Pamela's Conduct* published by Faulkner and Nelson.

27 June   James Parry's *True Anti-Pamela* published; 2nd edn follows on 26 Sept.

late June   Letter from London (dated Feb.) published in *Bibliothèque britannique* for Apr.–June, summarizing *Pamela* and announcing forthcoming French translation.

late June   Verses 'To the Author of *Shamela*' published in *London Magazine*.

23 July   'Sir *John Moore*'s Grey M[are] *Pamela*' runs at Reading; several other racehorses of this name compete in Britain and Ireland in later years.

24 July   1st instalment published of George Bennet's *Pamela Versified*, a heroic poem in 15 numbers. 2nd instalment announced for 18 Aug.; *Scots Magazine* reprints extract in Oct., commenting that 'the work now seems dropt'.

late July   R. D.'s verse defence, 'An Apology for the Censorious', published in *London Magazine*.

13 Aug.   SR advertises his continuation as 'In the Press'; Cheyne acknowledges sight of first two printed sheets on 24 Aug.

c. Aug.   Serialization begins of *The Life of Pamela*, dated 1741, in 21 weekly parts.

12 Sept.   2nd volume of Kelly's *Pamela's Conduct* published; 2nd edn of 1st volume published on 3 Oct.

22 Sept.   5th edn of *Pamela* published.

23 Sept.   Henry Giffard's *Pamela. A Comedy* announced as in rehearsal at Goodman's Fields Theatre.

29 Sept.   First instalment of *Pamela in High Life* (originally scheduled for 5 fortnightly instalments, but apparently completed in 3) published by Mary Kingman.

8 Oct.   SR reports to Ralph Allen that he has finished writing the continuation.

23 Oct.   Authorized French translation of *Pamela*, probably by Jean Baptiste de Freval with verse translations by César de Missy, published in London by John Osborn.

9 Nov.   First performance of Giffard's *Pamela. A Comedy* at Goodman's Fields; 17 further performances in the 1741–2 season.

16 Nov.   Publication of *Pamela: or, Virtue Triumphant*, possibly by James Dance, a play 'intended to be Acted at the Theatre Royal in *Drury-Lane*'.

17 Nov.   Publication of Giffard's *Pamela. A Comedy*; two separate piracies of the play follow in London, with another in Dublin; 2nd authorized edn published on 16 Nov. 1742.

23 Nov.   Charles Povey's *The Virgin in Eden* published, with a section denouncing *Pamela*.

4 Dec.   *Memoirs of the Life of Lady H------, The Celebrated Pamela* published.

7 Dec.   SR's continuation of *Pamela* published in two 12° volumes, dated 1742, having been registered in SR's name at the Stationers' Company on 4 Dec.

7 Dec.   First Dublin performance of Giffard's *Pamela. A Comedy* at Smock-Alley Theatre; text published by Nelson the same day.

21 Dec.   Solomon Lowe comments to SR on 'the Labours of the press in Piracies, in Criticisms, in Cavils, in Panegyrics, in Supplements, in Imitations, in Transformations, in Translations, &c, beyond anything I know of'; SR later annotates Lowe's letter with reference to 'no less than 16 Pieces under some of the above or the like Titles'.

28 Dec.   First Dublin edn of SR's continuation published by Faulkner and Ewing.

28 Dec.   Unidentified dramatization of *Pamela* (possibly *Pamela: or, Virtue Triumphant*) performed between two halves of a concert at French Theatre, Haymarket.

1742

13 Jan.   SR, Rivington and Osborn granted Royal Licence for the sole printing, publishing and vending of *Pamela* 'within our Kingdoms and Dominions'.

22 Feb.   Fielding's *Joseph Andrews* published; 2nd edn follows on 10 June; further edns on 24 Mar. 1743 and 5 Nov. 1748.

26 Feb.   Last performance of Giffard's *Pamela. A Comedy* at Goodman's Fields.

24 Apr.   *Universal Spectator* publishes first instalment of 'Pamela the Second'; continued 1 May; concluded 8 May.

c. Apr.–May   Earliest recorded remarks on *Pamela* by an American reader, Eliza Lucas Pinckney of Carolina, who comments on all four volumes in an undated letter before 1 June.

8 May   6th edn of *Pamela* published in 8° format, with 29 engravings by Hubert Gravelot and Francis Hayman, the first simultaneous publication of all four volumes as a unit.

11 May   1st Dublin edn of *Joseph Andrews* advertised by Faulkner, Ewing and Smith; 2nd Dublin edn follows in 1747.

16 Sept.   *Pamela* (probably an imported edn) advertised by William Bradford of Philadelphia in the *Pennsylvania Gazette*. Also in Philadelphia, at about this time, Benjamin Franklin begins printing 1st American edn, completed in 1744, based on 4th London edn and dated 1742–3.

1742   *Pamela: or, Virtue Rewarded. An Opera*, an adaptation of Giffard's play by 'Mr. Edge' (i.e. Joseph Dorman), published in Newcastle.

1742   *Lettre sur Pamela*, probably by the Abbé Marquet, published with a 'Londres' imprint, which may be false.

1742   Two scenes from *Pamela* painted by Hayman for Vauxhall Gardens at about this time. Two other *Pamela* paintings, by Gravelot and by the American portraitist Robert Feke, are of similar date.

1743

29 Jan.   2nd 12° edn of SR's continuation published, dated 1742; later reissued, again with the date 1742, as a 4th edn.

21 Dec.   *Pamela; or, The Fair Impostor. A Poem, in Five Cantos*, by 'J---- W----, Esq.' (perhaps John Winstanley), published in Dublin.

1744

5 Jan.   London edn of *Pamela; or, The Fair Impostor* published.

16 Feb.   Ten *Pamela* paintings advertised as on display at Joseph Highmore's London house; subscriptions are being taken for a set of twelve engravings.

15 Apr.   *Pamela* and Haywood's *Anti-Pamela* entered on the Roman Catholic *Index Librorum Prohibitorum*; French translations of both works added on 22 May 1745.

10 May   Highmore advertises that all twelve of his *Pamela* paintings are now complete.

1745

late Feb.   'To the Author of *Pamela*' (verse commendation by 'Belinda' of Salisbury) appears in *Gentleman's Magazine*.

Apr.–Dec.   *Pamela* waxworks exhibited near SR's Salisbury Court premises from 23 Apr. or earlier; expanded to include scenes from the continuation by 19 Nov.; still to be seen on 21 Dec.

15 July   Engravings by Antoine Benoist and Louis Truchy of Highmore's *Pamela* paintings published; reissued 1762.

1746

18 Oct.   6th 12° edn of *Pamela* published.

1747

1747   Verse commendation by the Revd Josiah Relph (d. 1743), 'Wrote after reading *Pamela*', appears in posthumous Glasgow edn of Relph's poems, perhaps following newspaper publication in his lifetime.

1747   'To the Unjust Author of *Pamela in High Life*', by Elizabeth Teft, appears in her *Orinthia's Miscellanies*, perhaps following prior magazine publication.

1749

16 June   First performance of Voltaire's *Nanine* at the Comédie française, Paris; later translated into English (1761–3).

1750

Mar.   Publication of Peter Shaw's *The Reflector*, with its account (from Ludvig Holberg's *Moralske tanker* (1744)) of *Pamela* dividing the world into 'two different Parties, *Pamelists* and *Antipamelists*'.

Spring   Goldoni's comedy *Pamela nubile* (published in English in 1756) first performed in Mantua; further performances in Venice from 28 Nov.

14 May   *A Dramatic Burlesque of Two Acts, Call'd Mock-Pamela* performed at Smock-Alley Theatre, Dublin, with publication the same day.

4 Aug.   *Mock-Pamela* performed at Richmond Theatre, Surrey.

21 Sept.   Publication of 'a Beautiful Print . . . of *Pamela* rising from her bed', engraved by Thomas Chambers from an original painting (probably of the mid 1740s) by Philip Mercier.

Notes

INTRODUCTION

1 Solomon Lowe to Richardson, 21 December 1741, Victoria and Albert Museum, London, Forster MSS, XVI, 1, f. 78.

2 Allen Michie, *Richardson and Fielding: The Dynamics of a Critical Rivalry* (Lewisburg, PA: Bucknell University Press, 1999), p. 13.

3 Thomas Keymer and Peter Sabor (eds), *The Pamela Controversy: Criticisms and Adaptations of Samuel Richardson's Pamela, 1740–1750*, 6 vols (London: Pickering & Chatto, 2001).

4 Moyra Haslett, *Pope to Burney, 1714–1779: Scriblerians to Bluestockings* (Basingstoke: Palgrave, 2003), pp. 223–4; see also Jenny Davidson, *Hypocrisy and the Politics of Politeness: Manners and Morals from Locke to Austen* (Cambridge: Cambridge University Press, 2004), ch. 4.

5 On Richardson's retained copy of his letter to James Leake, August 1741, Forster MSS, XVI, 1, f. 56.

6 Ralph Courtville to Richardson, 8 June 1741, Forster MSS, XVI, 1, f. 50 (referring specifically to the pubishers of *Pamela's Conduct in High Life*).

7 On *Mock-Pamela* and the lost play, see ch. 6 below; full details of the many other sources listed in this paragraph are given at relevant points in the chapters below.

8 *The Correspondence of Samuel Richardson*, ed. Anna Laetitia Barbauld, 6 vols (1804), 1, lviii, describing Ranelagh; on the Vauxhall decorations, see ch. 5 below.

9 John Cheny, *An Historical List of Horse-Matches Run* (1741), p. 36 ('Sir *John Moore*'s Grey M. *Pamela*').

10 Cheny, *Historical List* (1742), pp. 15 (Sir Henry Harpur's bay mare, Sir Thomas Peaton's grey (Newton Smith's grey), 24 (Newton Smith's grey), 29 (Crosdall Miller's chestnut).

11 Cheny, *Historical List* (1746), p. 22; (1748), pp. 49, 90.

12 David Blewett, 'Introduction', *Reconsidering the Rise of the Novel*, special issue of *Eighteenth-Century Fiction* 12 (2000), 144, citing Janet Todd, 'Fatal Fluency: Behn's Fiction and the Restoration Letter', 419.

13 John Richetti, *The English Novel in History, 1700–1780* (London: Routledge, 1999), pp. 84, 122.

14 See Albert J. Rivero, '*Pamela / Shamela / Joseph Andrews*: Henry Fielding and the Duplicities of Representation', in Rivero (ed.), *Augustan Subjects: Essays in Honor of Martin C. Battestin* (Newark: University of Delaware Press, 1997), pp. 207–28; Claude Rawson, 'Fielding's Richardson: *Shamela, Joseph Andrews* and Parody Revisited', *Bulletin de la société d'études anglo-américaines des XVIIe et XVIIIe siècles* 51 (2000), 77–94.

15 Terry Eagleton, *The Rape of Clarissa: Writing, Sexuality and Class Struggle in Samuel Richardson* (Oxford: Blackwell, 1982), p. 5.

16 Eagleton, *Rape of Clarissa*, p. 5; William B. Warner, *Licensing Entertainment: The Elevation of Novel Reading in Britain, 1684–1750* (Berkeley: University of California Press, 1998), pp. 176, 178.

17 Martin C. Battestin, with Ruthe R. Battestin, *Henry Fielding: A Life* (London: Routledge, 1989), p. 304.

18 Terry Castle, *Masquerade and Civilization: The Carnivalesque in Eighteenth-Century English Culture and Fiction* (London: Methuen, 1986), pp. 135–6.

19 George Cheyne to Richardson, 24 August 1741, *The Letters of Doctor George Cheyne to Samuel Richardson (1733–1743)*, ed. Charles F. Mullett (Columbia: University of Missouri, 1943), p. 69. On the persistence of rank and the emergence of class, see P. J. Corfield, 'Class by Name and Number in Eighteenth-Century Britain', *History* 72 (1987), 38–61; also Nicholas Hudson, *Samuel Johnson and the Making of Modern England* (Cambridge: Cambridge University Press, 2003), pp. 11–42.

20 Francis Coventry, *The History of Pompey the Little*, ed. Robert A. Day (London: Oxford University Press, 1974), p. 134; Susan Smythies, *The Brothers*, 2 vols (1758), I, 238; *London Magazine* 26 (1757), 269–70, summarizing *Centinel*, no. 22.

21 Lady Mary Wortley Montagu to Lady Bute, 23 July 1753, *The Complete Letters of Lady Mary Wortley Montagu*, ed. Robert Halsband, 3 vols (Oxford: Clarendon Press, 1965–7), III, 35–6.

22 Henry Fielding, *The History of Tom Jones, A Foundling*, ed. Martin C. Battestin and Fredson Bowers (Oxford: Clarendon Press, 1974), pp. 783, 826.

23 *A Satirical Review of the Manifold Falshoods and Absurdities Hitherto Publish'd Concerning the Earthquake* (1756), pp. 27, 28.

24 See T. C. Duncan Eaves and Ben D. Kimpel, *Samuel Richardson: A Biography* (Oxford: Clarendon Press, 1971), pp. 116–17; also, on Sidney, Gillian Beer, '*Pamela*: Rethinking *Arcadia*', in Margaret Anne Doody and Peter Sabor (eds), *Samuel Richardson: Tercentenary Essays* (Cambridge: Cambridge University Press, 1989), pp. 23–39.

25 Sarah Scott, *A Journey through Every Stage of Life*, 2 vols (1754), I, 50; Sarah Fielding, *The History of the Countess of Dellwyn*, 2 vols (1759), I, 226.

26 Henry Fielding, *Plays, Volume I, 1728–1731*, ed. Thomas Lockwood (Oxford: Clarendon Press, 2004), p. 720 ('Our modern Beaus in Vigour are so hearty | And modern Dames so very full of Vartue'). Hypocrites boast of their

vartue in several earlier comedies, including Sir John Vanbrugh, *The Confederacy* (1705), Act III: '[Mrs] *Amlet.* I think as the World goes, they may be proud of marrying their Daughter into a vartuous Family. *Dick.* Oons, Vartue is not the Case—' (ed. Thomas E. Lowderbraugh (New York: Garland, 1987), p. 134).

27 Peter Shaw, *The Reflector* (1750), pp. 14–15.
28 Ludvig Holberg, *Moralske Tansker,* ed. F. J. Billeskov Jansen and Jørgen Hunosøe (Copenhagen: Borgen, 1992), p. 12. Alan D. McKillop was the first to note Shaw's use of Holberg (*Samuel Richardson: Printer and Novelist* (Chapel Hill: University of North Carolina Press, 1936), pp. 101–2), but the original source remained known on the continent: 'L'Angleterre et l'Allemagne se partagèrent en *Pamélistes* et *anti-Pamélistes*', wrote a French playwright of 1793 (François de Neufchâteau, *Paméla, ou la vertu récompensée* (Paris, 1793), n. p.).
29 Though willing to satirize hierarchy elsewhere (as in his exuberant comedy of 1722, *Jeppe of the Hill; or, The Transformed Peasant*), Holberg shows his Antipamelist side in a different essay, likening Pamela's prudential virtue to the wily self-advancement of Ann Boleyn, whose 'affected resistance and coolness alone paved her way to the throne' (*Moral Reflections and Epistles,* trans. P. M. Mitchell (Norwich: Norvik Press, 1991), p. 59).
30 Henry Fielding, *Joseph Andrews and Shamela,* ed. Douglas Brooks-Davies, revised and intro. Thomas Keymer (Oxford: Oxford University Press, 1999), p. 309.
31 *Genuine and Impartial Memoirs of Elizabeth Canning* (1754), p. 5; *Truth Triumphant; or, The Genuine Account of the Whole Proceedings against Elizabeth Canning* (1754), p. 18 (with a play on 'Canaanites'); see also *The Chronicle of the Canningites and Egyptians or Gipseyites* (1754). Further analogies between the Canning literature and *Pamela* are proposed by Judith Moore, *The Appearance of Truth: The Story of Elizabeth Canning and Eighteenth-Century Narrative* (Newark: University of Delaware Press, 1994), pp. 240–55.
32 Henry Fielding, *An Enquiry into the Causes of the Late Increase of Robbers and Related Writings,* ed. Malvin R. Zirker (Oxford: Clarendon Press, 1988), p. 285.
33 W. D. Howells to J. R. Lowell, June 1879, in Roger Gard (ed.), *Henry James: The Critical Heritage* (London: Routledge, 1968), p. 74.
34 Jonathan Swift, *Gulliver's Travels,* ed. Paul Turner (Oxford: Oxford University Press, 1986), p. 36.
35 Samuel Richardson, *The Apprentice's Vade Mecum,* intro. Alan D. McKillop (Augustan Reprint Society nos 169–70. Los Angeles: Clark Memorial Library, 1975), p. ix; on the Collins, Woolston and Tindal controversies as market phenomena, see Isabel Rivers, 'Religious Publishing', in Michael Suarez and Michael Turner (eds), *The Cambridge History of the Book in Britain, 1695–1830* (Cambridge: Cambridge University Press, forthcoming).

36 See Fielding, *Joseph Andrews and Shamela*, p. 324 and n.
37 Charles Norris, *The Reconciler; or, The Bangorian Controversy Abridg'd* (1718); J. Philips, *The Inquisition: A Farce* (1717), p. 5.
38 *Memoirs of the Society of Grub-Street*, 2 vols (1737), 1, 303 (*Grub-street Journal*, no. 62, 11 March 1731).
39 Fielding, *Plays, Volume I*, p. 247 (*The Author's Farce*, 1. iv).
40 Maximillian E. Novak, *Daniel Defoe: Master of Fictions* (Oxford: Oxford University Press, 2001), pp. 491–2.
41 Novak, *Daniel Defoe*, pp. 466–7, quoting Pittis, *Considerations on the Mitre and Purse* (1714), 2–3; Defoe, *The Secret History of the Secret History of the White Staff* (1715), p. 8.
42 Translator's preface to *Pamela, ou la vertu récompensée*, 4 vols (Amsterdam, 1743–4), 1, 4–5; on the controversy over *Le Cid*, which involved at least thirty-seven responses, see Armand Gasté (ed.), *La Querelle du Cid: pièces et pamphlets publiés d'après les originaux* (Paris: Welter, 1899).
43 Samuel Johnson, *Lives of the English Poets*, ed. George Birkbeck Hill, 3 vols (Oxford: Clarendon Press, 1905), III, 188.
44 *Memoirs of the Society of Grub-Street*, 1, 93 (*Grub-street Journal*, no. 19, 14 May 1730).
45 Jonathan Swift, *A Tale of a Tub*, ed. A. C. Guthkelch and D. Nichol Smith, 2nd edn (Oxford: Clarendon Press, 1958), p. 40.
46 See J. V. Guerinot, *Pamphlet Attacks on Alexander Pope, 1711–44: A Descriptive Bibliography* (New York: New York University Press, 1969). The *Dunciad* is also a reminder that the fashionably themed merchandise surrounding *Pamela* was not unprecedented: see Pope's note on the consumer tat of fans and fire-screens marketed in response to *The Beggar's Opera* in 1728 (*The Dunciad in Four Books*, ed. Valerie Rumbold (London: Longman, 1999), p. 262, line 330 n.).
47 Laurence Sterne to Stephen Croft, 17 February 1761, *Letters of Laurence Sterne*, ed. L. P. Curtis (Oxford: Clarendon Press, 1935), p. 129.
48 *The Life of Pamela* (1741), p. 185 n.; for the allegation about *Pamela Censured*, see chapter 1 below.
49 Ian A. Bell, *Henry Fielding: Authorship and Authority* (London: Longman, 1994), p. 63.
50 Brean Hammond, *Professional Imaginative Writing in England, 1670–1740: 'Hackney for Bread'* (Oxford: Clarendon Press, 1997), p. 11.
51 John Hill, *The Adventures of Mr Loveill*, 2 vols (1750), 1, iii.
52 Bernard Kreissman, *Pamela-Shamela: A Study of the Criticisms, Burlesques, Parodies, and Adaptations of Richardson's Pamela* (Lincoln: University of Nebraska Press, 1960); Robert P. Utter and Gwendolyn B. Needham, *Pamela's Daughters* (New York: Macmillan, 1936).
53 William M. Sale, Jr, *Samuel Richardson: A Bibliographical Record of his Literary Career with Historical Notes* (New Haven: Yale University Press, 1936); McKillop, *Printer and Novelist*.

1 'THE SELLING PART': PUBLICATION, PROMOTION, PROFITS

1 *Memoirs of Laetitia Pilkington*, ed. A. C. Elias, Jr, 2 vols (Athens: University of Georgia Press, 1997), 1, 209.

2 On Richardson's official printing, see Keith Maslen, *Samuel Richardson of London, Printer* (Dunedin: University of Otago, 2001), pp. 22–6; Thomas Keymer, 'Parliamentary Printing, Paper Credit, and Corporate Fraud: A New Episode in Samuel Richardson's Early Career', *Eighteenth-Century Fiction* 17 (2005), 184–91; for his residences, see T. C. Duncan Eaves and Ben D. Kimpel, 'Samuel Richardson's London Houses', *Studies in Bibliography* 15 (1962), 135–48.

3 Richardson to Anne Dewes, 21 June 1752, *Selected Letters of Samuel Richardson*, ed. John Carroll (Oxford: Clarendon Press, 1964), p. 218. For Pope's earnings from his *Iliad* translation, see Maynard Mack, *Alexander Pope: A Life* (New Haven: Yale University Press, 1985), pp. 267–8; also Henry Fielding's comment in *Joseph Andrews and Shamela*, p. 187.

4 *The Parallel: or, Pilkington and Phillips Compared* (1748), p. 6; see Martin C. Battestin, 'On the Contemporary Reputations of *Pamela*, *Joseph Andrews*, and *Roderick Random*: Remarks by an "Oxford Scholar", 1748', *Notes and Queries* 213 (1968), 450–2.

5 C. Y. Ferdinand, *Benjamin Collins and the Provincial Newspaper Trade in the Eighteenth Century* (Oxford: Clarendon Press, 1997), p. 49; Sale, *Bibliographical Record*, p. 16.

6 Battestin, *Henry Fielding*, pp. 325–6. Millar paid Fielding £199 6s for three works, of which *Joseph Andrews* accounted for £183 11s.

7 *Boswell's Life of Johnson*, ed. G. B. Hill, rev. L. F. Powell, 6 vols (Oxford: Clarendon Press, 1934–50), 1, 288; see also 1, 287 n.

8 Ioan Williams (ed.), *Novel and Romance, 1700–1800: A Documentary Record* (London: Routledge, 1970), p. 373, quoting the *Monthly Review* for July 1791.

9 Samuel Richardson, *Pamela*, 2nd edn, 2 vols (1741), 1, xv. For publication dates of all editions of *Pamela* appearing before 1750, see the chronology appended to the present book, which is based on the earliest known newspaper advertisement in each case ('This day is published . . .').

10 'To satisfy the impatience of the public, you may tell them that I don't know how many presses are at work to get it printed off', scoffed Bonnell Thornton as Millar promoted *Amelia* a decade later (*Drury-Lane Journal*, 12 March 1752, cited in Henry Fielding, *Amelia*, ed. Martin C. Battestin (Oxford: Clarendon Press, 1983), p. xlvii).

11 Keith Maslen and John Lancaster, *The Bowyer Ledgers* (London: Bibliographical Society, 1991), p. 223 (item 2907).

12 Maslen and Lancaster, *Bowyer Ledgers*, p. 227 (item 2963).

13 See Martin C. Battestin's introduction to the Wesleyan edition of *Joseph Andrews* (Oxford: Clarendon Press, 1967), pp. xxix–xxxiv.

14 Richardson to Lady Bradshaigh, 14 February 1754, *Selected Letters*, ed. Carroll, p. 289.

15 Mary Davys, *The Reform'd Coquet, Familiar Letters betwixt a Gentleman and a Lady, and The Accomplish'd Rake*, ed. Martha F. Bowden (Lexington: University Press of Kentucky, 1999), pp. 11–12; on the market for amatory fiction before Richardson, see Sarah Prescott, *Women, Authorship and Literary Culture, 1690–1740* (Basingstoke: Palgrave, 2003), pp. 69–140.

16 'Eusebius' to Charles Rivington, 2 February 1741, Forster MSS, XVI, 1, f. 48.

17 'Eusebius' to Rivington, 2 February 1741, f. 47.

18 *Pamela Censured*, intro. Charles Batten, Jr (Augustan Reprint Society no. 175. Los Angeles: Clark Memorial Library, 1976), p. 2.

19 Hill to Richardson, 6 January 1741, Forster MSS, XIII, 2, f. 36, quoted by Peter Sabor, 'Did Richardson Bribe Dr. Slocock?', *Notes and Queries* 224 (1979), 29.

20 Povey, *The Virgin in Eden* (1741), p. i. *Shamela*'s title-page phrase, 'Necessary to be had in all FAMILIES', plays on the title-page caption ('Necessary for all Families') of *The Whole Duty of Man*: see *Joseph Andrews and Shamela*, n. to p. 305; also notes to pp. 20, 311, 332.

21 Georges-Louis de Bar, *Epîtres diverses sur des sujets différens*, 3 vols (Paris, 1745–55), II, 206, citing *Ars poetica*, lines 345–7. Here Horace discusses the artful blend of 'Profit and Pleasure' by which a work 'Shall gain all Votes; to Booksellers shall raise | No trivial Fortune, and across the Seas | To distant Nations spread the Writer's Fame' (Philip Francis, *A Poetical Translation of the Works of Horace*, 2nd edn, 4 vols (1747), IV, 253).

22 *A Voyage to Lethe* (1742), p. [ii]. The title page is dated 1741, but later publication is suggested by the reference to Richardson's octavo edition of 1742. The same joke was made of a new edition of Nicolas Vedette's *The Pleasures of Conjugal-Love Explain'd*, which was advertised as 'of the same Letter and Size with *Pamela*, and very proper to be bound with it' (*Daily Advertiser*, 9 April 1741).

23 Slocock's will, dated 2 December 1752, proved 3 February 1753, Public Record Office, PROB 10/2130; see also Eaves and Kimpel, *Biography*, pp. 123–4.

24 George Cheyne to Richardson, 12 February 1741, *Letters of Cheyne*, p. 65. Pope may also have been teasing Richardson with elements of faint praise: his wording leaves mischievously open whether the novel kept him awake or put him to sleep, and perhaps says as much about the new sermons – among them Slocock's – as about *Pamela* itself.

25 Daniel Defoe, *A Tour thro' the Whole Island of Great Britain*, 2nd edn, ed. Samuel Richardson, 4 vols (1738), II, 241; Orrery to Counsellor Kempe, 16 October 1731, *The Orrery Papers*, ed. the Countess of Cork and Orrery, 2 vols (London: Duckworth, 1903), I, 99.

26 Richardson, *Correspondence*, ed. Barbauld, i, lviii–lix.
27 William Cooke, *Memoirs of Samuel Foote* (1806), ii, 156, quoted by Peter M. Briggs, 'Laurence Sterne and Literary Celebrity in 1760', *Age of Johnson* 4 (1991), 276.
28 Eaves and Kimpel, *Biography*, p. 91. The first letter is initialled; one cannot dismiss Fielding's insinuation (in *Shamela*'s preliminary commendation from 'The EDITOR to *Himself*') that Richardson wrote the other himself.
29 Pope, *Dunciad*, p. 185 (ii. 258).
30 Richardson to George Cheyne, 31 August 1741, *Selected Letters*, ed. Carroll, p. 47. On the editorial policy of the *Weekly Miscellany*, see Michael Harris, *London Newspapers in the Age of Walpole* (Rutherford, NJ: Fairleigh Dickinson University Press, 1987), pp. 183, 186.
31 *Weekly Miscellany*, 27 June 1741, quoted by Harris, *London Newspapers*, p. 100; see also Eaves and Kimpel, *Biography*, pp. 58–60.
32 Richardson, *Apprentice's Vade Mecum*, pp. i–ii.
33 William M. Sale, Jr, *Samuel Richardson: Master Printer* (Ithaca, NY: Cornell University Press, 1950), pp. 193–4; *Pamela Censured*, p. 14.
34 Richardson to David Graham, 3 May 1750, *Selected Letters*, ed. Carroll, p. 159; Richardson to Johannes Stinstra, 2 June 1753, *Selected Letters*, ed. Carroll, p. 230.
35 Zach, 'Mrs. Aubin and Richardson's Earliest Literary Manifesto (1739)', *English Studies* 62 (1981), 271–85.
36 Reprinted in Zach, 'Mrs. Aubin and Richardson', pp. 282–3.
37 Richardson to Cheyne, 31 August 1741, *Selected Letters*, ed. Carroll, pp. 46–7.
38 Eliza Haywood, *Secret Histories, Novels, and Poems*, 3rd edn, 4 vols (1732), i, [iii, ii]. For Richardson's printing of volumes i and iv, see Maslen, *Richardson of London*, p. 90.
39 *Gentleman's Magazine* ii (January 1741), 56.
40 Cave, 'To Mr. Richardson', dated 19 January 1735/6, in John Nichols, *Literary Anecdotes of the Eighteenth Century*, 9 vols (1812–15), ii, 77.
41 Maslen, *Richardson of London*, pp. 35, 28; see also Sale, *Master Printer*, pp. 73, 320–1.
42 Elizabeth A. Kraft, '*The History of the Works of the Learned*', in Alvin Sullivan (ed.), *British Literary Magazines: The Augustan Age and the Age of Johnson, 1698–1788* (Westport, CT: Greenwood Press, 1983), p. 161.
43 *History of the Works of the Learned* 4.1 (May 1740), 346.
44 *History of the Works of the Learned* 4.2 (December 1740), 439.
45 See T. C. Duncan Eaves and Ben D. Kimpel, 'Richardson's Revisions of *Pamela*', *Studies in Bibliography* 20 (1967), 61–88; Philip Gaskell, *From Writer to Reader: Studies in Editorial Method* (Oxford: Clarendon Press, 1978), pp. 63–79; Peter Sabor, 'Richardson's Correspondence and His Final Revision of *Pamela*', *Transactions of the Samuel Johnson Society of the Northwest* 12 (1981), 114–31.

46 The changes are recorded in *Samuel Richardson's Introduction to Pamela*, ed. Sheridan W. Baker, Jr (Augustan Reprint Society no. 48. Los Angeles: Clark Memorial Library, 1954).

47 Thornton, *Drury-Lane Journal*, 9 April 1752, quoted in Fielding, *Amelia*, ed. Battestin, p. xlvii.

48 Hammond, *Professional Imaginative Writing*, p. 287. On Hill and Haywood, see Christine Gerrard, *Aaron Hill: The Muses' Projector, 1685–1750* (Oxford: Oxford University Press, 2003), pp. 66–77.

49 The introduction is reprinted as an appendix to Samuel Richardson, *Pamela*, ed. Thomas Keymer and Alice Wakely, intro. Thomas Keymer (Oxford: Oxford University Press, 2001), pp. 505–19; see p. 538 n. for identification of the original letters. Unless otherwise indicated, further references to *Pamela* in the chapters below are to this edition.

50 Anon. to Osborn, February 1741, Forster MSS, xvi, 1, f. 46.

51 The boy's sensibility stood him in good stead. Richardson promptly sent him a gift of illustrated books, including *Æsop's Fables*, and in 1751 (after Hill's death) took him for apprenticeship without the usual fee: see Sale, *Master Printer*, p. 21; *Stationers' Company Apprentices, 1701–1800*, ed. D. F. McKenzie (Oxford: Oxford Bibliographical Society, 1978), p. 290. Campbell later set up a printing business of his own, and was still trading in 1778 (*Stationers' Company Apprentices*, p. 63).

52 Anon. to Rivington, 15 November 1740, Forster MSS, xvi, 1, f. 34. On Richardson's use of these objections when revising, see Eaves and Kimpel, 'Richardson's Revisions of *Pamela*', pp. 63–5. Richardson quietly removed from his second edition the two sexual innuendoes noted by the objector (p. 509) as making Pamela too knowing: 'betwixt Fear and Delight' (p. 289) becomes 'betwixt Fear and Joy'; 'but I had no Appetite to any thing else' (p. 292) becomes 'but that was all'. The objector probably recognized the first of these formulations as Haywoodian code for erotic arousal, as in the 'enchanting Mixture of Delight and Fear' felt by the heroine of *The British Recluse* (*Secret Histories, Novels, and Poems*, ii, 38).

53 Advertisements in the *Daily Gazetteer* (20 November 1740) and *London Evening-Post* (11–13 December 1740); for Richardson's use of a newspaper advertisement to contact Lady Bradshaigh, see Thomas Keymer, 'Richardson, Incognita, and the *Whitehall Evening-Post*', *Notes and Queries* 237 (1992), 477–80.

54 Anon. to Osborn, February 1741, Forster MSS, xvi, 1, f. 46.

55 On the date of publication and Fielding's circumstances, see Battestin, *Henry Fielding*, pp. 303–4.

56 For the specific connections, see notes to *Joseph Andrews and Shamela*, pp. 404–10; also Eric Rothstein's classic article 'The Framework of *Shamela*', *ELH* 35 (1968), 381–402.

57 Fielding is also playing on the currency of this text in the contemporary critique of Methodism (see *Joseph Andrews and Shamela*, n. to p. 324), and

the objector quoted in Richardson's introduction was presumably doing the same. Richardson picked up the implication: 'the principal Complaints against me by many . . . are that I am too grave, too much of a Methodist, and make Pamela too pious' (*Selected Letters*, ed. Carroll, p. 47).

58 Many scholars have explored these diverse satirical targets and Fielding's connections between them; see especially J. Paul Hunter's chapter on 'Historical Registers for the Year 1740' (in his *Occasional Form: Henry Fielding and the Chains of Circumstance* (Baltimore: Johns Hopkins University Press, 1975), pp. 77–93).

59 See Melvyn New, '"At the Backside of the Door of Purgatory": A Note on Annotating *Tristram Shandy*', in Valerie Grosvenor Myer (ed.), *Laurence Sterne: Riddles and Mysteries* (London: Vision, 1984), p. 19.

60 Battestin, *Henry Fielding*, pp. 195–6.

61 Notably in 'Advice to Booksellers (After reading *Pamela*)', *Daily Advertiser*, 7 April 1741, reprinted in *Gentleman's Magazine* 11 (1741), 214.

62 *The Works of the Late Aaron Hill*, 2nd edn, 4 vols (1754), 11, 158 (Hill to Mallet, 13 January 1741).

63 *London Evening-Post*, 14–16 May 1741. The publication date of 25 April is from an advertisement in the *Daily Post* (Eaves and Kimpel, *Biography*, p. 129). The work sold for a shilling.

64 On the significance of this stage in the censurer's argument, which enables him to draw for the remainder of the pamphlet on an established 'antinovel discourse . . . haunted by the specter of the erotically aroused (usually female) body', see Warner, *Licensing Entertainment*, p. 211. *La Paysanne parvenue* was serially published in English, as *The Fortunate Country Maid*, between April 1740 and February 1741 (R. M. Wiles, *Serial Publication in England before 1750* (Cambridge: Cambridge University Press, 1957), p. 324).

65 John Kelly, *Pamela's Conduct in High Life*, 2 vols (1741), 1, xvi.

66 On this publication, *A New Description of Merryland* (1740), see David Foxon, *Libertine Literature in England, 1660–1745* (New York: University Books, 1965), p. 17 n.; also Ralph Strauss, *The Unspeakable Curll* (London: Chapman and Hall, 1927), pp. 308–11.

67 Eaves and Kimpel, *Biography*, p. 129; *Pamela Censured*, intro. Batten, p. ii.

68 Aaron Hill to Richardson (reporting the allegation of an acquaintance, and annotated with Richardson's denial), 25 May 1741, Forster MSS, xiii, 2, ff. 48–9.

69 As, for example, in the *London Evening-Post* for 14–16 May.

70 Edward Kimber, *The Juvenile Adventures of David Ranger, Esq.*, 2nd edn, 2 vols (1757), 11, 110. Cf. 'Adam Eden', *A Vindication of the Reformation, on Foot, among the Ladies, to Abolish Modesty and Chastity* (1755), which drily notes of the novels 'most in vogue among the Ladies, such as *Pamela*', that 'tho' the main Design is to excite to Virtue, there are many amorous Adventures interspersed, which were they to be told beforehand to the Ladies, they could not consistent with Modesty read them over' (p. 43).

71 See *The Richardson–Stinstra Correspondence and Stinstra's Prefaces to Clarissa*, ed. William C. Slattery (Carbondale: Southern Illinois University Press, 1969), pp. xxiii–xxiv.

72 Maslen, *Richardson of London*, pp. 122, 35.

73 James Grantham Turner, 'Novel Panic: Picture and Performance in the Reception of Richardson's *Pamela*', *Representations* 48 (1994), 94 n.; Sale, *Master Printer*, pp. 68–9; Eaves and Kimpel, *Biography*, pp. 58–9 n.

74 Sterne to David Garrick, 19 April 1762, *Letters of Sterne*, p. 162. For Sterne's possible connection with *The Clockmakers Outcry*, see Anne Bandry, 'Imitations of *Tristram Shandy*', in Melvyn New (ed.), *Critical Essays on Laurence Sterne* (New York: G. K. Hall, 1998), pp. 43, 51 n.

75 *Pamela Censured*, intro. Batten, p. vi; Batten is citing Richardson's fifth edition of 22 September 1741, letter xv (1, 31). The heroine rotates again in the text of 1801, which removes this added detail: see Samuel Richardson, *Pamela*, ed. Peter Sabor, intro. Margaret Anne Doody (Harmondsworth: Penguin, 1980), pp. 64 and 519 n.

76 Eaves and Kimpel, 'Richardson's Revisions of *Pamela*', p. 67.

77 Eaves and Kimpel, 'Richardson's Revisions of *Pamela*', p. 82, citing the removal from the 1801 text (p. 102 in Sabor's Penguin edition) of the pun on 'quick' in letter xxvii; see also, on this passage and *Pamela Censured*, Tassie Gwilliam, *Samuel Richardson's Fictions of Gender* (Stanford: Stanford University Press, 1993), pp. 37–41. Eaves and Kimpel underplay the significance for the 1801 edition of letters (now at Rice University) between Anne Richardson and Martha Bridgen in which the sisters agree that Richardson's final version is 'too imperfect for publication' (20 July 1784) and must be 're-revised' (10 July 1784). Only after this 're-revision' would they publish, as Anne duly did after Martha's death.

78 On 27 March a notice in the *Daily Post* reported that a translation was 'in the Press, and speedily will be published'; publication was advertised on 23 October 1741 (*Daily Gazetteer*), though printing seems to have been completed in August (Maslen and Lancaster, *Bowyer Ledgers*, p. 227 (item 2963)). The translator claimed to have worked 'avec la participation de l'Auteur' (*Pamela, ou la vertu récompensée*, 1, x), a claim substantiated by his inclusion of a passage not found in any English edition until the octavo sixth edition months later (Eaves and Kimpel, 'Richardson's Revisions of *Pamela*', 69).

79 *The Adventures of Lindamira*, ed. Benjamin Boyce (Minneapolis: University of Minnesota Press, 1949), p. xvi; P. des Maizeaux (tr.), *The Adventures of Telemachus*, 2 vols (1742), 1, [i].

80 Abbé Marquet (?), *Lettre sur Pamela* (1742), p. 3; *Pamela, ou la vertu récompensée*, 1, xv. Though sporting a 'Londres' imprint, *Lettre sur Pamela* was probably published in Paris.

81 *Pamela Censured*, p. 14. McKillop definitively eliminates the Abbé Prévost and Aubert de la Chesnaye-Desbois, notes that Nichols ascribes the passages of verse translation to César de Missy, an émigré in London (*Literary*

Anecdotes, III, 307), and speculates that a consortium of translators shared the work (*Printer and Novelist*, pp. 93–4). Jean Sgard quotes Charles de La Motte as suggesting in 1743 that Jean-Frédéric Bernard had translated the novel, assisted by de Missy for the verse (*Prévost romancier* (Paris: Librairie José Corti, 1968), pp. 539–40). Bernard lived and worked in Holland, however, and La Motte's informant was probably confusing the authorized London translation with the rival Amsterdam translation of 1742.

82 *London Evening-Post*, 8–10 June 1742. Richardson tacitly responds here to criticism of the material quality of early editions as being 'in so small a Type and so bad Paper' (13 December 1740, *Letters of Cheyne*, p. 63).

83 *History of the Works of the Learned*, 4.1 (May 1740), 346.

84 On the *Clarissa* synopsis, which Richardson provided for readers to guide 'their Understanding of it, in the Way I chose to have it understood in' (*Selected Letters*, ed. Carroll, p. 126), see *Samuel Richardson's Published Commentary on Clarissa, 1747–65, Volume II: Letters and Passages Restored*, intro. Peter Sabor (London: Pickering & Chatto, 1998), pp. vii–xxxvii.

85 Forster MSS, XVI, 1, ff. 10, 11; see also Sale, *Bibliographical Record*, p. 22.

86 Public Record Office (National Archives), SP 44/367, 250 (Warrant Book, 1736–48); see also Sale, *Bibliographical Record*, p. 21.

87 Wiles, *Serial Publication*, pp. 162–8.

88 *The Letterbook of Eliza Lucas Pinckney, 1739–1762*, ed. Elise Pinckney (Chapel Hill: University of North Carolina Press, 1972), p. 47; see also James Raven, *London Booksellers and American Customers: Transatlantic Literary Community and the Charleston Library Society, 1748–1811* (Columbia: University of South Carolina Press, 2002), p. 70. On Franklin and *Pamela*, see James N. Green, 'English Books and Printing in the Age of Franklin', in Hugh Amory and David D. Hall (eds), *The Colonial Book in the Atlantic World* (Cambridge: Cambridge University Press, 2000), pp. 267–8; Paul Giles, *Transatlantic Insurrections: British Culture and the Formation of American Literature, 1730–1860* (Philadelphia: University of Pennsylvania Press, 2001), pp. 70–91.

89 Serialization began before 20 May 1741, on which date a surviving number at Yale reprints a short instalment corresponding to p. 31 in the Keymer–Wakely edition of *Pamela*. It finished after 21 September 1742, when a number at Harvard reprints a passage corresponding to p. 441, but before mid-November, when the remaining Harvard survivals (12, 13, and 18 November) contain nothing from the novel.

90 *Thraliana*, ed. Katharine C. Balderston, 2nd edn, 2 vols (Oxford: Clarendon Press, 1951), I, 145; similar anecdotes are recorded in A. D. McKillop, 'Wedding Bells for Pamela', *Philological Quarterly* 28 (1949), 323–5.

91 Warner, *Licensing Entertainment*, p. 178.

92 *Göttingische Zeitungen von Gelehrten Sachen* (23 February 1741), 129–30, and *Bibliothèque britannique* (April–June 1741), 27–60: see McKillop, *Printer and Novelist*, pp. 36, 94.

93 Peter Sabor, 'Richardson's Index to His Correspondence on *Pamela*', *Notes and Queries* 224 (1979), 556–60. Other anonymous poems are listed, together with Hill's verses for the second edition and a later Hill poem (now lost), 'A. H. Esq His poetical Comparison of the Merits of Pamela, and the Complaint' (i.e. Young's *Night Thoughts*).

94 'To the Author of Pamela. By a Friend of Oxford', Forster MSS, XVI, 1, f. 24.

95 See Anthony D. Barker, 'Poetry from the Provinces: Amateur Poets in the *Gentleman's Magazine* in the 1730s and 1740s', in Alvaro Ribeiro and James G. Basker (eds), *Tradition in Transition: Women Writers, Marginal Texts, and the Eighteenth-Century Canon* (Oxford: Clarendon Press, 1996), pp. 241–56.

96 *Gentleman's Magazine* 10 (May 1740), 250. Thomas Kaminski suggests that this may be the wording of Samuel Johnson, who was still performing sub-editorial tasks for Cave at the time (*The Early Life of Samuel Johnson* (New York: Oxford University Press, 1987), p. 231 n.).

97 *Gentleman's Magazine* 11 (January 1741), 28, reprinting an item from the *Universal Spectator*, no. 641; *Queries upon Queries* (1743), quoted in Philip H. Highfill, Kalman A. Burnim and Edward A. Langhans, *A Biographical Dictionary of Actors, Actresses, Musicians, Dancers, Managers, and Other Stage Personnel in London, 1660–1800*, 16 vols (Carbondale: Southern Illinois University Press, 1973–93), V, 188.

98 *Grub-street Journal*, no. 417, 22 December 1737.

99 Further evidence to this effect lies in Aaron Hill's reference, a few days later, to the 'growing Renown of [Richardson's] Name', in a Great, Wicked, Town' (13 April 1741, Forster MSS, XVI, 1, f. 44), though perhaps his provincial renown took longer to achieve.

100 *London Magazine* 10 (May 1741), 250–1; (June 1741), 304; (July 1741), 358.

101 Sale discusses the evidence in *Bibliographical Record*, pp. 129–30; see also D. F. Foxon, *English Verse, 1701–1750* (Cambridge: Cambridge University Press, 1975), item B192.

102 Harris, *London Newspapers*, p. 96.

103 *Scots Magazine* 3 (October 1741), 453; the extract reprinted occupies pp. 453–4.

104 Sale, *Bibliographical Record*, p. 130. The quotation is from Ovid's *Ars amatoria*, i. 359–62.

105 Alexander Pope, *The Rape of the Lock and Other Poems*, ed. Geoffrey Tillotson, 3rd edn (London: Methuen, 1962), v. 25 and v. 34; see also ii. 21–2, in which Belinda's locks hang 'In equal Curls, and well conspir'd to deck | With shining Ringlets her smooth iv'ry Neck'.

106 Kelly, *Pamela's Conduct*, II, 191.

107 Roger Lonsdale identifies these poems as 'Orinthia's Plea' (September 1741) and 'Orinthia to Fido' (July 1742). See his biographical note on Teft in *Eighteenth-Century Women Poets: An Oxford Anthology* (Oxford: Oxford University Press, 1989), p. 217; also the entry in Virginia Blain, Isobel Grundy and Patricia Clements (eds), *The Feminist Companion to Literature in English* (New Haven: Yale University Press, 1990), p. 1061.

108 Elizabeth Teft, *Orinthia's Miscellanies; or, A Compleat Collection of Poems, Never before Published* (1747), p. 15. Teft's title for the poem is ambiguous (*Pamela in High Life* being the abbreviation widely used for Kelly's novel, but also the exact title of another continuation), but her text unmistakably alludes to the plot of Kelly's second volume.

109 'Epistle to Miss Blount, with the Works of Voiture', in Alexander Pope, *Minor Poems*, ed. Norman Ault and John Butt (London: Methuen, 1964), p. 63 (ll. 50, 53–4). It is probably because of *Pamela*'s success that the eight-line 'Pamela' section from this verse epistle subsequently seemed viable as a free-standing poem (reprinted as 'Wealth without Content; or, The Unhappy Marriage', in *The Accomplish'd Housewife* (1745), p. 73).

110 Three further editions of Relph's *Miscellany* were published in Carlisle, Newcastle and London in 1797–9, just as Wordsworth was arousing interest in the region as a poetic subject; one of Relph's Cumberland pastorals is in Roger Lonsdale's *New Oxford Book of Eighteenth-Century Verse* (Oxford: Oxford University Press, 1984), pp. 370–2.

111 Josiah Relph, *A Miscellany of Poems* (Glasgow, 1747), p. 187.

112 *Gentleman's Magazine* 15 (1745), 104.

113 Over a thousand poems were printed in the *Salisbury Journal* between 1736 and 1770 (Ferdinand, *Benjamin Collins and the Provincial Newspaper Trade*, p. 170); for the Harris circle, see Clive T. Probyn, *The Sociable Humanist: The Life and Works of James Harris, 1709–1780* (Oxford: Clarendon Press, 1991).

114 PRO, C 11/2283/45, cited in *The Correspondence of Henry and Sarah Fielding*, ed. Martin C. Battestin and Clive T. Probyn (Oxford: Clarendon Press, 1993), p. xxiii.

115 See, for example, *Gentleman's Magazine* 12 (October 1742), 600; 13 (September 1743), 488; 15 (September 1745), 495. There may also be a connection to the royal chaplain Edward Cobden (1684–1764), who addressed several poems to Belinda, including 'Belinda's Canary-Bird' (*Gentleman's Magazine* 3 (February 1733), 93), and later wrote verses comparing Elizabeth Canning to Richardson's *Clarissa* ('An Ode on E. C. alias Clarissa Exemplified', in *Discourses and Essays, in Prose and Verse* (1757), pp. 327–9).

116 Jürgen Habermas, *The Structural Transformation of the Public Sphere* (Cambridge: Polity Press, 1989), pp. 43, 49–50, 60.

117 Joseph Warton, *Fashion: An Epistolary Satire* (1742), p. 6; Henry Fielding, *Miscellanies, Volume One*, ed. Henry Knight Miller (Oxford: Clarendon Press, 1972), p. 99 (ll. 176–9).

118 William Whitehead, *On Nobility: An Epistle* (1744), p. 6 (ll. 69–70); César de Missy, *Bribery: A Satire* (1750), pp. 9, 10.

2 LITERARY PROPERTY AND THE TRADE IN CONTINUATIONS

1 Umberto Eco, *The Limits of Interpretation* (Bloomington: Indiana University Press, 1990), pp. 83–100.

2 See Ingrid E. Holmberg, 'Homer and the Beginning of the Sequel', in Paul Budra and Betty A. Schellenberg (eds), *Part Two: Reflections on the Sequel* (Toronto: University of Toronto Press, 1998), pp. 19–33; also Schellenberg's '"To Renew Their Former Acquaintance": Print, Gender, and Some Eighteenth-Century Serials', pp. 85–101 in the same volume.

3 J. Paul Hunter, 'Serious Reflections on Farther Adventures: Resistances to Closure in Eighteenth-Century English Novels', in Rivero (ed.), *Augustan Subjects*, p. 282. On Behn, see Warner, *Licensing Entertainment*, pp. 62–6; for eighteenth-century practices in general, see Keymer, *Sterne, the Moderns, and the Novel* (Oxford: Oxford University Press, 2002), pp. 122–32.

4 Castle, *Masquerade and Civilization*, p. 134.

5 Miguel de Cervantes Saavedra, tr. Tobias Smollett, *The History and Adventures of the Renowned Don Quixote*, ed. Martin C. Battestin and O M Brack, Jr (Athens: University of Georgia Press, 2003), p. 393 (II. iv).

6 Anon. to Charles Rivington (for forwarding to Richardson), 15 November 1740, Forster MSS, XVI, 1, f. 36.

7 To James Leake, *c.* August 1741, quoted at length below from Forster MSS, XVI, 1, ff. 55–7.

8 'Copy of a Letter to a Lady, Who Was Solicitous for an Additional Volume', in *Sir Charles Grandison*, ed. Jocelyn Harris, 3 vols (London: Oxford University Press, 1972), III, 467–70.

9 Richardson to Lady Bradshaigh, 25 February 1754, *Selected Letters*, ed. Carroll, p. 296.

10 *Pamela in High Life* was originally scheduled for publication 'in Five Numbers . . . every other Week 'till the whole is finish'd' (*London Daily Post and General Advertiser*, 29 September 1741, announcing publication of the first instalment that day), but by 15 October had been rescheduled as a three-part serial, with the second part to follow on 27 October (*Daily Advertiser*). Comparison between the second title page of *Pamela in High Life* (reproduced in Sale, *Bibliographical Record*, p. 121; see also McKillop, *Printer and Novelist*, p. 56) and the title page of the pirated *Pamela*, which suppresses the publisher's name, indicates a common provenance. Sale mentions the piracy (p. 16) but lacked access to a copy; the only copy known today is at the Houghton Library, Harvard. The date of the piracy can be inferred from Kingman's use of Richardson's fourth edition (5 May 1741) for *Pamela*'s introductory material, which was revised again in the fifth edition (22 September).

11 *Monthly Review* 23 (October 1760), 327; *Critical Review* 10 (September 1760), 237; see Anne Bandry, 'The Publication of the Spurious Volumes of *Tristram Shandy*', *Shandean* 3 (1991), 126–37.

12 'Forse altri canterà con migloir plettro' (*Don Quixote*, p. 366); the line (meaning 'perhaps others will sing with a better lyre') is from Ariosto's *Orlando Furioso*, itself an unauthorized continuation. On *Don Quixote*, Avellaneda, and the related case of Alemán's *Guzmán de Alfarache*

(1599–1604), see Edward H. Friedman, 'Insincere Flattery: Imitation and the Growth of the Novel', *Cervantes* 20 (2000), 99–114.

13 *Life of Pamela*, p. 2 n. Dated 1741 on its title page, *The Life of Pamela* is made up of twenty-one numbered instalments, which were probably issued weekly in the second half of the year: later instalments are based on Kelly's two-volume continuation, which was not completed until September, but no mention is made of Richardson's authorized continuation (7 December). The earliest known advertisement is in the *St James Evening Post* for 19–22 February 1743, by which time the entire work could be bought in bound form (Sale, *Bibliographical Record*, p. 127). The copy at the Beinecke Library, Yale, bears a dated ownership inscription: 'Ann Brookes Her Book 1742'.

14 Richard Griffin, *Specimens of the Novelists and Romancers*, 1st American edn (New York, 1831), II, 43; quoted by McKillop, *Printer and Novelist*, p. 86.

15 *Life of Pamela*, p. 185 n.; *Pamela in High Life* (1741), p. 436.

16 *Life of Pamela*, p. 451 n.

17 In the forepapers of *The Lady's Companion*, 4th edn, 2 vols. (1743), II.

18 *Pamela in High Life*, pp. 342, 136, 451–2. The tale of Theophana the slave is on pp. 8off.

19 Sale, *Bibliographical Record*, pp. 114–15. Each volume cost 3 shillings bound, which was also Richardson's price; the Dublin reprint was bound to match Faulkner's reprint of the original.

20 Sabor, 'Richardson's Index', p. 559.

21 See, for example, Edward Moore's comedy *The Foundling* (1748), which introduces an upwardly mobile character as 'the perfect Pamela in High Life' (p. 25); Richardson was left, on the crowded title page of his own continuation, with the awkward phrases 'in her Exalted Condition' and 'in Genteel Life'.

22 *Common Sense*, 30 May 1741; see also McKillop, *Printer and Novelist*, p. 54 (quoting *London Daily Post and General Advertiser* for the same day); also, on *Pamela*'s typeface, *Letters of Cheyne*, p. 63.

23 Anon. to Richardson, July 1741, Forster MSS, XVI, 1, f. 52; Mary Barber to Richardson, 26 August 1741, Forster MSS, XVI, 1, f. 53.

24 Sabor, 'Richardson's Index', p. 559.

25 The original letter is at Forster MSS, XVI, 1, ff. 55–7. Richardson's more guarded later rewording is transcribed by McKillop (*Printer and Novelist*, pp. 51–4) and Carroll (*Selected Letters*, pp. 42–5).

26 Henry Fielding, *Contributions to The Champion and Related Writings*, ed. W. B. Coley (Oxford: Clarendon Press, 2001), p. 474 (4 October 1740); Coley proposes Francis Cogan, but Chandler's recorded difficulties were closer in date. The *History and Proceedings* project, in three sets of three volumes, is advertised in the endpapers of *Pamela's Conduct*, II.

27 *The Life of Mr. Thomas Gent, Printer, of York*, ed. J. Hunter (1832), p. 192; see also C. Y. Ferdinand, 'The Economics of the Eighteenth-Century Provincial Book Trade: The Case of Ward and Chandler', in Maureen

Bell *et al.* (eds), *Re-constructing the Book: Literary Texts in Transmission* (Aldershot: Ashgate, 2001), pp. 42–56.

28 Warner, *Licensing Entertainment*, p. 200.

29 For Richardson's reliance on oral recommendation, see ch. 1 above; on the Roe campaign, see Eaves and Kimpel, *Biography*, pp. 81–3, 124.

30 Anon. to Richardson, July 1741, Forster MSS, XVI, 1, f. 52.

31 See Maslen, *Richardson of London*, pp. 30–1.

32 *Daily Gazetteer*, 30 May 1741, repeated 1 June. Roughly the same advertisement is in *London Daily Post and General Advertiser* (30 May, 1 June), *Daily Post* (1 June, 2 June), and two of the opposition weeklies favoured by Chandler, the *Craftsman* and the *Champion* for 6 June and 13 June.

33 Kelly was probably right in responding that Richardson, not himself, gets this wrong. Early in his second volume, he has Pamela remark that she will not be laughed out of her familiarity with Mrs Jervis 'by People, who, ignorant of what becomes Persons of the Rank to which Heaven has rais'd me, imagine that a haughty and distant Behaviour to their Inferiors and Dependents, are the Characteristicks of what is call'd *High Life*' (II, 2). Perhaps the insecure aloofness of Richardson's Pamela reflects the practice of his own rising class: he himself reportedly 'issued his orders to some of his servants in writing only' (Sir John Hawkins, *The Life of Samuel Johnson, LL. D.*, 2nd edn (1787), p. 384).

34 This advertisement is quoted by Eaves and Kimpel (*Biography*, p. 138) from issues of *Common Sense* (18 July–1 August 1741) absent from the British Library Burney Collection and the *Early English Newspapers* microfilm series.

35 Eaves and Kimpel, *Biography*, pp. 142, 144.

36 Richardson to Lady Bradshaigh, *c.* November 1749, *Selected Letters*, ed. Carroll, p. 133. On *Joseph Andrews* as responding to Richardson's continuation as well as the original, see Peter Sabor, '*Joseph Andrews* and *Pamela*', *British Journal for Eighteenth-Century Studies* 1 (1978), 169–81.

37 Henry Fielding, *Joseph Andrews and Shamela*, p. 303.

38 *The History of Tom Jones the Foundling, in His Married State*, 2nd edn (1750), A3.

39 In, respectively, *The Hotch-Potch* (1727); *Desolation* (1736); *John Medley* (1748–56).

40 Eaves and Kimpel, *Biography*, p. 137; Richard Gooding, '*Pamela, Shamela*, and the Politics of the *Pamela* Vogue', *Eighteenth-Century Fiction* 7 (1995), 119–20.

41 'The Islanders, or Mad Orphan, by John O Kelly Esqre of the Inner Temple', British Library, Kings MSS 301. According to Inner Temple records, 'John Kelly, son and heir of Smith Kelly, late of Aughrim in the island of Jamaica, deceased', was admitted on 13 December 1712.

42 *Calendar of State Papers, Colonial Series, America and West Indies, 1685–1688* (London: HMSO, 1899), item 1021. A substantial Irish planter class was established in Jamaica by 1670, when at least 10 per cent of property-owners were of Irish extraction (John J. Silke, 'The Irish Abroad', in T. W. Moody

et al. (eds), *Early Modern Ireland, 1534–1691* (Oxford: Clarendon Press, 1976), p. 603).

43 *Calendar of State Papers, 1685–1688*, items 1753–4, 1777, 1943; see also *Calendar of State Papers, Colonial Series, America and West Indies, 1689–1692* (London: HMSO, 1901), item 29. This may indicate that Smith Kelly had disavowed the pro-Stuart allegiance of his Irish kin, but no political inference need be drawn, and there is some evidence that he was distrusted after the Revolution. Both James II (in December 1688) and William III (in February 1689) ordered his restoration and cancelled other Albemarle measures, the issues at stake being local rather than dynastic (a fierce dispute between pro-Albemarle small planters and anti-Albemarle large planters, including Kelly): see Richard S. Dunne, 'The Glorious Revolution and America', in Nicholas Canny (ed.), *The Origins of Empire* (Oxford: Oxford University Press, 1998), p. 457.

44 PRO, PROB 11/501, 93.

45 PRO, C7/211, 33; C9/316, 80; C10/250, 48; C33/13, 555; *Calendar of State Papers, Colonial Series, America and West Indies, 1693–1696* (London: HMSO, 1903), item 1236. Further damage was done to the Kelly estate and factory during the French invasion of June 1694 (C10/250, 48).

46 John Kelly's younger sister was baptized at St Leonard's, Eastcheap, on 5 December 1688 (International Genealogical Index), while Smith Kelly was in London to lobby for restoration to his colonial office. His marriage licence application of 29 July 1700 (Lambeth Palace Library) gives his age as about twenty, but adjustment was probably dictated by the older age of his wife, Elizabeth Lane. In a deposition of May 1738, Kelly describes himself as aged fifty-three years and upwards, which indicates birth in 1684–5 (PRO, E134/13 Geo 2/Hil 10); this tallies roughly with his preface to *French Idioms* (published June 1736), where he writes that, having learned French 'almost as early as my Mother-Tongue', he had conversed and written in French at home and abroad for about forty-five years (p. vi).

47 Marriage of Susanna Kelly and Ralph Lambert, St Anne and St Agnes, Aldersgate, 17 December 1696 (IGI).

48 Kelly and Elizabeth Lane appear to have married soon after their licence application of July 1700 (IGI), and a document of February 1708 (PRO, PROB 8/101, 41) grants administration of Smith Kelly's will to George Lane on behalf of his son-in-law, John Kelly, then dwelling in Port Royal. Two children (George Kelly and Smith Kelly) had been born by 1717 (PRO, PROB 11/560, 193), but no London baptismal records have been found; they were probably born in Jamaica. Kelly was back in London by June 1710 (PRO, PROB 8/103, 122).

49 PRO, C7/211/33 (complaint of Ralph and Susan Lambert, March 1697); Kelly's mother had died by February 1708 (PRO, PROB 8/101, 41).

50 Cf. Alexander Pope, *Epistle to Bathurst* (1733), lines 103–4: 'The grave Sir Gilbert holds it for a rule, | That "ev'ry man in want is knave or fool".'

51 Chancery court orders of August 1710 (PRO, C33/313, 555) and May 1718 (C33/329, 254).
52 For Sadler's role, see PRO, PROB 11/501, 93 and C10/250, 48; British Library, Add. MSS 21931.
53 Performance in Jamaica remains a remote possibility: a theatre was probably operating in Spanish Town, but no records survive (Errol Hill, *The Jamaican Stage, 1655–1900* (Amherst: Massachusetts University Press, 1992), pp. 20–1).
54 'The Islanders, or Mad Orphan', f. 2.
55 St James, Westminster, parish register (entries between March 1712 and August 1717).
56 Chancery records of 1725–6 (C11/1766, 26; C11/1416, 5) involve a John Kelly, merchant, who was connected with the parish of St James, Westminster, and with the West Indies.
57 PRO, PRIS1/3, 350 (recording that Kelly was committed to the Fleet on 16 September 1727 and discharged on 25 May 1728).
58 *The Monthly Catalogue, 1727–1730* (London: Gregg Press Ltd, 1964), no. 55 (November 1727), pp. 127–8; for *The Hotch-Potch*, see no. 54 (October 1727), p. 113. Prudently, both works appeared with a fictitious bookseller's name, 'A. Moore', on the imprint.
59 PRO, SP 36/5, 181 (examination of Phyllis Leveridge, a pamphlet-seller, 10 March 1728).
60 PRO, SP 36/5, 135 (examination of James Watson, 6 March 1728); see also SP 36/5, 183. On Richardson and *Mist's*, see Eaves and Kimpel, *Biography*, pp. 31–4.
61 Wiles, *Serial Publication*, pp. 106, 108, 285–6.
62 Richardson printed another Pluche work the same year, *The History of the Heavens*, translated by *Pamela*'s promoter Jean Baptiste de Freval (Sale, *Master Printer*, pp. 193–4; Maslen, *Richardson of London*, p. 117).
63 Baker's attributions of authorship for the first 149 numbers of the *Universal Spectator* are listed in Walter Graham, *English Literary Periodicals* (New York: Thomas Nelson and Sons, 1930), p. 106 n.; see also David M. Greenhalgh's entry for the *Universal Spectator* in Sullivan, *British Literary Magazines*, pp. 346–9. Kelly may have continued to contribute after the Baker attributions run out, and received credit in 1747 for a four-volume reprint of early numbers.
64 Thomas Lockwood, 'John Kelly's "Lost" Play "The Fall of Bob" (1736)', *English Language Notes* 22 (1984), 27.
65 Arthur H. Scouten (ed.), *The London Stage, 1660–1800, Part 3, 1729–1747*, 2 vols (Carbondale: Southern Illinois University Press, 1961), pp. 201, 203, 205, 207; *Gentleman's Magazine*, 2 (April 1732), 729. Unless otherwise indicated, further publication dates are from the *Gentleman's Magazine* monthly register.
66 Scouten, *London Stage*, p. 281.

67 Scouten, *London Stage*, p. cxlvi; see also Pierre Danchin (ed.), *The Prologues and Epilogues of the Eighteenth Century* (Nancy: Presses Universitaires de Nancy, 1990–), IV, 502.

68 Scouten, *London Stage*, pp. 344, 345.

69 The prologue reappears in Hill's *Works* (1754), IV, 25–7: see Danchin (ed.), *Prologues and Epilogues*, IV, 598.

70 Scouten, *London Stage*, pp. 453, 454, 455. The published version was advertised as *The Plot; or Pill and Drop; a New Pantomimical Entertainment* (*Gentleman's Magazine*, 5 (January 1735), 55), exploiting the currency as a satirical target of Joshua Ward, the quack, and his famous nostrum.

71 Scouten, *London Stage*, pp. 628, 631.

72 Lockwood, 'Kelly's "Lost" Play', p. 28. The connection with *The Fall of Phaeton* is made by Vincent J. Liesenfeld, *The Licensing Act of 1737* (Madison: University of Wisconsin Press, 1984), p. 212 n.

73 Lockwood details the overwhelming case for Kelly's authorship of both *The Fall of Bob* and *Desolation* ('Kelly's "Lost" Play', 32). Earlier sources (e.g. Scouten, *London Stage*, p. 631; Foxon, *English Verse*, item B556) give them to Eustace Budgell, whose old pseudonym, 'Timothy Scrubb, of Ragg-Fair, Esq.', Kelly had tactically appropriated in both publications.

74 *Daily Advertiser*, 7 January 1737, quoted in Scouten, *London Stage*, pp. 628–9; see also Lockwood, 'Kelly's "Lost" Play', pp. 30–1, and Robert D. Hume and Judith Milhous (eds), *A Register of English Theatrical Documents, 1660–1737* (Carbondale: Southern Illinois University Press, 1991), items 4046, 4050. The earlier puff was in *Fog's Weekly Journal* for 1 January 1737.

75 Robert D. Hume, *Henry Fielding and the London Theatre, 1728–1737* (Oxford: Clarendon Press, 1988), p. 222.

76 It should be added that ownership of this pseudonym remains somewhat obscure, and that Kelly (as conjectured in ESTC) may have been using it to write on Budgell's behalf, and with his approval, in 1730–1.

77 *Gentleman's Magazine*, 7 (July 1737), 432. The episode is discussed in Lockwood, 'Kelly's "Lost" Play', 31; see also Harris, *London Newspapers*, pp. 99, 107, 125, 141.

78 PRO, SP 36/41, 240 (examination of John Purser, 25 July 1737); see also SP 36/41, 206; also *London Magazine* 6 (1738), 397. On the connection between John Purser and Richardson's journeyman James Purser, see T. C. Duncan Eaves and Ben D. Kimpel, 'Two Notes on Samuel Richardson', *The Library* 23 (1968), 242–7.

79 PRO, SP 36/45, 326 (Nicholas Paxton's memorandum of 20 June 1738; Caroline had died in the interim).

80 PRO, SP 36/41, 133 ('The humble petition of John Kelly', *c.* July 1737).

81 *Gentleman's Magazine*, 7 (August 1737), 513; on the contemporaneous case of Henry Haines, printer of the *Craftsman*, see Harris, *London Newspapers*, pp. 141–5.

82 PRO, SP 36/45, 326 (Paxton's memorandum of 20 June 1738).
83 PRO, PRIS 1/7, 204, entry 622, recording Kelly's committal on 28 June 1738 and discharge on 8 March 1739.
84 PRO, E134/13 Geo 2/Hil 10 (1738); C33/383, 408 (1745).
85 J. S. Burn, *History of Fleet Marriages*, 3rd edn (1846), entry for 5 November 1735.
86 *London Magazine*, 8 (July 1739), 364.
87 See L. W. Conolly, *The Censorship of English Drama, 1737–1824* (San Marino: Huntington Library, 1976), pp. 62–3.
88 John Kelly, *The Levee* (1741), p. 6.
89 John Kelly (?), *Memoirs of the Life of John Medley, Esq.*, 2 vols (1747–56), II, 176.
90 *London Magazine*, 20 (July 1751); St Pancras, parish register.
91 Hammond, *Professional Imaginative Writing*, pp. 8–9.
92 *Life of Pamela*, p. 416 n.
93 Kreissman, *Pamela-Shamela*, p. 66; Eaves and Kimpel, *Biography*, p. 140; Gooding, '*Pamela, Shamela*', pp. 117–18.
94 Barber to Richardson, 26 August 1741, Forster MSS, XVI, 1, f. 53; Teft, *Orinthia's Miscellanies*, p. 15; anon. to Richardson, July 1741, Forster MSS, XVI, 1, f. 52; Matilda Postlethwaite to Barbara Kerrich, 15 January 1742, Parker Library, Corpus Christi College, Cambridge, MS 588, f. 168.
95 Richardson, *Correspondence*, ed. Barbauld, I, lxxvii.
96 Eagleton, *Rape of Clarissa*, p. 39.
97 Witness 'poor Mrs Jinks, your ladyship's sempstress and clear-starcher' in Eliza Haywood, *The History of Miss Betsy Thoughtless*, ed. Christine E. Blouch (Peterborough, ON: Broadview, 1998), p. 402.
98 Gooding, '*Pamela, Shamela*', pp. 117, 119.
99 *Life of Pamela*, p. 451 n.
100 Eaves and Kimpel, *Biography*, p. 139; Gooding, '*Pamela, Shamela*', p. 118.
101 *Miscellaneous Works of the Late Philip Dormer Stanhope, Earl of Chesterfield*, 2 vols (1777), I, 239.
102 Richardson to Stephen Duck, October–November 1741, *Selected Letters*, ed. Carroll, p. 53; see also Eaves and Kimpel, *Biography*, pp. 143–5.
103 Cheyne to Richardson, 24 August 1741, *Letters of Cheyne*, p. 68.
104 See Keymer, *Sterne, the Moderns, and the Novel*, p. 103.
105 Anon. to Richardson, July 1741, Forster MSS, XVI, 1, f. 52. Without citing this letter, Florian Stuber argues for the influence of Cervantes on Richardson's continuation ('*Pamela II*: "Written in Imitation of the Manner of Cervantes"', in Albert J. Rivero (ed.), *New Essays on Samuel Richardson* (New York: St Martin's Press, 1996), pp. 53–68). In line with his correspondent's advice, however, Richardson refuses to make the crucial metaleptic move of *Don Quixote*, which is to allow the original novel and its spurious continuation to enter his sequel as objects printed, circulated and debated within the fictional world.
106 *Life of Pamela*, p. 249 n.

3 COUNTER-FICTIONS AND NOVEL PRODUCTION

1 See Keymer, *Sterne, the Moderns, and the Novel*, pp. 49, 56; and the chart in James Raven, *British Fiction, 1750–1770: A Chronological Check-List of Prose Fiction Printed in Britain and Ireland* (Newark: University of Delaware Press, 1987), p. 8.

2 The most accurate account of Haywood's life to date is Christine Blouch's biographical introduction to *Selected Works of Eliza Haywood*, ed. Alexander Pettit *et al.* (London: Pickering & Chatto, 2000–1), Part 1, vol. 1, pp. xxi–lxxxii. See also Patrick Spedding, *A Bibliography of Eliza Haywood* (London: Pickering & Chatto, 2004).

3 Some of the anonymous and pseudonymous authors of responses to *Pamela* might also, of course, have been women. One such was 'Belinda' of Salisbury, who published a verse commendation, 'To the Author of *Pamela*' (*Gentleman's Magazine* 15 (February 1745), p. 104).

4 Maslen, *Richardson of London*, p. 90; Spedding, *Bibliography of Haywood*, pp. 78, 131; Katherine Ruth Williams, 'Samuel Richardson and Amatory Fiction', diss., Oxford University, 2004.

5 Richardson to Aaron Hill, *c.* 1 February 1741, *Selected Letters*, ed. Carroll, p. 41.

6 Richardson to George Cheyne, 31 August 1741, *Selected Letters*, ed. Carroll, pp. 46–7.

7 Richardson to Sarah Chapone, 6 December 1750, *Selected Letters*, ed. Carroll, p. 173 n. Although Pilkington's *Memoirs* praise Richardson for his generosity towards her, he was apparently offended by her publicizing what he considered a private affair. For Richardson's dealings with Pilkington, see *Memoirs of Laetitia Pilkington*, ed. Elias, pp. xliv–xlix.

8 Blouch contends that 'the question of a direct influence' of *Shamela* on *Anti-Pamela* 'is moot, since the novels were published within a few months of one another' (Haywood, *Selected Works*, ed. Blouch, 1, 1 lxvi). Given Haywood's ability to publish ten or more novels per year, however, as she had done during the 1720s, she might well have begun writing *Anti-Pamela* only after the publication of Fielding's satire.

9 Gerrard, *Aaron Hill*, pp. 61–101, and Prescott, *Women, Authorship and Literary Culture*, pp. 26–30.

10 Scouten, *London Stage*, p. 674.

11 Haywood, *Betsy Thoughtless*, pp. 66–7.

12 Eaves and Kimpel, *Biography*, p. 130.

13 Gooding, '*Pamela, Shamela*', p. 110 n.

14 De Mauvillon, listed only as 'D. M****' on the title page, is identified by McKillop, *Printer and Novelist*, p. 80, and by Sale, *Bibliographical Record*, p. 116.

15 De Mauvillon, 'Avertissement des Libraires', *L'Anti-Pamela* (Amsterdam, 1743), pp. 1–4.

16 See Richardson to Lady Bradshaigh, 14 February 1754: 'It is not fair to say –
I, identically I, am any-where, while I keep within the character' (*Selected Letters*, ed. Carroll, p. 286).

17 Haywood, *Anti-Pamela* and Fielding, *Shamela*, ed. Catherine Ingrassia
(Peterborough, ON: Broadview, 2004), p. [51].

18 The title pages of many of the eighteenth-century editions of *Pamela* are
reproduced in Sale, *Bibliographical Record*, pp. 11–34.

19 Gerrard, *Aaron Hill*, pp. 92–3, and *Clio: The Autobiography of Martha
Fowke Sansom (1689–1736)*, ed. Phyllis J. Guskin (Newark: University of
Delaware Press, 1997), pp. 28–31.

20 Kate Williams, '"The Force of Language, and the Sweets of Love": Eliza
Haywood and the Erotics of Reading in Samuel Richardson's *Clarissa*',
Lumen 23 (2004), 316.

21 In a discussion of Mrs Jervis's role in *Shamela*, Carl Wood points out that
'Fielding's seemingly arbitrary and outrageous changes in the characters of
Richardson's housekeepers . . . are really not so arbitrary and outrageous
after all' ('*Shamela*'s Subtle Satire: Fielding's Characterization of Mrs.
Jewkes and Mrs. Jervis', *English Language Notes* 13 (1976), 270). See also
Scarlet Bowen, '"A Sawce-box and Boldface Indeed": Refiguring the Female
Servant in the Pamela–Antipamela Debate', *Studies in Eighteenth-Century
Culture* 28 (1999), 257–85.

22 Sale, *Bibliographical Record*, pp. 116–17.

23 Wiles, *Serial Publication*, pp. 44–50. The British Library possesses a run of
the newspaper from 20 October 1741, in which the serialization had already
begun, to 2 January 1742, in which it had not yet been completed. The
extract in the issue of 20 October is from pp. 166–7 of *Anti-Pamela*; that of
2 January is from pp. 216–17. Thus, even allowing for longer extracts in
earlier issues and the possibility that parts of the text were omitted,
serialization probably began shortly after *Anti-Pamela* was first published on
16 June 1741 and continued until at least March 1742. Complicating the
situation is what Wiles terms a 'curious kind of skullduggery' (p. 48): the
existence of two different versions of *All-Alive and Merry*, the second being
either a piracy published by a rival or a concurrent edition issued by
'Merryman' himself. On 10 November, one version of *All-Alive and Merry*
contained pp. 181–2 of *Anti-Pamela*; the other version bearing the same date
contained pp. 187–8. The first version printed the later episode (pp. 187–8)
on 19 November.

24 Spedding, *Bibliography of Haywood*, pp. 361–4. Spedding has not located the
Dublin edition or the Danish translation mentioned by McKillop, *Printer
and Novelist*, p. 80.

25 Richard H. Thornton, 'English Authors Placed on the Roman "Index"
(1600 to 1750)', *Notes and Queries* 11th series 12 (1915), 333; Florian J. Schleck,
'Richardson on the Index', *Times Literary Supplement*, 25 April 1935, p. 272;
and Eaves and Kimpel, *Biography*, p. 126.

26 Haywood, *Selected Works*, ed. Blouch, I, 1 lxvi.

27 Catherine Ingrassia, *Authorship, Commerce, and Gender in Early Eighteenth-Century England: A Culture of Paper Credit* (Cambridge: Cambridge University Press, 1998), p. 110.

28 A sale of Cogan's stock in July 1746 calls him a bankrupt; see Fielding, *Contributions to the Champion*, ed. Coley, p. 474 n.

29 McKillop, *Printer and Novelist*, p. 80, and Spedding, *Bibliography of Haywood*, p. 354. Spedding suggests that 'the lack of interest in the copyright was probably due to the fact that the book was out of print', and in addition that it may have been 'seen as being out of date'. Cogan's catalogue, listing 'Anti-Pamela, by Mrs. Haywood (out of Print) — the Whole', is also the source for attributing *Anti-Pamela* to Haywood. This was noted by McKillop (*Printer and Novelist*, p. 80) in 1936, but as Blouch observes, *Anti-Pamela* has often been 'attributed to Haywood only tentatively, for reasons that are not clear' (Introduction to *Betsy Thoughtless*, p. 18 n.).

30 The first edition of *The Virtuous Villager* was published 'at the Sign of Fame' on 18 March 1742; a second issue, published by Francis Cogan, followed on 20 March. See Spedding, *Bibliography of Haywood*, pp. 369–70.

31 *Pamela Censured*, intro. Batten, p. ix.

32 Haywood, *The Virtuous Villager* (1742), p. x.

33 Haywood, *A Present for a Servant-Maid* (1743), in *Selected Works*, ed. Blouch, I, I, 242. The work is discussed in relationship to *Pamela* by Margaret Anne Doody in *A Natural Passion: A Study of the Novels of Samuel Richardson* (Oxford: Oxford University Press, 1974), pp. 43–4.

34 Blouch, intro. to *Betsy Thoughtless*, p. 12.

35 See *The Yale Edition of Horace Walpole's Correspondence*, ed. W. S. Lewis (New Haven: Yale University Press, 1937–83), XVII, 434 n. In her 'Life of Richardson', Barbauld confirms the association between the pleasure garden and *Pamela*; see Introduction above.

36 Sale, *Bibliographical Record*, p. 117.

37 Lord Hervey to Lady Mary Wortley Montagu, 16 July 1741, *Letters of Montagu*, II, 244–5.

38 See W. J. T. Collins, 'A Scandal of Old Monmouthshire', *Monmouthshire Review* I (1933), 9–12, and Sale, *Bibliographical Record*, pp. 117–20. All but one of the five editions are held in the Haines Collection, Newport Central Library, and are of local Welsh provenance, including two copies with extensive manuscript identifications of suppressed names. The fifth, the pirated London edition, is reproduced from an annotated copy in the Beinecke Library, Yale, in *Richardsoniana* VII (New York: Garland, 1974).

39 Eaves and Kimpel, *Biography*, p. 130; McKillop, *Printer and Novelist*, pp. 80–1.

40 Terri Nickel, '*Pamela* as Fetish: Masculine Anxiety in Henry Fielding's *Shamela* and James Parry's *The True Anti-Pamela*', *Studies in Eighteenth-Century Culture* 22 (1992), 43.

41 See Nickel, '*Pamela* as Fetish', pp. 44–5.

42 On the vogue for 'providing farther adventures (or at least leaving the door ajar for them)', see Hunter, 'Serious Reflections', p. 281.

43 Moira Dearnley, *Distant Fields: Eighteenth-Century Fictions of Wales* (Cardiff: University of Wales Press, 2001), p. 63.

44 In the posthumously published 1742 edition of *The True Anti-Pamela*, for which Parry was not responsible, these letters are incorporated into the body of the memoirs; see Sale, *Bibliographical Record*, p. 120.

45 See Mark G. Spencer's entry on Povey in the *Oxford Dictionary of National Biography* (hereafter *ODNB*). Eaves and Kimpel's belief that Povey was aged eighty in 1741 (*Biography*, p. 131) stems from a misreading of his Preface to *The Virgin in Eden*, in which he states that he has 'arrived at the Period of fourscore': i.e. at the end, not the beginning, of his eighties.

46 See, for example, the postscript to *Clarissa*'s third edition: 'He has lived to see Scepticism and Infidelity openly avowed, and even endeavoured to be propagated from the *Press*' (VIII, 279).

47 Povey required his will to be printed after his death in a public newspaper, as it duly was in the *London Daily Post and General Advertiser* for 1 and 8 July 1743; see McKillop, *Printer and Novelist*, p. 81, and Eaves and Kimpel, *Biography*, p. 131.

48 Sale notes that Cooper's 'pamphlet shop served as distributing agent' for various periodicals printed by Richardson (*Master Printer*, p. 73). Cooper was publisher of the *Daily Gazetteer*, possibly but not certainly printed by Richardson from its inception in 1735 until 1746; see Keith Maslen, 'Samuel Richardson as Printer', in R. C. Alston (ed.), *Order and Connexion: Studies in Bibliography and Book History* (Cambridge: D. S. Brewer, 1997), pp. 8–9.

49 Hill to Richardson, 15 January 1741, Forster MSS, XIII, 2, f. 42; see McKillop, *Printer and Novelist*, p. 24.

50 Richardson to Hill, *c.* 1 February 1741, *Selected Letters*, ed. Carroll, pp. 39–40.

51 Richardson to Johannes Stinstra, 2 June 1753, *Richardson–Stinstra Correspondence*, p. 28.

52 Richardson to Hill, 26 January 1747, *Selected Letters*, ed. Carroll, pp. 78–9; Richardson to Lady Bradshaigh, 25 February 1754, *Selected Letters*, ed. Carroll, p. 296.

53 Richardson to Thomas Edwards, 21 April 1753, *Selected Letters*, p. 225.

54 Richardson, Preface to *Pamela*, III (1741), iv.

55 Richardson, draft dedication for *Pamela*, Forster MSS, XVI, 1, f. 11.

56 Mercier's portraits of Sir Arthur and Lady Hesilrige are reproduced in Robert Raines and John Ingamells, *Philip Mercier* (London: Paul Mellon Foundation, 1969), p. 37. The originals, and another portrait of Sir Arthur by Mercier, are at Noseley Hall, Leicestershire, seat of the present Lord Hazlerigg. Turner conjectures that Mercier's commission to paint the Hesilriges might have contributed 'to his later fascination with Pamela' ('Novel Panic', p. 95 n.).

57 Aleyn Lyell Reade, 'Richardson's Pamela: Her Original', *Notes and Queries* 10th series 9 (1908), 361–3, 503–5. McKillop (*Printer and Novelist*, p. 27 n.) draws attention to an obituary of the Hesilriges' daughter Hannah in the *Gentleman's Magazine* 92 (1822), ii, 571, which states that 'the character of Pamela was drawn from that of Lady Hesilrige'.

58 Eaves and Kimpel, *Biography*, pp. 32, 130 n.; they misdate the issue with the announcement as 4 August. The notice reads: 'We hear that Sir Arthur Haslerigg of Nosely in the County of Leicester, Bart. was lately married to Mrs. Sturgis, his Coachman's Daughter.'

59 They include Elizabeth Chapman, who married the Earl of Gainsborough in 1739, and Sarah Boothby of Tooley Park; see Reade, 'Richardson's Pamela'. McKillop provides several other examples of cross-class marriages recorded in the Earl of Egmont's Diary for February 1745 (*Printer and Novelist*, p. 29).

60 *Universal Magazine* 78 (1786), 73. For the attribution to Brooke, see ch. 4 below.

61 The *Spectator* parallel was first noted by William Bowyer in John Nichols, *Biographical and Literary Anecdotes of William Bowyer* (1782), II, 443. For this and for Richardson's possible use of Marivaux, see McKillop, *Printer and Novelist*, pp. 30–1, 35–8.

62 The final page, numbered 67, should be 59, since the pagination skips from 24 to 33.

63 Haslett, *Pope to Burney*, p. 216.

64 See the British Library copy of *Memoirs of the Life of Lady H------*, p. 1.

65 Watt, *The Rise of the Novel*, p. 173.

66 See John Cleland, *Memoirs of a Woman of Pleasure*, ed. Peter Sabor (Oxford: Oxford University Press, 1985), p. 135; John Sutherland, 'Where does Fanny Hill keep her Contraceptives?' in Sutherland, *Can Jane Eyre be Happy?: More Puzzles in Classic Fiction* (Oxford: Oxford University Press, 1997), pp. 17–18; and Corrinne Harol, 'Faking It: Female Virginity and Pamela's Virtue', *Eighteenth-Century Fiction* 16 (2004), 197–216.

67 'Six Reading Ladies' to Richardson, January–February 1742, Forster MSS, XVI, 1, f. 17; Richardson's draft reply, Forster MSS, XVI, 1, ff. 18–19.

68 Sarah Chapone to Richardson, 25 February 1751, Forster MSS, XII, 2, f. 20; Richardson to Chapone, 25 March 1751, *Selected Letters*, ed. Carroll, p. 180.

69 Richardson's term for Fielding's *Joseph Andrews* in a letter of late 1749 to Lady Bradshaigh, *Selected Letters*, ed. Carroll, p. 133.

70 Sabor, intro. to *Memoirs of a Woman of Pleasure*, p. vii.

71 Edward Copeland contends that 'Cleland must be enrolled in the ranks of the anti-Pamelists', but goes on to list various parallels between *Pamela* and *Memoirs of a Woman of Pleasure* ('*Clarissa* and *Fanny Hill*: Sisters in Distress', *Studies in the Novel* 4 (1972), 343, 351 n.). Further parallels between *Memoirs of a Woman of Pleasure* and both *Pamela* and some of the Antipamelas are suggested by William Epstein, *John Cleland: Images of a Life* (New York: Columbia University Press, 1974), pp. 99–101, and by Sabor, intro. to *Memoirs of a Woman of Pleasure*, pp. xxii–xxvi.

72 This translation was published in Paris in February 1750, with a false London imprint. Richardson's old friend Jean de Freval conveyed the bad news from France, in April 1751, that the book 'has had a vast run here this good while' (Richardson, *Correspondence*, ed. Barbauld, V, 277); see Battestin, intro. to Fielding, *Tom Jones*, I, lii–liii.

73 William B. Ober, *Bottoms Up! A Pathologist's Essays on Medicine and the Humanities* (Carbondale: Southern Illinois University Press, 1987), pp. 161–3. Gravelot's illustrations have been reproduced, from the apparently unique surviving copy in the British Library, in *Eighteenth-Century British Erotica II*, vol. IV, ed. Lena Olsson (London: Pickering & Chatto, 2004), pp. 363–96.

74 In his pioneering account of *The Surprises of Love*, Epstein writes that 'the "Pamela question"' was 'a matter which in 1765 still plagued writers of romantic fiction' (*John Cleland*, p. 154). James Basker notes that the London edition of *The Surprises of Love*, while bearing the date 1765, was first published on 15 December 1764. A Dublin edition, dated 1764, was in fact published after the London edition ('"The Wages of Sin": The Later Career of John Cleland', *Etudes anglaises* 40 (1987), 190).

75 Ann Louise Kibbie, 'Sentimental Properties: *Pamela* and *Memoirs of a Woman of Pleasure*', *ELH* 58 (1991), 567.

76 See Dianne Dugaw, intro. to *The Female Soldier; or, The Surprising Life and Adventures of Hannah Snell* (Augustan Reprint Society no. 257. Los Angeles: Clark Memorial Library, 1989), p. v. This is a facsimile reprint of the shorter version.

77 Dugaw, intro. to *The Female Soldier*, pp. vi–vii.

78 John Jones to Spence, 3 September 1761; Austin Wright, *Joseph Spence: A Critical Biography* (Chicago: University of Chicago Press, 1950), p. 123.

79 The manuscript, not known to Wright, is in the Osborn Collection, Beinecke Library.

80 Isobel Grundy, '"Trash, Trumpery, and Idle Time": Lady Mary Wortley Montagu and Fiction', *Eighteenth-Century Fiction* 5 (1993), 302.

81 Montagu to Lady Bute, 17 October 1750, 8 December 1754, *Letters of Montagu*, II, 470; III, 70.

82 Lady Mary Wortley Montagu, *Romance Writings*, ed. Isobel Grundy (Oxford: Clarendon Press, 1996), p. III.

83 Montagu to Lady Bute, 20 October 1755, 9 August 1760, *Letters of Montagu*, III, 97, 244.

84 Raven, *British Fiction*, p. 173.

85 See Peter Marr, 'John Alcock and Fanny Brown', *Musical Times* 118 (February 1977), 118–20; and H. Diack Johnstone's entry on Alcock in *ODNB*. A disgruntled reader of the British Library's copy of the novel expressed his dissatisfaction by writing, at the end of the dedication to the 'worthy Subscribers': 'A damn'd foolish History and yet Piper found greater fools than himself to become Subscribers. O tempora O mores' (p. x). The same reader deleted the words 'Subscribers Names' at the head of the subscription list, replacing them with 'Fools' (p. xlvii).

86 *Aris's Birmingham Gazette*, 19 February 1759; see Marr, 'John Alcock', p. 118 n.

87 Kreissman's suggestion (*Pamela-Shamela*, p. 6) that Alcock's title is an allusion to *Fanny Hill* is unpersuasive: the name Fanny appears in many eighteenth-century novels before and after Cleland's.

88 Keymer, *Sterne, the Moderns, and the Novel*, p. 72.

89 Antonia Forster and James Raven note that although Georgiana Cavendish, Duchess of Devonshire, claimed authorship of *The Sylph*, it might be by Sophia Briscoe (Peter Garside, James Raven and Rainer Schöwerling (eds), *The English Novel 1770–1829: A Bibliographical Survey of Prose Fiction Published in the British Isles* (Oxford: Oxford University Press, 2000), I, 277). Contemporary rumours attributed *The Sylph* to Frances Burney; for her indignant denial, see her journal for 11 January 1779, *Early Journals and Letters of Fanny Burney*, III, ed. Lars E. Troide and Stewart J. Cooke (Montreal and Kingston: McGill-Queen's University Press, 1994), 231–2. In her introduction to a reprint of the novel (York: Henry Parker, 2001), Amanda Foreman attributes it without reservations to the Duchess of Devonshire, as does Jonathan David Gross in his introduction to *Emma; or, The Unfortunate Attachment* (Albany: State University of New York Press, 2004, pp. 10–14), which he also attributes to the Duchess.

90 Shaw, *The Reflector*, p. 14; see Introduction above.

91 Gerard Barker, *Grandison's Heirs: The Paragon's Progress in the Late Eighteenth-Century Novel* (Newark: University of Delaware Press, 1985); Isobel Grundy, '"A novel in a series of a letters by a lady": Richardson and some Richardsonian Novels', in Margaret Anne Doody and Peter Sabor (eds), *Samuel Richardson: Tercentenary Essays* (Cambridge: Cambridge University Press, 1989), pp. 223–36; Jerry C. Beasley, 'Richardson's Girls: The Daughters of Patriarchy in *Pamela, Clarissa,* and *Sir Charles Grandison*', and Joseph F. Bartolomeo, 'Female Quixotism v. "Feminine" Tragedy: Lennox's Comic Revision of *Clarissa*', in Rivero (ed.), *New Essays on Richardson*, pp. 35–52, 163–75.

4 DOMESTIC SERVITUDE AND THE LICENSED STAGE

1 See George Winchester Stone, Jr and George M. Kahrl, *David Garrick: A Critical Biography* (Carbondale: Southern Illinois University Press, 1979), p. 24; and Highfill *et al.*, *Biographical Dictionary of Actors*, VI, 4. 'Lyddal' was the maiden name of Giffard's wife.

2 Cited by McKillop, *Printer and Novelist*, p. 45.

3 See Rosie Broadley *et al.*, *Every Look Speaks: Portraits of David Garrick* (Bath: Holburne Museum of Art, 2003), p. 33, and ch. 5 below.

4 Garrick was billed as a 'Gentleman' when playing Clodio in Colley Cibber's *Love Makes a Man* on 28 October, Chamont in Otway's *The Orphan* on 6 November, and Jack Smatter in Giffard's *Pamela* on 9 November. He would use his own name for the first time in a production of *The Orphan* on 28 November; see Highfill *et al.*, *Biographical Dictionary of Actors*, VI, 7, and Stone and Kahrl, *David Garrick*, p. 26.

5 Joseph Dorman, *Pamela; or, Virtue Rewarded* (Newcastle, 1742), p. vii.

6 See A. D. McKillop, 'Richardson's Early Writings – Another Pamphlet', *Journal of English and Germanic Philology* 53 (1954), 72–5, and Thomas Keymer, *Richardson's Clarissa and the Eighteenth-Century Reader* (Cambridge: Cambridge University Press, 1992) pp. 142–50.

7 See Scouten, *London Stage*, pp. xlviii–liii; Liesenfeld, *The Licensing Act of 1737*; and Hume, *Henry Fielding and the London Theatre*, pp. 39–44, 192–9.
8 Forster MSS, XVI, I, f. 44; McKillop, *Printer and Novelist*, pp. 50–1.
9 *London Daily Post and General Advertiser*, 23 September 1741; Scouten, *London Stage*, p. 929.
10 For their ages (they are a year older by the end of the novel), see Dorothy Parker, 'The Time Scheme of *Pamela* and the Character of B.', *Texas Studies in Language and Literature* II (1969), 695–704.
11 Highfill *et al.*, *Biographical Dictionary of Actors*, VI, 189.
12 Allardyce Nicoll claims that Giffard's *Pamela* was 'the first dramatisation in English of a regular novel, testifying to the enormous contemporary popularity of Richardson's work' (*A History of English Drama, 1660–1900*, vol. II, *Early Eighteenth Century Drama*, 3rd edn (Cambridge: Cambridge University Press, 1952), p. 206). This begs the question, however, of what is a 'regular novel'. Among earlier works of prose fiction made into plays, the most famous is Thomas Southerne's dramatization of Aphra Behn's *Oroonoko* (1695).
13 In addition, the anonymous *Life of Pamela* was probably appearing in serial form at this time.
14 Scouten, *London Stage*, pp. 941–6, 948, 951–2, 971. Of the ninety-six roles that Garrick performed between 1741 and 1776, Jack Smatter was 34th in order of frequency, and among his most frequently performed roles in new plays; see Stone and Kahrl, *David Garrick*, pp. 656–8.
15 Garrick to Peter Garrick, 30 January 1742, *The Letters of David Garrick*, ed. David M. Little and George M. Kahrl (London: Oxford University Press, 1963), I, 36. Peter had apparently enquired about the authorship of the comedy in a missing letter to Garrick.
16 Richardson to Aaron Hill, 27 October 1748, *Selected Letters*, ed. Carroll, p. 99; *Clarissa*, ed. Angus Ross (Harmondsworth: Penguin, 1985), p. 1497. Richardson also tells Hill that he has recently become 'pretty well acquainted' with Garrick.
17 Highfill *et al.*, *Biographical Dictionary of Actors*, II, 150.
18 The lesbian innuendo is noticed by the anonymous author of *Pamela Censured* (1741), who states: 'There are at present, I am sorry to say it, too many who assume the Characters of Women of Mrs. *Jewkes's* Cast, I mean *Lovers of their own Sex*' (p. 50).
19 See Davidson, *Hypocrisy*, pp. 135–6.
20 Kreissman notes that in Giffard's play, Mr B. 'benefits by the presence of Jack Smatter, a dandified, mincing, effeminate fop who also tries to seduce Pamela. In comparison with this noxious fellow, B. is a hero' (*Pamela-Shamela*, pp. 56–7).
21 The romance remained popular in several chapbook versions. Pamela's later comment on Colbrand's stride (p. 181) points specifically to the versification by Samuel Rowlands, in which Colbrand is a 'Monster of a man . . . Treading at every step two yards of ground' (*The Famous History of Guy*

Earle of Warwicke (1607), xii, 83–4); noted by D. C. Muecke, 'Beauty and Mr. B.', *Studies in English Literature* 7 (1967), 467–74.

22 Sale, *Bibliographical Record,* p. 123.

23 *London Evening-Post,* 28 November 1741; see McKillop, *Printer and Novelist,* p. 69.

24 Scouten, *London Stage,* p. 954. Dodsley's afterpiece, *Sir John Cockle at Court,* had been performed on four previous occasions at Drury Lane. Since *Pamela; or, Virtue Triumphant* also claimed to have Drury Lane associations, it is the most likely of the *Pamela* plays to have been performed together with Dodsley's afterpiece.

25 William M. Sale, 'The First Dramatic Version of *Pamela*', *Yale University Library Gazette* 9 (1935), 84–5, and *Bibliographical Record,* pp. 12–23.

26 *Daily Advertiser,* 19 November 1741; see Sale, *Bibliographical Record,* p. 123.

27 See Sale, *Bibliographical Record,* pp. 123–4. Sale also speculates that the reduced price might be explained by the play's absence from the stage in the 1742–3 theatre season, with a consequent 'waning appeal of the printed version'. The book had, however, appeal enough to justify a new edition.

28 *The History of the Stage. In which is included the Theatrical Characters of the most Celebrated Actors who have adorn'd the Theatre* (1742), p. 104.

29 In all five copies of *The History of the Stage* examined – two at the British Library and three at the Theatre Collection, Harvard – the play is absent from the volume.

30 Sale, *Bibliographical Record,* p. 65, and McKillop, *Printer and Novelist,* p. 214.

31 Paul Burditt, 'The Authorship of *Sir Charles Goodvillé*', *Notes and Queries* 249 (2004), 406–7. The attribution was made by Ralph Griffiths, founder of the *Monthly Review,* in his annotated file copy.

32 Sale, 'First Dramatic Version', pp. 86–7, citing David Erskine Baker, *Biographia Dramatica,* ed. Isaac Reed (1782), s.v. 'Love'.

33 Part of Sale's argument is that at the age of nineteen Dance was already a hack writer, having published *Yes, They Are: Being an Answer to Are these Things so?* (1740) 'in fatuous praise of Robert Walpole', and that 'with equal lack of compunction and ability he might well have prostituted *Pamela*' too ('First Dramatic Version', pp. 87–8). As Foxon has shown, however, *Yes, They Are* is not by Dance but by Robert Morris (*English Verse,* I, 486). The attribution to Dance was first made by Isaac Reed, whose knowledge of Dance's career in the 1740s is thus seen to be suspect at best.

34 Sale, 'First Dramatic Version', p. 85.

35 One page was misnumbered (16 for 14, so that 16 appears twice); characters' names are abbreviated inconsistently and confused on several occasions; and, as Sale notes, 'in order to crowd the text within the four pages' of the final gathering, 'a smaller type size is used on p. 92' (*Bibliographical Record,* p. 122). So much smaller is the type here that the page contains fifty lines, instead of the thirty-eight or so found elsewhere.

36 Eaves and Kimpel, *Biography,* p. 134.

37 See David M. Greenhalgh's entry on the *Universal Spectator* in Sullivan (ed.), *British Literary Magazines*, p. 346.

38 Harris, *London Newspapers*, p. 187.

39 *No Screen!*, final leaf; see Spedding, *Bibliography of Haywood*, pp. 677–8. Spedding suggests that *No Screen!* might have been a collaborative venture by Haywood and J. Huggonson.

40 In a list of 'All the Plays ever printed in the *English* Language' (p. 87) up to 1747, appended to Thomas Whincop's *Scanderberg, Or, Love and Liberty. A Tragedy* (1747), *Pamela; or Virtue Rewarded* is said to have been 'not acted, but printed in the Year 1742', while Giffard's *Pamela* is listed as 'acted at the Theatre in *Goodmans-Fields*, 1742' (p. 311).

41 Victor Link, 'The First Operatic Versions of *Pamela*', *Studies on Voltaire and the Eighteenth Century* 267 (1989), 280. Link also notes that this work is 'the first full-length operatic version of . . . any English novel' (p. 273).

42 Turner, 'Novel Panic', p. 95 n.

43 Edward Moore, *The Foundling: A Comedy and The Gamester: A Tragedy*, ed. Anthony Amberg (Newark: University of Delaware Press, 1996), p. 144.

44 Frank H. Ellis, *Sentimental Comedy: Theory and Practice* (Cambridge: Cambridge University Press, 1991), p. 59.

45 See Amberg, intro. to *The Foundling*, pp. 49–82, for a comprehensive study of the play's reception and publication history.

46 Richardson to Moore, 3 October 1748; *The Foundling*, ed. Amberg, p. 396.

47 Mary Delany to Richardson, 24 April 1751, and Richardson *Correspondence*, ed. Barbauld, I, cvii; see *The Foundling*, pp. 82–3.

48 *The Maid of the Mill*, in *The Plays of Isaac Bickerstaff*, ed. Peter A. Tasch (New York: Garland, 1981), I, v–vi.

49 *Gentleman's Magazine* 35 (February 1765), 78; see Peter Tasch, *The Dramatic Cobbler: The Life and Works of Isaac Bickerstaff* (Lewisburg, PA: Bucknell University Press, 1971), p. 75.

50 *Monthly Review* 32 (February 1765), 156. In *Pamela*, Mr B. tells his sister Lady Davers that his marrying a servant is very different from a lady of her rank 'marrying a sordid Groom' (p. 422).

51 *Pamela*, 4 vols (1740), III, 7.

52 Bickerstaff's modern critics, in contrast to Bickerstaff himself, tend to underestimate his indebtedness to *Pamela*. Tasch, for example, contends that Bickerstaff's preface was designed to 'shelter his work under the popularity of Richardson's novel' (*Plays of Isaac Bickerstaff*, I, xvi), while Roger Fiske believes that despite Bickerstaff's claims 'the basic situation in *Pamela* is completely left out' (*English Theatre Music in the Eighteenth Century*, 2nd edn (Oxford: Oxford University Press, 1986), p. 333).

53 George Winchester Stone, Jr (ed.), *The London Stage, 1660–1800, Part 4, 1747–1776*, 3 vols (Carbondale: Southern Illinois University Press, 1962), pp. xxvii, cci.

54 Tasch, *Dramatic Cobbler*, pp. 80–2, and Fiske, *English Theatre Music*, p. 336.

55 Link, 'First Operatic Versions', p. 277.

56 Frances Brooke, *Rosina*, ed. John Drummond (London: Stainer and Bell, 1998), p. xxi.

57 See Lorraine McMullen, *An Odd Attempt in a Woman: The Literary Life of Frances Brooke* (Vancouver: University of British Columbia Press, 1983), pp. 187–9. McMullen conjectures that Brooke's essay on Richardson was the one published in the *Universal Magazine* (January–February 1786). She also provides a useful account of *Rosina*, but does not consider the opera's link with *Pamela*.

58 Brooke, *The Excursion*, ed. Paula R. Backscheider and Hope D. Cotton (Lexington: University Press of Kentucky, 1997), p. 11.

59 McMullen, *An Odd Attempt*, pp. 201–3, and Fiske, *English Theatre Music*, p. 456.

60 *Samuel Foote's Primitive Puppet-Shew Featuring Piety in Pattens: A Critical Edition*, ed. Samuel N. Bogorad and Robert Gale Noyes, *Theatre Survey* 14, no. 1a (Fall, 1973), 42. This edition transcribes both the Folger Library and the Huntington Library manuscripts of *Piety in Pattens*, which had previously remained unpublished. Quotations here are from the Folger text, which was probably a prompt copy; the Huntington text is that submitted for approval for licensing, and thus further removed from the stage performance.

61 *Piety in Pattens*, pp. 97–100.

62 *The Early Diary of Frances Burney 1768–1778*, ed. Annie Raine Ellis (London: Bell, 1913), 11, 279–80.

63 Simon Trefman, *Sam. Foote, Comedian, 1720–1777* (New York: New York University Press, 1971), p. 214, and Elizabeth N. Chatten, *Samuel Foote* (Boston: Twayne, 1980), pp. 135–8.

64 The author claims, as Turner notes, 'that Pamela is "connoisseuse en oeuillades" when reporting the way milord looked at her in the summerhouse (*Lettre sur Pamela*, 8); unfortunately the suggestive word *oeuillades* (seductive glances) appears only in the translation' ('Novel Panic', p. 96 n.). The word is from *Pamela, ou la vertu récompensée* (1741), 1, 20; for the corresponding English phrase, see *Pamela*, p. 22.

65 *Pamela*, ed. Sabor, p. 75 and n.

66 Marie-Rose de Labriolle and Colin Duckworth, intro. to *Nanine* (The Complete Works of Voltaire, 31B. Oxford: Voltaire Foundation, 1994), p. 4.

67 Turner, 'Novel Panic', p. 89. Turner is perhaps the only critic to have written positively about de Boissy's much maligned play, which achieves, he contends, a 'sublime apotheosis' in its finale (p. 90).

68 Gustave Lanson, *Nivelle de la Chaussée et la comédie larmoyante* (Paris: Hachette, 1903), p. 163.

69 André Magnan, 'Pour saluer *Paméla*: une oeuvre inconnue de Voltaire', *Dix-huitième siècle* 15 (1983), 357–68; Magnan, *Dossier Voltaire en Prusse (1750–1753)*, Studies on Voltaire and the Eighteenth Century 224 (1986); and *L'Affaire Paméla: lettres de Monsieur de Voltaire à Madame Denis, de Berlin*, ed. Magnan (Paris: Paris Mediterranée, 2004).

70 Jonathan Mallinson, 'What's in a Name? Reflections on Voltaire's *"Paméla"*, forthcoming in *Eighteenth-Century Fiction* 18.2 (January 2006).
71 Voltaire to Charles Augustin Feriol, 24 July 1749, *Correspondence*, ed. Theodore Besterman, 51 vols (1968–77), Complete Works of Voltaire, vols 85–135, 95, p. III.
72 Voltaire, *Lettre à messieurs les auteurs des Etrennes de la Saint-Jean et autres beaux ouvrages*, ed. Mark Waddicor, Complete Works of Voltaire, 31B, p. 193. This work, first published in 1770, was probably written in about 1750; see Waddicor, p. 183.
73 Peter Hynes, 'From Richardson to Voltaire: *Nanine* and the Novelization of Comedy', *The Eighteenth Century: Theory and Interpretation* 31 (1990), 124.
74 Liliane Willens, *Voltaire's Comic Theatre: Composition, Conflict and Critics*, *Studies on Voltaire and the Eighteenth Century* 136 (1975), pp. 116–17.
75 Voltaire to Frederick II, 17 August 1749, Complete Works of Voltaire, 95, p. 133.
76 Voltaire to Charles Augustin Feriol, 16 May 1767, Complete Works of Voltaire, 116, pp. III–12.
77 *Nanine*, p. 33.
78 *Nanine*, pp. 57–9, and H. L. Bruce, 'Voltaire on the English Stage', *University of California Publications in Modern Philology* 8 (1918), 112–16.
79 Ginette Herry, intro. to Goldoni, *Pamela* (Arles: Actes Sud-Papiers, 1995), p. 5.
80 Goldoni's play appeared under several different titles. In 1750, it was performed as *Pamela, o sia la virtù premiata* (*Pamela, or virtue rewarded*). In 1753, it was first published as *La Pamela*. In 1761, it appeared as *Pamela fanciulla* (*Pamela as a young girl*) to distinguish it from Goldoni's own continuation, *Pamela maritata* (1760); in 1788, the title *Pamela nubile* was used. The English translation (1756) was entitled *Pamela. A Comedy*.
81 *Journal étranger* (February 1755), p. 197.
82 Goldoni, *Mémoires*, ed. Norbert Jonard (Paris: Aubier, 1992), p. 280.
83 For Goldoni's operatic versions of *Pamela*, see Mary Hunter, '*Pamela*: The Offspring of Richardson's Heroine in Eighteenth-Century Opera', *Mosaic* 18 (1985), 61–76; Ted A. Emery, 'Goldoni's *Pamela* from Play to Libretto', *Italica* 64 (1987), 572–82; and Jane V. Bertolino, *The Many Faces of Pamela* (Brooklyn: Vegas, 1990), pp. 37–45.
84 See Colin Duckworth, 'Madame Denis's unpublished *Pamela*: A Link between Richardson, Goldoni and Voltaire', *Studies on Voltaire and the Eighteenth Century* 76 (1970), 37–53; Kathleen M. Lynch, '*Pamela Nubile*, *L'Ecossaise*, and *The English Merchant*', *Modern Language Notes* 47 (1932), 94–6; and Edna Purdie, 'Some Adventures of *Pamela* on the Continental Stage', in *German Studies Presented to Professor H. G. Fiedler* (Oxford: Clarendon Press, 1938), pp. 352–84.
85 See Bertolino, *Many Faces*, pp. 53–60; Laurence Marsden Price, 'On the Reception of Richardson in Germany', *JEGP* 25 (1926), 7–33; and Paul Patrick Rogers, *Goldoni in Spain* (Oberlin, OH: Academy Press, 1941).
86 Sale, *Bibliographical Record*, p. 130.

87 Richardson to Erasmus Reich, 2 April 1757; McKillop, *Printer and Novelist*, p. 271. Nourse was also Fielding's bookseller, and puffed by Fielding in *The Champion* (21 October 1740); see Fielding, *Contributions to the Champion*, ed. Coley, p. 485.

88 *Monthly Review* 17 (July 1757), 40–50. For the attribution to James Grainger, a physician and poet, see Benjamin Christie Nangle, *The Monthly Review First Series 1749–1789: Indexes of Contributors and Articles* (Oxford: Clarendon Press, 1934), p. 115.

89 Link, 'First Operatic Versions', p. 278.

90 An Italian reviewer, Giuseppe Baretti, criticized Goldoni's alterations; see *La frusta letteraria*, nos. 17, 22 (1 June, 15 August 1764). But Baretti, who lived in England from 1751 to 1760, was a friend of Richardson, and might have been privy to Richardson's own attitude to Goldoni's lack of fidelity to the novel.

91 Emery, 'Goldoni's *Pamela*', p. 574.

92 After hearing of Olivia's attack on Sir Charles, Harriet Byron writes to Miss Selby that 'she appears to me as a Medusa' (*Sir Charles Grandison*, II, 388).

93 Fidelis Morgan and Giles Havergal, *Pamela or the Reform of a Rake* (Oxford: Amber Lane Press, 1987), p. 5.

94 Polesso herself directed the actors, the Robinson Dramatic Society of Cambridge, and took the part of Goldoni, a role that she created; see Paola Polesso, 'The Character of Pamela from Richardson's Novel to Goldoni's Comedy', *Restoration and Eighteenth-Century Theatre Research* 2nd series 10 (1995), 50 n.

5   *PAMELA* ILLUSTRATIONS AND THE VISUAL CULTURE
OF THE NOVEL

1 The *Sentimental Journey* fan is reproduced in Peter de Voogd, 'Sterne All the Fashion: A Sentimental Fan', *Shandean* 8 (1996), 133–6.

2 Ronald Paulson and Thomas Lockwood (eds), *Henry Fielding: The Critical Heritage* (London: Routledge, 1969), p. 155; Foxon, *English Verse*, I, 266 (F55).

3 Postlethwaite letters, MS 588, f. 166.

4 Postlethwaite letters, MS 589, f. 34; *'Your Affectionate and Loving Sister': The Correspondence of Barbara Kerrich and Elizabeth Postlethwaite, 1733 to 1751*, ed. Nigel Surry (Dereham: Larks Press, 2000), p. 44. In this selection from a massive family correspondence, Surry prints the letter describing the fan but not the others cited here on *Pamela*.

5 Stephanie Fysh, one of the few critics to take an interest in the *Pamela* fan, suggests that it 'probably contained several vignettes, anywhere from three (the most common) to the ten or twelve sometimes found' at the end of the century (*The Work(s) of Samuel Richardson* (Newark: University of Delaware Press, 1997), p. 77).

6 Pamela had previously escaped through her bedroom window, 'not without some Difficulty, sticking a little at my Shoulders and Hips' (p. 170), when a

captive at Mr B.'s Lincolnshire house, but since Mrs Jewkes is absent here, the later scene is more likely to have embellished the fan.

7 *Gentleman's Magazine* 10 (December 1740), 616. The poem appears to have been lifted from Sarah Dixon's *Poems on Several Occasions* (Canterbury, 1740); see Donald F. Bond, '*The Gentleman's Magazine*', *Modern Philology* 38 (1940), 94.

8 Fysh, *Work(s)*, p. 77.

9 Matilda Postlethwaite to Barbara Kerrich, 15 January 1742, MS 588, f. 168.

10 Matilda Postlethwaite to Barbara Kerrich, 5 March 1742, MS 588, f. 171; Elizabeth Postlethwaite to Barbara Kerrich, 27 March 1744, MS 589, f. 37.

11 See Sale, *Bibliographical Record*, p. 127. His observations are based on the copy of *The Life of Pamela* at Yale. The copy at the Houghton Library, Harvard, contains two additional engravings, which, as the catalogue notes, have apparently been inserted from another source, having nothing to do with *The Life of Pamela*.

12 Hanns Hammelmann and T. S. R. Boase, *Book Illustrators in Eighteenth-Century England* (New Haven: Yale University Press, 1975), p. 24.

13 Janet E. Aikins, 'Re-presenting the Body in *Pamela II*', in Jeffrey N. Cox and Larry J. Reynolds (eds), *New Historical Literary Study: Essays on Reproducing Texts, Representing History* (Princeton: Princeton University Press, 1993), p. 157.

14 Until recently, the only known copy of this spurious continuation was one without illustrations at the Houghton Library, Harvard. A copy acquired in 2002 by the Clark Library, Los Angeles, however, possesses the previously unrecorded frontispiece.

15 Sale, *Bibliographical Record*, pp. 3–4.

16 Samuel Richardson, *Aesop's Fables* (1739), p. xii.

17 Eaves and Kimpel, *Biography*, pp. 120–1.

18 Richardson adopted a similar strategy with his edition of *The Negotiations of Sir Thomas Roe* (1740), to which he added, in 1741, a frontispiece engraved by George Vertue, a year or so after the book was first published; see Sale, *Bibliographical Record*, pp. 6–7.

19 Hill to Richardson, 29 December 1740, Richardson, *Correspondence*, ed. Barbauld, I, 56.

20 Twenty years later, Laurence Sterne too resolved to gain an illustration by Hogarth as a frontispiece for the London edition of *Tristram Shandy*, and succeeded in doing so; see Ian Campbell Ross, *Laurence Sterne: A Life* (Oxford: Oxford University Press, 1999), pp. 5–6.

21 Hill to Richardson, *Works*, II, 164–5. The date given in Hill's *Works* (9 February 1741) may be inaccurate; part of the letter surviving in a manuscript copy (Forster MSS, XIII, 2, f. 45) is undated, and another part, printed in Richardson, *Correspondence*, ed. Barbauld, I, 59–66, is dated December 1740.

22 The 'ingenious Gentleman' is Aaron Hill, whose letter to Richardson of 9 February 1741 is quoted here.

23 T. C. Duncan Eaves, 'Graphic Illustration of the Novels of Samuel Richardson, 1740–1810', *Huntington Library Quarterly* 14 (1950–1), 351–2.

24 Marcia Epstein Allentuck, 'Narration and Illustration: The Problem of Richardson's *Pamela*', *Philological Quarterly* 51 (1972), 877.

25 Ronald Paulson, *Hogarth*, 3 vols (New Brunswick, NJ: Rutgers University Press, 1991–3), II, 187–8. Paulson asserts (p. 187), without providing evidence, that the engraver employed by Richardson for the second edition of *Pamela* was Gerard Vandergucht.

26 Janet E. Aikins suggests that Richardson's change of plans 'was not a rejection of Hogarth but of the frontispiece as a genre too limited in power' ('Richardson's "Speaking Pictures"', in Doody and Sabor (eds), *Tercentenary Essays*, p. 152).

27 Richardson to Allen, 8 October 1741, *Selected Letters*, ed. Carroll, p. 52.

28 Eaves, 'Graphic Illustration', p. 353.

29 No correspondence between either Gravelot or Hayman and Richardson has survived. Hayman painted a portrait of Richardson and his family, reproduced and dated 'towards the end of 1740' by Brian Allen (*Francis Hayman* (New Haven: Yale University Press, 1987), p. 30), but a date during or after Hayman's work on the *Pamela* illustrations is also possible.

30 Allen, *Francis Hayman*, p. 108.

31 Mark Girouard, 'Coffee at Slaughter's: English Art and the Rococo', in Girouard, *Town and Country* (New Haven: Yale University Press, 1992), p. 18.

32 Allentuck, 'Narration and Illustration', p. 880.

33 Peter Sabor, 'What Did Pamela Look Like?', *Notes and Queries* 228 (1983), 48–9.

34 Eaves, 'Graphic Illustration', p. 353.

35 Allentuck, 'Narration and Illustration', p. 880.

36 Raynie, 'Hayman and Gravelot's Anti-*Pamela* Designs for Richardson's Octavo Edition of *Pamela I* and *II*', *Eighteenth-Century Life* 23 (1999), 79.

37 Stephen A. Raynie, 'Hayman and Gravelot's Anti-*Pamela*', pp. 85, 89.

38 Richardson to Cheyne, early January 1742, Richardson, *Selected Letters*, ed. Carroll, p. 54.

39 As Aikins contends, in her pioneering study of Gravelot and Hayman's engravings for the final volumes, the artists take pains to emphasize Richardson's 'concern with pregnancy and sexual intimacy' that plays so large a role in the continuation of *Pamela* ('Re-presenting the Body', p. 166).

40 Sepia drawings for six of Gravelot's and one of Hayman's designs are at the British Museum, Department of Prints and Drawings. Sepia drawings for four of Gravelot's designs are at the Houghton Library, Harvard. Hayman's drawing is reproduced in Allen, *Francis Hayman*, p. 150.

41 *The Diary of Joseph Farington*, VIII, ed. Kathryn Cave (New Haven: Yale University Press, 1982), p. 2800; cited by Paulson, *Hogarth*, II, 65.

42 Hammelmann and Boase, *Book Illustrators*, p. 40.

43 For a complete list of Hayman's supper-box paintings of *c*. 1741–2, see Allen, *Francis Hayman*, pp. 180–2. Fysh writes well on the placing of the

Pamela paintings in relation to others at Vauxhall, and on the significance of Hayman's choice of subjects for the Vauxhall clientele (*Work(s)*, pp. 71–5). She wrongly supposes, however (p. 71), that both of the *Pamela* paintings have been lost. The painting at Sizergh Castle has been newly restored.

44 Eaves ('Graphic Illustration', p. 357) terms this a 'small, exquisite piece'.

45 The petition is reprinted in John B. Shipley, 'Samuel Richardson and *Pamela*', *Notes and Queries* 199 (1954), 28–9.

46 Allen, *Francis Hayman*, pp. 152–3. Allen discusses the surviving contract between Hanmer and Hayman, and Hanmer's remarkably detailed written instructions to Hayman concerning the Shakespeare engravings, which suggest the kind of guidance that Richardson might have given his own illustrators. See also W. M. Merchant, 'Francis Hayman's Illustrations of Shakespeare', *Shakespeare Quarterly* 9 (1958), 141–7, and Marcia Epstein Allentuck, 'Sir Thomas Hanmer Instructs Francis Hayman: An Editor's Notes to His Illustrator (1744)', *Shakespeare Quarterly* 27 (1976), 288–315.

47 Sale, *Bibliographical Record*, pp. 14–34.

48 Cheyne to Richardson, 13 December 1740, 2 May 1742, *Letters of Cheyne*, pp. 63, 93.

49 Warburton to Richardson, 28 December 1742, Richardson, *Correspondence*, ed. Barbauld, I, 133.

50 *The Correspondence of Edward Young, 1683–1765*, ed. Henry Pettit (Oxford: Clarendon Press, 1971), pp. 223–4.

51 Richardson to Osborne, 14 February 1759, Houghton Library, Harvard University.

52 Sale, *Bibliographical Record*, p. 22.

53 For *Clarissa*, however, Richardson printed an engraved folding plate, containing music to accompany Elizabeth Carter's 'Ode to Wisdom'. For an analysis of this plate and the expenses it entailed, see Janine Barchas, *Graphic Design, Print Culture, and the Eighteenth-Century Novel* (Cambridge: Cambridge University Press, 2003), pp. 92–117.

54 Eaves, 'Graphic Illustration', p. 357. The copy of the edition he describes (University of Chicago Library) contains, oddly, no engravings in volumes I–II of the novel, but all fifteen of the plates in volumes III–IV. In the British Library copy, volumes I–II are dated 1744 and volumes III–IV 1743, but the plates in volume I are dated 1742; plates in the other volumes are undated.

55 Yver's engraving is also used, without acknowledgment, as the frontispiece to a 1744 Italian edition of *Pamela*, translated by Giuseppe Bettinelli. A copy of this very rare edition, unseen by McKillop (*Printer and Novelist*, p. 100 n.), is now in the Clark Library.

56 The exception is an engraving used as the frontispiece for volume II, in which the engraver's name is listed as Wicker. This plate, depicting Pamela with her children in the nursery, based on Gravelot's final illustration for volume IV, is strangely misplaced as the frontispiece to a volume of the original novel.

57 Warren Mild, *Joseph Highmore of Holborn Row* (Ardmore, PA: Kingswood Group, 1990), p. 255.

58 Paulson, *Hogarth*, II, 239–45.

59 See Mario Praz, *Conversation Pieces: A Survey of the Informal Group Portrait in Europe and America* (University Park: Pennsylvania State University Press, 1971); and Ellen D'Oench, *The Conversation Piece: Arthur Devis and His Contemporaries* (New Haven: Yale University Press, 1980). Janet Aikins notes that in Richardson's continuation of *Pamela*, Lady Davers applies the term 'conversation piece' to Pamela's own letters ('Picturing "Samuel Richardson": Francis Hayman and the Intersections of Word and Image', *Eighteenth-Century Fiction* 14 (2002), 467–70).

60 *London Daily Post and General Advertiser*, 16–18, 20, 22–25 February 1744; Mild, *Joseph Highmore*, p. 259.

61 See Mild, *Joseph Highmore*, pp. 259–60.

62 An announcement in the *Daily Advertiser* for 15 July 1745 stated that the prints were now available; see Mild, *Joseph Highmore*, p. 262.

63 Each artist engraved six of the plates: Truchy numbers 1, 2, 7, 8, 10, and 11; Benoist the remainder. Paulson writes that they 'worked in a loose, informal style in imitation of Lépicié [who executed engravings after Chardin] or the engravings after Watteau' (*Hogarth*, II, 241).

64 Highmore kept the paintings in his studio until they were sold at his retirement sale of 5 March 1762; see Elizabeth Einberg and Judy Egerton, 'Joseph Highmore 1692–1780', in their *The Age of Hogarth: British Painters Born 1675–1709* (London: Tate Gallery, 1988), p. 50. The paintings are now divided among the Tate Gallery, London (1, 7, 9, 11), the Fitzwilliam Museum, Cambridge (2, 5, 6, 12), and the National Gallery of Victoria, Melbourne (3, 4, 8, 10).

65 See Mild, *Joseph Highmore*, pp. 255–8, and Louise M. Miller, 'Author, Artist, Reader: "The Spirit of the Passages" and the Illustrations to *Pamela*', *QWERTY* 4 (1994), 121–30.

66 For Highmore's later dealings with Richardson, see Mild, *Joseph Highmore*, pp. 284–324. The extant *Clarissa* painting, 'The Harlowe Family', is at the Yale Center for British Art. Mild suggests (p. 324) that a drawing in Highmore's scrapbook (Tate Gallery) is a sketch for his lost portrait of Clementina. Other preliminary sketches in the Tate scrapbook indicate that Highmore may at some point have contemplated a series of *Clarissa* illustrations along the lines of his *Pamela* paintings.

67 Eaves, 'Graphic Illustration', p. 362.

68 Einberg and Egerton, 'Joseph Highmore', p. 51. The broadsheet is reprinted, as they note, in Hugh Phillips, *Mid-Georgian London* (London: Collins, 1964), p. 68.

69 *Daily Advertiser*, 23 April 1745, repeated on 8 August. Richard D. Altick discusses the exhibition briefly as one of many evanescent eighteenth-century waxwork shows (*The Shows of London* (Cambridge, MA: Harvard University Press, 1978), p. 53). The Shoe Lane exhibition of *Pamela*, however, had a remarkably long run of sixteen months.

70 The advertisement was first quoted by Austin Dobson, *Samuel Richardson* (London: Macmillan, 1902), p. 47 n. Subsequent commentators provide sketchier versions.

71 Fysh, *Work(s)*, pp. 69–70.

72 *Daily Advertiser*, 19 November 1745, repeated on 21 December.

73 See Moore, *The Foundling*, ed. Amberg, p. 303.

74 McKillop (*Printer and Novelist*, p. 89) notes that in September 1742, 'William Bradford of Philadelphia was advertising *Pamela* in a long list of religious books.' Benjamin Franklin began printing his Philadelphia edition in 1742 but completed it only in 1744, sending 100 copies to be sold in Willamsburg and smaller lots to Boston and New York boooksellers (see James N. Green, 'Benjamin Franklin as Publisher and Bookseller', in J. A. Leo Lemay (ed.), *Reappraising Benjamin Franklin: A Bicentennial Perspective* (Newark: University of Delaware Press, 1993), pp. 102–3). Henry Wilder Foote suggests a date for Feke's portrait of 'a little later' than 1741–2, 'as the maturity of manner with which it is painted would seem to indicate' (*Robert Feke: Colonial Portrait Painter* (Cambridge, MA: Harvard University Press, 1930), p. 121). The painting, which remained in Feke's possession during his lifetime, was bequeathed by a descendant to the Rhode Island School of Design.

75 See John Ingamells and Robert Raines, 'A Catalogue of the Paintings, Drawings and Etchings of Philip Mercier', *Walpole Society* 46 (1976–8), p. 45, no. 174, who tentatively date the painting 1743–5. Examining Mercier's paintings of Pamela is difficult, since all are in private hands.

76 Only one of these is listed in Ingamells and Raines, 'Catalogue', no. 175, also dated 1743–5.

77 This version, not in Ingamells and Raines, was sold at Christie's, 14 July 1989, lot 72. The catalogue states that it was 'probably commissioned by the [anonymous] vendor's family when the artist was working in Ireland in 1746/7'. The other versions might have been painted at about the same time.

78 These two paintings, not in Ingamells and Raines, were sold at Christie's, 24 November 1978, lots 103, 102. Turner ('Novel Panic', p. 86) links the stockings in the second painting to Mr B.'s gift of 'Stockens' in the novel (*Pamela*, p. 19). He adds that 'Mercier (like Highmore) captures her taking those garments off'; she seems clearly, however, to be pulling the stockings on.

79 Another portrait by Mercier, painted in four versions (Ingamells and Raines, nos. 205–8), uses the same artist's model. Ingamells and Raines (p. 49) suggest that the subject 'is possibly taken from Richardson's *Pamela*', but there is nothing to link the paintings with the novel. C. L. Berry shows that the former identification of the subject as Clementine Walkinshaw is also erroneous ('Portraits of Clementine Walkinshaw', *Notes and Queries* 196 (1951), 491–5).

80 Turner, 'Novel Panic', p. 85.

81 *Daily Advertiser*, 21 September 1750. For an account of the Fleet Street printshop, owned by Elizabeth Griffin, see Timothy Clayton, *The English Print, 1688–1802* (New Haven: Yale University Press, 1997), pp. 108–9.

82 A copy of Heudelot's engraving was sold with the first version of Mercier's painting of Pamela getting out of bed at Christie's, 29 June 1934, lot 35. We have not located copies of the Chambers or the Heudelot print.

83 Eaves, 'Graphic Illustration', p. 364.

84 *London Magazine* 25 (1756), 379–81.

85 The subjects and headings of Lodge's engravings are listed by Eaves, 'Graphic Illustration', p. 364 n. A facsimile reprint of this edition was published in 1929 by A. Edward Newton, Berwyn, Pennsylvania. An unsigned note in the *Times Literary Supplement*, 6 March 1930, 'Newbery's Edition of "Pamela", 1769', describes Lodge's work as 'six delightful little full-page illustrations' (p. 196), but the piece was written to promote Newton's facsimile reprint.

86 Eaves, 'Graphic Illustration', pp. 364–5, and 'An Unrecorded Children's Book Illustrated by Thomas Bewick', *The Library* 5th series 5 (1951), 272–3.

87 See Robert D. Mayo, *The English Novel in the Magazines, 1740–1815* (Evanston, IL: Northwestern University Press, 1962), pp. 363–7; G. E. Bentley, Jr, *Blake Books* (Oxford: Clarendon Press, 1977), pp. 597–602; and Carol de Saint Victor, '*The Novelist's Magazine*', in Sullivan (ed.), *British Literary Magazines*, pp. 261–3.

88 Charles Lamb, 'To T. Stothard, Esq.', *Athenaeum*, 21 December 1833, p. 871; see Eaves, 'Graphic Illustration', p. 366.

89 See T. C. Duncan Eaves, 'Edward Burney's Illustrations to *Evelina*', *PMLA* 62 (1947), 995–9.

90 Hammelmann and Boase, *Book Illustrators*, pp. 21–3.

91 For the conjectural date, see Hester Davenport, *Faithful Handmaid: Fanny Burney at the Court of George III* (Stroud, Gloucestershire: Sutton, 2000), pp. 191–3. The portrait is in the National Portrait Gallery, London.

6 COMMERCIAL MORALITY, COLONIAL NATIONALISM, AND *PAMELA*'S IRISH RECEPTION

1 Swift estimated in 1732 that Margaret Tenison was worth £1,600 a year (Swift to Gay and the Duchess of Queensbury, 12 August 1732, *The Correspondence of Jonathan Swift*, ed. David Woolley (Frankfurt: Peter Lang, 2000–), III, 524). She died in December 1741, and in 1743 Delany married another wealthy English widow of superior rank, the talented Mary Granville Pendarves.

2 T. C. Barnard, *A New Anatomy of Ireland: The Irish Protestants, 1649–1770* (New Haven: Yale University Press, 2003), p 25, quoting Delany's *Twenty Sermons on Social Duties* (1747), p. 428; *Sixteen Discourses upon Doctrines and Duties* (1754), p. 235.

3 *Memoirs of Laetitia Pilkington*, I, 283; Andrew Carpenter (ed.), *Verse in English from Eighteenth-Century Ireland* (Cork: Cork University Press, 1998), p. 29.

4 Patrick Delany to Richardson, 21 January 1741, Forster MSS, XVI, 1, f. 42; 7 January 1742, f. 41. Alternatively, Swift may have seen or heard of the novel by way of George Faulkner, as suggested by Peter Sabor, '"A large Portion of our ethereal Fire": Swift and Samuel Richardson', in Hermann J. Real and Helgard Stöver-Leidig (eds), *Reading Swift: Papers from the Fourth Münster Symposium on Jonathan Swift* (Munich: Wilhelm Fink, 2003), p. 368 n.

5 Mary Barber, *Poems on Several Occasions* (1735), pp. vii (Swift's dedicatory letter), 17 ('An Unanswerable Apology for the Rich', lines 3–4). See also Adam Budd, '"Merit in Distress": The Troubled Success of Mary Barber', *Review of English Studies* 53, No. 210 (2002), 206.

6 *Shamela* was issued in Dublin by Oliver Nelson on 15 April 1741, a mere thirteen days after the London edition, priced sixpence and thus severely undercutting the London price of 1s 6d. The first volume of *Pamela's Conduct* was published in London on 28 May 1741 for three shillings; a Faulkner–Nelson edition was on sale in Dublin within a month, undercutting the London price by sixpence and bound to match the Irish reprint of *Pamela. Joseph Andrews*, like *Pamela* itself, cost six shillings when published in London in February 1742; in this case, the Irish publishers – Faulkner, George Ewing and William Smith – sold their edition three months later, in May 1742, at the knockdown price of 2s 8d, but a second Dublin edition was not called for until 1747.

7 Mary Barber to Richardson, 26 August 1741, Forster MSS, XVI, 1, f. 53.

8 Samuel Richardson, *An Address to the Public, on the Treatment Which the Editor of . . . Sir Charles Grandison Has Met with from Certain Booksellers and Printers in Dublin* (1754), p. 9, quoting a letter to him of 12 November 1741 from an unnamed Dublin printer.

9 *Faulkner's Dublin Journal*, 27–31 January 1741. The same technique of addressing purchasers by rank was to return in the case of *Clarissa*, when Faulkner offered a special binding service to the 'great Numbers of Nobility and Gentry' who had purchased the first instalment (*Faulkner's Dublin Journal*, 3 May 1748, quoted by Richard Cargill Cole, *Irish Booksellers and English Writers, 1740–1800* (London: Mansell, 1986), p. 64).

10 The prejudices displayed on both sides of the *Grandison* quarrel echo in modern scholarship. For Eaves and Kimpel, the Irish booksellers' justification for literary theft as national entitlement was made 'to Richardson's bewilderment though perhaps not to the bewilderment of those better acquainted with that nation' (*Biography*, p. 380); for Kathryn Temple, 'Richardon's response to Irish contamination, to its "vileness" and "wickedness", represents a textual playing out of . . . the brutality behind English tolerance' ('Printing Like a Post-Colonialist: The Irish Piracy of *Sir Charles Grandison*', *Novel* 33 (2000), 169). For an even-handed account of this 'case of grand biblio-larceny' in which Richardson, though 'indeed the victim of moral turpitude', was also guilty of reacting with 'frothy madness', see James W. Phillips, *Printing and Bookselling in Dublin, 1670–1800: A Bibliographical Enquiry* (Dublin: Irish Academic Press, 1998), pp. 111–14.

11 Book-smuggling from Ireland persisted after this date, however; see Cole, *Irish Booksellers*, pp. 66–87.
12 *Faulkner's Dublin Journal*, 22–5 December 1741.
13 Richardson, *Address to the Public*, p. 22. See also his letter to Lady Echlin at the height of his outrage over the *Grandison* theft: 'The two last Volumes of Pamela had been stolen from my Press before Publication, but the Theft was not attended with such flagrant Circumstances of Baseness as this was' (24 November 1753, Berg Library).
14 *Faulkner's Dublin Journal*, 20–4 April 1742.
15 Mary Pollard, *Dictionary of Members of the Dublin Book Trade* (London: Bibliographical Society, 2000), p. 19; see also Phillips, *Printing and Bookselling*, pp. 111–12, 132–4.
16 Barber to Richardson, 26 August 1741, Forster MSS, XVI, 1, f. 53.
17 *The Reformer*, No. 1 (28 January 1748), partly quoted by Thomas McLoughlin, *Contesting Ireland: Irish Voices Against England in the Eighteenth Century* (Dublin: Four Courts Press, 1999), p 168.
18 T. C. Barnard, '"Grand Metropolis" or "The Anus of the World"? The Cultural Life of Eighteenth-Century Dublin', in Peter Clark and Raymond Gillespie (eds), *Two Capitals: London and Dublin, 1500–1840* (Proceedings of the British Academy 107. Oxford: Oxford University Press, 2001), p. 206.
19 T. C. Barnard, *New Anatomy of Ireland*, pp. 2, 256. On Swift's ambivalence towards the indigenous Irish, see Claude Rawson, *God, Gulliver, and Genocide: Barbarism and the European Imagination, 1492–1945* (Oxford: Oxford University Press, 2001), pp. 182–255.
20 J. C. Beckett, 'Literature in English, 1691–1800', in T. W. Moody and W. E. Vaughan (eds), *Eighteenth-Century Ireland, 1691–1800* (Oxford: Clarendon Press, 1986), p. 424.
21 Nicholas Canny, 'Identity Formation in Ireland: The Emergence of the Anglo-Irish', in Nicholas Canny and Anthony Pagden (eds), *Colonial Identity in the Atlantic World, 1500–1800* (Princeton: Princeton University Press, 1987), p. 159.
22 For this phenomenon see J. G. Simms, *Colonial Nationalism, 1698–1776* (Cork: Cork University Press, 1976), and J. L. McCracken, 'Protestant Ascendancy and the Rise of Colonial Nationalism, 1714–60', in Moody and Vaughan (eds), *Eighteenth-Century Ireland*, pp. 105–22; for the literary dimension, see also McLoughlin, *Contesting Ireland*, pp. 9–40, 211–38.
23 See Beckett, 'Literature in English', pp. 458–9. For an acrimonious instance of the confusion caused in literary studies by this usage in Swift, see the debate generated by Warren Montag's attempt to correct Carole Fabricant in *Eighteenth-Century Fiction* 9 (1996), 101–2, 337–41; 11 (1997), 101–6, 363–6.
24 McLoughlin, *Contesting Ireland*, p. 11.
25 *Vertue Rewarded; or, The Irish Princess*, ed. Hubert McDermott (Gerrards Cross: Smythe, 1992), p. xi.
26 Canny, 'Identity Formation', p. 206; see also pp. 201–2.
27 Christopher Morash, *A History of Irish Theatre, 1601–2000* (Cambridge: Cambridge University Press, 2002), pp. 40, 41.

28 Charles Shadwell, *Irish Hospitality; or, Virtue Rewarded* (1717), in *The Works of Mr. Charles Shadwell* (Dublin, 1720), I, 246.

29 Ewha Chung, *Samuel Richardson's New Nation: Paragons of the Domestic Sphere and 'Native' Virtue* (New York: Peter Lang, 1998), pp. 23–4; see also Gerald Newman, *The Rise of English Nationalism: A Cultural History, 1740–1830* (New York: St Martin's Press, 1987).

30 Cheny, *Historical List* (1742), pp. 29, 64; (1744), p. 71; (1746), p. 77; (1747), p. 51; (1748), pp. 58, 84. On the penal legislation and Sir Edward O'Brien, see Moody and Vaughan (eds), *Eighteenth-Century Ireland*, pp. 16, 47.

31 John C. Greene and Gladys L. H. Clark, *The Dublin Stage, 1720–1745: A Calendar of Plays, Entertainments, and Afterpieces* (Bethlehem, PA: Lehigh University Press, 1993), pp. 294–5.

32 Greene and Clark, *Dublin Stage*, p. 45; Morash, *History of Irish Theatre*, pp. 37–8.

33 W. R. Chetwood, *A General History of the Stage* (1749), quoted in Highfill et al., *Biographical Dictionary*, III, 193.

34 *Faulkner's Dublin Journal*, 16–20 June 1741.

35 *Remarks on Two Letters Signed Theatricus and Hibernicus* (Dublin, 1754), quoted by Morash, *History of Irish Theatre*, pp. 65–6.

36 Benjamin Victor, *The History of the Theatres of London and Dublin* (1761), I, 97–8, quoted by Esther K. Sheldon, *Thomas Sheridan of Smock-Alley* (Princeton: Princeton University Press, 1967), p. 86.

37 *A Full Vindication of Thomas Sheridan, Esq.* (Dublin, 1758), p. 17.

38 Morash, *History of Irish Theatre*, p. 46.

39 Sheldon, *Thomas Sheridan*, p. 26; Sheldon cites Sheridan's holograph version from the LeFanu MSS, in private hands.

40 *Daily Gazetteer*, 5 January 1744; McKillop, *Printer and Novelist*, p. 88, citing *Flying Post*, 31 March 1744.

41 Sale, *Bibliographical Record*, p. 129; Foxon, *English Verse*, items P25, P26.

42 J---- W----, *Pamela; or, The Fair Impostor* (Dublin, 1743), i. 40; iii. 86; iii. 121–2. On eighteenth-century Irish pronunciation as deployed by Swift, see Jonathan Pritchard, 'Swift's Irish Rhymes', *Studies in Philology*, forthcoming; on 'Dean' specifically, see Pat Rogers's edition of Swift's *Complete Poems* (Harmondsworth: Penguin, 1983), p. 781 n. ('the common Irish pronunciation "dane" . . . became a regular practice in Swift's later verse').

43 *Poems Written Occasionally by John Winstanley* (Dublin, 1742), p. 125; a second volume appeared posthumously in 1751. Several Winstanley poems are reprinted in Carpenter (ed.), *Verse in English*, pp. 271–7; he also makes the *Field Day Anthology*.

44 Claude Rawson, 'An Epidemical Phrenzy', *Times Literary Supplement* (14 December 2001), p. 4.

45 Terry Eagleton, *Crazy John and the Bishop and Other Essays on Irish Culture* (Cork: Cork University Press, 1998), p. 2.

46 It further indicates the sequence of publication that the London reprint tidies up the floating syntax here: 'Feign fearful Flights, yet gain Advantage too, |

And sometimes this, and sometimes that pursue'. Stylistic revision is quite extensive in the London text, which may even record authorial correction.

47 Pope, *The Rape of the Lock* (hereafter *RL*), i. 63–4; i. 65–6.

48 See Valerie Rumbold, *Women's Place in Pope's World* (Cambridge: Cambridge University Press, 1989), pp. 48–82.

49 Christine Gerrard, *The Patriot Opposition to Walpole: Poetry, Politics, and National Myth, 1725–1742* (Oxford: Clarendon Press, 1994); see especially pp. 3–18 and her remarks on Aaron Hill's role, pp. 49–54.

50 Jerry C. Beasley, *Novels of the 1740s* (Athens: University of Georgia Press, 1982), p. 172.

51 Quoted by Betty Rizzo in her biography of McCarthy in Janet Todd (ed.), *A Dictionary of British and American Women Writers, 1660–1800* (Totowa, NJ: Rowman & Littlefield, 1987), p. 204.

52 Charlotte McCarthy, *The Fair Moralist; or, Love and Virtue*, 2nd edn (1746), p. 205.

53 McCarthy, *Fair Moralist*, 2nd edn, p. 82; cf. p. 39. On this trope and its complication in Swift, see Rawson, *God, Gulliver, and Genocide*, pp. 79–91.

54 Beasley, *Novels of the 1740s*, p. 174.

55 In Todd (ed.), *Dictionary of Women Writers*, p. 205.

56 Lady Mary Wortley Montagu to Lady Bute, 17–25 October 1750, *Complete Letters*, II, 470; Emmett L. Avery, 'The Summer Theatrical Seasons at Richmond and Twickenham, 1746–1753', *Notes and Queries* 173 (1937), 313.

57 Sheldon, *Thomas Sheridan*, p. 346.

58 *A Dramatic Burlesque of Two Acts, Call'd Mock-Pamela* (Dublin, 1750), p. 36.

59 *Joseph Andrews and Shamela*, pp. 310, 317. Fielding is scoring off Aaron Hill in these adjectival pile-ups (see, e.g., *Pamela*, p. 506: 'a poor Girl's little, innocent, Story'), and the technique returns elsewhere in *Mock-Pamela*, e.g. p. 9, where Gudgeon is interrupted in saying 'My charming, sweet, lovely, everlasting – hey!'

60 Richardson to Sarah Wescomb, 6 August 1750, Forster MSS, XIV, 3, f. 53.

61 Richardson, *Aesop's Fables*, p. 62 (fable 77).

62 Undated note, Forster MSS, XVI, 1, f. 78; see also XVI, 1, f. 56.

AFTERWORD

1 Clara Reeve, *The Progress of Romance* (Colchester, 1785), I, 135. Reeve also appeals to the authority of Martha Bridgen in a fawning dedication to the 1780 edition of her novel, *The Old English Baron*, first published as *The Champion of Virtue* (1777). Jeanine M. Casler suggests that Reeve's 'strong feeling of kinship with Pamela' stems from her own experience of domestic service (Reeve, *The School for Widows*, ed. Casler (Newark: University of Delaware Press, 2003), p. 27).

2 *Gentleman's Magazine* 56 (1786), 15–17, 117–18.

3 Macaulay's volume received an extensive, favourable review by Mary Wollstonecraft in the *Analytical Review*, 1790; see Bridget Hill, *The*

Republican Virago: The Life and Times of Catharine Macaulay, Historian (Oxford: Clarendon Press, 1992), p. 162.

4 Derek Hughes (ed.), *Eighteenth-Century Women Playwrights*, vol. VI, *Elizabeth Inchbald*, ed. Angela J. Smallwood (London: Pickering & Chatto, 2001), p. 127. Smallwood provides a fuller account of Mercier's and Inchbald's contrasting use of *Pamela* in a forthcoming essay, 'Jacobites and Jacobins: Fielding's Legacy in the Later 18th-Century London Theatre' in the proceedings of the Fielding commemorative conference held at Yale University in October 2004, ed. Claude Rawson (Newark: University of Delaware Press).

5 Mary Hays, 'On Novel Writing', *Monthly Magazine* 4 (1797), 180–1; see Eleanor Ty, *Unsex'd Revolutionaries: Five Women Novelists of the 1790s* (Toronto: University of Toronto Press, 1993), p. 65.

6 Mary Robinson, *A Letter to the Women of England and The Natural Daughter*, ed. Sharon M. Setzer (Peterborough, ON: Broadview, 2003), pp. 210–11. Eleanor Ty, discussing this passage, suggests that 'a girl who maintains her innocence was no longer a feasible model for women of the 1790s' (*Empowering the Feminine: The Narratives of Mary Robinson, Jane West, and Amelia Opie, 1796–1812* (Toronto: University of Toronto Press, 1998), p. 74).

7 Marilyn Butler, *Jane Austen and the War of Ideas* (Oxford: Clarendon Press, rev. edn, 1987).

8 The obscure Miss Pilkington is often confused with the better-known miscellaneous writer, Mary Pilkington.

9 'Character of the Life and Writings of Mr. Samuel Richardson', *Lady's Magazine* 24 (1793), 202.

10 Hogg had already, the announcement declared, published new editions of Richardson's three 'celebrated Novels'; purchasers could now obtain these separately or order them in sixpenny weekly instalments, as printed in the *New Novelist's Magazine* (9, 4).

11 See Robert R. Bataille, '*The New Lady's Magazine*', in Sullivan (ed.), *British Literary Magazines*, p. 247; and Mayo, *English Novel in the Magazines*, p. 569. Bataille describes this decision by Alexander Hogg, the magazine's publisher, as 'a desperate strategy to save his publication'.

12 In March 1795, Hogg again addressed these subscribers, informing them that they could obtain *Pamela* either by buying the run of the *New Novelist's Magazine* for the previous year or by backdating their current subscriptions to the *New Lady's Magazine* to July 1794, the first instalment of the current serialization, which included both parts of the novel and was continuing with 'universal Applause' (10, 34).

13 Frank Gees Black, *The Epistolary Novel in the Late Eighteenth Century: A Descriptive and Bibliographical Study* (Eugene: University of Oregon Press, 1940), p. 99.

14 *Anthologia Hibernica* 1 (May 1793), 366; cited by Tasch, *Dramatic Cobbler*, p. 80.

15 *Nanine*, ed. Labriolle and Duckworth, pp. 33–4, and Phyllis S. Robinove, 'Voltaire's Theater on the Parisian Stage, 1789–1799', *French Review* 32 (1958–9), 534–8.

16 *Nanine*, ed. Labriolle and Duckworth, p. 33; R. S. Ridgway, *Voltaire and Sensibility* (Montreal: McGill-Queen's University Press, 1973), p. 217.

17 See Cecilia Feilla, 'Performing Virtue: *Pamela* on the French Revolutionary Stage, 1793', *The Eighteenth Century* 43 (2002), 286–305, and Lynn Festa, 'Sentimental Bonds and Revolutionary Characters: Richardson's *Pamela* in England and France', in Margaret Cohen and Carolyn Dever (eds), *The Literary Channel: The Inter-National Invention of the Novel* (Princeton: Princeton University Press, 2002), pp. 73–105.

18 Henry Seidel Canby, '*Pamela* Abroad', *Modern Language Notes* 18 (1903), 211–12.

19 Neufchâteau, *François de Neufchâteau, auteur de Paméla, à la Convention nationale* (Paris, 1793).

20 Festa, 'Sentimental Bonds', p. 91. Many of the documents concerning Neufchâteau's arrest and hearing are reprinted in *Archives parlementaires de 1787 à 1860* 74 (Paris, 1879). Various other sources are cited by Feilla and Festa.

21 Barbauld, intro. to Richardson, *Correspondence*, ed. Barbauld, I, lxiii, lxvi–lxvii, lxxvii.

22 *Critical Review* 3rd series 3 (1804), 162; *Monthly Review* 2nd series 46 (1805), 29; *The Sentinel*, December 1804, pp. 372–6; *Edinburgh Review* 5 (1804), 27.

23 James Lackington, *Memoirs of the First Forty-Five Years of the Life of James Lackington*, 2nd edn. (London, 1791), pp. 386–7.

24 Peter Sabor, 'The Cooke–Everyman Edition of *Pamela*', *The Library* 32 (1977), 360.

25 *Hanes Pamela: Neu Ddiweirdeb Wedi ei Wobrwyo* (Caerfyrddin, 1818). A copy is in the British Library.

26 This edition was reprinted, with further slight corrections, in 1810, and then issued as an expurgated Routledge 'yellow-back' edition in 1873; see Eaves and Kimpel, 'Richardson's Revisions of *Pamela*', and Gaskell, *From Writer to Reader*, p. 77. In his Introduction to *Pamela* (pp. xxxiii–xxxiv) Keymer suggests that both Anne Richardson and her sister Martha Bridgen may have played a significant part in revising the text.

27 Among the editions based on Cooke's abridgment was one published by R. Evans in Spitalsfields, London, in 1816, with six illustrations depicting the characters in elegant Regency dress. It was one in a series of stereotyped, double-column editions, all first published in inexpensive numbered parts: *Pamela* in twenty-five sixpenny instalments.

28 See Sabor, 'Cooke–Everyman', p. 366, and Gaskell, *From Writer to Reader*, pp. 77–8.

29 *Byron's Letters and Journals*, ed. Leslie A. Marchand, VIII (Cambridge, MA: Harvard University Press, 1978), 11.

30 Swift, *Tale of a Tub*, p. 206.
31 A copy was recently acquired by the Clark Library, Los Angeles; no other copies have been recorded.
32 This copy, now at Stanford, was first described by John E. Mustain, 'Eighteenth-Century Highlights of the Kline/Roethke Collection at Stanford University', *East-Central Intelligencer* n.s. 16.3 (2002), 4.

Select bibliography

The emphasis of the bibliography is on works directly related to the *Pamela* controversy. Other works are cited in the notes to each chapter but excluded here, as are minor items such as magazine verses, book reviews, and newspaper advertisements and leaders. Items in the primary bibliography marked with an asterisk are reprinted in Thomas Keymer and Peter Sabor (eds), *The Pamela Controversy: Criticisms and Adaptations of Samuel Richardson's Pamela, 1740–1750*, 6 vols (London: Pickering & Chatto, 2001).

MANUSCRIPTS

Highmore, Joseph. Scrapbook, Tate Gallery, London.

Kelly, John. 'The Islanders, or Mad Orphan', British Library, Kings MSS, 301.

Postlethwaite, Elizabeth. Family Correspondence, Corpus Christi College, Cambridge, Parker Library, MSS 588–9.

Richardson, Samuel. Correspondence, Harvard University, Houghton Library.

Correspondence, New York Public Library, Henry W. and Albert A. Berg Collection.

Correspondence, Rice University, Fondren Library.

Correspondence and related papers, Victoria and Albert Museum, London, Forster MSS, 48 E5–48 E10 (vols XI–XVI).

Spence, Joseph. 'Letters from a Maid-Servant Lately Come to Town, To Her Relations in Hamshire', Yale University, Beinecke Library, Osborn Collection.

Miscellaneous documents relating to the lives of John Kelly, Samuel Richardson and Benjamin Slocock, Public Record Office (National Archives), London.

PRIMARY

Alcock, John ['John Piper']. *The Life of Miss Fanny Brown*. London, 1761.

Bar, Georges-Louis de. *Epîtres diverses sur des sujets différens*. 3 vols. Paris, 1745–55.

Beckford, William ['Jacquetta Agneta Mariana Jenks']. *Azemia. A Descriptive and Sentimental Novel.* 2 vols. London, 1797.

['Lady Harriet Marlow']. *Modern Novel Writing; or, The Elegant Enthusiast.* 2 vols. London, 1798.

*Bennet, George. *Pamela Versified; or, Virtue Rewarded. An Heroic Poem.* London, 1741; extract in *Scots Magazine* 3 (October 1741), 453–4.

Bickerstaff, Isaac. *The Plays of Isaac Bickerstaff,* ed. Peter A. Tasch. New York: Garland, 1981.

Boissy, Louis de. *Paméla en France, ou la vertu mieux éprouvée.* Paris, 1743.

Brooke, Frances. *The Excursion,* ed. Paula R. Backscheider and Hope D. Cotton. Lexington: University Press of Kentucky, 1997.

[?]. 'Memoirs of the Life and Writings of Mr. Samuel Richardson'. *Universal Magazine* 78 (January 1786), 16–21, and (February 1786), 73–7.

Rosina, ed. John Drummond. London: Stainer and Bell, 1998.

Brooke, Henry. *Juliet Grenville; or, The History of the Human Heart.* 3 vols. London, 1774.

Byron, George Gordon, Lord. *Byron's Letters and Journals,* ed. Leslie A. Marchand. 13 vols. Cambridge, MA: Harvard University Press, 1973–94.

Carpenter, Andrew (ed.). *Verse in English from Eighteenth-Century Ireland.* Cork: Cork University Press, 1998.

Cavendish, Georgiana, Duchess of Devonshire [?]. *The Sylph,* intro. Amanda Foreman. York: Henry Parker, 2001.

'Character of the Life and Writings of Mr. Samuel Richardson'. *Lady's Magazine* 24 (April 1793), 202–4.

Cheny, John. *An Historical List of Horse-Matches Run.* London, 1741 and later years.

Cheyne, George. *The Letters of Doctor George Cheyne to Samuel Richardson (1733–1743),* ed. Charles F. Mullett. Columbia: University of Missouri, 1943.

The Chronicle of the Canningites and Egyptians or Gipseyites. London, 1754.

Cleland, John. *Memoirs of a Woman of Pleasure,* ed. Peter Sabor. Oxford: Oxford University Press, 1985.

The Surprises of Love. London, 1764.

'Cock, Samuel' [pseud.]. *A Voyage to Lethe.* London, 1742.

Coventry, Francis. *The History of Pompey the Little,* ed. Robert A. Day. London: Oxford University Press, 1974.

Critical Remarks on Sir Charles Grandison, Clarissa and Pamela, 'By a Lover of Virtue', intro. Alan Dugald McKillop. Augustan Reprint Society no. 21. Los Angeles: Clark Memorial Library, 1950.

*Dance, James [?]. *Pamela; or, Virtue Triumphant.* London, 1741.

Danchin, Pierre (ed.). *The Prologues and Epilogues of the Eighteenth Century.* Nancy: Presses Universitaires de Nancy, 1990– .

D'Aucour, Claude Godard. *La Déroute des Paméla.* Paris, 1744.

Davys, Mary. *The Reform'd Coquet, Familiar Letters betwixt a Gentleman and a Lady, and The Accomplish'd Rake,* ed. Martha F. Bowden. Lexington: University Press of Kentucky, 1999.

Desfontaines, Pierre François Guyot. Letter 429. *Observations sur les écrits modernes* 29 (June 1742), 193–214.

*Dorman, Joseph ['Mr. Edge']. *Pamela; or, Virtue Rewarded. An Opera.* Newcastle, 1742.

A Dramatic Burlesque of Two Acts, Call'd Mock-Pamela: or, A Kind Caution to Country Coxcombs. Dublin, 1750.

'Eden, Adam' [pseud.]. *A Vindication of the Reformation, on Foot, among the Ladies, to Abolish Modesty and Chastity.* London, 1755.

The Feelings of the Heart; or, The History of a Country Girl. 2 vols. London, 1772.

The Female Soldier; or, The Surprising Life and Adventures of Hannah Snell, intro. Dianne Dugaw. Augustan Reprint Society no. 257. Los Angeles: Clark Memorial Library, 1989.

Fielding, Henry. *Amelia*, ed. Martin C. Battestin. Oxford: Clarendon Press, 1988.

Contributions to the Champion and Related Writings, ed. W. B. Coley. Oxford: Clarendon Press, 2001.

An Enquiry into the Causes of the Late Increase of Robbers and Related Writings, ed. Malvin R. Zirker. Oxford: Clarendon Press, 1988.

The History of Tom Jones, A Foundling, ed. Martin C. Battestin and Fredson Bowers. 2 vols. Oxford: Clarendon Press, 1974.

Joseph Andrews, ed. Martin C. Battestin. Oxford: Clarendon Press, 1967.

Joseph Andrews and Shamela, ed. Douglas Brooks-Davies, revd and intro. by Thomas Keymer. Oxford: Oxford University Press, 1999.

Miscellanies, Volume One, ed. Henry Knight Miller. Oxford: Clarendon Press, 1972.

Plays, Volume I, 1728–1731, ed. Thomas Lockwood. Oxford: Clarendon Press, 2004.

Fielding, Sarah. *The History of the Countess of Dellwyn.* 2 vols. London, 1759.

Foote, Samuel. *Samuel Foote's Primitive Puppet-Shew Featuring Piety in Pattens: A Critical Edition*, ed. Samuel N. Bogorad and Robert Gale Noyes. *Theatre Survey* 14. 1a (Fall, 1973).

The Fortunate Country Maid. 2 vols. London, 1741.

Fowkes, Martha. *Clio: The Autobiography of Martha Fowkes Sansom (1689–1736)*, ed. Phyllis J. Guskin. Newark: University of Delaware Press, 1997.

A Full Vindication of Thomas Sheridan, Esq. Dublin, 1758.

Garrick, David. *The Letters of David Garrick*, ed. David M. Little and George M. Kahrl. 3 vols. London: Oxford University Press, 1963.

Genuine and Impartial Memoirs of Elizabeth Canning. London, 1754.

Giffard, Henry. *Memoirs of Sir Charles Goodville and his Family, in a Series of Letters to a Friend.* 2 vols. London, 1753.

Pamela. A Comedy. London, 1741.

Goldoni, Carlo. *Mémoires*, ed. Norbert Jonard. Paris: Aubier, 1992.

Pamela, ed. Ginette Herry. Arles: Actes Sud-Papiers, 1995.

Pamela. A Comedy. London, 1756.

Hays, Mary. *Letters and Essays, Moral and Miscellaneous.* London, 1793.

'On Novel Writing'. *Monthly Magazine* 4 (1797), 180–1.

*Haywood, Eliza. *Anti-Pamela*, and Henry Fielding, *Shamela*, ed. Catherine Ingrassia. Peterborough, ON: Broadview, 2004.

The History of Jemmy and Jenny Jessamy. 3 vols. London, 1753.

The History of Miss Betsy Thoughtless, ed. Christine E. Blouch. Peterborough, ON: Broadview, 1998.

Secret Histories, Novels, and Poems, 3rd edn. 4 vols. London, 1732.

Selected Works of Eliza Haywood, ed. Alexander Pettit *et al.*, 6 vols. London: Pickering & Chatto, 2000–1.

The Virtuous Villager. 2 vols. London, 1742.

Hill, Aaron. *The Works of the Late Aaron Hill*, 2nd edn. 4 vols. London, 1754.

The History of the Stage. In which is included the Theatrical Characters of the most Celebrated Actors who have adorn'd the Theatre. London, 1742.

Holberg, Ludvig. *Moral Reflections and Epistles*, trans. P. M. Mitchell. Norwich: Norvik Press, 1991.

Moralske Tanker, ed. F. J. Billeskov Jansen and Jørgen Hunosøe. Copenhagen: Borgen, 1992.

Inchbald, Elizabeth. *Next Door Neighbours*. In Derek Hughes (ed.), *Eighteenth-Century Women Playwrights*, vol. VI, *Elizabeth Inchbald*, ed. Angela J. Smallwood. London: Pickering & Chatto, 2001.

Kelly, John. *The Levee*. London, 1741.

*[?]. 'Pamela the Second'. *The Universal Spectator, or Weekly Journal*, 24 April– 8 May 1742.

Pamela's Conduct in High Life. 2 vols. London, 1741.

Kerrich, Barbara, and Elizabeth Postlethwaite. *'Your Affectionate and Loving Sister': The Correspondence of Barbara Kerrich and Elizabeth Postlethwaite, 1733 to 1751*, ed. Nigel Surry. Dereham: Larks Press, 2000.

Keymer, Thomas, and Peter Sabor (eds). *The Pamela Controversy: Criticisms and Adaptations of Samuel Richardson's Pamela, 1740–1750*. 6 vols. London: Pickering & Chatto, 2001.

Kidgell, John. *The Card*. 2 vols. London, 1755.

La Chaussée, Nivelle de. *Pamela*. Paris, 1743.

Lackington, James. *Memoirs of the First Forty-Five Years of the Life of James Lackington*, 2nd edn. London, 1791.

Lettre à Monsieur l'Abbé Des Fontaines sur Pamela. Paris, 1742.

The Life and Extraordinary Adventures of Pamela, Daughter of Goodman Andrews, a Labourer. Clerkenwell Green, *c.* 1817–29.

The Life of Pamela. London, 1741.

Lonsdale, Roger (ed.). *Eighteenth-Century Women Poets: An Oxford Anthology*. Oxford: Oxford University Press, 1989.

New Oxford Book of Eighteenth-Century Verse. Oxford: Oxford University Press, 1984.

Macaulay, Catharine. *Letters on Education*. London, 1790.

*Marquet, Abbé [?]. *Lettre sur Pamela*. London, 1742.

Mauvillon, Eléazar de. *L'Anti-Pamela*. Amsterdam, 1743.

McCarthy, Charlotte. *The Fair Moralist; or, Love and Duty*. Dublin, 1747.

The Fair Moralist; or, Love and Virtue, 2nd edn. London, 1746.

*Memoirs of the Life of Lady H----, The Celebrated Pamela. From her Birth to the Present Time. London, 1741.

Mercier, Louis-Sébastien. *L'Indigent*. Paris, 1782.

Miller, James. *The Picture*. London, 1745.

Missy, César de. *Bribery: A Satire*. London, 1750.

Montagu, Lady Mary Wortley. *The Complete Letters of Lady Mary Wortley Montagu*, ed. Robert Halsband. 3 vols. Oxford: Clarendon Press, 1965–7.

Romance Writings, ed. Isobel Grundy. Oxford: Clarendon Press, 1996.

Moore, Edward. *The Foundling: A Comedy and The Gamester: A Tragedy*, ed. Anthony Amberg. Newark: University of Delaware Press, 1996.

Morgan, Fidelis, and Giles Havergal. *Pamela or the Reform of a Rake*. Oxford: Amber Lane Press, 1987.

Neufchâteau, François de. *François de Neufchâteau, auteur de Paméla, à la Convention nationale*. Paris, 1793.

Paméla, ou la vertu récompensée. Paris, 1793.

Nichols, John. *Literary Anecdotes of the Eighteenth Century*. 9 vols. London, 1812–15.

*Pamela Censured, intro. Charles Batten, Jr. Augustan Reprint Society no. 175. Los Angeles: Clark Memorial Library, 1976.

Pamela in High Life; or, Virtue Rewarded. London, 1741.

The Parallel; or, Pilkington and Phillips Compared. London, 1748.

Parry, James. *The True Anti-Pamela; or, Memoirs of Mr. James Parry*. 2 vols. London, 1741.

The Paths of Virtue Delineated; or, The History in Miniature of the Celebrated Pamela, Clarissa Harlowe, and Sir Charles Grandison, Familiarised and Adapted to the Capacities of Youth. London, 1756.

Paulson, Ronald, and Thomas Lockwood (eds). *Henry Fielding: The Critical Heritage*. London: Routledge, 1969.

Pilkington, Laetitia. *Memoirs of Laetitia Pilkington*, ed. A. C. Elias, Jr. 2 vols. Athens: University of Georgia Press, 1997.

Pilkington, Miss. *Rosina*. 5 vols. London, 1793.

Pinckney, Eliza. *The Letterbook of Eliza Lucas Pinckney, 1739–1762*, ed. Elise Pinckney. Chapel Hill: University of North Carolina Press, 1972.

Pope, Alexander. *The Dunciad in Four Books*, ed. Valerie Rumbold. London: Longman, 1999.

The Rape of the Lock and Other Poems, ed. Geoffrey Tillotson, 3rd edn. London: Methuen, 1962.

**Povey, Charles. *The Virgin in Eden; or, The State of Innocency*. London, 1741.

Reeve, Clara. Letter to the Editor. *Gentleman's Magazine* 56 (1786), 117–18.

The Progress of Romance. 2 vols. Colchester, 1785.

The School for Widows, ed. Jeanine M. Casler. Newark: University of Delaware Press, 2003.

Relph, Josiah. *A Miscellany of Poems*. Glasgow, 1747.

Richardson, Samuel. *Aesop's Fables*. London, 1739.

The Apprentice's Vade Mecum, intro. Alan Dugald McKillop. Augustan Reprint Society nos 169–70. Los Angeles: Clark Memorial Library, 1975.

Clarissa, ed. Angus Ross. Harmondsworth: Penguin, 1985.

The Correspondence of Samuel Richardson, ed. Anna Laetitia Barbauld. 6 vols. London, 1804.

Pamela. 4 vols. London, 1740–1.

Pamela. 4 vols. Sixth edn. London, 1742.

Pamela, ed. Peter Sabor, intro. Margaret Anne Doody. Harmondsworth: Penguin, 1980.

Pamela, ed. Thomas Keymer and Alice Wakely, intro. Thomas Keymer. Oxford: Oxford University Press, 2001.

The Richardson–Stinstra Correspondence and Stinstra's Prefaces to Clarissa, ed. William C. Slattery. Carbondale: Southern Illinois University Press, 1969.

Samuel Richardson's Introduction to Pamela, ed. Sheridan W. Baker, Jr. Augustan Reprint Society no. 48. Los Angeles: Clark Memorial Library, 1954.

A Seasonable Examination of the Pleas and Pretensions of the Proprietors of, and Subscribers to, Play-houses, Erected in Defiance of Royal License. London, 1735.

Selected Letters of Samuel Richardson, ed. John Carroll. Oxford: Clarendon Press, 1964.

Sir Charles Grandison, ed. Jocelyn Harris. 3 vols. Oxford: Oxford University Press, 1972.

Richardsoniana. 16 vols. New York: Garland, 1974–5.

Robinson, Mary. *A Letter to the Women of England and The Natural Daughter*, ed. Sharon M. Setzer. Peterborough, ON: Broadview, 2003.

A Satirical Review of the Manifold Falshoods and Absurdities Hitherto Publish'd Concerning the Earthquake. London, 1756.

Scott, Sarah. *A Journey through Every Stage of Life*. 2 vols. London, 1754.

Seward, Anna. Letter to the Editor. *Gentleman's Magazine* 56 (1786), 15–17.

Shadwell, Charles. *Irish Hospitality; or, Virtue Rewarded*. In *The Works of Mr. Charles Shadwell*. 2 vols. Dublin, 1720, I, 206–304.

Shaw, Peter. *The Reflector*. London, 1750.

Sheridan, Thomas. *The Brave Irishman; or, Captain O'Blunder. A Farce*. Dublin, ?1746.

Smythies, Susan. *The Brothers*. 2 vols. London, 1758.

Spence, Joseph ['Sir Harry Beaumont']. *Moralities; or, Essays, Letters, Fables; and Translations*. London, 1753.

Sterne, Laurence. *Letters of Laurence Sterne*, ed. L. P. Gertis. Oxford: Clarendon Press, 1935.

Stevens, George Alexander. *The History of Tom Fool*. 2 vols. London, 1760.

Swift, Jonathan. *A Tale of a Tub*, ed. A. C. Guthkelch and D. Nichol Smith, 2nd edn. Oxford: Clarendon Press, 1958.

Teft, Elizabeth. *Orinthia's Miscellanies; or, A Compleat Collection of Poems, Never Before Published*. London, 1747.

The Theatre of Love. London, 1758.

Thrale, Hester Lynch. *Thraliana*, ed. Katharine C. Balderston, 2nd edn. 2 vols. Oxford: Clarendon Press, 1951.

Truth Triumphant; or, The Genuine Account of the Whole Proceedings against Elizabeth Canning. London, 1754.

Vertue Rewarded; or, The Irish Princess, ed. Hubert McDermott. Gerrards Cross: Smythe, 1992.

Voltaire. *L'Affaire Paméla: lettres de Monsieur de Voltaire à Madame Denis, de Berlin*, ed. André Magnan. Paris: Paris Mediterranée, 2004.

Correspondence, ed. Theodore Besterman, 51 vols, The Complete Works of Voltaire, vols 85–135. Oxford: Voltaire Foundation, 1968–77.

Lettre à messieurs les auteurs des Etrennes de la Saint-Jean et autres beaux ouvrages, ed. Mark Waddicor, The Complete Works of Voltaire, 31B. Oxford: Voltaire Foundation, 1994.

Nanine, ed. Marie-Rose de Labriolle and Colin Duckworth, The Complete Works of Voltaire, 31B. Oxford: Voltaire Foundation, 1994.

W----, J---- [?John Winstanley]. *Pamela; or, The Fair Imposter*. London, 1744.

Pamela; or, The Fair Impostor. Dublin, 1743.

Warton, Joseph. *Fashion: An Epistolary Satire*. London, 1742.

Whitehead, William. *On Nobility: An Epistle*. London, 1744.

Williams, Ioan (ed.). *Novel and Romance, 1700–1800: A Documentary Record*. London: Routledge, 1970.

Young, Edward. *The Correspondence of Edward Young, 1683–1765*, ed. Henry Pettit. Oxford: Clarendon Press, 1971.

SECONDARY

Aikins, Janet E. 'Picturing "Samuel Richardson": Francis Hayman and the Intersections of Word and Image'. *Eighteenth-Century Fiction* 14 (2002), 465–505.

'Re-presenting the Body in *Pamela II*'. In Jeffrey N. Cox and Larry J. Reynolds (eds), *New Historical Literary Study: Essays on Reproducing Texts, Representing History*. Princeton: Princeton University Press, 1993, pp. 151–77.

'Richardson's "Speaking Pictures"'. In Margaret Anne Doody and Peter Sabor (eds), *Samuel Richardson: Tercentenary Essays*. Cambridge: Cambridge University Press, 1989, pp. 146–66.

Allen, Brian. *Francis Hayman*. New Haven: Yale University Press, 1987.

Allentuck, Marcia Epstein. 'Narration and Illustration: The Problem of Richardson's *Pamela*'. *Philological Quarterly* 51 (1972), 874–86.

Altick, Richard D. *The Shows of London*. Cambridge, MA: Harvard University Press, 1978.

Avery, Emmett L. 'The Summer Theatrical Seasons at Richmond and Twickenham, 1746–1753'. *Notes and Queries* 173 (1937), 312–15.

Barchas, Janine. *Graphic Design, Print Culture, and the Eighteenth-Century Novel.* Cambridge: Cambridge University Press, 2003.

Bartolomeo, Joseph. *Matched Pairs: Gender and Intertextual Dialogue in Eighteenth-Century Fiction.* Newark: University of Delaware Press, 2002.

Basker, James. '"The Wages of Sin": The Later Career of John Cleland'. *Etudes anglaises* 40 (1987), 178–94.

Bataille, Robert R. '*The New Lady's Magazine*'. In Alvin Sullivan (ed.), *British Literary Magazines: The Augustan Age and the Age of Johnson, 1698–1788.* Westport, CT: Greenwood Press, 1983, pp. 243–8.

Battestin, Martin C. 'On the Contemporary Reputations of *Pamela, Joseph Andrews* and *Roderick Random*: Remarks by an "Oxford Scholar", 1748'. *Notes and Queries* 213 (1968), 450–2.

Battestin, Martin C., with Ruthe R. Battestin. *Henry Fielding: A Life.* London: Routledge, 1989.

Beasley, Jerry C. *Novels of the 1740s.* Athens: University of Georgia Press, 1982.

Beer, Gillian. '*Pamela:* Rethinking *Arcadia*'. In Margaret Anne Doody and Peter Sabor (eds), *Samuel Richardson: Tercentenary Essays.* Cambridge: Cambridge University Press, 1989, pp. 23–39.

Bell, Ian A. *Henry Fielding: Authorship and Authority.* London: Longman, 1994.

Berry, C. L. 'Portraits of Clementine Walkinshaw'. *Notes and Queries* 196 (1951), 491–5.

Bertolino, Jane V. *The Many Faces of Pamela.* Brooklyn: Vegas, 1990.

Black, Frank Gees. *The Epistolary Novel in the Late Eighteenth Century: A Descriptive and Bibliographical Study.* Eugene: University of Oregon Press, 1940.

Blewett, David. 'Introduction' to *Reconsidering the Rise of the Novel.* Special edition of *Eighteenth-Century Fiction* 12 (2000), 141–5.

Blouch, Christine. 'Eliza Haywood'. In *Selected Works of Eliza Haywood*, ed. Alexander Pettit *et al.* London: Pickering & Chatto, 2000–1, I, I, xxi–lxxxii.

Bowen, Scarlett. '"A Sawce-box and Boldface Indeed": Refiguring the Female Servant in the Pamela–Antipamela Debate'. *Studies in Eighteenth-Century Culture* 28 (1999), 257–85.

Briggs, Peter M. 'Laurence Sterne and Literary Celebrity in 1760'. *Age of Johnson* 4 (1991), 251–80.

Broadley, Rosie, *et al. Every Look Speaks: Portraits of David Garrick.* Bath: Holburne Museum of Art, 2003.

Bruce, H. L. 'Voltaire on the English Stage'. *University of California Publications in Modern Philology* 8 (1918), 112–16.

Burditt, Paul. 'The Authorship of *Sir Charles Goodville*'. *Notes and Queries* 249 (2004), 406–7.

Butler, Marilyn. *Jane Austen and the War of Ideas*, revd edn. Oxford: Clarendon Press, 1987.

Canby, Henry Seidel. '*Pamela* Abroad'. *Modern Language Notes* 18 (1903), 206–13.

Castle, Terry. *Masquerade and Civilization: The Carnivalesque in Eighteenth-Century English Culture and Fiction.* London: Methuen, 1986.

Chatten, Elizabeth N. *Samuel Foote.* Boston: Twayne, 1980.

Chung, Ewha. *Samuel Richardson's New Nation: Paragons of the Domestic Sphere and 'Native' Virtue*. New York: Peter Lang, 1998.

Clayton, Timothy. *The English Print, 1688–1802*. New Haven: Yale University Press, 1997.

Cole, Richard Cargill. *Irish Booksellers and English Writers, 1740–1800*. London: Mansell, 1986.

Collins, W. J. T. 'A Scandal of Old Monmouthshire'. *Monmouthshire Review* 1 (1933), 9–12.

Copeland, Edward. '*Clarissa* and *Fanny Hill*: Sisters in Distress'. *Studies in the Novel* 4 (1972), 343–52.

Davidson, Jenny. *Hypocrisy and the Politics of Politeness: Manners and Morals from Locke to Austen*. Cambridge: Cambridge University Press, 2004.

Dearnley, Moira. *Distant Fields: Eighteenth-Century Fictions of Wales*. Cardiff: University of Wales Press, 2001.

Dick, Miriam. 'Joseph Highmore's Vision of *Pamela*'. *English Language Notes* 24 (1987), 33–42.

Dobson, Austin. *Samuel Richardson*. London: Macmillan, 1902.

D'Oench, Ellen. *The Conversation Piece: Arthur Devis and His Contemporaries*. New Haven: Yale University Press, 1980.

Doody, Margaret Anne. *A Natural Passion: A Study of the Novels of Samuel Richardson*. Oxford: Oxford University Press, 1974.

Duckworth, Colin. 'Madame Denis's unpublished *Pamela*: A Link between Richardson, Goldoni and Voltaire'. *Studies on Voltaire and the Eighteenth Century* 76 (1970), 37–53.

Eagleton, Terry. *Crazy John and the Bishop and Other Essays on Irish Culture*. Cork: Cork University Press, 1998.

The Rape of Clarissa: Writing, Sexuality and Class Struggle in Samuel Richardson. Oxford: Blackwell, 1982.

Eaves, T. C. Duncan. 'Graphic Illustration of the Novels of Samuel Richardson, 1740–1810'. *Huntington Library Quarterly* 14 (1950–1), 349–83.

'An Unrecorded Children's Book Illustrated by Thomas Bewick'. *The Library* 5th ser. 5 (1951), 272–3.

Eaves, T. C. Duncan, and Ben D. Kimpel. 'The Publisher of *Pamela* and Its First Audience'. *Bulletin of the New York Public Library* 64 (1960), 143–6.

'Richardson's Revisions of *Pamela*'. *Studies in Bibliography* 20 (1967), 61–88.

Samuel Richardson: A Biography. Oxford: Clarendon Press, 1971.

'Samuel Richardson's London Houses'. *Studies in Bibliography* 15 (1962), 135–48.

Eco, Umberto. *The Limits of Interpretation*. Bloomington: Indiana University Press, 1990.

Einberg, Elizabeth, and Judy Egerton. *The Age of Hogarth: British Painters Born 1675–1709*. London: Tate Gallery, 1988.

Ellis, Frank H. *Sentimental Comedy: Theory and Practice*. Cambridge: Cambridge University Press, 1991.

Emery, Ted A. 'Goldoni's *Pamela* from Play to Libretto'. *Italica* 64 (1987), 572–82.

Epstein, William. *John Cleland: Images of a Life.* New York: Columbia University Press, 1974.

Feilla, Cecilia. 'Performing Virtue: *Pamela* on the French Revolutionary Stage, 1793'. *The Eighteenth Century* 43 (2002), 286–305.

Ferdinand, C. Y. *Benjamin Collins and the Provincial Newspaper Trade in the Eighteenth Century.* Oxford: Clarendon Press, 1997.

'The Economics of the Eighteenth-Century Provincial Book Trade: The Case of Ward and Chandler'. In Maureen Bell *et al.* (eds), *Re-constructing the Book: Literary Texts in Transmission.* Aldershot: Ashgate, 2001, pp. 42–56.

Festa, Lynn. 'Sentimental Bonds and Revolutionary Characters: Richardson's *Pamela* in England and France'. In Margaret Cohen and Carolyn Dever (eds), *The Literary Channel: The Inter-National Invention of the Novel.* Princeton: Princeton University Press, 2002, pp. 73–105.

Fiske, Roger. *English Theatre Music in the Eighteenth Century,* 2nd edn. Oxford: Oxford University Press, 1986.

Foote, Henry Wilder. *Robert Feke: Colonial Portrait Painter.* Cambridge, MA: Harvard University Press, 1930.

Foxon, David F. *English Verse, 1701–1750.* Cambridge: Cambridge University Press, 1975.

Libertine Literature in England, 1660–1745. New York: University Books, 1965.

Fysh, Stephanie. *The Work(s) of Samuel Richardson.* Newark: University of Delaware Press, 1997.

Garside, Peter, James Raven, and Rainer Schöwerling (eds). *The English Novel, 1770–1829: A Bibliographical Survey of Prose Fiction Published in the British Isles.* 2 vols. Oxford: Oxford University Press, 2000.

Gaskell, Philip. *From Writer to Reader: Studies in Editorial Method.* Oxford: Clarendon Press, 1978.

Gerrard, Christine. *Aaron Hill: The Muses' Projector, 1685–1750.* Oxford: Oxford University Press, 2003.

The Patriot Opposition to Walpole: Poetry, Politics, and the National Myth, 1725–1742. Oxford: Clarendon Press, 1994.

Giles, Paul. *Transatlantic Insurrections: British Culture and the Formation of American Literature, 1730–1860.* Philadelphia: University of Pennsylvania Press, 2001.

Girouard, Mark. 'Coffee at Slaughter's: English Art and the Rococo'. In Girouard, *Town and Country.* New Haven: Yale University Press, 1992, pp. 15–34.

Gooding, Richard. '*Pamela, Shamela,* and the Politics of the *Pamela* Vogue'. *Eighteenth-Century Fiction* 7 (1995), 109–30.

Green, James N. 'Benjamin Franklin as Publisher and Bookseller'. In J. A. Leo Lemay (ed.), *Reappraising Benjamin Franklin: A Bicentennial Perspective.* Newark: University of Delaware Press, 1993, pp. 98–114.

'English Books and Printing in the Age of Franklin'. In Hugh Amory and David D. Hall (eds), *The Colonial Book in the Atlantic World*. Cambridge: Cambridge University Press, 2000, pp. 248–98.

Greene, John C., and Gladys L. H. Clark. *The Dublin Stage, 1720–1745: A Calendar of Plays, Entertainments, and Afterpieces*. Bethlehem, PA: Lehigh University Press, 1993.

Greenhalgh, David M. '*The Universal Spectator*'. In Alvin Sullivan (ed.), *British Literary Magazines: The Augustan Age and the Age of Johnson, 1698–1788*. Westport, CT: Greenwood Press, 1983, pp. 346–9.

Grundy, Isobel. '"Trash, Trumpery, and Idle Time": Lady Mary Wortley Montagu and Fiction'. *Eighteenth-Century Fiction* 5 (1993), 293–310.

Gwilliam, Tassie. *Samuel Richardson's Fictions of Gender*. Stanford: Stanford University Press, 1993.

Habermas, Jürgen. *The Structural Transformation of the Public Sphere*. Cambridge: Polity Press, 1989.

Hammelmann, Hanns, and T. S. R. Boase. *Book Illustrators in Eighteenth-Century England*. New Haven: Yale University Press, 1975.

Hammond, Brean. *Professional Imaginative Writing in England, 1670–1740: 'Hackney for Bread'*. Oxford: Clarendon Press, 1997.

Harol, Corrinne. 'Faking It: Female Virginity and Pamela's Virtue'. *Eighteenth-Century Fiction* 16 (2004), 197–216.

Harris, Michael. *London Newspapers in the Age of Walpole*. Rutherford, NJ: Fairleigh Dickinson University Press, 1987.

Haslett, Moyra. *Pope to Burney, 1714–1779: Scriblerians to Bluestockings*. Basingstoke: Palgrave, 2003.

Highfill, Philip H., Kalman A. Burnim and Edward A. Langhans. *A Biographical Dictionary of Actors, Actresses, Musicians, Dancers, Managers, and Other Stage Personnel in London, 1660–1800*. 16 vols. Carbondale: Southern Illinois University Press, 1973–93.

Hume, Robert D. *Henry Fielding and the London Theatre, 1728–1737*. Oxford: Clarendon Press, 1988.

Hume, Robert D., and Judith Milhous (eds). *A Register of English Theatrical Documents, 1660–1737*. Carbondale: Southern Illinois University Press, 1991.

Hunter, J. Paul. *Occasional Form: Henry Fielding and the Chains of Circumstance*. Baltimore: Johns Hopkins University Press, 1975.

'Serious Reflections on Farther Adventures: Resistances to Closure in Eighteenth-Century English Novels'. In Albert J. Rivero (ed.), *Augustan Subjects: Essays in Honor of Martin C. Battestin*. Newark: University of Delaware Press, 1997, pp. 276–94.

Hunter, Mary. '*Pamela*: The Offspring of Richardson's Heroine in Eighteenth-Century Opera'. *Mosaic* 18 (1985), 61–76.

Hynes, Peter. 'From Richardson to Voltaire: *Nanine* and the Novelization of Comedy'. *The Eighteenth Century: Theory and Interpretation* 31 (1990), 117–35.

Ingamells, John, and Robert Raines. 'A Catalogue of the Paintings, Drawings, and Etchings of Philip Mercier'. *Walpole Society* 46 (1976–8), 1–70.

Ingrassia, Catherine. *Authorship, Commerce, and Gender in Early Eighteenth-Century England: A Culture of Paper Credit*. Cambridge: Cambridge University Press, 1998.

Keymer, Thomas. 'Parliamentary Printing, Paper Credit, and Corporate Fraud: A New Episode in Samuel Richardson's Early Career'. *Eighteenth-Century Fiction* 17 (2005), 183–206.

'Reception, and *The Rape of the Lock*, and Richardson'. In Howard Erskine-Hill (ed.), *Alexander Pope: World and Word*. Oxford: Oxford University Press, 1998, pp. 147–75.

Richardson's Clarissa and the Eighteenth-Century Reader. Cambridge: Cambridge University Press, 1992.

Sterne, The Moderns, and the Novel. Oxford: Oxford University Press, 2002.

Kibbie, Ann Louise. 'Sentimental Properties: *Pamela* and *Memoirs of a Woman of Pleasure*'. *ELH* 58 (1991), 561–77.

Kraft, Elizabeth A. '*The History of the Works of the Learned*'. In Alvin Sullivan (ed.), *British Literary Magazines: The Augustan Age and the Age of Johnson, 1698–1788*. Westport, CT: Greenwood Press, 1983, pp. 160–3.

Kreissman, Bernard. *Pamela-Shamela: A Study of the Criticisms, Burlesques, Parodies, and Adaptations of Richardson's Pamela*. Lincoln: University of Nebraska Press, 1960.

Lanson, Gustave. *Nivelle de la Chaussée et la comédie larmoyante*. Paris: Hachette, 1903.

Liesenfeld, Vincent J. *The Licensing Act of 1737*. Madison: University of Wisconsin Press, 1984.

Link, Victor. 'The First Operatic Versions of *Pamela*'. *Studies on Voltaire and the Eighteenth Century* 267 (1989), 273–81.

Lockwood, Thomas. 'John Kelly's "Lost" Play "The Fall of Bob" (1736)'. *English Language Notes* 22 (1984), 27–32.

Lynch, Kathleen M. '*Pamela Nubile, L'Ecossaise*, and *The English Merchant*'. *Modern Language Notes* 47 (1932), 94–6.

Mack, Maynard. *Alexander Pope: A Life*. New Haven: Yale University Press, 1985.

Magnan, André. *Dossier Voltaire en Prusse (1750–1753)*. *Studies on Voltaire and the Eighteenth Century* 224 (1986).

'Pour saluer *Paméla*: une oeuvre inconnue de Voltaire'. *Dix-huitième siècle* 15 (1983), 357–68.

Mallinson, Jonathan. 'What's In A Name? Reflections on Voltaire's "*Paméla*"'. forthcoming in *Eighteenth-Century Fiction* 18 (2006).

Marr, Peter. 'John Alcock and Fanny Brown'. *Musical Times* 118 (February 1977), 118–20.

Maslen, Keith. 'Samuel Richardson as Printer'. In R. C. Alston (ed.), *Order and Connexion: Studies in Bibliography and Book History*. Cambridge: D. S. Brewer, 1997, pp. 1–16.

Samuel Richardson of London, Printer. Dunedin: University of Otago, 2001.

Maslen, Keith, and John Lancaster. *The Bowyer Ledgers*. London: Bibliographical Society, 1991.

Matthew, H. C. G., and Brian Harrison (eds). *Oxford Dictionary of National Biography*. 60 vols. Oxford: Oxford University Press, 2004.

Mayo, Robert D. *The English Novel in the Magazines, 1740–1815*. Evanston, IL: Northwestern University Press, 1962.

McKillop, Alan Dugald. 'Richardson's Early Writings – Another Pamphlet'. *Journal of English and Germanic Philology* 53 (1954), 72–5.

Samuel Richardson: Printer and Novelist. Chapel Hill: University of North Carolina Press, 1936.

'Wedding Bells for Pamela'. *Philological Quarterly* 28 (1949), 323–5.

McLoughlin, Thomas. *Contesting Ireland: Irish Voices Against England in the Eighteenth Century*. Dublin: Four Courts Press, 1999.

McMullen, Lorraine. *An Odd Attempt in a Woman: The Literary Life of Frances Brooke*. Vancouver: University of British Columbia Press, 1983.

Michie, Allen. *Richardson and Fielding: The Dynamics of a Critical Rivalry*. Lewisburg, PA: Bucknell University Press, 1999.

Mild, Warren. *Joseph Highmore of Holborn Row*. Ardmore, PA: Kingswood Group, 1990.

Miller, Louise M. 'Author, Artist, Reader: "The Spirit of the Passages" and the Illustrations to *Pamela*'. *QWERTY* 4 (1994), 121–30.

Moore, Judith. *The Appearance of Truth: The Story of Elizabeth Canning and Eighteenth-Century Narrative*. Newark: University of Delaware Press, 1994.

Morash, Christopher. *A History of Irish Theatre, 1601–2000*. Cambridge: Cambridge University Press, 2002.

Muecke, D. C. 'Beauty and Mr. B.' *Studies in English Literature* 7 (1967), 467–74.

Mustain, John E. 'Eighteenth-Century Highlights of the Kline/Roethke Collection at Stanford University'. *East-Central Intelligencer* n.s. 16.3 (2002), 2–8.

'Newbery's Edition of "Pamela", 1769'. *Times Literary Supplement*, 6 March 1930, p. 196.

Nickel, Terri. '*Pamela* as Fetish: Masculine Anxiety in Henry Fielding's *Shamela* and James Parry's *The True Anti-Pamela*'. *Studies in Eighteenth-Century Culture* 22 (1992), 37–49.

Nicoll, Allardyce. *A History of English Drama, 1660–1900*, vol. II, *Early Eighteenth Century Drama*, 3rd edn. Cambridge: Cambridge University Press, 1952.

Ober, William. *Bottoms Up! A Pathologist's Essays on Medicine and the Humanities*. Carbondale: Southern Illinois University Press, 1987.

Parker, Dorothy. 'The Time Scheme of *Pamela* and the Character of B.' *Texas Studies in Language and Literature* 11 (1969), 695–704.

Paulson, Ronald. *Hogarth*. 3 vols. New Brunswick, NJ: Rutgers University Press, 1991–3.

Phillips, James W. *Printing and Bookselling in Dublin, 1670–1800: A Bibliographical Enquiry*. Dublin: Irish Academic Press, 1998.

Polesso, Paola. 'The Character of Pamela from Richardson's Novel to Goldoni's Comedy'. *Restoration and Eighteenth-Century Theatre Research* 2nd ser. 10 (1995), 42–51.

Pollard, Mary. *Dictionary of Members of the Dublin Book Trade*. London: Bibliographical Society, 2000.

Dublin's Trade in Books, 1550–1800. Oxford: Clarendon Press, 1989.

Praz, Mario. *Conversation Pieces: A Survey of the Informal Group Portrait in Europe and America*. University Park: Pennsylvania State University Press, 1971.

Prescott, Sarah. *Women, Authorship and Literary Culture, 1690–1740*. Basingstoke: Palgrave, 2003.

Price, Laurence Marsden. 'On the Reception of *Pamela* in Germany'. *JEGP* 25 (1926), 7–33.

Purdie, Edna. 'Some Adventures of *Pamela* on the Continental Stage'. In *German Studies Presented to Professor H. G. Fiedler*. Oxford: Clarendon Press, 1938, pp. 352–84.

Raines, Robert, and John Ingamells. *Philip Mercier*. London: Paul Mellon Foundation, 1969.

Raven, James. *British Fiction, 1750–1770: A Chronological Check-List of Prose Fiction Printed in Britain and Ireland*. Newark: University of Delaware Press, 1987.

London Booksellers and American Customers: Transatlantic Literary Community and the Charleston Library Society, 1748–1811. Columbia: University of South Carolina Press, 2002.

Rawson, Claude. 'An Epidemical Phrenzy'. *Times Literary Supplement*, 14 December 2001, pp. 3–5.

'Fielding's Richardson: *Shamela*, *Joseph Andrews* and Parody Revisited'. *Bulletin de la société d'études anglo-américaines des XVIIe et XVIIIe siècles* 51 (2000), 77–94.

God, Gulliver, and Genocide: Barbarism and the European Imagination, 1492–1945. Oxford: Oxford University Press, 2001.

Raynie, Stephen A. 'Hayman and Gravelot's Anti-*Pamela* Designs for Richardson's Octavo Edition of *Pamela I* and *II*'. *Eighteenth-Century Life* 23 (1999), 77–93.

Reade, Aleyn Lyell. 'Richardson's Pamela: Her Original'. *Notes and Queries* 10th ser. 9 (1908), 361–3, 503–5.

Richetti, John. *The English Novel in History, 1700–1800*. London: Routledge, 1999.

Popular Fiction Before Richardson: Narrative Patterns 1700–1739. Oxford: Clarendon Press, 1969.

'The Public Sphere and the Eighteenth-Century Novel: Social Criticism and Narrative Enactment'. *Eighteenth-Century Life* 16 (1992), 114–29.

Ridgway, R. S. *Voltaire and Sensibility*. Montreal: McGill-Queen's University Press, 1973.

Rivero, Albert J. '*Pamela/Shamela/Joseph Andrews*: Henry Fielding and the Duplicities of Representation'. In Rivero (ed.), *Augustan Subjects: Essays in Honor of Martin C. Battestin*. Newark: University of Delaware Press, 1997, pp. 207–28.

Rizzo, Betty. 'Charlotte McCarthy'. In Janet Todd (ed.), *A Dictionary of British and American Women Writers, 1660–1800*. Totowa, NJ: Rowman & Littlefield, 1987, p. 204.

Robinove, Phyllis S. 'Voltaire's Theater on the Parisian Stage, 1789–1799'. *French Review* 32 (1958–9), 534–8.

Rogers, Paul Patrick. *Goldoni in Spain*. Oberlin, OH: Academy Press, 1941.

Ross, Ian Campbell. *Laurence Sterne: A Life*. Oxford: Oxford University Press, 1999.

Rothstein, Eric. 'The Framework of *Shamela*'. *ELH* 35 (1968), 381–402.

Rumbold, Valerie. *Women's Place in Pope's World*. Cambridge: Cambridge University Press, 1989.

Sabor, Peter. 'The Cooke–Everyman Edition of *Pamela*'. *The Library* 32 (1977), 360–6.

'Did Richardson Bribe Dr. Slocock?' *Notes and Queries* 224 (1979), 29–31.

'*Joseph Andrews* and *Pamela*'. *British Journal for Eighteenth-Century Studies* 1 (1978), 169–81.

'"A large Portion of our ethereal Fire": Swift and Samuel Richardson'. In Hermann J. Real and Helgard Stöver-Leidig (eds), *Reading Swift: Papers from the Fourth Münster Symposium on Jonathan Swift*. Munich: Wilhelm Fink, 2003, pp. 387–401.

'Richardson and His Readers'. *Humanities Association Review* 30 (1979), 161–73.

'Richardson's Correspondence and His Final Revision of *Pamela*'. *Transactions of the Samuel Johnson Society of the Northwest* 12 (1981), 114–31.

'Richardson's Index to His Correspondence on *Pamela*'. *Notes and Queries* 224 (1979), 556–60.

'What Did Pamela Look Like?' *Notes and Queries* 228 (1983), 48–9.

Sale, William Merritt, Jr. 'The First Dramatic Version of *Pamela*'. *Yale University Library Gazette* 9 (1935), 83–8.

Samuel Richardson: A Bibliographical Record of His Literary Career with Historical Notes. New Haven: Yale University Press, 1936.

Samuel Richardson: Master Printer. Ithaca, NY: Cornell University Press, 1950.

Schellenberg, Betty A. ' "To Renew Their Former Acquaintance": Print, Gender, and Some Eighteenth-Century Serials'. In Paul Budra and Betty A. Schellenberg (eds), *Part Two: Reflections on the Sequel*. Toronto: University of Toronto Press, 1998, pp. 85–101.

Schleck, Florian J. 'Richardson on the Index'. *Times Literary Supplement*, 25 April 1935, p. 272.

Scouten, Arthur H. (ed.) *The London Stage, 1660–1800, Part 3, 1729–1747*, 2 vols. Carbondale: Southern Illinois University Press, 1961.

Sgard, Jean. *Prévost romancier*. Paris: Librairie José Corti, 1968.

Sheldon, Esther K. *Thomas Sheridan of Smock-Alley*. Princeton: Princeton University Press, 1967.

Shipley, John B. 'Samuel Richardson and *Pamela*'. *Notes and Queries* 199 (1954), 28–9.

Smallwood, Angela J. 'Jacobites and Jacobins: Fielding's Legacy in the Later 18th-Century London Theatre', forthcoming in the proceedings of the Fielding commemorative conference held at Yale University in October 2004, ed. Claude Rawson (Newark: University of Delaware Press).

Spedding, Patrick. *A Bibliography of Eliza Haywood.* London: Pickering & Chatto, 2004.

Stone, George Winchester, Jr (ed). *The London Stage, 1660–1800, Part 4, 1747–1776,* 3 vols. Carbondale: Southern Illinois University Press, 1962.

Stone, George Winchester, Jr, and George M. Kahrl. *David Garrick: A Critical Biography.* Carbondale: Southern Illinois University Press, 1979.

Strauss, Ralph. *The Unspeakable Curll.* London: Chapman and Hall, 1927.

Stuber, Florian. '*Pamela II:* "Written in Imitation of the Manner of Cervantes"'. In Albert J. Rivero (ed.), *New Essays on Samuel Richardson.* New York: St Martin's Press, 1996, pp. 53–68.

Sutherland, John. 'Where Does Fanny Hill Keep Her Contraceptives?' In Sutherland, *Can Jane Eyre Be Happy?: More Puzzles in Classic Fiction.* Oxford: Oxford University Press, 1997, pp. 11–18.

Tasch, Peter A. *The Dramatic Cobbler: The Life and Works of Isaac Bickerstaff.* Lewisburg, PA: Bucknell University Press, 1971.

Temple, Kathryn. 'Printing Like a Post-Colonialist: The Irish Piracy of *Sir Charles Grandison'. Novel* 33 (2000), 157–74.

Thornton, Richard H. 'English Authors Placed on the Roman "Index" (1600 to 1750)'. *Notes and Queries* 11th ser. 12 (1915), 333.

Todd, Janet. 'Fatal Fluency: Behn's Fiction and the Restoration Letter'. *Eighteenth-Century Fiction* 12 (2000), 417–34.

Trefman, Simon. *Sam. Foote, Comedian, 1720–1777.* New York: New York University Press, 1971.

Turner, James Grantham. 'Novel Panic: Picture and Performance in the Reception of Richardson's *Pamela'. Representations* 48 (1994), 70–96.

Ty, Eleanor. *Empowering the Feminine: The Narratives of Mary Robinson, Jane West, and Amelia Opie, 1796–1812.* Toronto: University of Toronto Press, 1998.

Unsex'd Revolutionaries: Five Women Novelists of the 1790s. Toronto: University of Toronto Press, 1993.

Utter, Robert P., and Gwendolyn B. Needham. *Pamela's Daughters.* New York: Macmillan, 1936.

Warner, William B. *Licensing Entertainment: The Elevation of Novel Reading in Britain, 1684–1750.* Berkeley: University of California Press, 1998.

Watt, Ian. *The Rise of the Novel: Studies in Defoe, Richardson and Fielding.* Berkeley: University of California Press, 1957.

Wiles, R. M. *Serial Publication in England before 1750.* Cambridge: Cambridge University Press, 1957.

Willens, Liliane. *Voltaire's Comic Theatre: Composition, Conflict and Critics. Studies on Voltaire and the Eighteenth Century* 136 (1975).

Williams, Kate [Katherine Ruth]. '"The Force of Language, and the Sweets of Love": Eliza Haywood and the Erotics of Reading in Samuel Richardson's *Clarissa*. *Lumen* 23 (2004), 309–23.

'Samuel Richardson and Amatory Fiction'. Diss. Oxford University, 2004.

Wilputte, Earla A. 'Ambiguous Language and Ambiguous Gender: The "Bisexual" Text of *Shamela*. *Modern Language Review* 89 (1994), 561–71.

Wood, Carl. '*Shamela*'s Subtle Satire: Fielding's Characterization of Mrs. Jewkes and Mrs. Jervis'. *English Language Notes* 13 (1976), 266–70.

Wright, Austin. *Joseph Spence: A Critical Biography*. Chicago: University of Chicago Press, 1950.

Zach, Wolfgang. 'Mrs. Aubin and Richardson's Earliest Literary Manifesto (1739)'. *English Studies* 62 (1981), 271–85.

Index

References in italics are to the illustrations.

Made in the USA
Lexington, KY
18 May 2014